THE COMPLETE WORKS OF SWAMI VIVEKANANDA

VOLUME VI

Discovery Publisher

2019, Discovery Publisher

No part of this book may be reproduced in any form or by any electronic or mechanical means including information storage and retrieval systems, without permission in writing from the publisher.

Author: Swami Vivekananda

616 Corporate Way, Suite 2-4933
Valley Cottage, New York, 10989
www.discoverypublisher.com
edition@discoverypublisher.com
facebook.com/discoverypublisher
twitter.com/discoverypb

New York • Paris • Dublin • Tokyo • Hong Kong

TABLE OF CONTENTS

Lectures and Discourses — 3

- THE METHODS AND PURPOSE OF RELIGION — 4
- THE NATURE OF THE SOUL AND ITS GOAL — 10
- THE IMPORTANCE OF PSYCHOLOGY — 14
- NATURE AND MAN — 16
- CONCENTRATION AND BREATHING — 17
- INTRODUCTION TO JNANA-YOGA — 19
- THE VEDANTA PHILOSOPHY AND CHRISTIANITY — 21
- WORSHIPPER AND WORSHIPPED — 22
- FORMAL WORSHIP — 26
- DIVINE LOVE — 30

Notes of Class Talks and Lectures — 35

- Religion And Science — 36
- Religion Is Realisation — 36
- Religion Is Self-Abnegation — 36
- Unselfish Work Is True Renunciation — 37
- Freedom Of The Self — 37
- Notes On Vedanta — 37
- Hindu And Greek — 38
- Thoughts On The Vedas And Upanishads — 38
- On Raja-Yoga — 39

On Bhakti-Yoga	39
On Jnana-Yoga	40
The Reality And Shadow	40
How To Become Free	41
Soul And God	41
The Goal	41
On Proof Of Religion	42
The Design Theory	43
Spirit And Nature	43
The Practice Of Religion	44
Fragmentary Notes On The Ramayana	45
Notes Taken Down In Madras, 1892-93	45
Concentration	54
The Power Of The Mind	55
Lessons On Raja-Yoga	56
Prana	56
The Practice of Yoga	57
The Ojas	57
Pranayama	58
Metagnosticism	58
Thought, Imagination, and Meditation	58
Lessons On Bhakti-Yoga	60
The Yoga Through Devotion	60
Worships Through Words and Love	61
On Doing Good to the World	63

Mother-Worship	63
Narada-Bhakti-Sutras	65
Chapter I	65
Chapter II	66
Chapter III	66
Chapter IV	66
Chapter V	67

Writings: Prose and Poems (Original and Translated) 69

HISTORICAL EVOLUTION OF INDIA	70
OM TAT SAT	70
Om Namo Bhagavate Râmakrishnâya	
THE STORY OF THE BOY GOPALA	74
MY PLAY IS DONE	77
Written in the Spring of 1895 in New York	
THE CUP	79
A BENEDICTION	79
Written to Sister Nivedita	
THE HYMN OF CREATION	79
A translation of the Nâsadiya-Sukta, Rig-Veda, X. 129.	
ON THE SEA'S BOSOM	80
HINDUISM AND SHRI RAMAKRISHNA	80
Translated from Bengali	
THE BENGALI LANGUAGE	82
Written for the "Udbodhan"	
MATTER FOR SERIOUS THOUGHT	84
Translated from Bengali	
SHIVA'S DEMON	86

Epistles - Second Series

1 — SIR	90	31 — SIR	107
2 — SIR	90	32 — SIR	107
3 — SIR	90	33 — SIR	107
4 — SIR	91	34 — SHARAT	109
5 — M—	91	35 — GOVINDA SAHAY	109
6 — SIR	91	36 — GOVINDA SAHAY	110
7 — SIR	92	37 — GOVINDA SAHAY	110
8 — SIR	93	38 — DOCTOR	110
9 — SIR	94	39 — MOTHER	110
10 — SIR	96	40 — MAHARAJA OF KHETRI	111
11 — SIR	96	41 — SHASHI	112
12 — SIR	96	42 — SIR	115
13 — SIR	97	43 — SISTERS	115
14 — SIR	97	44 — SISTERS	116
15 — SIR	97	45 — BROTHERS	118
16 — SIR	98	46 — MOTHER SARA	120
17 — SIR	98	47 — BROTHER DISCIPLES	120
18 — SIR	99	48 — MRS. BULL	124
19 — SIR	99	49 — RAMAKRISNANANDA	124
20 — SIR	100	50 — MRS. BULL	124
21 — SIR	100	51 — DEAR AND BELOVED	125
22 — SIR	100	52 — GOVINDA SAHAY	126
23 — AKHANDANANDA	101	53 — GOVINDA SAHAY	126
24 — SIR	103	54 — RAMAKRISHNANDA	126
25 — SIR	103	55 — AKHANDANANDA	128
26 — SIR	104	56 — DEAR AND BELOVED	129
27 — AKHANDANANDA	104	57 — MRS. BULL	132
28 — AKHANDANANDA	105	58 — SARADA	132
29 — SIR	106	59 — SANYAL	133
30 — KALI	106	60 — MRS. BULL	133

61 — MRS. BULL	134		92 — YOGEN	158
62 — MRS. BULL	135		93 — MRS. BULL	158
63 — SHASHI	135		94 — SARADA	159
64 — MRS. BULL	136		95 — MRS. BULL	159
65 — MRS. BULL	137		96 — MRS. BULL	160
66 — MRS. BULL	137		97 — SARADA	160
67 — MRS. BULL	138		98 — MRS. BULL	160
68 — MRS. BULL	138		99 — MRS. BULL	161
69 — SHASHI	138		100 — SHASHI	161
70 — ALBERTA	139		101 — SHASHI	161
71 — RAKHAL	140		102 — FRANKINCENSE	162
72 — AKHANDANANDA	143		103 — MRS. BULL	163
73 — BROTHER DISCIPLES	143		104 — MRS. BULL	163
74 — RAKHAL	144		105 — SAHJI	163
75 — SHASHI	145		106 — SHASHI	163
76 — RAKHAL	149		107 — MRS. BULL	164
77 — SHASHI	150		108 — SISTER	165
78 — RAKHAL	151		109 — JOE JOE	166
79 — MRS. BULL	152		110 — MISS S. E. WALDO	167
80 — MRS. BULL	152		111 — MRS. BULL	167
81 — MOTHER	152		112 — MARY	167
82 — DEAR—	153		113 — MRS. BULL	169
83 — RAKHAL	153		114 — LALAJI	170
84 — MRS. BULL	154		115 — DEAR—	170
85 — AKHANDANANDA	154		116 — SISTERS	170
86 — MRS. BULL	155		117 — ALBERTA	171
87 — MRS. ALBERTA	155		118 — MRS. BULL	171
88 — MRS. BULL	156		119 — FRANKINCENSE	171
89 — MRS. BULL	156		120 — ALBERTA	171
90 — SISTER	157		121 — MARY	172
91 — SARADA	157		122 — MRS. BULL	172

123 — MARY	173	146 — DEAR	185
124 — SIR	174	147 — MRS. BULL	185
125 — SHUDDHANANDA	175	148 — MARGOT	185
126 — MISS NOBLE	176	149 — MARGOT	185
127 — RAKHAL	176	150 — MRS. BULL	185
128 — AKHANDANANDA	177	151 — MARGOT	186
129 — RAKHAL	177	152 — MARGOT	186
130 — RAKHAL	178	153 — NIVEDITA	187
131 — AKHANDANANDA	178	154 — AKHANDANANDA	188
132 — AKHANDANANDA	179	155 — NIVEDITA	189
133 — MRS. BULL	180	156 — NIVEDITA	189
134 — MOTHER	180	157 — MARGOT	190
135 — SARADA	181	158 — JOE	190
136 — AKHANDANANDA	181	159 — NIVEDITA	191
137 — RAKHAL	182	160 — NIVEDITA	191
138 — M—	182	161 — NIVEDITA	192
139 — MOTHER	182	162 — NIVEDITA	192
140 — MOTHER	183	163 — MOTHER	193
141 — MARGOT	183	164 — ALBERTA	194
142 — FRIEND	183	165 — JOE	194
143 — MARGOT	184	166 — NIVEDITA	194
144 — DEAR	184	167 — JOE	194
145 — DHIRA MATA	184	168 — NIVEDITA	195

Conversations and Dialogues   198

I	200	VII	217
II	203	VIII	219
III	206	IX	222
IV	209	X	225
V	211	XI	229
VI	213	XII	230

THE **COMPLETE WORKS** OF **SWAMI VIVEKANANDA**

VOLUME VI

LECTURES AND DISCOURSES

THE METHODS AND PURPOSE OF RELIGION

In studying the religions of the world we generally find two methods of procedure. The one is from God to man. That is to say, we have the Semitic group of religions in which the idea of God comes almost from the very first, and, strangely enough, without any idea of soul. It was very remarkable amongst the ancient Hebrews that, until very recent periods in their history, they never evolved any idea of a human soul. Man was composed of certain mind and material particles, and that was all. With death everything ended. But, on the other hand, there was a most wonderful idea of God evolved by the same race. This is one of the methods of procedure. The other is through man to God. The second is peculiarly Aryan, and the first is peculiarly Semitic.

The Aryan first began with the soul. His ideas of God were hazy, indistinguishable, not very clear; but, as his idea of the human soul began to be clearer, his idea of God began to be clearer in the same proportion. So the inquiry in the Vedas was always through the soul. All the knowledge the Aryans got of God was through the human soul; and, as such, the peculiar stamp that has been left upon their whole cycle of philosophy is that introspective search after divinity. The Aryan man was always seeking divinity inside his own self. It became, in course of time, natural, characteristic. It is remarkable in their art and in their commonest dealings. Even at the present time, if we take a European picture of a man in a religious attitude, the painter always makes his subject point his eyes upwards, looking outside of nature for God, looking up into the skies. In India, on the other hand, the religious attitude is always presented by making the subject close his eyes. He is, as it were, looking inward.

These are the two subjects of study for man, external and internal nature; and though at first these seem to be contradictory, yet external nature must, to the ordinary man, be entirely composed of internal nature, the world of thought. The majority of philosophies in every country, especially in the West, have started with the assumption that these two, matter and mind, are contradictory existences; but in the long run we shall find that they converge towards each other and in the end unite and form an infinite whole. So it is not that by this analysis I mean a higher or lower standpoint with regard to the subject. I do not mean that those who want to search after truth through external nature are wrong, nor that those who want to search after truth through internal nature are higher. These are the two modes of procedure. Both of them must live; both of them must be studied; and in the end we shall find that they meet. We shall see that neither is the body antagonistic to the mind, nor the mind to the body, although we find, many persons who think that this body is nothing. In old times, every country was full of people who thought this body was only a disease, a sin, or something of that kind. Later on, however, we see how, as it was taught in the Vedas, this body melts into the mind, and the mind into the body.

You must remember the one theme that runs through all the Vedas: "Just as by the knowledge of one lump of clay we know all the clay that is in the universe, so what is that, knowing which we know everything else?" This, expressed more or less clearly, is the theme of all human knowledge. It is the finding of a unity towards which we are all going. Every action of our lives—the most material, the grossest as well as the finest, the highest, the most spiritual—is alike tending towards this one ideal, the finding of unity. A man is single. He marries. Apparently it may be a selfish act, but at the same time, the impulsion, the motive power, is to find that unity. He has children, he has friends, he loves his country, he loves the world, and ends by loving the whole universe. Irresistibly we are impelled towards that perfection which consists in finding the unity, killing this little self and making ourselves broader and broader. This is the goal, the end towards which the universe is rushing. Every atom is trying to go and join itself to the next atom. Atoms after atoms combine, making huge balls, the earths, the suns, the moons, the stars, the planets. They in their turn, are trying to rush towards each other, and at last, we know that the whole universe, mental and material, will be fused into one.

The process that is going on in the cosmos on a large scale, is the same as that going on in the microcosm on a smaller scale. Just as this universe has its existence in separation, in distinction, and all the while is rushing towards unity, non-separation, so in our little worlds each soul is born, as it were, cut off from the rest of the world. The more ignorant, the more unenlightened the soul, the more it thinks that it is separate from the rest of the universe. The more ignorant the person, the more he thinks, he will die or will be born, and so forth—ideas that are an expression of this separateness. But we find that, as knowledge comes, man grows, morality is evolved and the idea of non-separateness begins. Whether men understand it or not, they are impelled by that power behind to become unselfish. That is the foundation of all morality. It is the quintessence of all ethics, preached in any language, or in any religion, or by any prophet in the world. "Be thou unselfish", "Not 'I', but 'thou'"—that is the background of all ethical codes. And what is meant by this is the recognition of non-individuality—that you are a part of me, and I of you; the recognition that in hurting you I hurt myself, and in helping you I help myself; the recognition that there cannot possibly be death for me when you live. When one worm lives in this universe, how can I die? For my life is in the life of that worm. At the same time it will teach us that we cannot leave one of our fellow-beings without helping him, that in his good consists my good.

This is the theme that runs through the whole of Vedanta, and which runs through every other religion. For, you must remember, religions divide themselves generally into three parts. There is the first part, consisting of the philosophy, the essence, the principles of every religion. These principles find expression in mythology—lives of saints or heroes, demi-gods, or gods, or divine beings; and the whole idea of this mythology is that of power. And in the lower class of mythologies—the primitive— the expression of this power is in the muscles; their heroes are strong, gigantic. One hero conquers the whole world. As man advances, he must find expression for his energy higher than in the muscles; so his heroes also find expression in something higher. The higher mythologies have heroes who are gigantic moral men. Their strength is manifested in becoming moral and pure. They can stand alone, they can beat back the surging tide of selfishness and immorality. The third portion of all religions is symbolism, which you call ceremonials and forms. Even the expression through mythology, the lives of heroes, is not sufficient for all. There are minds still lower. Like children they must have their kindergarten of religion, and these symbologies are evolved—concrete examples which they can handle and grasp and understand, which they can see and feel as material things.

So in every religion you find there are the three stages: philosophy, mythology, and ceremonial. There is one advantage which can be pleaded for the Vedanta, that in India, fortunately, these three stages have been sharply defined. In other religions the principles are so interwoven with the mythology that it is very hard to distinguish one from the other. The mythology stands supreme, swallowing up the principles; and in course of centuries the principles are lost sight of. The explanation, the illustration of the principle, swallows up the principle, and the people see only the explanation, the prophet, the preacher, while the principles have gone out of existence almost—so much so that even today, if a man dares to preach the principles of Christianity apart from Christ, they will try to attack him and think he is wrong and dealing blows at Christianity. In the same way, if a man wants to preach the principles of Mohammedanism, Mohammedans will think the same; because concrete ideas, the lives of great men and prophets, have entirely overshadowed the principles.

In Vedanta the chief advantage is that it was not the work of one single man; and therefore, naturally, unlike Buddhism, or Christianity, or Mohammedanism, the prophet or teacher did not entirely swallow up or overshadow the principles. The principles live, and the prophets, as it were, form a secondary group, unknown to Vedanta. The Upanishads speak of no particular prophet, but they speak of various prophets and prophetesses. The old Hebrews had something of that idea; yet we find Moses occupying most of the space of the Hebrew literature. Of course I do not mean that it is bad that these prophets should take religious hold of a nation; but it certainly is very injurious if the whole field of principles is lost sight of. We can very much agree as to principles, but not very much as to persons. The persons appeal to our emotions; and the principles, to something higher, to our calm judgement. Principles must conquer in the long run, for that is the manhood of man. Emotions many times drag us down to the level of animals. Emotions have more connection with the senses than with the faculty of reason; and, therefore, when principles are entirely lost sight of and emotions prevail, religions degenerate into fanaticism and sectarianism. They are no better than party politics and such things. The most horribly ignorant notions will be taken up, and for these ideas thousands will be ready to cut the throats of their brethren. This is the reason that, though these great personalities and prophets are tremendous motive powers for good, at the same time their lives are altogether dangerous when they lead to the disregard of the principles they represent. That has always led to fanaticism, and has deluged the world in blood. Vedanta can avoid this difficulty, because it has not one special prophet. It has many Seers, who are called Rishis or sages. Seers—that is the literal translation—those who see these truths, the Mantras.

The word Mantra means "thought out", cogitated by the mind; and the Rishi is the seer of these thoughts. They are neither the property of particular persons, nor the exclusive property of any man or woman, however great he or she may be; nor even the exclusive property of the greatest spirits—the Buddhas or Christs—whom the world has produced. They are as much the property of the lowest of the low, as they are the property of a Buddha, and as much the property of the smallest worm that crawls as of the Christ, because they are universal principles. They were never created. These principles have existed throughout time; and they will exist. They are non-create—uncreated by any laws which science teaches us today. They remain covered and become discovered, but are existing through all eternity in nature. If Newton had not been born, the law of gravitation would have remained all the same and would have worked all the same. It was Newton's genius which formulated it, discovered it, brought it into consciousness, made it a conscious thing to the human race. So are these religious laws, the grand truths of spirituality. They are working all the time. If all the Vedas and the Bibles and the Korans did not exist at all, if seers and prophets had never been born, yet these laws would exist. They are only held in abeyance, and slowly but surely would work to raise the human race, to raise human nature. But they are the prophets who see them, discover them, and such prophets are discoverers in the field of spirituality. As Newton and Galileo were prophets of physical science, so are they prophets of spirituality. They can claim no exclusive right to any one of these laws; they are the common property of all nature.

The Vedas, as the Hindus say, are eternal. We now understand what they mean by their being eternal, i.e. that the laws have neither beginning nor end, just as nature has neither beginning nor end. Earth after earth, system after system, will evolve, run for a certain time, and then dissolve back again into chaos; but the universe remains the same. Millions and millions of systems are being born, while millions are being destroyed. The universe remains the same. The beginning and the end of time can be told as regards a certain planet; but as regards the universe, time has no meaning at all. So are the laws of nature, the physical laws, the mental laws, the spiritual laws. Without beginning and without end are they; and it is within a few years, comparatively speaking, a few thousand years at best, that man has tried to reveal them. The infinite mass remains before us. Therefore the one great lesson that we learn from the Vedas, at the start, is that religion has just begun. The infinite ocean of spiritual truth lies before us to be worked on, to be discovered, to be brought into our lives. The world has seen thousands of prophets, and the world has yet to see millions.

There were times in olden days when prophets were many in every society. The time is to come when prophets will walk through every street in every city in the world. In olden times, particular, peculiar persons were, so to speak, selected by the operations of the laws of society to become prophets. The time is coming when we shall understand that to become religious means to become a prophet, that none can become religious until he or she becomes a prophet. We shall come to understand that the secret of religion is not being able to think and say all these thoughts; but, as the Vedas teach, to realise them, to realise newer and higher one than have ever been realised, to discover them, bring them to society; and the study of religion should be the training to make prophets. The schools and colleges should be training grounds for prophets. The whole universe must become prophets; and until a man becomes a prophet, religion is a mockery and a byword unto him. We must see religion, feel it, realise it in a thousand times more intense a sense than that in which we see the wall.

But there is one principle which underlies all these various manifestations of religion and which has been already mapped out for us. Every science must end where it finds a unity, because we cannot go any further. When a perfect unity is reached, that science has nothing more of principles to tell us. All the work that religions have to do is to work out the details. Take any science, chemistry, for example. Suppose we can find one element out of which we can manufacture all the other elements. Then chemistry, as a science, will have become perfect. What will remain for us is to discover every day new combinations of that one material and the application of those combinations for all the purposes of life. So with religion. The gigantic principles, the scope, the plan of religion were already discovered ages ago when man found the last words, as they are called, of the Vedas—"I am He"—that there is that One in whom this whole universe of matter and mind finds its unity, whom they call God, or Brahman, or Allah, or Jehovah, or any other name. We cannot go beyond that. The grand principle has been already mapped out for us. Our work lies in filling it in, working it out, applying it to every part of our lives. We have to work now so that every one will become a prophet. There is a great work before us.

In old times, many did not understand what a prophet meant. They thought it was something by chance, that just by a fiat of will or some superior intelligence, a man gained superior knowledge. In modern times, we are prepared to demonstrate that this knowledge is the birthright of every living being, whosoever and wheresoever he be, and that there is no chance in this universe. Every man who, we think, gets something by chance, has been working for it slowly and surely through ages. And the whole question devolves upon us: "Do we want to be prophets?" If we want, we shall be.

This, the training of prophets, is the great work that lies before us; and, consciously or unconsciously, all the great systems of religion are working toward this one great goal, only with this difference, that in many religions you will find they declare that this direct perception of spirituality is not to be had in this life, that man must die, and after his death there will come a time in another world, when he will have visions of spirituality, when he will realise things which now he must believe. But Vedanta will ask all people who make such assertions, "Then how do you know that spirituality exists?" And they will have to answer that there must have been always certain particular people who, even in this life, have got a glimpse of things which are unknown and unknowable.

Even this makes a difficulty. If they were peculiar people, having this power simply by chance, we have no right to believe in them. It would be a sin to believe in anything that is by chance, because we cannot know it. What is meant by knowledge? Destruction of peculiarity. Suppose a boy goes into a street or a menagerie, and sees a peculiarly shaped animal. He does not know what it is. Then he goes to a country where there are hundreds like that one, and he is satisfied, he knows what the species is. Our knowledge is knowing the principle. Our non-knowledge is finding the particular without reference to principle. When we find one case or a few cases separate from the principle, without any reference to the principle, we are in darkness and do not know. Now, if these prophets, as they say, were peculiar persons who alone had the right to catch a glimpse of that which is beyond and no one else has the right, we should not believe in these prophets, because they are peculiar cases without any reference to a principle. We can only believe in them if we ourselves become prophets.

You, all of you, hear about the various jokes that get into the newspapers about the sea-serpent; and why should it be so? Because a few persons, at long intervals, came and told their stories about the sea-serpent, and others never see it. They have no particular principle to which to refer, and therefore the world does not believe. If a man comes to me and says a prophet disappeared into the air and went through it, I have the right to see that. I ask him, "Did your father or grandfather see it?" "Oh, no," he replies, "but five thousand years ago such a thing happened." And if I do not believe it, I have to be barbecued through eternity!

What a mass of superstition this is! And its effect is to degrade man from his divine nature to that of brutes. Why was reason given us if we have to believe? Is it not tremendously blasphemous to believe against reason? What right have we not to use the greatest gift that God has given to us? I am sure God will pardon a man who will use his reason and cannot believe, rather than a man who believes blindly instead of using the faculties He has given him. He simply degrades his nature and goes down to the level of the beasts—degrades his senses and dies. We must reason; and when reason proves to us the truth of these prophets and great men about whom the ancient books speak in every country, we shall believe in them. We shall believe in them when we see such prophets among ourselves. We shall then find that they were not peculiar men, but only illustrations of certain principles. They worked, and that principle expressed itself naturally, and we shall have to work to express that principle in us. They were prophets, we shall believe, when we become prophets. They were seers of things divine. They could go beyond the bounds of senses and catch a glimpse of that which is beyond. We shall believe that when we are able to do it ourselves and not before.

That is the one principle of Vedanta. Vedanta declares that religion is here and now, because the question of this life and that life, of life and death, this world and that world, is merely one of superstition and prejudice. There is no break in time beyond what we make. What difference is there between ten and twelve o'clock, except what we make by certain changes in nature? Time flows on the same. So what is meant by this life or that life? It is only a question of time, and what is lost in time may be made up by speed in work. So, says Vedanta, religion is to be realised now. And for you to become religious means that you will start without any religion work your way up and realise things, see things for yourself; and when you have done that, then, and then alone, you have religion. Before that you are no better than atheists, or worse, because the atheist is sincere—he stands up and says, "I do not know about these things—while those others do not know but go about the world, saying, "We are very religious people." What religion they have no one knows, because they have swallowed some grandmother's story, and priests have asked them to believe these things; if they do not, then let them take care. That is how it is going.

Realisation of religion is the only way. Each one of us will have to discover. Of what use are these books, then, these Bibles of the world? They are of great use, just as maps are of a country. I have seen maps of England all my life before I came here, and they were great helps to me informing some sort of conception of England. Yet, when I arrived in this country, what a difference between the maps and the country itself! So is the difference between realisation and the scriptures. These books are only the maps, the experiences of past men, as a motive power to us to dare to make the same experiences and discover in the same way, if not better.

This is the first principle of Vedanta, that realisation is religion, and he who realises is the religious man; and he who does not is no better than he who says, "I do not know", if not worse, because the other says, "I do not know", and is sincere. In this realisation, again, we shall be helped very much by these books, not only as guides, but as giving instructions and exercises; for every science has its own particular method of investigation. You will find many persons in this world who will say. "I wanted to become religious, I wanted to realise these things, but I have not been able, so I do not believe anything." Even among the educated you will find these. Large numbers of people will tell you, "I have tried to be religious all my life, but there is nothing in it." At the same time you will find this phenomenon: Suppose a man is a chemist, a great scientific man. He comes and tells you this. If you say to him, "I do not believe anything about chemistry, because I have all my life tried to become a chemist and do not find anything in it", he will ask, "When did you try?" "When I went to bed, I repeated, 'O chemistry, come to me', and it never came." That is the very same thing. The chemist laughs at you and says, "Oh, that is not the way. Why did you not go to the laboratory and get all the acids and alkalis and burn your hands from time to time? That alone would have taught you." Do you take the same trouble with religion? Every science has its own method of learning, and religion is to be learnt the same way. It has its own methods, and here is something we can learn, and must learn, from all the ancient prophets of the world, every one who has found something, who has realised religion. They will give us the methods, the particular methods, through which alone we shall be able to realise the truths of religion. They struggled all their lives, discovered particular methods of mental culture, bringing the mind to a certain state, the finest perception, and through that they perceived the truths of religion. To become religious, to perceive religion, feel it, to become a prophet, we have to take these methods and practice them; and then if we find nothing, we shall have the right to say, "There is nothing in religion, for I have tried and failed."

This is the practical side of all religions. You will find it in every Bible in the world. Not only do they teach principles and doctrines, but in the lives of the saints you find practices; and when it is not expressly laid down as a rule of conduct, you will always find in the lives of these prophets that even they regulated their eating and drinking sometimes. Their whole living, their practice, their method, everything was different from the masses who surrounded them; and these were the causes that gave them the higher light, the vision of the Divine. And we, if we want to have this vision, must be ready to take up these methods. It is practice, work, that will bring us up to that. The plan of Vedanta, therefore, is: first, to lay down the principles, map out for us the goal, and then to teach us the method by which to arrive at the goal, to understand and realise religion.

Again, these methods must be various. Seeing that we are so various in our natures, the same method can scarcely be applied to any two of us in the same manner. We have idiosyncrasies in our minds, each one of us; so the method ought to be varied. Some, you will find, are very emotional in their nature; some very philosophical, rational; others cling to all sorts of ritualistic forms—want things which are concrete. You will find that one man does not care for any ceremony or form or anything of the sort; they are like death to him. And another man carries a load of amulets all over his body; he is so fond of these symbols! Another man who is emotional in his nature wants to show acts of charity to everyone; he weeps, he laughs, and so on. And all of these certainly cannot have the same method. If there were only one method to arrive at truth, it would be death for everyone else who is not similarly constituted. Therefore the methods should be various. Vedanta understands that and wants to lay before the world different methods through which we can work. Take up any one you like; and if one does not suit you, another may. From this standpoint we see how glorious it is that there are so many religions in the world, how good it is that there are so many teachers and prophets, instead of there being only one, as many persons would like to have it. The Mohammedans want to have the whole world Mohammedan; the Christians, Christian; and the Buddhists, Buddhist; but Vedanta says, "Let each person in the world be separate, if you will; the one principle, the units will be behind. The more prophets there are, the more books, the more seers, the more methods, so much the better for the world." Just as in social life the greater the number of occupations in every society, the better for that society, the more chance is there for everyone of that society to make a living; so in the world of thought and of religion. How much better it is today when we have so many divisions of science—how much more is it possible for everyone to have great mental culture, with this great variety before us! How much better it is, even on the physical plane, to have the opportunity of so many various things spread before us, so that we may choose any one we like, the one which suits us best! So it is with the world of religions. It is a most glorious dispensation of the Lord that there are so many religions in the world; and would to God that these would increase every day, until every man had a religion unto himself!

Vedanta understands that and therefore preaches the one principle and admits various methods. It has nothing to say against anyone—whether you are a Christian, or a Buddhist, or a Jew, or a Hindu, whatever mythology you believe, whether you owe allegiance to the prophet of Nazareth, or of Mecca, or of India, or of anywhere else, whether you yourself are a prophet—it has nothing to say. It only preaches the principle which is the background of every religion and of which all the prophets and saints and seers are but illustrations and manifestations. Multiply your prophets if you like; it has no objection. It only preaches the principle, and the method it leaves to you. Take any path you like; follow any prophet you like; but have only that method which suits your own nature, so that you will be sure to progress.

THE NATURE OF THE SOUL AND ITS GOAL

The earliest idea is that a man, when he dies, is not annihilated. Something lives and goes on living even after the man is dead. Perhaps it would be better to compare the three most ancient nations—the Egyptians, the Babylonians, and the ancient Hindus—and take this idea from all of them. With the Egyptians and the Babylonians, we find a sort of soul idea—that of a double. Inside this body, according to them, there is another body which is moving and working here; and when the outer body dies, the double gets out and lives on for a certain length of time; but the life of the double is limited by the preservation of the outer body. If the body which the double has left is injured in any part, the double is sure to be injured in that part. That is why we find among the ancient Egyptians such solicitude to preserve the dead body of a person by embalming, building pyramids, etc. We find both with the Babylonians and the ancient Egyptians that this double cannot live on through eternity; it can, at best, live on for a certain time only, that is, just so long as the body it has left can be preserved.

The next peculiarity is that there is an element of fear connected with this double. It is always unhappy and miserable; its state of existence is one of extreme pain. It is again and again coming back to those that are living, asking for food and drink and enjoyments that it can no more have. It is wanting to drink of the waters of the Nile, the fresh waters which it can no more drink. It wants to get back those foods it used to enjoy while in this life; and when it finds it cannot get them, the double becomes fierce, sometimes threatening the living with death and disaster if it is not supplied with such food.

Coming to Aryan thought, we at once find a very wide departure. There is still the double idea there, but it has become a sort of spiritual body; and one great difference is that the life of this spiritual body, the soul, or whatever you may call it, is not limited by the body it has left. On the contrary, it has obtained freedom from this body, and hence the peculiar Aryan custom of burning the dead. They want to get rid of the body which the person has left, while the Egyptian wants to preserve it by burying, embalming, and building pyramids. Apart from the most primitive system of doing away with the dead, amongst nations advanced to a certain extent, the method of doing away with the bodies of the dead is a great indication of their idea of the soul. Wherever we find the idea of a departed soul closely connected with the idea of the dead body, we always find the tendency to preserve the body, and we also find burying in some form or other. On the other hand, with those in whom the idea has developed that the soul is a separate entity from the body and will not be hurt if the dead body is even destroyed, burning is always the process resorted to. Thus we find among all ancient Aryan races burning of the dead, although the Parsees changed it to exposing the body on a tower. But the very name of the tower (Dakhma) means a burning-place, showing that in ancient times they also used to burn their bodies. The other peculiarity is that among the Aryans there was no element of fear with these doubles. They are not coming down to ask for food or help; and when denied that help, they do not become ferocious or try to destroy those that are living. They rather are joyful, are glad at getting free. The fire of the funeral pyre is the symbol of disintegration. The symbol is asked to take the departed soul gently up and to carry it to the place where the fathers live, where there is no sorrow, where there is joy for ever, and so on.

Of these two ideas we see at once that they are of a similar nature, the one optimistic, and the other pessimistic—being the elementary. The one is the evolution of the other. It is quite possible that the Aryans themselves had, or may have had, in very ancient times exactly the same idea as the Egyptians. In studying their most ancient records, we find the possibility of this very idea. But it is quite a bright thing, something bright. When a man dies, this soul goes to live with the fathers and lives there enjoying their happiness. These fathers receive it with great kindness; this is the most ancient idea in India of a soul. Later on, this idea becomes higher and higher. Then it was found out that what they called the soul before was not really the soul. This bright body, fine body, however fine it might be, was a body after all; and all bodies must be made up of materials, either gross or fine. Whatever had form or shape must be limited, and could not be eternal. Change is inherent in every form. How could that which is changeful be eternal? So, behind this bright body, as it were, they found something which was the soul of man. It was called the Âtman, the Self. This Self idea then began. It had also to undergo various changes. By some it was thought that this Self was eternal; that it was very minute, almost as minute as an atom; that it lived in a certain part of the body, and when a man died, his Self went away, taking along with it the bright body. There were other people who denied the atomic nature of the soul on the same ground on which they had denied that this bright body was the soul.

Out of all these various opinions rose Sânkhya philosophy, where at once we find immense differences. The idea there is that man has first this gross body; behind the gross body is the fine body, which is the vehicle of the mind, as it were; and behind even that is the Self, the Perceiver, as the Sânkhyas call it, of the mind; and this is omnipresent. That is, your soul, my soul, everyone's soul is everywhere at the same time. If it is formless, how can it be said to occupy space? Everything that occupies space has form. The formless can only be infinite. So each soul is everywhere. The second theory put forward is still more startling. They all saw in ancient times that human beings are progressive, at least many of them. They grew in purity and power and knowledge; and the question was asked: Whence was this knowledge, this purity, this strength which men manifested? Here is a baby without any knowledge. This baby grows and becomes a strong, powerful, and wise man. Whence did that baby get its wealth of knowledge and power? The answer was that it was in the soul; the soul of the baby had this knowledge and power from the very beginning. This power, this purity, this strength were in that soul, but they were unmanifested; they have become manifested. What is meant by this manifestation or unmanifestation? That each soul is pure and perfect, omnipotent and omniscient, as they say in the Sankhya; but it can manifest itself externally only according to the mind it has got. The mind is, as it were, the reflecting mirror of the soul. My mind reflects to a certain extent the powers of my soul; so your soul, and so everyone's. That mirror which is clearer reflects the soul better. So the manifestation varies according to the mind one possesses; but the souls in themselves are pure and perfect.

There was another school who thought that this could not be. Though souls are pure and perfect by their nature, this purity and perfection become, as they say, contracted at times, and expanded at other times. There are certain actions and certain thoughts which, as it were, contract the nature of the soul; and then also other thoughts and acts, which bring its nature out, manifest it. This again is explained. All thoughts and actions that make the power and purity of the soul get contracted are evil actions, evil thoughts; and all those thoughts and actions which make the soul manifest itself—make the powers come out, as it were—are good and moral actions. The difference between the two theories is very slight; it is more of less a play on the words expansion and contraction. The one that holds that the variation only depends on the mind the soul has got is the better explanation, no doubt, but the contracting and expanding theory wants to take refuge behind the two words; and they should be asked what is meant by contraction of soul, or expansion. Soul is a spirit. You can question what is meant by contraction or expansion with regard to material, whether gross which we call matter, or fine, the mind; but beyond that, if it is not matter, that which is not bound by space or by time, how to explain the words contraction and expansion with regard to that? So it seems that this theory which holds that the soul is pure and perfect all the time, only its nature is more reflected in some minds than in others, is the better. As the mind changes, its character grows, as it were, more and more clear and gives a better reflection of the soul. Thus it goes on, until the mind has become so purified that it reflects fully the quality of the soul; then the soul becomes liberated.

This is the nature of the soul. What is the goal? The goal of the soul among all the different sects in India seems to be the same. There is one idea with all, and that is liberation. Man is infinite; and this limitation in which he exists now is not his nature. But through these limitations he is struggling upward and forward until he reaches the infinite, the unlimited, his birthright, his nature. All these combinations and recombinations and manifestations that we see round us are not the aim or the goal, but merely by the way and in passing. These combinations as earths and suns, and moons and stars, right and wrong, good and bad, our laughter and our tears, our joys and sorrows, are to enable us to gain experience through which the soul manifests its perfect nature and throws off limitation. No more, then, is it bound by laws either of internal or external nature. It has gone beyond all law, beyond all limitation, beyond all nature. Nature has come under the control of the soul, not the soul under the control of nature, as it thinks it is now. That is the one goal that the soul has; and all the succeeding steps through which it is manifesting, all the successive experiences through which it is passing in order to attain to that goal—freedom—are represented as its births. The soul is, as it were, taking up a lower body and trying to express itself through that. It finds that to be insufficient, throws it aside, and a higher one is taken up. Through that it struggles to express itself. That also is found to be insufficient, is rejected, and a higher one comes; so on and on until a body is found through which the soul manifests its highest aspirations. Then the soul becomes free.

Now the question is: If the soul is infinite and exists everywhere, as it must do, if it is a spirit, what is meant by its taking up bodies and passing through body after body? The idea is that the soul neither comes nor goes, neither is born nor dies. How can the omnipresent be born? It is meaningless nonsense to say that the soul lives in a body. How can the unlimited live in a limited space? But as a man having a book in his hands reads one page and turns it over, goes to the next page, reads that, turns it over, and so on, yet it is the book that is being turned over, the pages that are revolving, and not he—he is where he is always—even so with regard to the soul. The whole of nature is that book which the soul is reading. Each life, as it were, is one page of that book; and that read, it is turned over, and so on and on, until the whole of the book is finished, and that soul becomes perfect, having got all the experiences of nature. Yet at the same time it never moved, nor came, nor went; it was only gathering experiences. But it appears to us that we are moving. The earth is moving, yet we think that the sun is moving instead of the earth, which we know to be a mistake, a delusion of the senses. So is also this, delusion that we are born and that we die, that we come or that we go. We neither come nor go, nor have we been born. For where is the soul to go? There is no place for it to go. Where is it not already?

Thus the theory comes of the evolution of nature and the manifestation of the soul. The processes of evolution, higher and higher combinations, are not in the soul; it is already what it is. They are in nature. But as nature is evolving forward into higher and higher combinations, more and more of the majesty of the soul is manifesting itself. Suppose here is a screen, and behind the screen is wonderful scenery. There is one small hole in the screen through which we can catch only a little bit of that scenery behind. Suppose that hole becomes increased in size. As the hole increases in size, more and more of the scenery behind comes within the range of vision; and when the whole screen has disappeared, there is nothing between the scenery and you; you see the whole of it. This screen is the mind of man. Behind it is the majesty, the purity, the infinite power of the soul, and as the mind becomes clearer and clearer, purer and purer, more of the majesty of the soul manifests itself. Not that the soul is changing, but the change is in the screen. The soul is the unchangeable One, the immortal, the pure, the ever-blessed One.

So, at last, the theory comes to this. From the highest to the lowest and most wicked man, in the greatest of; human beings and the lowest of crawling worms under our feet, is the soul, pure and perfect, infinite and ever-blessed. In the worm that soul is manifesting only an infinitesimal part of its power and purity, and in the greatest man it is manifesting most of it. The difference consists in the degree of manifestation, but not in the essence. Through all beings exists the same pure and perfect soul.

There are also the ideas of heavens and other places, but these are thought to be second-rate. The idea of heaven is thought to be a low idea. It arises from the desire for a place of enjoyment. We foolishly want to limit the whole universe with our present experience. Children think that the whole universe is full of children. Madmen think the whole universe a lunatic asylum, and so on. So those to whom this world is but sense-enjoyment, whose whole life is in eating and feasting, with very little difference between them and brute beasts—such are naturally found to conceive of places where they will have more enjoyments, because this life is short. Their desire for enjoyment is infinite, so they are bound to think of places where they will have unobstructed enjoyment of the senses; and we see, as we go on, that those who want to go to such places will have to go; they will dream, and when this dream is over, they will be in another dream where there is plenty of sense-enjoyment; and when that dream breaks, they will have to think of something else. Thus they will be driving about from dream to dream.

Then comes the last theory, one more idea about the soul. If the soul is pure and perfect in its essence and nature, and if every soul is infinite and omnipresent, how is it that there can be many souls? There cannot be many infinites. There cannot be two even, not to speak of many. If there were two infinites, one would limit the other, and both become finite. The infinite can only be one, and boldly the last conclusion is approached— that it is but one and not two.

Two birds are sitting on the same tree, one on the top, the other below, both of most beautiful plumage. The one eats the fruits, while the other remains, calm and majestic, concentrated in its own glory. The lower bird is eating fruits, good and evil, going after sense-enjoyments; and when it eats occasionally a bitter fruit, it gets higher and looks up and sees the other bird sitting there calm and majestic, neither caring for good fruit nor for bad, sufficient unto itself, seeking no enjoyment beyond itself. It itself is enjoyment; what to seek beyond itself? The lower bird looks at the upper bird and wants to get near. It goes a little higher; but its old impressions are upon it, and still it goes about eating the same fruit. Again an exceptionally bitter fruit comes; it gets a shock, looks up. There the same calm and majestic one! It comes near but again is dragged down by past actions, and continues to eat the sweet and bitter fruits. Again the exceptionally bitter fruit comes, the bird looks up, gets nearer; and as it begins to get nearer and nearer, the light from the plumage of the other bird is reflected upon it. Its own plumage is melting away, and when it has come sufficiently near, the whole vision changes. The lower bird never existed, it was always the upper bird, and what it took for the lower bird was only a little bit of a reflection.

Such is the nature of the soul. This human soul goes after sense-enjoyments, vanities of the world; like animals it lives only in the senses, lives only in momentary titillations of the nerves. When there comes a blow, for a moment the head reels, and everything begins to vanish, and it finds that the world was not what it thought it to be, that life was not so smooth. It looks upward and sees the infinite Lord a moment, catches a glimpse of the majestic One, comes a little nearer, but is dragged away by its past actions. Another blow comes, and sends it back again. It catches another glimpse of the infinite Presence, comes nearer, and as it approaches nearer and nearer, it begins to find out that its individuality—its low, vulgar, intensely selfish individuality—is melting away; the desire to sacrifice the whole world to make that little thing happy is melting away; and as it gets gradually nearer and nearer, nature begins to melt away. When it has come sufficiently near, the whole vision changes, and it finds that it was the other bird, that this infinity which it had viewed as from a distance was its own Self, this wonderful glimpse that it had got of the glory and majesty was its own Self, and it indeed was that reality. The soul then finds That which is true in everything. That which is in every atom, everywhere present, the essence of all things, the God of this universe— know that thou art He, know that thou art free.

THE IMPORTANCE OF PSYCHOLOGY

The idea of psychology in the West is very much degraded. Psychology is the science of sciences; but in the West it is placed upon the same plane as all other sciences; that is, it is judged by the same criterion—utility.

How much practical benefit will it do to humanity? How much will it add to our rapidly growing happiness? How much will it detract from our rapidly increasing pain? Such is the criterion by which everything is judged in the West.

People seem to forget that about ninety per cent of all our knowledge cannot, in the very nature of things, be applied in a practical way to add to our material happiness or to lessen our misery. Only the smallest fraction of our scientific knowledge can have any such practical application to our daily lives. This is so because only an infinitely small percentage of our conscious mind is on the sensuous plane. We have just a little bit of sensuous consciousness and imagine that to be our entire mind and life; but, as a matter of fact, it is but a drop in the mighty ocean of subconscious mind. If all there is of us were a bundle of sense-perceptions, all the knowledge we could gain could be utilised in the gratification of our sense-pleasures. But fortunately such is not the case. As we get further and further away from the animal state, our sense-pleasures become less and less; and our enjoyment, in a rapidly increasing consciousness of scientific and psychological knowledge, becomes more and more intense; and "knowledge for the sake of knowledge", regardless of the amount of sense-pleasures it may conduce to, becomes the supreme pleasure of the mind.

But even taking the Western idea of utility as a criterion by which to judge, psychology, by such a standard even, is the science of sciences. Why? We are all slaves to our senses, slaves to our own minds, conscious and subconscious. The reason why a criminal is a criminal is not because he desires to be one, but because he has not his mind under control and is therefore a slave to his own conscious and subconscious mind, and to the mind of everybody else. He must follow the dominant trend of his own mind; he cannot help it; he is forced onward in spite of himself, in spite of his own better promptings, his own better nature; he is forced to obey the dominant mandate of his own mind. Poor man, he cannot help himself. We see this in our own lives constantly. We are constantly doing things against the better side of our nature, and afterwards we upbraid ourselves for so doing and wonder what we could have been thinking of, how we could do such a thing! Yet again and again we do it, and again and again we suffer for it and upbraid ourselves. At the time, perhaps, we think we desire to do it, but we only desire it because we are forced to desire it. We are forced onward, we are helpless! We are all slaves to our own and to everybody else's mind; whether we are good or bad, that makes no difference. We are led here and there because we cannot help ourselves. We say we think, we do, etc. It is not so. We think because we have to think. We act because we have to. We are slaves to ourselves and to others. Deep down in our subconscious mind are stored up all the thoughts and acts of the past, not only of this life, but of all other lives we have lived. This great boundless ocean of subjective mind is full of all the thoughts and actions of the past. Each one of these is striving to be recognised, pushing outward for expression, surging, wave after wave, out upon the objective mind, the conscious mind. These thoughts, the stored-up energy, we take for natural desires, talents, etc. It is because we do not realise their true origin. We obey them blindly, unquestioningly; and slavery, the most helpless kind of slavery, is the result; and we call ourselves free. Free! We who cannot for a moment govern our own minds, nay, cannot hold our minds on a subject, focus it on a point to the exclusion of everything else for a moment! Yet we call ourselves free. Think of it! We cannot do as we know we ought to do even for a very short space of time. Some sense-desire will crop up, and immediately we obey it. Our conscience smites us for such weakness, but again and again we do it, we are always doing it. We cannot live up to a high standard of life, try as we will. The ghosts of past thoughts, past lives hold us down. All the misery of the world is caused by this slavery to the senses. Our inability to rise above the sense-life—the striving for physical pleasures, is the cause of all the horrors and miseries in the world.

It is the science of psychology that teaches us to hold in check the wild gyrations of the mind, place it under the control of the will, and thus free ourselves from its tyrannous mandates. Psychology is therefore the science of sciences, without which all sciences and all other knowledge are worthless.

The mind uncontrolled and unguided will drag us down, down, for ever—rend us, kill us; and the mind controlled and guided will save us, free us. So it must be controlled, and psychology teaches us how to do it.

To study and analyse any material science, sufficient data are obtained. These facts are studied and analysed and a knowledge of the science is the result. But in the study and analysis of the mind, there are no data, no facts acquired from without, such as are equally at the command of all. The mind is analysed by itself. The greatest science, therefore, is the science of the mind, the science of psychology.

In the West, the powers of the mind, especially unusual powers, are looked upon as bordering on witchcraft and mysticism. The study of higher psychology has been retarded by its being identified with mere alleged psychic phenomena, as is done by some mystery-mongering order of Hindu fakirs.

Physicists obtain pretty much the same results the world over. They do not differ in their general facts, nor in the results which naturally follow from such facts. This is because the data of physical science are obtainable by all and are universally recognised, and the results are logical conclusions based upon these universally recognised facts. In the realm of the mind, it is different. Here there are no data, no facts observable by the physical senses, and no universally recognised materials therefore, from which to build a system of psychology after their being equally experimented upon by all who study the mind.

Deep, deep within, is the soul, the essential man, the Âtman. Turn the mind inward and become united to that; and from that standpoint of stability, the gyrations of the mind can be watched and facts observed, which are to be found in all persons. Such facts, such data, are to be found by those who go deep enough, and only by such. Among that large class of self-styled mystics the world over, there is a great difference of opinion as to the mind, its nature, powers, etc. This is because such people do not go deep enough. They have noticed some little activity of their own and others' minds and, without knowing anything about the real character of such superficial manifestations, have published them as facts universal in their application; and every religious and mystical crank has facts, data, etc., which, he claims, are reliable criteria for investigation, but which are in fact nothing more or less than his own imaginings

If you intend to study the mind, you must have systematic training; you must practice to bring the mind under your control, to attain to that consciousness from which you will be able to study the mind and remain unmoved by any of its wild gyrations. Otherwise the facts observed will not be reliable; they will not apply to all people and therefore will not be truly facts or data at all.

Among that class who have gone deeply into the study of the mind, the facts observed have been the same, no matter in what part of the world such persons may be or what religious belief they may have. The results obtained by all who go deep enough into the mind are the same.

The mind operates by perception and impulsion. For instance, the rays of the light enter by eyes, are carried by the nerves to the brain, and still I do not see the light. The brain then conveys the impulse to the mind, but yet I do not see the light; the mind then reacts, and the light flashes across the mind. The mind's reaction is impulsion, and as a result the eye perceives the object.

To control the mind you must go deep down into the subconscious mind, classify and arrange in order all the different impressions, thoughts, etc., stored up there, and control them. This is the first step. By the control of the subconscious mind you get control over the conscious.

NATURE AND MAN

The modern idea of nature includes only that part of the universe that is manifested on the physical plane. That which is generally understood to be mind is not considered to be nature.

Philosophers endeavouring to prove the freedom of the will have excluded the mind from nature; for as nature is bound and governed by law, strict unbending law, mind, if considered to be in nature, would be bound by law also. Such a claim would destroy the doctrine of free will; for how can that be free which is bound by law?

The philosophers of India have taken the reverse stand. They hold all physical life, manifest and unmanifest, to be bound by law. The mind as well as external nature, they claim, is bound by law, and by one and the same law. If mind is not bound by law, if the thoughts we think are not the necessary results of preceding thoughts, if one mental state is not followed by another which it produces, then mind is irrational; and who can claim free will and at the same time deny the operation of reason? And on the other hand, who can admit that the mind is governed by the law of causation and claim that the will is free?

Law itself is the operation of cause and effect. Certain things happen according to certain other things which have gone before. Every precedent has its consequent. Thus it is in nature. If this operation of law obtains in the mind, the mind is bound and is therefore not free. No, the will is not free. How can it be? But we all know, we all feel, that one are free. Life would have no meaning, it would not be worth living, if we were not free.

The Eastern philosophers accepted this doctrine, or rather propounded it, that the mind and the will are within time, space, and causation, the same as so-called matter; and that they are therefore bound by the law of causation. We think in time; our thoughts are bound by time; all that exists, exists in time and space. All is bound by the law of causation.

Now that which we call matter and mind are one and the same substance. The only difference is in the degree of vibration. Mind at a very low rate of vibration is what is known as matter. Matter at a high rate of vibration is what is known as mind. Both are the same substance; and therefore, as matter is bound by time and space and causation, mind which is matter at a high rate of vibration is bound by the same law.

Nature is homogeneous. Differentiation is in manifestation. The Sanskrit word for nature is Prakriti, and means literally differentiation. All is one substance, but it is manifested variously.

Mind becomes matter, and matter in its turn becomes mind, it is simply a question of vibration.

Take a bar of steel and charge it with a force sufficient to cause it to vibrate, and what would happen? If this were done in a dark room, the first thing you would be aware of would be a sound, a humming sound. Increase the force, and the bar of steel would become luminous; increase it still more, and the steel would disappear altogether. It would become mind.

Take another illustration: If I do not eat for ten days, I cannot think. Only a few stray thoughts are in my mind. I am very weak and perhaps do not know my own name. Then I eat some bread, and in a little while I begin to think; my power of mind has returned. The bread has become mind. Similarly, the mind lessens its rate of vibration and manifests itself in the body, becomes matter.

As to which is first—matter or mind, let me illustrate: A hen lays an egg; the egg brings out another hen; that hen lays another egg; that egg brings out another hen, and so on in an endless chain. Now which is first—the egg or the hen? You cannot think of an egg that was not laid by a hen, or a hen that was not hatched out of an egg. It makes no difference which is first. Nearly all our ideas run themselves into the hen and egg business.

The greatest truths have been forgotten because of their very simplicity. Great truths are simple because they are of universal application. Truth itself is always simple. Complexity is due to man's ignorance.

Man's free agency is not of the mind, for that is bound. There is no freedom there. Man is not mind, he is soul. The soul is ever free, boundless, and eternal. Herein is man's freedom, in the soul. The soul is always free, but the mind identifying itself with its own ephemeral waves, loses sight of the soul and becomes lost in the maze of time, space, and causation—Maya.

This is the cause of our bondage. We are always identifying ourselves with the mind, and the mind's phenomenal changes.

Man's free agency is established in the soul, and the soul, realising itself to be free, is always asserting the fact in spite of the mind's bondage: "I am free! I am what I am! I am what I am!" This is our freedom. The soul— ever free, boundless, eternal—through aeons and aeons is manifesting itself more and more through its instrument, the mind.

What relation then does man bear to nature? From the lowest form of life to man, the soul is manifesting itself through nature. The highest manifestation of the soul is involved in the lowest form of manifest life and is working itself outward through the process called evolution.

The whole process of evolution is the soul's struggle to manifest itself. It is a constant struggle against nature. It is a struggle against nature, and not conformity to nature that makes man what he is. We hear a great deal about living in harmony with nature, of being in tune with nature. This is a mistake. This table, this pitcher, the minerals, a tree, are all in harmony with nature. Perfect harmony there, no discord. To be in harmony with nature means stagnation, death. How did man build this house? By being in harmony with nature? No. By fighting against nature. It is the constant struggle against nature that constitutes human progress, not conformity with it.

CONCENTRATION AND BREATHING

The main difference between men and the animals is the difference in their power of concentration. All success in any line of work is the result of this. Everybody knows something about concentration. We see its results every day. High achievements in art, music, etc., are the results of concentration. An animal has very little power of concentration. Those who have trained animals find much difficulty in the fact that the animal is constantly forgetting what is told him. He cannot concentrate his mind long upon anything at a time. Herein is the difference between man and the animals—man has the greater power of concentration. The difference in heir power of concentration also constitutes the difference between man and man. Compare the lowest with the highest man. The difference is in the degree of concentration. This is the only difference.

Everybody's mind becomes concentrated at times. We all concentrate upon those things we love, and we love those things upon which we concentrate our minds. What mother is there that does not love the face of her homeliest child? That face is to her the most beautiful in the world. She loves it because she concentrates her mind on it; and if every one could concentrate his mind on that same face, every one would love it. It would be to all the most beautiful face. We all concentrate our minds upon those things we love. When we hear beautiful music, our minds become fastened upon it, and we cannot take them away. Those who concentrate their minds upon what you call classical music do not like common music, and vice versa. Music in which the notes follow each other in rapid succession holds the mind readily. A child loves lively music, because the rapidity of the notes gives the mind no chance to wander. A man who likes common music dislikes classical music, because it is more complicated and requires a greater degree of concentration to follow it.

The great trouble with such concentrations is that we do not control the mind; it controls us. Something outside of ourselves, as it were, draws the mind into it and holds it as long as it chooses. We hear melodious tones or see a beautiful painting, and the mind is held fast! We cannot take it away.

If I speak to you well upon a subject you like, your mind becomes concentrated upon what I am saying. I draw your mind away from yourself and hold it upon the subject in spite of yourself. Thus our attention is held, our minds are concentrated upon various things, in spite of ourselves. We cannot help it.

Now the question is: Can this concentration be developed, and can we become masters of it? The Yogis say, yes. The Yogis say that we can get perfect control of the mind. On the ethical side there is danger in the development of the power of concentration—the danger of concentrating the mind upon an object and then being unable to detach it at will. This state causes great suffering. Almost all our suffering is caused by our not having the power of detachment. So along with the development of concentration we must develop the power of detachment. We must learn not only to attach the mind to one thing exclusively, but also to detach it at a moment's notice and place it upon something else. These two should be developed together to make it safe.

This is the systematic development of the mind. To me the very essence of education is concentration of mind, not the collecting of facts. If I had to do my education over again, and had any voice in the matter, I would not study facts at all. I would develop the power of concentration and detachment, and then with a perfect instrument I could collect facts at will. Side by side, in the child, should be developed the power of concentration and detachment.

My development has been one-sided all along I developed concentration without the power of detaching my mind at will; and the most intense suffering of my life has been due to this. Now I have the power of detachment, but I had to learn it in later life.

We should put our minds on things; they should not draw our minds to them. We are usually forced to concentrate. Our minds are forced to become fixed upon different things by an attraction in them which we cannot resist. To control the mind, to place it just where we want it, requires special training. It cannot be done in any other way. In the study of religion the control of the mind is absolutely necessary. We have to turn the mind back upon itself in this study.

In training the mind the first step is to begin with the breathing. Regular breathing puts the body in a harmonious condition; and it is then easier to reach the mind. In practicing breathing, the first thing to consider is Âsana or posture. Any posture in which a person can sit easily is his proper position. The spine should be kept free, and the weight of the body should be supported by the ribs. Do not try by contrivances to control the mind; simple breathing is all that is necessary in that line. All austerities to gain concentration of the mind are a mistake. Do not practice them.

The mind acts on the body, and the body in its turn acts upon the mind. They act and react upon each other. Every mental state creates a corresponding state in the body, and every action in the body has its corresponding effect on the mind. It makes no difference whether you think the body and mind are two different entities, or whether you think they are both but one body— the physical body being the gross part and the mind the fine part. They act and react upon each other. The mind is constantly becoming the body. In the training of the mind, it is easier to reach it through the body. The body is easier to grapple with than the mind.

The finer the instrument, the greater the power. The mind is much finer and more powerful than the body. For this reason it is easier to begin with the body.

The science of breathing is the working through the body to reach the mind. In this way we get control of the body, and then we begin to feel the finer working of the body, the finer and more interior, and so on till we reach the mind. As we feel the finer workings of the body, they come under our control. After a while you will be able to feel the operation of the mind on the body. You will also feel the working of one half of the mind upon the other half, and also feel the mind recruiting the nerve centres; for the mind controls and governs the nervous system. You will feel the mind operating along the different nerve currents.

Thus the mind is brought under control—by regular systematic breathing, by governing the gross body first and then the fine body.

The first breathing exercise is perfectly safe and very healthful. It will give you good health, and better your condition generally at least. The other practices should be taken up slowly and carefully.

INTRODUCTION TO JNANA-YOGA

This is the rational and philosophic side of Yoga and very difficult, but I will take you slowly through it.

Yoga means the method of joining man and God. When you understand this, you can go on with your own definitions of man and God, and you will find the term Yoga fits in with every definition. Remember always, there are different Yogas for different minds, and that if one does not suit you, another may. All religions are divided into theory and practice. The Western mind has given itself up to the theory and only sees the practical part of religion as good works. Yoga is the practical part of religion and shows that religion is a practical power apart from good works.

At the beginning of the nineteenth century man tried to find God through reason, and Deism was the result. What little was left of God by this process was destroyed by Darwinism and Millism. Men were then thrown back upon historical and comparative religion. They thought, religion was derived from element worship (see Max Müller on the sun myths etc.); others thought that religion was derived from ancestor worship (see Herbert Spencer). But taken as a whole, these methods have proved a failure. Man cannot get at Truth by external methods.

"If I know one lump of clay, I know the whole mass of clay." The universe is all built on the same plan. The individual is only a part, like the lump of clay. If we know the human soul—which is one atom—its beginning and general history, we know the whole of nature. Birth, growth, development, decay, death—this is the sequence in all nature and is the same in the plant and the man. The difference is only in time. The whole cycle may be completed in one case in a day, in the other in three score years and ten; the methods are the same. The only way to reach a sure analysis of the universe is by the analysis of our own minds. A proper psychology is essential to the understanding of religion. To reach Truth by reason alone is impossible, because imperfect reason cannot study its own fundamental basis. Therefore the only way to study the mind is to get at facts, and then intellect will arrange them and deduce the principles. The intellect has to build the house; but it cannot do so without bricks and it cannot make bricks. Jnana-Yoga is the surest way of arriving at facts.

First we have the physiology of mind. We have organs of the senses, which are divided into organs of action and organs of perception. By organs I do not mean the external sense-instruments. The ophthalmic centre in the brain is the organ of sight, not the eye alone. So with every organ, the function is internal. Only when the mind reacts, is the object truly perceived. The sensory and motor nerves are necessary to perception.

Then there is the mind itself. It is like a smooth lake which when struck, say by a stone, vibrates. The vibrations gather together and react on the stone, and all through the lake they will spread and be felt. The mind is like the lake; it is constantly being set in vibrations, which leave an impression on the mind; and the idea of the Ego, or personal self, the "I", is the result of these impressions. This "I" therefore is only the very rapid transmission of force and is in itself no reality.

The mind-stuff is a very fine material instrument used for taking up the Prâna. When a man dies, the body dies; but a little bit of the mind, the seed, is left when all else is shattered; and this is the seed of the new body called by St. Paul "the spiritual body". This theory of the materiality of the mind accords with all modern theories. The idiot is lacking in intelligence because his mind-stuff is injured. Intelligence cannot be in matter nor can it be produced by any combinations of matter. Where then is intelligence? It is behind matter; it is the Jiva, the real Self, working through the instrument of matter. Transmission of force is not possible without matter, and as the

Jiva cannot travel alone, some part of mind is left as a transmitting medium when all else is shattered by death.

How are perceptions made? The wall opposite sends an impression to me, but I do not see the wall until my mind reacts, that is to say, the mind cannot know the wall by mere sight. The reaction that enables the mind to get a perception of the wall is an intellectual process. In this way the whole universe is seen through our eyes plus mind (or perceptive faculty); it is necessarily coloured by our own individual tendencies. The real wall, or the real universe, is outside the mind, and is unknown and unknowable. Call this universe X, and our statement is that the seen universe is X plus mind.

What is true of the external must also apply to the internal world. Mind also wants to know itself, but this Self can only be known through the medium of the mind and is, like the wall, unknown. This self we may call Y. and the statement would then be, Y plus mind is the inner self. Kant was the first to arrive at this analysis of mind, but it was long ago stated in the Vedas. We have thus, as it were, mind standing between X and Y and reacting on both.

If X is unknown, then any qualities we give to it are only derived from our own mind. Time, space, and causation are the three conditions through which mind perceives. Time is the condition for the transmission of thought, and space for the vibration of grosser matter. Causation is the sequence in which vibrations come. Mind can only cognise through these. Anything therefore, beyond mind must be beyond time, space, and causation.

To the blind man the world is perceived by touch and sound. To us with five senses it is another world. If any of us developed an electric sense and the faculty seeing electric waves, the world would appear different. Yet the world, as the X to all of these, is still the same. As each one brings his own mind, he sees his own world. There is X plus one sense; X plus two senses, up to five, as we know humanity. The result is constantly varied, yet X remains always unchanged. Y is also beyond our minds and beyond time, space, and causation.

But, you may ask, "How do we know there are two things (X and Y) beyond time, space, and causation?" Quite true, time makes differentiation, so that, as both are really beyond time, they must be really one. When mind sees this one, it calls it variously—X, when it is the outside world, and Y, when it is the inside world. This unit exists and is looked at through the lens of minds.

The Being of perfect nature, universally appearing to us, is God, is Absolute. The undifferentiated is the perfect condition; all others must be lower and not permanent.

What makes the undifferentiated appear differentiated to mind? This is the same kind of question as what is the origin of evil and free will? The question itself is contradictory and impossible, because the question takes for granted cause and effect. There is no cause and effect in the undifferentiated; the question assumes that the undifferentiated is in the same condition as the differentiated. "Whys" and "wherefores" are in mind only. The Self is beyond causation, and It alone is free. Its light it is which percolates through every form of mind. With every action I assert I am free, and yet every action proves that I am bound. The real Self is free, yet when mixed with mind and body, It is not free. The will is the first manifestation of the real Self; the first limitation therefore of this real Self is the will. Will is a compound of Self and mind. Now, no compound can be permanent, so that when we will to live, we must die. Immortal life is a contradiction in terms, for life, being a compound, cannot be immortal. True Being is undifferentiated and eternal. How does this Perfect Being become mixed up with will, mind, thought—all defective things? It never has become mixed. You are the real you (the Y of our former statement); you never were will; you never have changed; you as a person never existed; It is illusion. Then on what, you will say, do the phenomena of illusion rest? This is a bad question. Illusion never rests on Truth, but only on illusion. Everything struggles to go back to what was before these illusions, to be free in fact. What then is the value of life? It is to give us experience. Does this view do away with evolution? On the contrary, it explains it. It is really the process of refinement of matter allowing the real Self to manifest Itself. It is as if a screen or a veil were between us and some other object. The object becomes clear as the screen is gradually withdrawn. The question is simply one of manifestation of the higher Self.

THE VEDANTA PHILOSOPHY AND CHRISTIANITY

Notes of a lecture delivered at the Unitarian Church, in Oakland, California, on February 28, 1900

Between all great religions of the world there are many points of similarity; and so startling is this likeness, at times, as to suggest the idea that in many particulars the different religions have copied from one another.

This act of imitation has been laid at the door of different religions; but that it is a superficial charge is evident from the following facts:

Religion is fundamental in the very soul of humanity; and as all life is the evolution of that which is within, it, of necessity, expresses itself through various peoples and nations.

The language of the soul is one, the languages of nations are many; their customs and methods of life are widely different. Religion is of the soul and finds expression through various nations, languages, and customs. Hence it follows that the difference between the religions of the world is one of expression and not of substance; and their points of similarity and unity are of the soul, are intrinsic, as the language of the soul is one, in whatever peoples and under whatever circumstances it manifests itself. The same sweet harmony is vibrant there also, as it is on many and diverse instruments.

The first thing in common in all great religions of the world is the possession of an authentic book. When religious systems have failed to have such a book, they have become extinct. Such was the fact of the religions of Egypt. The authentic book is the hearthstone, so to speak, of each great religious system, around which its adherents gather, and from which radiates the energy and life of the system.

Each religion, again, lays the claim that its particular book is the only authentic word of God; that all other sacred books are false and are impositions upon poor human credulity; and that to follow another religion is to be ignorant and spiritually blind.

Such bigotry is characteristic of the orthodox element of all religions. For instance, the orthodox followers of the Vedas claim that the Vedas are the only authentic word of God in the world; that God has spoken to the world only through the Vedas; not only that, but that the world itself exists by virtue of the Vedas. Before the world was, the Vedas were. Everything in the world exists because it is in the Vedas. A cow exists because the name cow is in the Vedas; that is, because the animal we know as a cow is mentioned in the Vedas. The language of the Vedas is the original language of God, all other languages are mere dialects and not of God. Every word and syllable in the Vedas must be pronounced correctly, each sound must be given its true vibration, and every departure from this rigid exactness is a terrible sin and unpardonable.

Thus, this kind of bigotry is predominant in the orthodox element of all religions. But this fighting over the letter is indulged in only by the ignorant, the spiritually blind. All who have actually attained any real religious nature never wrangle over the form in which the different religions are expressed. They know that the life of all religions is the same, and, consequently, they have no quarrel with anybody because he does not speak the same tongue.

The Vedas are, in fact, the oldest sacred books in the world. Nobody knows anything about the time when they were written or by whom. They are contained in many volumes, and I doubt that any one man ever read them all.

The religion of the Vedas is the religion of the Hindus, and the foundation of all Oriental religions; that is, all other Oriental religions are offshoots of the Vedas; all Eastern systems of religion have the Vedas as authority.

It is an irrational claim to believe in the teachings of Jesus Christ and at the same time to hold that the greater part of his teachings have no application at the present time. If you say that the reason why the powers do not follow them that believe (as Christ said they would) is because you have not faith enough and are not pure enough—that will be all right. But to say that they have no application at the present time is to be ridiculous.

I have never seen the man who was not at least my equal. I have travelled all over the world; I have been among the very worst kind of people—among cannibals—and I have never seen the man who is not at least my equal. I have done as they do—when I was a fool. Then I did not know any better; now I do. Now they do not know any better; after a while they will. Every one acts according to his own nature. We are all in process of growth. From this standpoint one man is not better than another.

WORSHIPPER AND WORSHIPPED

This lecture is reproduced from the Vedanta and the West. *See Vol. IV.*

Delivered in San Francisco area, April 9, 1900

We have been taking up the more analytical side of human nature. In this course we [shall] study the emotional side... The former deals with man as unlimited being, [as] principle, the latter with man as limited being... The one has no time to stop for a few tear-drops or pangs; the other cannot proceed without wiping the tear-drop, without healing that misery. One is great, so great and grand that sometimes we are staggered by the magnitude; the other [is] commonplace, and yet most beautiful and dear to us. One gets hold of us, takes us up to the heights where our lungs almost burst. We cannot breathe [in] that atmosphere. The other leaves us where we are and tries to see the objects of life, [takes the limited] view. One will accept nothing until it has the shining seal of reason; the other has faith, and what it cannot see it believes. Both are necessary. A bird cannot fly with only one wing...

What we want is to see the man who is harmoniously developed ... great in heart, great in mind, [great in deed] ... We want the man whose heart feels intensely the miseries and sorrows of the world... And [we want] the man who not only can feel but can find the meaning of things, who delves deeply into the heart of nature and understanding. [We want] the man who will not even stop there, [but] who wants to work out [the feeling and meaning by actual deeds]. Such a combination of head, heart, and hand is what we want. There are many teachers in this world, but you will find [that most of them] are one-sided. [One] sees the glorious midday sun of intellect [and] sees nothing else. Another hears the beautiful music of love and can hear nothing else. Another is [immersed] in activity, and has neither time to feel nor time to think. Why not [have] the giant who is equally active, equally knowing, and equally loving? Is it impossible? Certainly not. This is the man of the future, of whom there are [only a] few at present. [The number of such will increase] until the whole world is humanised.

I have been talking to you so long about intellect [and] reason. We have heard the whole of Vedanta. The veil of Maya breaks: wintry clouds vanish, and the sunlight shines on us. I have been trying to climb the heights of the Himalayas, where the peaks disappear beyond the clouds. I propose lip study with you the other side: the most beautiful valleys, the most marvellous exquisiteness in nature. [We shall study the] love that holds us here in spite of all the miseries of the world, [the] love that has made us forge the chain of misery, this eternal martyrdom which man is suffering willingly, of his own accord. We want to study that for which man has forged the chain with his own hands, that for which he suffers, that eternal love. We do not mean to forget the other. The glacier of the Himalayas must join hands with the rice fields of Kashmir. The thunderbolt must blend its base note with the warbling of the birds.

This course will have to do with everything exquisite and beautiful. Worship is everywhere, in every soul. Everyone worships God. Whatever be the name, they are all worshipping God. The beginnings of worship—like the beautiful lotus, like life itself—are in the dirt of the earth... There is the element of fear. There is the hungering for this world's gain. There is the worship of the beggar. These are the beginnings of [the] world worshipping, [culminating in] loving God and worshipping God through man.

Is there any God? Is there anyone to be loved, any such one capable of being loved? Loving the stone would not be much good. We only love that which understands love, that which draws our love. So with worship. Never say [that] there is a man in this world of ours who worshipped a piece of stone [as stone]. He always worshipped [the omnipresent being in the stone].

We find out that the omnipresent being is in us. [But] how can we worship, unless that being is separate from us? I can only worship Thee, and not me. I can only pray to Thee, and not me. Is there any "Thou"?

The One becomes many. When we see the One, any limitations reflected through Maya disappear; but it is quite true that the manifold is not valueless. It is through the many that we reach the one...

Is there any Personal God—a God who thinks, who understands, a God who guides us? There is. The Impersonal God cannot have any one of these attributes. Each one of you is an individual: you think, you love, [you] hate, [you] are angry, sorry, etc.; yet you are impersonal, unlimited. [You are] personal and impersonal in one. You have the personal and the impersonal aspects. That [impersonal reality] cannot be angry, [nor] sorry, [nor] miserable—cannot even think misery. It cannot think, cannot know. It is knowledge itself. But the personal [aspect] knows, thinks, and dies, etc. Naturally the universal Absolute must have two aspects; the one representing the infinite reality of all things; the other, a personal aspect, the Soul of our souls, Lord of all lords. [It is] He who creates this universe. Under [His] guidance this universe exists...

He, the Infinite, the Ever-Pure, the Ever-[Free,]... He is no judge, God cannot be [a] judge. He does not sit upon a throne and judge between the good and the wicked... He is no magistrate, [no] general, [nor] master. Infinitely merciful, infinitely loving is the Personal [God].

Take it from another side. Every cell in your body has a soul conscious of the cell. It is a separate entity. It has a little will of its own, a little sphere of action of its own. All [cells] combined make up an individual. [In the same way,] the Personal God of the universe is made up of all these [many individuals].

Take it from another side. You, as I see you, are as much of your absolute nature as has been limited and perceived by one. I have limited you in order to see you through the power of my eyes, my senses. As much of you as my eyes can see, I see. As much of you as my mind can grasp is what I know to be you, and nothing more. In the same way, I am reading the Absolute, the Impersonal [and see Him as Personal]. As long as we have body and mind, we always see this triune being: God, nature, and soul. There must always be the three in one, inseparable... There is nature. There are human souls. There is again That in which nature and the human souls [are contained]

The universal soul has become embodied. My soul itself is a part of God. He is the eye of our eyes, the life of our life, the mind of our mind, the soul of our soul. This is the highest ideal of the Personal God we can have.

If you are not a dualist, [but are] a monist, you can still have the Personal God... There is the One without a second. That One wanted to love Himself. Therefore, out of that One, He made [many]... It is the big Me, the real Me, that that little me is worshipping. Thus in all systems you can have the Personal [God].

Some people are born under circumstances that make them happier than others: why should this be in the reign of a just being? There is mortality in this world. These are the difficulties in the way [These problems] have never been answered. They cannot be answered from any dualistic plane. We have to go back to philosophy to treat things as they are. We are suffering from our own Karma. It is not the fault of God. What we do is our own fault, nothing else. Why should God be blamed?...

Why is there evil? The only way you can solve [the problem] is [by saying that God is] the cause of both good and evil. The great difficulty in the theory of the

Personal God is that if you say He is only good and not evil, you will be caught in the trap of your own argument. How do you know there is [a] God? You say [that He is] the Father of this universe, and you say He is good; and because there is [also] evil in the world, God must be evil... The same difficulty!

There is no good, and there is no evil. God is all there is ... How do you know what is good? You feel [it]. [How do you know what is evil? If evil comes, you feel it... We know good and evil by our feelings. There is not one man who feels only good, happy feelings. There is not one who feels only unhappy feelings...

Want and anxiety are the causes of all unhappiness and happiness too. Is want increasing or decreasing? Is life becoming simple or complex? Certainly complex. Wants are being multiplied. Your great-grandfathers did not want the same dress or the same amount of money [you do]. They had no electric cars, [nor] railroads, etc. That is why they had to work less. As soon as these things come, the want arises, and you have to work harder. More and more anxiety, and more and more competition.

It is very hard work to get money. It is harder work to keep it. You fight the whole world to get a little money together [and] fight all your life to protect it. [Therefore] there is more anxiety for the rich than for the poor... This is the way it is...

There are good and evil every where in this world. Sometimes evil becomes good, true; but other times good becomes evil also. All our senses produce evil some time or other. Let a man drink wine. It is not bad [at first], but let him go on drinking, [and] it will produce evil... A man is born of rich parents; good enough. He becomes a fool, never exercises his body or brain. That is good producing evil. Think of this love of life: We go away and jump about and live a few moments; we work hard. We are born babies, entirely incapable. It takes us years to understand things again. At sixty or seventy we open our eyes, and then comes the word, "Get out!" And there you are.

We have seen that good and evil are relative terms. The thing [that is] good for me is bad for you. If you eat the dinner that I eat, you will begin to weep, and I shall laugh... We [may] both dance, but I with joy and you with pain... The same thing is good at one part of our life and bad at another part. How can you say [that] good and evil are all cut and dried— [that] this is all good and that is all evil?

Now, who is responsible for all this good and evil, if God is ever the good? The Christians and the Mohammedans say there is a gentleman called Satan. How can you say there are two gentlemen working? There must be one... The fire that burns the child also cooks the meal. How can you call the fire good or bad, and how can you say it was created by two different persons? Who creates all [so-called] evil? God. There is no other way out. He sends death and life, plague and epidemics, and everything. If such is God, He is the good; He is the evil; He is the beautiful; He is the terrible; He is life; and He is death.

How can such a God be worshipped? We shall come to [understand] how the soul can really learn to worship the terrible; then that soul will have peace... Have you peace? Do you get rid of anxieties? Turn around, first of all, and face the terrible. Tear aside the mask and find the same [God]. He is the personal—all that is [apparently] good and all that is [apparently] bad. There is none else. If there were two Gods, nature could not stand a moment. There is not another one in nature. It is all harmony. If God played one side and the devil the other, the whole [of] nature would be [in chaos]. Who can break the law? If I break this glass, it will fall down. If anyone succeeds in throwing one atom out of place, every other atom will go out of balance... The law can never be broken. Each atom is kept in its place. Each is weighed and measured and fulfils its [purpose] and place. Through His command the winds blow, the sun shines. Through His rule the worlds are kept in place. Through His orders death is sporting upon the earth. Just think of two or three Gods having a wrestling match in this world! It cannot be.

We now come to see that we can have the Personal God, the creator of this universe, who is merciful and also cruel... He is the good, He is the evil. He smiles, and He frowns. And none can go beyond His law. He is the creator of this universe.

What is meant by creation, something coming out of nothing? Six thousand years ago God woke up from His dream and created the world [and] before that there was nothing? What was God doing then, taking a good nap? God is the cause of the universe, and we can know the cause through the effect. If the effect is not present, the cause is not [the] cause. The cause is always known in and through the effect... Creation is infinite... You cannot think of the beginning in time or in space.

Why does He create it? Because He likes to; because He is free... You and I are bound by law, because we can work [only] in certain ways and not in others. "Without hands, He can grasp everything. Without feet, [He moves fast]." Without body, He is omnipotent. "Whom no eyes can see, but who is the cause of sight in every eye, know Him to be the Lord." You cannot worship anything else. God is the omnipotent supporter of this universe. What is called "law" is the manifestation of His will. He rules the universe by His laws.

So far [we have discussed] God and nature, eternal God and eternal nature. What about souls? They also are eternal. No soul was [ever] created; neither can [the] soul die. Nobody can even imagine his own death. The soul is infinite, eternal. How can it die? It changes bodies. As a man takes off his old, worn-out garments and puts on new and fresh ones, even so the worn-out body is thrown away and [a] fresh body is taken.

What is the nature of the soul? The soul is also [omnipotent] and omnipresent. Spirit has neither length, nor breadth, nor thickness... How can it be said to be here and there? This body falls; [the soul] works [through] another body. The soul is a circle of which the circumference is nowhere, but the centre is in the body. God is a circle whose circumference is nowhere, but whose centre is everywhere. The soul by its [very] nature is blessed, pure, and perfect; it could never be pure if its nature was impure... The soul's nature is purity; that is why souls [can] become pure. It is blessed [by nature]; that is why it [can] become blessed. It is peace; [that is why it can become peaceful]...

All of us who find ourselves in this plane, attracted to the body, work hard for a living, with jealousies and quarrels and hardships, and then death. That shows we are not what we should be. We are not free, perfectly pure, and so on. The soul, as it were, has become degraded. Then what the soul requires is expansion...

How can you do it? Can you work it out yourself? No. If a man's face is dusty, can you wash it out with dust? If I put a seed in the ground, the seed produces a tree, the tree produces a seed, the seed another tree, etc. Hen and egg, egg and hen. If you do something good, you will have to reap the result of that, be born again and be sorry. Once started in this infinite chain, you cannot stop. You go on, ... up and down, [to] heavens and earths, and all these [bodies]... There is no way out.

Then how can you get out of all this, and what are you here for? One idea is to get rid of misery. We are all struggling day and night to get rid of misery... We cannot do it by work. Work will produce more work. It is only possible if there is someone who is free himself and lends us a hand. "Hear, ye children of immortality, all those that reside in this plane and all those that reside in the heavens above, I have found the secret", says the great sage. "I have found Him who is beyond all darkness. Through His mercy alone we cross this ocean of life."

In India, the idea of the goal is this: There are heavens, there are hells, there are earths, but they are not permanent. If I am sent to hell, it is not permanent. The same struggle goes on and on wherever I am. How to get beyond all this struggle is the problem. If I go to heaven, perhaps there will be a little bit of rest. If I get punished for my misdeeds, that cannot last [for ever either] ... The Indian ideal is not to go to heaven. Get out of this earth, get out of hell, and get out of heaven! What is the goal? It is freedom. You must all be free. The glory of the soul is covered up. It has to be uncovered again. The soul exists. It is everywhere. Where shall it go? ... Where can it go? It can only go where it is not. If you understand [that] it is ever present, ... [there will be] perfect happiness for ever afterwards. No more births and deaths... No more disease, no body. [The] body itself is the biggest disease...

The soul shall stand [as] soul. Spirit shall live as spirit. How is this to be done? By worshipping [the Lord in] the soul, who, by his [very] nature is ever present, pure, and perfect. There cannot be two almighty beings in this world. [Imagine having] two or three Gods; one will create the world, another says, "I will destroy the world." It [can] never happen. There must be one God. The soul attains to perfection; [it becomes] almost omnipotent [and] omniscient. This is the worshipper. Who is the worshipped? He, the Lord God Himself, the Omnipresent, the Omniscient, and so on. And above all, He is Love. How is [the soul] to attain this perfection? By worship.

Vedanta and the West, July-Aug. 1955.

FORMAL WORSHIP

This lecture is reproduced from the Vedanta and the West. *See Vol. IV.*

Delivered in San Francisco area, April 10, 1900

All of you who are students of the Bible . . . . .understand that the whole [of] Jewish history and Jewish thought have been produced by two [types of] teachers—priests and prophets, the priests representing the power of conservatism, the prophets the power of progress. The whole thing is that a conservative ritualism creeps in; formality gets hold of everything. This is true of every country and every religion. Then come some new seers with new visions; they preach new ideals and ideas and give a new push to society. In a few generations the followers become so faithful to their masters' ideas that they cannot see anything else. The most advanced, liberal preachers of this age within a few years will be the most conservative priests. The advanced thinkers, in their turn, will begin to hinder the man who goes a little farther. They will not let anyone go farther than what they themselves have attained. They are content to leave things as they are.

The power which works through the formative principles of every religion in every country is manifested in the forms of religion. . . . Principles and books, certain rules and movements—standing up, sitting down—all these belong to the same category of worship Spiritual worship becomes materialised in order that the majority of mankind can get hold of it. The vast majority of mankind in every country are never [seen] to worship spirit as spirit. It is not yet possible. I do not know if there ever will be a time when they can. How many thousands in this city are ready to worship God as spirit? Very few. They cannot; they live in the senses. You have to give them cut and dried ideas. Tell them to do something physical: Stand up twenty times; sit down twenty times. They will understand that. Tell them to breathe in through one nostril and breathe out through the other. They will understand that. All this idealism about spirit they cannot accept at all. It is not their fault. . . . If you have the power to worship God as spirit, good! But there was a time when you could not. . . . If the people are crude, the religious conceptions are crude, and the forms are uncouth and gross. If the people are refined and cultured, the forms are more beautiful. There must be forms, only the forms change according to the times.

It is a curious phenomenon that there never was a religion started in this world with more antagonism . . . [to the worship of forms] than Mohammedanism. . . . The Mohammedans can have neither painting, nor sculpture, nor music. . . . That would lead to formalism. The priest never faces his audience. If he did, that would make a distinction. This way there is none. And yet it was not two centuries after the Prophet's death before saint worship [developed]. Here is the toe of the saint! There is the skin of the saint! So it goes. Formal worship is one of the stages we have to pass through.

Therefore, instead of crusading against it, let us take the best in worship and study its underlying principles.

Of course, the lowest form of worship is what is known as [tree and stone worship]. Every crude, uncultured man will take up anything and add to it some idea [of his own]; and that will help him. He may worship a bit of bone, or stone—anything. In all these crude states of worship man has never worshipped a stone as stone, a tree as tree. You know that from common sense. Scholars sometimes say that men worshipped stones and trees. That is all nonsense. Tree worship is one of the stages through which the human race passed. Never, really, was there ever worship of anything but the spirit by man.

He is spirit [and] can feel nothing but spirit. Divine mind could never make such a gross mistake as [to worship spirit as matter]. In this case, man conceived the stone as spirit or the tree as spirit. He [imagined] that some part of that Being resides in [the stone] or the tree, that [the stone or] the tree has a soul.

Tree worship and serpent worship always go together. There is the tree of knowledge. There must always be the tree, and the tree is somehow connected with the serpent. These are the oldest [forms of worship]. Even there you find that some particular tree or some particular stone is worshipped, not all the [trees or] stones in the world.

A higher state in [formal worship is that of] images [of ancestors and God]. People make images of men who have died and imaginary images of God. Then they worship those images.

Still higher is the worship of saints, of good men and women who have passed on. Men worship their relics. [They feel that] the presence of the saints is somehow in the relics, and that they will help them. [They believe that] if they touch the saint's bone, they will be healed—not that the bone itself heals, but that the saint who resides there does. . . .

These are all low states of worship and yet worship. We all have to pass through them. It is only from an intellectual standpoint that they are not good enough. In our hearts we cannot get rid of them. [If] you take from a man all the saints and images and do not allow him to go into a temple, [he will still] imagine all the gods. He has to. A man of eighty told me he could not conceive God except as an old man with a long beard sitting on a cloud. What does that show? His education is not complete. There has not been any spiritual education, and he is unable to conceive anything except in human terms.

There is still a higher order of formal worship—the world of symbolism. The forms are still there, but they are neither trees, nor [stones], nor images, nor relics of saints. They are symbols. There are all sorts [of symbols] all over the world. The circle is a great symbol of eternity. . . . There is the square; the well-known symbol of the cross; and two figures like S and Z crossing each other.

Some people take it into their heads to see nothing in symbols. . . . [Others want] all sorts of abracadabra. If you tell them plain, simple truths, they will not accept them. . . . Human nature being [what it is], the less they understand the better—the greater man [they think] you are. In all ages in every country such worshippers are deluded by certain diagrams and forms. Geometry was the greatest science of all. The vast majority of the people knew nothing [of it. They believed that if] the geometrist just drew a square and said abracadabra at the four corners, the whole world would begin to turn, the heavens would open, and God would come down and jump about and be a slave. There is a whole mass of lunatics today poring over these things day and night. All this is a sort of disease. It is not for the metaphysician at all; it is for the physician.

I am making fun, but I am so sorry. I see this problem so [grave] in India These are signs of the decay of the race, of degradation and duress. The sign of vigour, the sign of life, the sign of hope, the sign of health, the sign of everything that is good, is strength. As long as the body lives, there must be strength in the body, strength in the mind, [and strength] in the hand. In wanting to get spiritual power through [all this abracadabra] there is fear, fear of life. I do not mean that sort of symbolism.

But there is some truth in symbolistic. There cannot be any falsehood without some truth behind it. There cannot be any imitation without something real.

There is the symbolic form, of worship in the different religions. There are fresh, vigorous, poetic, healthy symbols Think of the marvellous power the symbol of the cross has had upon millions of people! Think of the symbol of the crescent! Think of the magnetism of this one symbol! Everywhere there are good and great symbols in the world. They interpret the spirit and bring [about] certain conditions of the mind; as a rule we find [they create] a tremendous power of faith and love.

Compare the Protestant with the Catholic [Church]. Who has produced more saints, more martyrs within the last four hundred years [during which] both have been in existence? The tremendous appeal of Catholic ceremonialism— all those lights, incense, candles, and the robes of the priests—has a great effect in itself. Protestantism is quite austere and unpoetic. The Protestants have gained many things, have granted a great deal more freedom in certain lines than the Catholics have, and so have a clear, more individualized conception. That is all right, but they have lost a good deal. . . . Take the paintings in the churches. That is an attempt at poetry. If we are hungry for poetry, why not have it? Why not give the soul what it wants? We have to have music. The Presbyterians were even against music. They are the "Mohammedans" of the Christians. Down with all poetry! Down with all ceremonials! Then they produce music. It appeals to the senses. I have seen how collectively they strive for the ray of light there over the pulpit.

Let the soul have its fill of poetry and religion represented on the external plane. Why not . . . ? You cannot fight [formal worship]. It will conquer again and again. . . . If you do not like what the Catholics do, do better. But we will neither do anything better nor have the poetry that already exists. That is a terrible state of things! Poetry is absolutely necessary. You may be the greatest philosopher in the world. But philosophy is the highest poetry. It is not dry bones It is essence of things. The Reality itself is more poetic than any dualism. . . .

Learning has no place in religion; for the majority learning is a block in the way. . . . A man my have read all the libraries in the world and many not be religious at all, and another, who cannot perhaps write his own name, senses religion and realises it. The whole of religion is our own inner perception. When I use the words "man-making religion", I do not mean books, nor dogmas, nor theories. I mean the man who has realised, has fully perceived, something of that infinite presence in his own heart.

The man at whose feet I sat all my life—and it is only a few ideas of his that try to teach—could [hardly] write his name at all. All my life I have not seen another man like that, and I have travelled all over the world. When I think of that man, I feel like a fool, because I want to read books and he never did. He never wanted to lick the plates after other people had eaten. That is why he was his own book. All my life I am repeating what Jack said and John said, and never say anything myself. What glory is it that you know what John said twenty-five years ago and what Jack said five years ago? Tell me what you have to say.

Mind you, there is no value in learning. You are all mistaken in learning. The only value of knowledge is in the strengthening, the disciplining, of the mind. By all this eternal swallowing it is a wonder that we are not all dyspeptics. Let us stop, and burn all the books, and get hold of ourselves and think. You all talk [about] and get distracted over losing your "individuality". You are losing it every moment of your lives by this eternal swallowing. If any one of you believes what I teach, I will be sorry. I will only be too glad if I can excite in you the power of thinking for yourselves. . . . My ambition is to talk to men and women, not to sheep. By men and women, I mean individuals. You are not little babies to drag all the filthy rags from the street and bind them up into a doll!

"This is a place for learning! That man is placed in the university! He knows all about what Mr. Blank said!" But Mr. Blank said nothing! If I had the choice I would . . . say to the professor, "Get out! You are nobody!" Remember this individualism at any cost! Think wrong if you will, no matter whether you get truth or not. The whole point is to discipline the mind. That truth which you swallow from others will not be yours. You cannot teach truth from my mouth; neither can you learn truth from my mouth. None can teach another. You have to realise truth and work it out for yourself according to your own nature. . . . All must struggle to be individuals— strong, standing on your own feet, thinking your own thoughts, realising your own Self. No use swallowing doctrines others pass on—standing up together like soldiers in jail, sitting down together, all eating the same food, all nodding their heads at the same time. Variation is the sign of life. Sameness is the sign of death.

Once I was in an Indian city, and an old man came

to me. He said, "Swami, teach me the way." I saw that that man was as dead as this table before me. Mentally and spiritually he was really dead. I said, "will you do what I ask you to do? Can you steal? Can you drink wine? Can you eat meat?"

The man [exclaimed], "What are you teaching!"

I said to him, "Did this wall ever steal? Did the wall ever drink wine?"

"No, sir."

Man steals, and he drinks wine, and becomes God. "I know you are not the wall, my friend. Do something! Do something!" I saw that if that man stole, his soul would be on the way to salvation.

How do I know that you are individuals—all saying the same thing, all standing up and sitting down together? That is the road to death! Do something for your souls! Do wrong if you please, but do something! You will understand me by and by, if you do not just now. Old age has come upon the soul, as it were. It has become rusty. The rust must be [rubbed off], and then we go on. Now you understand why there is evil in the world. Go home and think of that, just to take off that rustiness!

We pray for material things. To attain some end we worship God with shopkeeping worship. Go on and pray for food and clothes! Worship is good. Something is always better than nothing. "A blind uncle is better than no uncle at all." A very rich young man becomes ill, and then to get rid of his disease he begins to give to the poor. That is good, but it is not religion yet, not spiritual religion. It is all on the material plane. What is material, and what is not? When the world is the end and God the means to attain that end, that is material. When God is the end and the world is only the means to attain that end, spirituality has begun.

Thus, to the man who wants this [material] life enough, all his heavens are a continuance of this life. He wants to see all the people who are dead, and have a good time once more.

There was one of those ladies who bring the departed spirits down to us—a medium. She was very large, yet she was called medium. Very good! This lady liked me very much and invited me to come. The spirits were all very polite to me. I had a very peculiar experience. You understand, it was a [seance], midnight. The medium said, ". . . I see a ghost standing here. The ghost tells me that there is a Hindu gentleman on that bench." I stood up and said, "It required no ghost to tell you that."

There was a young man present who was married, intelligent, and well educated. He was there to see his mother. The medium said, "So-and-so's mother is here." This young man had been telling me about his mother. She was very thin when she died, but the mother that came out of the screen! You ought to have seen her! I wanted to see what this young man would do. To my surprise he jumped up and embraced this spirit and said. "Oh mother, how beautiful you have grown in the spirit land!" I said, "I am blessed that I am here. It gives me an insight into human nature!"

Going back to our formal worship. . . . it is a low state of worship when you worship God as a means to the end, which is this life and this world. . . . The vast majority of [people] have never had any conception of anything higher than this lump of flesh and the joys of the senses. Even in this life, all the pleasures these poor souls have are the same as the beasts. . . . They eat animals. They love their children. Is that all the glory of man? And we worship God Almighty! What for? Just to give us these material things and defend them all the time. . . . It means we have not gone beyond the [animals and] birds. We are no better. We do not know any better. And woe unto us, we should know better! The only difference is that they do not have a God like ours. . . We have the same five senses [as the animals], only theirs are better. We cannot eat a morsel of food with the relish that a dog chews a bone. They have more pleasure in life than we; so we are a little less than animals.

Why should you want to be something that any power in nature can operate better? This is the most important question for you to think about. What do you want—this life, these senses, this body, or something infinitely higher and better, something from which there is no more fall, no more change?

So what does it mean . . . ? You say, "Lord, give me my bread, my money! Heal my diseases! Do this and that!" Every time you say that, you are hypnotising yourselves with the idea, "I am matter, and this matter is the goal." Every time you try to fulfil a material desire, you tell yourselves that you are [the] body, that you are not spirit. . . .

Thank God, this is a dream! Thank God, for it will vanish! Thank God, there is death, glorious death, because it ends all this delusion, this dream, this fleshiness, this anguish. No dream can be eternal; it must end sooner or later. There is none who can keep his dream for ever. I thank God that it is so! Yet this form of worship is all right. Go on! To pray for something is better than nothing. These are the stages through which we pass. These are the first lessons. Gradually, the mind begins to think of something higher than the senses, the body, the enjoyments of this world.

How does [man] do it? First he becomes a thinker. When you think upon a problem, there is no sense enjoyment there, but [the] exquisite delight of thought. . . . It is that that makes the man. . . . Take one great idea! It deepens. Concentration comes. You no longer feel your body. Your senses have stopped. You are above all physical senses. All that was manifesting itself through the senses is concentrated upon that one idea. That moment you are higher than the animal. You get the revelation none can take from you—a direct perception of something higher than the body. . . . Therein is the gold of mind, not upon the plane of the senses.

Thus, working through the plane of the senses, you get more and more entry into the other regions, and then this world falls away from you. You get one glimpse of that spirit, and then your senses and your sense-enjoyments, your dinging to the flesh, will all melt away from you. Glimpse after glimpse will come from the realm of spirit. You will have finished Yoga, and spirit will stand revealed as spirit. Then you will begin the worship of God as spirit. Then you will begin to understand that worship is not to gain something. At heart, our worship was that infinite-finite element, love, which [is] an eternal sacrifice at the feet of the Lord by the soul. "Thou and not I. I am dead. Thou art, and I am not. I do not want wealth nor beauty, no, nor even learning. I do not want salvation. If it be Thy will, let me go into twenty million hells. I only want one thing: Be Thou my love!"

Vedanta and the West, Nov.-Dec. 1955.

DIVINE LOVE

This lecture is reproduced from the Vedanta and the West. *See Vol. IV.*

Delivered in San Francisco area, April 12, 1900

[Love may be symbolised by a triangle. The first angle is,] love questions not. It is not a beggar. . . . Beggar's love is no love at all. The first sign of love is when love asks nothing, [when it] gives everything. This is the real spiritual worship, the worship through love. Whether God is merciful is no longer questioned. He is God; He is my love. Whether God is omnipotent and almighty, limited or unlimited, is no longer questioned. If He distributes good, all right; if He brings evil, what does it matter? All other attributes vanish except that one—infinite love.

There was an old Indian emperor who on a hunting expedition came across a great sage in the forest. He was so pleased with this sage that he insisted that the latter come to the capital to receive some presents. [At first] the sage refused. [But] the emperor insisted, and at last the sage consented. When he arrived [at the palace], he was announced to the emperor who said, "Wait a minute until I finish my prayer." The emperor prayed, "Lord, give me more wealth, more [land, more health], more children." The sage stood up and began to walk out of the room. The emperor said, "You have not received my presents." The sage replied, "I do not beg from beggars. All this time you have been praying for more land, [for] more money, for this and that. What can you give me? First satisfy your own wants!"

Love never asks; it always gives. . . . When a young man goes to see his sweetheart, . . . there is no business relationship between them; theirs is a relationship of love, and love is no beggar. [In the same way], we understand that the beginning of real spiritual worship means no begging. We have finished all begging: "Lord, give me this and that." Then will religion begin.

The second [angle of the triangle of love] is that love knows no fear. You may cut me to pieces, and I [will] still love you. Suppose one of you mothers, a weak woman, sees a tiger in the street snatching your child. I know where you will be: you will face the tiger. Another time a dog appears in the street, and you will fly. But you jump at the mouth of the tiger and snatch your child away. Love knows no fear. It conquers all evil. The fear of God is the beginning of religion, but the love of God is the end of religion. All fear has died out.

The third [angle of the love-triangle is that] love is its own end. It can never be the means. The man who says, "I love you for such and such a thing", does not love. Love can never be the means; it must be the perfect end. What is the end and aim of love? To love God, that is all. Why should one love God? [There is] no why, because it is not the means. When one can love, that is salvation, that is perfection, that is heaven. What more? What else can be the end? What can you have higher than love?

I am not talking about what every one of us means by love. Little namby-pamby love is lovely. Man rails in love with woman, and woman goes to die for man. The chances are that in five minutes John kicks Jane, and Jane kicks John. This is a materialism and no love at all. If John could really love Jane, he would be perfect that moment. [His true] nature is love; he is perfect in himself. John will get all the powers of Yoga simply by loving Jane, [although] he may not know a word about religion, psychology, or theology. I believe that if a man and woman can really love, [they can acquire] all the powers the Yogis claim to have, for love itself is God. That God is omnipresent, and [therefore] you have that love, whether you know it or not.

I saw a boy waiting for a girl the other evening.... I thought it a good experiment to study this boy. He developed clairvoyance and clairaudience through the intensity of his love. Sixty or seventy times he never made a mistake, and the girl was two hundred miles away. [He would say], "She is dressed this way." [Or,] "There she goes." I have seen that with my own eyes.

This is the question: Is not your husband God, your child God? If you can love your wife, you have all the religion in the world. You have the whole secret of religion and Yoga in you. But can you love? That is the question. You say, "I love . . . Oh Mary, I die for you!" [But if you] see Mary kissing another man, you want to cut his throat. If Mary sees John talking to another girl, she cannot sleep at night, and she makes life hell for John. This is not love. This is barter and sale in sex. It is blasphemy to talk of it as love. The world talks day and night of God and religion—so of love. Making a sham of everything, that is what you are doing! Everybody talks of love, [yet in the] columns in the newspapers [we read] of divorces every day. When you love John, do you love John for his sake or for your sake? [If you love him for your sake], you expect something from John. [If you love him for his sake], you do not want anything from John. He can do anything he likes, [and] you [will] love him just the same.

These are the three points, the three angles that constitute the triangle [of love]. Unless there is love, philosophy becomes dry bones, psychology becomes a sort of [theory], and work becomes mere labour. [If there is love], philosophy becomes poetry, psychology becomes [mysticism], and work the most delicious thing in creation. [By merely] reading books [one] becomes barren. Who becomes learned? He who can feel even one drop of love. God is love, and love is God. And God is everywhere. After seeing that God is love and God is everywhere, one does not know whether one stands on one's head or [on one's] feet—like a man who gets a bottle of wine and does not know where he stands. . . . If we weep ten minutes for God, we will not know where we are for the next two months. . . . We will not remember the times for meals. We will not know what we are eating. [How can] you love God and always be so nice and businesslike? . . . The . . . all-conquering, omnipotent power of love—how can it come? . . .

Judge people not. They are all mad. Children are [mad] after their games, the young after the young, the old [are] chewing the cud of their past years; some are mad after gold. Why not some after God? Go crazy over the love of God as you go crazy over Johns and Janes. Who are they? [people] say, "Shall I give up this? Shall I give up that?" One asked, "Shall I give up marriage?" Do not give up anything! Things will give you up. Wait, and you will forget them.

[To be completely] turned into love of God—there is the real worship! You have a glimpse of that now and then in the Roman Catholic Church—some of those wonderful monks and nuns going mad with marvellous love. Such love you ought to have! Such should be the love of God—without asking anything, without seeking anything. . . .

The question was asked: How to worship? Worship Him as dearer than all your possessions, dearer than all your relatives, [dearer than] your children. [Worship Him as] the one you love as Love itself. There is one whose name is infinite Love. That is the only definition of God. Do not care if this . . . universe is destroyed. What do we care as long as He is infinite love? [Do you see what worship means? All other thoughts must go. Everything must vanish except God. The love the father or mother has for the child, [the love] the wife [has] for the husband, the husband, for the wife, the friend for the friend—all these loves concentrated into one must be given to God. Now, if the woman loves the man, she cannot love another man. If the man loves the woman, he cannot love another [woman]. Such is the nature of love.

My old Master used to say, "Suppose there is a bag of gold in this room, and in the next room there is a robber. The robber is well aware that there is a bag of gold. Would the robber be able to sleep? Certainly not. All the time he would be crazy thinking how to reach the gold." . . . [Similarly], if a man loves God, how can he love anything else? How can anything else stand before that mighty love of God? Everything else vanishes [before it]. How can the mind stop without going crazy to find [that love], to realise, to feel, to live in that?

This is how we are to love God: "I do not want wealth, nor [friends, nor beauty], nor possessions, nor learning, nor even salvation. If it be Thy will, send me a thousand deaths. Grant me, this—that I may love Thee and that for love's sake. That love which materialistic persons have for their worldly possessions, may that strong love come into my heart, but only for the Beautiful. Praise to God! Praise to God the Lover!" God is nothing else than that. He does not care for the wonderful things many Yogis can do. Little magicians do little tricks. God is the big magician; He does all the tricks. Who cares how many worlds [there are]? . . .

There is another [way. It is to] conquer everything, [to] subdue everything —to conquer the body [and] the mind. . . . "What is the use of conquering everything? My business is with God!" [says the devotee.]

There was one Yogi, a great lover. He was dying of cancer of the throat. He [was] visited [by] another Yogi, who was a philosopher. [The latter] said, "Look here, my friend, why don't you concentrate your mind on that sore of yours and get it cured?" The third time this question was asked [this great Yogi] said, "Do you think it possible that the [mind] which I have given entirely to the Lord [can be fixed upon this cage of flesh and blood]?" Christ refused to bring legions of angels to his aid. Is this little body so great that I should bring twenty thousand angels to keep it two or three days more?

[From the worldly standpoint,] my all is this body. My world is this body. My God is this body. I am the body. If you pinch me, I am pinched. I forget God the moment I have a headache. I am the body! God and everything must come down for this highest goal— the body. From this standpoint, when Christ died on the cross and did not bring angels [to his aid], he was a fool. He ought to have brought down angels and gotten himself off the cross! But from the standpoint of the lover, to whom this body is nothing, who cares for this nonsense? Why bother thinking about this body that comes and goes? There is no more to it than the piece of cloth the Roman soldiers cast lots for.

There is a whole gamut of difference between [the worldly standpoint] and the lover's standpoint. Go on loving. If a man is angry, there is no reason why you should be angry; if he degrades himself, that is no reason why you should degrade yourself. . . . "Why should I become angry just because another man has made a fool of himself. Do thou resist not evil!" That is what the lovers of God say. Whatever the world does, wherever it goes, has no influence [on them].

One Yogi had attained supernatural powers. He said, "See my power! See the sky; I will cover it with clouds." It began to rain. [Someone] said, "My lord, you are wonderful. But teach me that, knowing which, I shall not ask for anything else." ... To get rid even of power, to have nothing, not to want power! [What this means] cannot be understood simply by intellect. . . . You cannot understand by reading thousands of books. ... When we begin to understand, the whole world opens before us. ... The girl is playing with her dolls, getting new husbands all the time; but when her real husband comes, all the dolls will be put away [for ever]. ... So [with] all these goings-on here. [When] the sun of love rises, all these play-suns of power and these [cravings] all pass [away]. What shall we do with power? Thank God if you can get rid of the power that you have. Begin to love. Power must go. Nothing must stand between me and God except love. God is only love and nothing else—love first, love in the middle, and love at the end.

[There is the] story of a queen preaching [the love of God] in the streets. Her enraged husband persecuted her, and she was hunted up and down the country. She used to sing songs describing her [love]. Her songs have been sung everywhere. "With tears in my eyes I [nourished the everlasting creeper] of love. ..." This is the last, the great [goal]. What else is there? [People] want this and that. They all want to have and possess. That is why so few understand [love], so few come to it. Wake them and tell them! They will get a few more hints.

Love itself is the eternal, endless sacrifice. You will have to give up everything. You cannot take possession of anything. Finding love, you will never [want] anything [else]. ... "Only be Thou my love for ever!" That is what love wants. "My love, one kiss of those lips! [For him] who has been kissed by Thee, all sorrows vanish. Once kissed by Thee, man becomes happy and forgets love of everything else. He praises Thee alone and he sees Thee alone." In the nature of human love even, [there lurk divine elements. In] the first moment of intense love the whole world seems in tune with your own heart. Every bird in the universe sings your love; the flowers bloom for you. It is infinite, eternal love itself that [human] love comes from.

Why should the lover of God fear anything—fear robbers, fear distress, fear even for his life? ... The lover [may]go to the utmost hell, but would it be hell? We all have to give up these ideas of heaven [and hell] and get greater [love]. ... Hundreds there are seeking this madness of love before which everything [but God vanishes].

At last, love, lover, and beloved become one. That is the goal. ... Why is there any separation between soul and man, between soul and God? . . . Just to have this enjoyment of love. He wanted to love Himself, so He split Himself into many . . . "This is the whole reason for creation", says the lover. "We are all one. 'I and my Father are one.' Just now I am separate in order to love God. ... Which is better—to become sugar or to eat sugar? To become sugar, what fun is that:? To eat sugar—that is infinite enjoyment of love."

All the ideals of love—[God] as [our] father, mother, friend, child—[are conceived in order to strengthen devotion in us and make us feel nearer and dearer to God]. The intensest love is that between the sexes. God must be loved with that sort of love The woman loves her father; she loves her mothers she loves her child; she loves her friend. But she cannot express herself all to the father, nor to the mother, nor to the child, nor to the friend. There is only one person from whom she does not hide anything. So with the man. ... The [husband-] wife relationship is the all-rounded relationship. The relationship of the sexes [has] all the other loves concentrated into one. In the husband, the woman has the father, the friend, the child. In the wife, the husband has mother, daughter, and something else. That tremendous complete love of the sexes must come [for God]—that same love with which a woman opens herself to a man without any bond of blood—perfectly, fearlessly, and shamelessly. No darkness! She would no more hide anything from her lover than she would from her own self. That very love must come [for God]. These things are hard and difficult to understand. You will begin to understand by and by, and all idea of sex will fall away. "Like the water drop on the sand of the river bank on a summer day, even so is this life and all its relations."

All these ideas [like] "He is the creator", are ideas fit for children. He is my love, my life itself—that must be the cry of my heart! ...

"I have one hope. They call Thee the Lord of the world, and—good or evil, great or small—I am part of the world, and Thou art also my love. My body, my mind, and my soul are all at Thy altar. Love, refuse these gifts not!"

Vedanta and the West, Sept.-Oct. 1955.

NOTES OF CLASS TALKS AND LECTURES

Religion And Science

Experience is the only source of knowledge. In the world, religion is the only source where there is no surety, because it is not taught as a science of experience. This should not be. There is always, however, a small group of men who teach religion from experience. They are called mystics, and these mystics in every religion speak the same tongue and teach the same truth. This is the real science of religion. As mathematics in every part of the world does not differ, so the mystics do not differ. They are all similarly constituted and similarly situated. Their experience is the same; and this becomes law.

In the church, religionists first learn a religion, then begin to practise it; they do not take experience as the basis of their belief. But the mystic starts out in search of truth, experiences it first, and then formulates his creed. The church takes the experience of others; the mystic has his own experience. The church goes from the outside in; the mystic goes from the inside out.

Religion deals with the truths of the metaphysical world just as chemistry and the other natural sciences deal with the truths of the physical world. The book one must read to learn chemistry is the book of nature. The book from which to learn religion is your own mind and heart. The sage is often ignorant of physical science, because he reads the wrong book—the book within; and the scientist is too often ignorant of religion, because he too reads the wrong book—the book without.

All science has its particular methods; so has the science of religion. It has more methods also, because it has more material to work upon. The human mind is not homogeneous like the external world. According to the different nature, there must be different methods. As some special sense predominates in a person—one person will see most, another will hear most—so there is a predominant mental sense; and through this gate must each reach his own mind. Yet through all minds runs a unity, and there is a science which may be applied to all. This science of religion is based on the analysis of the human soul. It has no creed.

No one form of religion will do for all. Each is a pearl on a string. We must be particular above all else to find individuality in each. No man is born to any religion; he has a religion in his own soul. Any system which seeks to destroy individuality is in the long run disastrous. Each life has a current running though it, and this current will eventually take it to God. The end and aim of all religions is to realise God. The greatest of all training is to worship God alone. If each man chose his own ideal and stuck to it, all religious controversy would vanish.

Religion Is Realisation

The greatest name man ever gave to God is Truth. Truth is the fruit of realisation; therefore seek it within the soul. Get away from all books and forms and let your soul see its Self. "We are deluded and maddened by books", Shri Krishna declares. Be beyond the dualities of nature. The moment you think creed and form and ceremony the "be-all" and "end-all", then you are in bondage. Take part in them to help others, but take care they do not become a bondage. Religion is one, but its application must be various. Let each one, therefore, give his message; but find not the defects in other religions. You must come out from all form if you would see the Light. Drink deep of the nectar of the knowledge of God. The man who realises, "I am He", though clad in rags, is happy. Go forth into the Eternal and come back with eternal energy. The slave goes out to search for truth; he comes back free.

Religion Is Self-Abnegation

One cannot divide the rights of the universe. To talk of "right" implies limitation. It is not "right" but "responsibility". Each is responsible for the evil anywhere in the world. No one can separate himself from his brother. All that unites with the universal is virtue; all that separates is sin. You are a part of the Infinite. This is your nature. Hence you are your brother's keeper.

The first end of life is knowledge; the second end of life is happiness. Knowledge and happiness lead to freedom. But not one can attain liberty until every being (ant or dog) has liberty. Not one can be happy until all are happy. When you hurt anyone you hurt yourself, for you and your brother are one. He is indeed a Yogi who sees himself in the whole universe and the whole universe in himself. Self-sacrifice, not self-assertion, is the law of the highest universe. The world is so evil because Jesus' teaching, "Resist not evil", has never been tried. Selflessness alone will solve the problem. Religion comes with intense self-sacrifice. Desire nothing for yourself. Do all for others. This is to live and move and have your being in God.

Unselfish Work Is True Renunciation

This world is not for cowards. Do not try to fly. Look not for success or failure. Join yourself to the perfectly unselfish will and work on. Know that the mind which is born to succeed joins itself to a determined will and perseveres. You have the right to work, but do not become so degenerate as to look for results. Work incessantly, but see something behind the work. Even good deeds can find a man in great bondage. Therefore be not bound by good deeds or by desire for name and fame. Those who know this secret pass beyond this round of birth and death and become immortal.

The ordinary Sannyasin gives up the world, goes out, and thinks of God. The real Sannyasin lives in the world, but is not of it. Those who deny themselves, live in the forest, and chew the cud of unsatisfied desires are not true renouncers. Live in the midst of the battle of life. Anyone can keep calm in a cave or when asleep. Stand in the whirl and madness of action and reach the Centre. If you have found the Centre, you cannot be moved.

Freedom Of The Self

As we cannot know except through effects that we have eyes, so we cannot see the Self except by Its effects. It cannot be brought down to the low plane of sense-perception. It is the condition of everything in the universe, though Itself unconditioned. When we know that we are the Self, then we are free. The Self can never change. It cannot be acted on by a cause, because It is Itself the cause. It is self-caused. If we can find in ourself something that is not acted on by any cause, then we have known the Self.

Freedom is inseparably connected with immortality. To be free one must be above the laws of nature. Law exists so long as we are ignorant. When knowledge comes, then we find that law nothing but freedom in ourselves. The will can never be free, because it is the slave of cause and effect. But the "I" behind the will is free; and this is the Self. "I am free"—that is the basis on which to build and live. And freedom means immortality.

Notes On Vedanta

The cardinal features of the Hindu religion are founded on the meditative and speculative philosophy and on the ethical teachings contained in the various books of the Vedas, which assert that the universe is infinite in space and eternal in duration. It never had a beginning, and it never will have an end. Innumerable have been the manifestations of the power of the Spirit in the realm of matter, of the force of the Infinite in the domain of the finite, but the Infinite Itself is self - existent, eternal, and unchangeable. The passage of time makes no mark whatever on the dial of eternity. In its supersensuous region, which cannot be comprehended at all by the human understanding, there is no past and there is no future.

The Vedas teach that the soul of man is immortal. The body is subject to the law of growth and decay; what grows must of necessity decay. But the indwelling spirit is related to the infinite and eternal life; it never had a beginning, and it will never have an end. One of the chief distinctions between the Vedic and the Christian religion is that the Christian religion teaches that each human soul had its beginning at its birth into this world; whereas the Vedic religion asserts that the spirit of man is an emanation of the Eternal Being and had no more a beginning than God Himself. Innumerable have been and will be its manifestations in its passage from one personality to another, subject to the great law of spiritual evolution, until it reaches perfection, when there is no more change.

Hindu And Greek

Three mountains stand as typical of progress — the Himalayas of Indo-aryan, Sinai of Hebrew, and Olympus of Greek civilisation. When the Aryans reached India, they found the climate so hot that they could not work incessantly, so they began to think; thus they became introspective and developed religion. They discovered that there was no limit to the power of mind; they therefore sought to master that; and through it they learnt that there was something infinite coiled up in the frame we call man, which was seeking to become kinetic. To evolve this became their chief aim. Another branch of the Aryans went into the smaller and more picturesque country of Greece, where the climate and natural conditions were more favorable; so their activity turned outwards, and they developed the external arts and outward liberty. The Greek sought political liberty. The Hindu has always sought spiritual liberty. Both are one - sided. The Indian cares not enough for national protection or patriotism, he will defend only his religion; while with the Greek and in Europe (where the Greek civilisation finds its continuation) the country comes first. To care only for spiritual liberty and not for social liberty is a defect, but the opposite is a still greater defect. Liberty of both soul and body is to be striven for.

Thoughts On The Vedas And Upanishads

The Vedic sacrificial altar was the origin of Geometry.

The invocation of the Devas, or bright ones, was the basis of worship. The idea is that one invoked is helped and helps.

Hymns are not only words of praise but words of power, being pronounced with the right attitude of mind.

Heaven are only other states of existence with added senses and heightened powers.

All higher bodies also are subject to disintegration as is the physical. Death comes to all forms of bodies in this and other lives. Devas are also mortal and can only give enjoyment.

Behind all Devas there is the Unit Being—god, as behind this body there is something higher that feels and sees.

The powers of creation, preservation, and destruction of the Universe, and the attributes, such as omnipresence, omniscience, and omnipotence, make God of gods. "Hear ye children of Immortality! Hear ye Devas who live in higher spheres!" (Shvetashvatara, II.5). "I have found out a ray beyond all darkness, beyond all doubt. I have found the Ancient One" (ibid. III.8). The way to this is contained in the Upanishads.

On earth we die. In heaven we die. In the highest heaven we die. It is only when we reach God that we attain life and become immortal.

The Upanisads treat of this alone. The path of the Upanishads is the pure path. Many manners, customs, and local allusions cannot be understood today. Through them, however, truth becomes clear. Heavens and Earth are all thrown off in order to come to Light.

The Upanisads declare:

"He the Lord has interpenetrated the universe. It is all His."

"He the Omnipresent, the One without a second, the One without a body, pure, the great poet of the universe, whose metre is the suns and stars, is giving to each what he deserves" (Isha Upanishad, 8, adapted).

"They are groping in utter darkness who try to reach the Light by ceremonials. And they who think this nature is all are in darkness. They who wish to come out of nature through this thought are groping in still deeper darkness" (Isha, 9).

Are then ceremonials bad? No, they will benefit those who are coming on.

In one of the Upanishads (i.e. Katha) this question is asked by Nachiketa, a youth: "Some say of a dead man, he is gone; others, he is still living. You are Yama, Death.

You know the truth; do answer me." Yama replied, "Even the Devas, many of them, know not—much less men. Boy, do not ask of me this answer." But Nachiketa persists. Yama again replies, "The enjoyments of the gods, even these I offer you. Do not insist upon your query." But Nachiketa was firm as a rock. Then the god of death said, "My boy, you have declined, for the third time, wealth, power, long life, fame, family. You are brave enough to ask the highest truth. I will teach you. There are two ways, one of truth, one of enjoyment. You have choosen the former."

Now note here the conditions of imparting the truth. First, the purity—a boy, a pure, unclouded soul, asking the secret of the universe. Second, that he must take truth for truth's sake alone. Until the truth has come through one who has had realisation, from one who has perceived it himself, it cannot become fruitful. Books cannot give it, argument cannot establish it. Truth comes unto him who knows the secret of it.

After you have received it, be quiet. Be not ruffled by vain argument. Come to your own realisation. You alone can do it.

Neither happiness nor misery, vice nor virtue, knowledge nor non-knowledge is it. You must realise it. How can I describe it to you?

He who cries out with his whole heart, "O Lord, I want but Thee"—to him the Lord reveals Himself. Be pure, be calm; the mind when ruffled cannot reflect the Lord. "He whom the Vedas declare, He, to reach whom, we serve with prayer and sacrifice, Om is the sacred name of that indescribable One. This word is the holiest of all words. He who knows the secret of this word receives that which he desires." Take refuge in this word. Whoso takes refuge in this word, to him the way opens.

On Raja-Yoga

The first stage of Yoga is Yama.

To master Yama five things are necessary:

1. Non-injuring any being by thought, word, and deed.
2. Speaking the truth in thought, word, and deed.
3. Non-covetousness in thought, word, and deed.
4. Perfect chastity in thought, word, and deed.
5. Perfect sinlessness in thought, word, and deed.

Holiness is the greatest power. Everything else quails before it. Then comes Asana, or posture, of a devotee. The seat must be firm, the head, ribs, and body in a straight line, erect. Say to yourself that you are firmly seated, and that nothing can move you. Then mention the perfection of the body, bit by bit, from head to foot. Think of it as being clear as crystal, and as a perfect vessel to sail over the sea of life.

Pray to God and to all the prophets and saviors of the world and holy spirits in the universe to help you.

Then for half an hour practice Pranayama or the suspending, restraining, and controlling of the breath, mentally repeating the word Om as you inhale and exhale the breath. Words charged with spirit have wonderful power.

The other stages of Yoga are: (1) Pratyahara or the restraint of the organs of sense from all outward things, and directing them entirely to mental impressions; (2) Dharana or steadfast concentration; (3) Dhyana or meditation; (4) Samadhi or abstract meditation. It is the highest and last stage of Yoga. Samadhi is perfect absorption of thought into the Supreme Spirit, when one realises, "I and my Father are one."

Do one thing at a time and while doing it put your whole soul into it to the exclusion of all else.

On Bhakti-Yoga

Bhakti-Yoga is the path of systematised devotion for the attainment of union with the Absolute. It is the easiest and surest path to religion or realisation.

Love to God is the one essential to be perfect in this path.

There are five stages of love.

- First, man wants help and has a little fear.
- Second, when God is seen as Father.
- Third, when God is seen as Mother. Then all women are looked upon as reflections of the Mother-god. With the idea of Mother-god real love begins.
- Fourth, love for love's sake. Love for love's sake transcends all qualities.
- Fifth, love in Divine-union. It leads to oneness or superconsciousness.

God is both Personal and Impersonal as we are personal and impersonal.

Prayer and praise are the first means of growth. Repeating the names of God has wonderful power.

Mantra is a special word, or sacred text, or name of God choosen by the Guru for repetition and reflection by the disciple. The disciple must concentrate on a personality for prayer and praise, and that is his Ishta.

These words (Mantras) are not sounds of words but God Himself, and we have them within us. Think of Him, speak of Him. No desire for the world! Buddhas's Sermon on the Mount was, "As thou thinkest, so art thou."

After attaining superconsiousness the Bhakta descends again to love and worship.

Pure love has no motive. It has nothing to gain.

After prayer and praise comes meditation. Then comes reflection on the name and on the Ishta of the individual.

Pray that that manifestation which is our Father, our Mother, may cut our bonds.

Pray, "Take us by the hand as a father takes his son, and leave us not."

Pray, "I do not want wealth or beauty, this world or another, but Thee, O God! Lord! I have become weary. Oh, take me by the hand, Lord, I take shelter with Thee. Make me Thy servant. Be Thou my refuge."

Pray, "Thou our Father, our Mother, our dearest Friend! Thou who bearest this universe, help us to bear the little burden of this our life. Leave us not. Let us never be separated from Thee. Let us always dwell in Thee."

When love to God is revealed and is all, this world appears like a drop.

Pass from non-existence to existence, from darkness to light.

On Jnana-Yoga

First, meditation should be of a negative nature. Think away everything. Analyse everything that comes in the mind by the sheer action of the will.

Next, assert what we really are—existence, knowledge, and bliss—being, knowing, and loving.

Meditation is the means of unification of the subject and object. Meditate:

Above, it is full of me; below, it is full of me; in the middle, it is full of me. I am in all beings, and all beings are in me. Om Tat Sat, I am It. I am existence above mind. I and the one spirit of the universe. I am neither pleasure nor pain.

The body drinks, eats, and so on. I am not the body. I am not mind. I am He.

I am the witness. I look on. When health comes I am the witness. When disease comes I am the witness.

I am Existence, Knowledge, Bliss.

I am the essence and nectar of knowledge. Through eternity I change not. I am calm, resplendent, and unchanging.

The Reality And Shadow

That which differentiates one thing from another is time, space, and causation.

The differentiation is in the form, not in the substance. You may destroy the form and it disappears for ever; but the substance remains the same. You can never destroy the substance.

Evolution is in nature, not in the soul—evolution of nature, manifestation of the soul.

Maya is not illusion as it is popularly interpreted. Maya is real, yet it is not real. It is real in that the Real is behind it and gives it its appearance of reality. That which is real in Maya is the Reality in and through Maya. Yet the Reality is never seen ; and hence that which is seen is unreal, and it has no real independent existence of itself, but is dependent upon the Real for its existence.

Maya then is a paradox—real, yet not real, an illusion, yet not an illusion.

He who knows the Real sees in Maya not illusion, but reality. He who knows not the Real sees in Maya illusion and thinks it real.

How To Become Free

All things in nature work according to law. Nothing is excepted. The mind as well as everything in external nature is governed and controlled by law.

Internal and external nature, mind and matter, are in time and space, and are bound by the law of causation.

The freedom of the mind is a delusion. How can the mind be free when it is controlled and bound by law?

The law of Karma is the law of causation.

We must become free. We are free; the work is to know it. We must give up all slavery, all bondage of whatever kind. We must not only give up our bondage to earth and everything and everybody on earth, but also to all ideas of heaven and happiness.

We are bound to earth by desire and also to God, heaven, and the angels. A slave is a slave whether to man, to God, or to angels.

The idea of heaven must pass away. The idea of heaven after death where the good live a life of eternal happiness is a vain dream, without a particle of meaning or sense in it. Wherever there is happiness there must follow unhappiness sometime. Wherever there is pleasure there must be pain. This is absolutely certain, every action has its reaction somehow.

The idea of freedom is the only true idea of salvation—freedom from everything, the senses, whether of pleasure or pain, from good as well as evil.

More than this even, we must be free from death; and to be free from death, we must be free from life. Life is but a dream of death. Where there is life, there will be death; so get away from life if you would be rid of death.

We are ever free if we would only believe it, only have faith enough. You are the soul, free and eternal, ever free, ever blessed. Have faith enough and you will be free in a minute.

Everything in time, space, and causation is bound. The soul is beyond all time, all space, all causation. That which is bound is nature, not the soul.

Therefore proclaim your freedom and be what you are—ever free, ever blessed.

Time, space, and causation we call Maya.

Soul And God

Anything that is in space has form. Space itself has form. Either you are in space, or space is in you. The soul is beyond all space. Space is in the soul, not the soul in space.

Form is confined to time and space and is bound by the law of causation. All time is in us, we are not in time. As the soul is not in time and space, all time and space are within the soul. The soul is therefore omnipresent.

Our idea of God is the reflection of ourselves.

Old Persian and Sanskrit have affinities.

The primitive idea of God was identifying God with different forms of nature—nature-worship. The next stage was the tribal God. The next stage, the worship of kings.

The idea of God in heaven is predominant in all nations except in India. The idea is very crude.

The idea of the continuity of life is foolish. We can never get rid of death until we get rid of life.

The Goal

Dualism recognises God and nature to be eternally separate: the universe and nature eternally dependent upon God.

The extreme monists make no such distinction. In the last analysis, they claim, all is God: the universe becomes lost in God; God is the eternal life of the universe.

With them infinite and finite are mere terms. The universe, nature, etc. exist by virtue of differentiation. Nature is itself differentiation.

Such questions as, "Why did God create the universe?" "Why did the All-perfect create the imperfect?" etc., can never be answered, because such questions are logical absurdities. Reason exists in nature; beyond nature it has no existence. God is omnipotent, hence to ask why He did so and so is to limit Him; for it implies that there is a purpose in His creating the universe. If He has a purpose, it must be a means to an end, and this would mean that He could not have the end without the means. The questions, why and wherefore, can only be asked of something which depends upon something else.

On Proof Of Religion

The great question about religion is: What makes it so unscientific? If religion is a science, why is it not as certain as other sciences? All beliefs in God, heaven, etc., are mere conjectures, mere beliefs. There seems to be nothing certain about it. Our ideas concerning religion are changing all the time. The mind is in a constant state of flux.

Is man a soul, an unchanging substance, or is he a constantly changing quantity? All religions, except primitive Buddhism, believe that man is a soul, an identity, a unit that never dies but is immortal.

The primitive Buddhists believe that man is a constantly changing quantity, and that his consciousness consists in an almost infinite succession of incalculably rapid changes, each change, as it were, being unconnected with the others, standing alone, thus precluding the theory of the law of sequence or causation.

If there is a unit, there is a substance. A unit is always simple. A simple is not a compound of anything. It does not depend on anything else. It stands alone and is immortal.

Primitive Buddhists contend that everything is unconnected; nothing is a unit; and that the theory of man being a unit is a mere belief and cannot be proved.

Now the great question is : Is man a unit, or is he a constantly changing mass?

There is but one way to prove this, to answer this question. Stop the gyrations of the mind, and the theory that a man is a unit, a simple, will be demonstrated. All changes are in me, in the Chitta, the mind-substance. I am not the changes. If I were, I could not stop them.

Everyone is trying to make himself and everybody else believe that this world is all very fine, that he is perfectly happy. But when man stops to question his motives in life, he will see that the reason he is struggling after this and that is because he cannot help himself. He must move on. He cannot stop, so he tries to make himself believe that he really wants this and that. The one who actually succeeds in making himself believe that he is having a good time is the man of splendid physical health. This man responds to his desires instantly, without question. He acts in response to that power within him, urging him on without a thought, as though he acted because he wanted to. But when he has been knocked about a good deal by nature, when he has received a good many wounds and bruises, he begins to question the meaning of all this; and as he gets hurt more and thinks more, he sees that he is urged on by a power beyond his control and that he acts simply because he must. Then he begins to rebel, and the battle begins.

Now if there is a way out of all this trouble, it is within ourselves. We are always trying to realise the Reality. Instinctively we are always trying to do that. It is creation in the human soul that covers up God; that is why there is so much difference in God-ideals. Only when creation stops can we find the Absolute. The Absolute is in the soul, not in creation. So by stopping creation, we come to know the Absolute. When we think of ourselves, we think of the body; and when we think of God, we think of Him as body. To stop the gyrations of the mind, so that the soul may become manifested, is the work. Training begins with the body. Breathing trains the body, gets it into a harmonious condition. The object of the breathing exercises is to attain meditation and concentration. If you can get absolutely still for just one moment, you have reached the goal. The mind may go on working after that; but it will never be the same mind again. You will know yourself as you are—your true Self. Still the mind but for one moment, and the truth of your real nature will flash upon you, and freedom is at hand: no more bondage after that. This follows from the theory that if you can know an instant of time, you know all time, as the whole is the rapid succession of one. Master the one, know thoroughly one instant—and freedom is reached.

All religions believe in God and the soul except the

primitive Buddhist. The modern Buddhists believe in God and the soul. Among the primitive Buddhists are the Burmese, Siamese, Chinese, etc.

Arnold's book, *The Light of Asia*, represents more of Vedantism than Buddhism.

The Design Theory

The idea that nature in all her orderly arrangements shows design on the part of the Creator of the universe is good as a kindergarten teaching to show the beauty, power, and glory of God, in order to lead children in religion up to a philosophical conception of God; but apart from that, it is not good, and perfectly illogical. As a philosophical idea, it is entirely without foundation, if God is taken to be omnipotent.

If nature shows the power of God in creating the universe, (then) to have a design in so doing also shows His weakness. If God is omnipotent, He needs no design, no scheme, to do anything. He has but to will it, and it is done. No question, no scheme, no plan, of God in nature.

The material universe is the result of the limited consciousness of man. When man becomes conscious of his divinity, all matter, all nature, as we know it, will cease to exist.

The material world, as such, has no place in the consciousness of the All-presence as a necessity of any end. If it had, God would be limited by the universe. To say that nature exists by His permission is not to say that it exists as a necessity for Him to make man perfect, or for any other reason.

It is a creation for man's necessity, not God's. There is no scheme of God in the plan of the universe. How could there be any if He is omnipotent? Why should He have need of a plan, or a scheme, or a reason to do anything? To say that He has is to limit Him and to rob Him of His character of omnipotence.

For instance, if you came to a very wide river, so wide that you could not get across it except by building a bridge, the very fact that you would have to build the bridge to get across the river would show your limitation, would show your weakness, even if the ability to build the bridge did show your strength.

If you were not limited but could just fly or jump across, you would not be under the necessity of building a bridge; and to build the bridge just to exhibit your power to do so would show your weakness again by showing your vanity, more than it would show anything else.

Monism and dualism are essentially the same. The difference consists in the expression. As the dualists hold the Father and Son to be two, the monists hold them to be really one. Dualism is in nature, in manifestation, and monism is pure spirituality in the essence.

The idea of renunciation and sacrifice is in all religions as a means to reach God.

Spirit And Nature

Religion is the realisation of Spirit as Spirit; not Spirit as matter.

Religion is a growth. Each one must experience it himself. The Christians believe that Jesus Christ died to save man. With you it is belief in a doctrine, and this belief constitutes your salvation. With us doctrine has nothing whatever to do with salvation. Each one may believe in whatever doctrine he likes; or in no doctrine.

What difference does it make to you whether Jesus Christ lived at a certain time or not? What has it to do with you that Moses saw God in the burning bush? The fact that Moses saw God in the burning bush does not constitute your seeing Him, does it? If it does, then the fact that Moses ate is enough for you; you ought to stop eating. One is just as sensible as the other. Records of great spiritual men of the past do us no good whatever except that they urge us onward to do the same, to experience religion ourselves. Whatever Christ or Moses or anybody else did does not help us in the least, except to urge us on.

Each one has a special nature peculiar to himself, which he must follow and through which he will find his way to freedom. Your teacher should be able to tell you what your particular path in nature is and to put you in it. He should know by your face where you belong and should be able to indicate it to you. You should never try to follow another's path, for that is his way, not yours. When that path is found, you have nothing to do but fold your arms, and the tide will carry you to freedom. Therefore when you find it, never swerve from it. You way is the best for you, but that is no sign that it is the best for others.

The truly spiritual see Spirit as Spirit, not as matter. It is Spirit that makes nature move; It is the reality in nature. So action is in nature; not in the Spirit. Spirit is always the same, changeless, eternal. Spirit and matter are in reality the same; but Spirit, as such, never becomes matter; and matter, as such, never becomes Spirit.

The Spirit never acts. Why should it? It merely is, and that is sufficient. It is pure existence absolute and has no need of action.

You are not bound by law. That is in your nature. The mind is in nature and is bound by law. All nature is bound by law, the law of its own action; and this law can never be broken. If you could break a law of nature, all nature would come to an end in an instant. There would be no more nature. He who attains freedom breaks the law of nature, and for him nature fades away and has no more power over him. Each one will break the law but once and for ever; and that will end his trouble with nature.

Governments, societies, etc. are comparative evils. All societies are based on bad generalisation. The moment you form yourselves into an organissation, you begin to hate everybody outside of that organisation. When you join an organisation, you are putting bounds upon yourself, you are limiting your own freedom. The greatest goodness is the highest freedom. Our aim should be to allow the individual to move towards this freedom. More of goodness, less of artificial laws. Such laws are not laws at all. If it were a law, it could not be broken. The fact that these so-called laws are broken, shows clearly that they are not laws. A law is that which cannot be broken.

Whenever you suppress a thought, it is simply pressed down out of sight, in a coil like a spring, only to spring out again at a moment's notice, with all the pent-up force resulting from the suppression, and do in a few moments what it would have done in a much longer period.

Every ounce of pleasure brings its pound of pain. It is the same energy that at one time manifests itself as pleasure, at another time as pain. As soon as one set of sensations stops, another begins. But in some cases, in more advanced persons, one may have two, yea, even a hundred different thoughts entering into active operation at the same time.

Mind is action of its own nature. Mind-activity means creation. The thought is followed by the word, and the word by the form. All of this creating will have to stop, both mental and physical, before the mind can reflect the soul.

The Practice Of Religion

At Alameda, Calif., March 18, 1900

We read many books, but that does not bring us knowledge. We may read all the Bibles in the world, but that will not give us religion. Theoretical religion is easy enough to get, any one may get that. What we want is practical religion.

The Christian idea of a practical religion is in doing good works—worldly utility.

What good is utility? Judged from a utilitarian standpoint, religion is a failure. Every hospital is a prayer that more people may come there. What is meant by charity? Charity is not fundamental. It is really helping on the misery of the world, not eradicating it. One looks for name and fame and covers his efforts to obtain them with the enamel of charity and good works. He is working for himself under the pretext of working for others. Every so-called charity is an encouragement of the very evil it claims to operate against.

Men and women go to balls and dance all night in honor of some hospital or other charitable institution, then go home, behave like beasts, and bring devils into the world to fill jails, insane asylums, and hospitals. So it goes on, and it is called good works—building hospital, etc. The ideal of good works is to lessen, or eradicate, the misery of the world. The Yogi says, all misery comes from not being able to control the mind. The Yogi's ideal is freedom from nature. Conquest of nature is his standard of work. The Yogi says that all power is in the soul, and by the controlling of the mind and body one conquers nature by the power of the soul.

Every ounce of muscle in excess of what is beyond the needs of one's physical work is that much less of brain. Do not exercise too hard; it is injurious. The one who does not work hard will live the longest. Eat less food and work less. Store up brain food.

Household work is enough for women.

Do not make the lamp burn fast; let it burn slowly.

Proper diet means simple diet, not highly spiced.

Fragmentary Notes On The Ramayana

Worship Him who alone stands by us, whether we are doing good or are doing evil; who never leaves us even; as love never pulls down, as love knows no barter, no selfishness.

Rama was the soul of the old king; but he was a king, and he could not go back on his word. "Wherever Rama goes, there go I", says Lakshmana, the younger brother.

The wife of the elder brother to us Hindus is just like a mother. At last he found Sita, pale and thin, like a bit of the moon that lies low at the foot of the horizon.

Sita was chastity itself; she would never touch the body of another man except that of her husband. "Pure? She is chastity itself", says Rama.

Drama and music are by themselves religion; any song, love song or any song, never mind; if one's whole soul is in that song, he attains salvation, just by that; nothing else he has to do; if a man's whole soul is in that, his soul gets salvation. They say it leads to the same goal.

Wife—the co-religionist. Hundreds of ceremonies the Hindu has to perform, and not one can be performed if he has not a wife. You see the priests tie them up together, and they go round temples and make very great pilgrimages tied together.

Rama gave up his body and joined Sita in the other world.

Sita—the pure, the pure, the all-suffering!

Sita is the name in India for everything that is good, pure, and holy; everything that in woman we call woman.

Sita—the patient, all-suffering, ever-faithful, ever-pure wife! Through all the suffering she had, there was not one harsh word against Rama.

Sita never returned injury.

"Be Sita!"

Notes Taken Down In Madras, 1892-93

The three essentials of Hinduism are belief in God, in the Vedas as revelation, in the doctrine of Karma and transmigration.

If one studies the Vedas between the lines, one sees a religion of harmony.

One point of difference between Hinduism and other religions is that in Hinduism we pass from truth to truth—from a lower truth to a higher truth—and never from error to truth.

The Vedas should be studied through the eye-glass of evolution. They contain the whole history of the progress of religious consciousness, until religion has reached perfection in unity.

The Vedas are Anadi, eternal. The meaning of the statement is not, as is erroneously supposed by some, that the words of the Vedas are Anadi, but that the spiritual laws inculcated by the Vedas are such. These laws which are immutable and eternal have been discovered at various times by great men or Rishis, though some of them are forgotten now, while others are preserved.

When a number of people from various angles and distances have a look at the sea, each man sees a portion of it according to his horizon. Though each man may say that what he sees is the real sea, all of them speak the truth, for all of them see portions of the same wide expanse. So the religious scriptures, though they seem to contain varying and conflicting statements, speak the truth, for they are all descriptions of that one infinite Reality.

When one sees a mirage for the first time, he mistakes it for a reality, and after vainly trying to quench his thirst in it, learns that it is a mirage. But whenever he sees such a phenomenon in future, in spite of the apparent reality, the idea that he sees a mirage always presents itself to him. So is the world of Maya to a Jivanmukta (the liberated in life).

Some of the Vedic secrets were known to certain families only, as certain powers naturally exist in some families. With the extinction of these families, those secrets have died away.

Vedic anatomy was no less perfect than the Ayurvedic.

There were many names for many parts of the organs, because they had to cut up animals for sacrifice. The sea is described as full of ships. Sea voyage was prohibited later on, partly because there came the fear that people might thereby become Buddhists.

Buddhism was the rebellion of newly-formed Kshatriyas against Vedic priestcraft.

Hinduism threw away Buddhism after taking its sap. The attempt of all the Southern Acharyas was to effect a reconciliation between the two. Shankaracharya's teaching shows the influence of Buddhism. His disciples perverted his teaching and carried it to such an extreme point that some of the later reformers were right in calling the Acharya's followers "crypto-buddhists".

***

What is Spencer's unknowable? It is our Maya. Western philosophers are afraid of the unknowable, but our philosophers have taken a big jump into the unknown, and they have conquered.

Western philosophers are like vultures soaring high in the sky, but all the while, with their eye fixed on the carrion beneath. They cannot cross the unknown, and they therefore turn back and worship the almighty dollar.

There have been two lines of progress in this world—political and religious. In the former the Greeks are everything, the modern political institutions being only the development of the Grecian; in the latter the Hindus are everything.

My religion is one of which Christianity is an offshoot and Buddhism a rebel child.

Chemistry ceases to improve when one element is found from which all others are deductible. Physics ceases to progress when one force is found of which all others are manifestations. So religion ceases to progress when unity is reached, which is the case with Hinduism.

There is no new religious idea preached anywhere which is not found in the Vedas.

In everything, there are two kinds of development—analytical and synthetical. In the former the Hindus excel other nations. In the latter they are nil[1].

The Hindus have cultivated the power of analysis and abstraction. No nation has yet produced a grammar like that of Panini.

Ramanuja's important work is the conversion of Jains and Buddhists to Hinduism. He is a great advocate of image-worship. He introduced love and faith as potent means of salvation.

Even in the Bhagavata, twenty-four Avatars are mentioned corresponding to the twenty-four Tirthankaras of the Jains, the name of Rishabhadeva being common to both.

The practice of Yoga gives the power of abstraction. The superiority of a Siddha over others consists in his being able to separate attributes from objects and think of them independently, giving them objective reality.

***

The opposite extremes always meet and resemble each other. The greatest self-forgotten devotee whose mind is absorbed in the contemplation of the infinite Brahman and the most debased, drunken maniac present the same externals. At times we are surprised with the analogical transition from one to the other.

Extremely nervous men succeed as religious men. They become fervent over whatever they take into their head. "All are mad in this world; some are mad after gold, others after women, and some are after God; if drowning is to be the fate of man, it is better to be drowned in an ocean of milk than in a pool of dung", a devotee replied who was charged with mad-

---

1. Here by the term "synthesis" is meant a scientific generalisation, and by the term "analysis" an ontological reduction of facts and objects to their immanent principles.—Ed.

ness.

The God of Infinite Love and the object of Love sublime and infinite are painted blue. Krishna is painted blue, so also Solomon's[1] God of Love. It is a natural law that anything sublime and infinite is associated with blue colour. Take a handful of water, it is absolutely colourless. But look at the deep wide ocean; it is as blue as anything. Examine the space near you; it is colourless. But look at the infinite expanse of the sky; it is blue.

That the Hindus, absorbed in the ideal, lacked in realistic observation is evident from this. Take painting and sculpture. What do you see in the Hindu paintings? All sorts of grotesque and unnatural figures. What do you see in a Hindu temple? A Chaturbhanga[2] Narayana or some such thing. But take into consideration any Italian picture or Grecian statue—what a study of nature you find in them! A gentleman for twenty years sat burning a candle in his hand, in order to paint a lady carrying a candle in her hand.

The Hindus progressed in the subjective sciences.

There are as many different conducts taught in the Vedas as there are differences in human nature. What is taught to an adult cannot be taught to a child.

A Guru should be a doctor of men. He should understand the nature of his disciple and teach him the method which suits him best.

There are infinite ways of practicing Yoga. Certain methods have produced successful result with certain men. But two are of general importance with all: (1) Reaching the reality by negativing every known experience, (2) Thinking that you are everything, the whole universe. The second method, though it leads to the goal sooner than the first, is not the safest one. It is generally attended with great dangers which may lead a man astray and deter him from obtaining his aim.

There is this difference between the love taught by Christianity and that taught by Hinduism: Christianity teaches us to love our neighbours as we should wish them to love us; Hinduism asks us to love them as ourselves, in fact to see ourselves in them.

---

1. See Old Testament, The Song of Solomon, I. 5,7,14.
2. Lit. bent at four places or joints of the body.

A mongoose is generally kept in a glass-case with a long chain attached to it, so that it may go about freely. When it scents danger as it wanders about, with one jump it goes into the glass case. So is a Yogi in this world.

***

The whole universe is one chain of existence, of which matter forms one pole and God the other; the doctrine of Vishishtadvaitism may be explained by some such ideas.

The Vedas are full of passages which prove the existence of a Personal God. The Rishis, who through long devotion saw God, had a peep into the unknown and threw their challenge to the world. It is only presumptuous men, who have not walked in the path described by the Rishis and who have not followed their teachings, that criticise them and oppose them. No man has yet come forward who would dare to say that he has properly followed their directions and has not seen anything and that these men are liars. There are men who have been under trial at various times and have felt that they have not been forsaken by God. The world is such that if faith in God does not offer us any consolation, it is better to commit suicide.

A pious missionary went out on business. All of a sudden his three sons died of cholera. His wife covered the three dead bodies of her beloved children with a sheet and was awaiting her husband at the gate. When he returned, she detained him at the gate and put him the question, "My dear husband, some one entrusts something to you and in your absence suddenly takes it back. Will you feel sorry?" He replied, "Certainly I would not". Then she took him in, removed the sheet and showed the three corpses. He bore this calmly and buried the bodies. Such is the strength of mind of those who hold firm faith in the existence of an all-merciful God who disposes of everything in the universe.

The Absolute can never be thought of. We can have no idea of a thing unless it is finite. God the infinite can only be conceived and worshipped as the finite.

John the Baptist was an Essene—a sect of Buddhists. The Christian cross is nothing but the Shivalinga converted into two across. Remnants of Buddhist worship are still to be found among the relics of ancient Rome.

In South India, some of the Ragas (tunes) are sung and remembered as independent Ragas, whereas they are derivations of the six primary ones. In their music, there is very little of Murchhana, or oscillating touches of sound.

Even the use of the perfect instrument of music is rare. The Vina of the South is not the real Vina. We have no martial music, no martial poetry either. Bhavabhuti is a little martial.

***

Christ was a Sannyasin, and his religion is essentially fit for Sannyasins only. His teachings may be summed up as: "Give up"; nothing more—being fit for the favoured few. "Turn the other cheek also!"—impossible, impracticable! The Westerners know it. It is meant for those who hunger and thirst after righteousness, who aim at perfection. "Stand on your rights", is the rule for the ordinary men. One set of moral rules cannot be preached to all—sadhus and householders.

All sectarian religions take for granted that all men are equal. This is not warranted by science. There is more difference between minds than between bodies. One fundamental doctrine of Hinduism is that all men are different, there being unity in variety. Even for a drunkard, there are some Mantras—even for a man going to a prostitute!

Morality is a relative term. Is there anything like absolute morality in this world? The idea is a superstition. We have no right to judge every man in every age by the same standard.

Every man, in every age, in every country is under peculiar circumstances. If the circumstances change, ideas also must change. Beef-eating was once moral. The climate was cold, and the cereals were not much known. Meat was the chief food available. So in that age and clime, beef was in a manner indispensable. But beef-eating is held to be immoral now.

The one thing unchangeable is God. Society is moving.

Jagat (world) means that which is moving. God is Achala (immovable).

What I say is not, "Reform", but, "Move on". Nothing is too bad to reform. Adaptability is the whole mystery of life—the principle underneath which serves to unfold it. Adjustment or adaptation is the outcome of the Self pitted against external forces tending to suppress It. He who adjusts himself best lives the longest. Even if I do not preach this, society is changing, it must change. It is not Christianity nor science, it is necessity, that is working underneath, the necessity that people must have to live or starve.

***

The best scenery in the world can be seen on the sublime heights of the Himalayas. If one lives there for a time, he is sure to have mental calmness, however restless he might have been before. God is the highest form of generalised law. When once this law is known, all others can be explained as being subordinate to it. God is to religion what Newton's law of gravity is to falling bodies.

Every worship consists of prayer in the highest form. For a man who cannot make Dhyana or mental worship, Puja or ceremonial worship is necessary. He must have the thing concrete.

The brave alone can afford to be sincere. Compare the lion and the fox.

Loving only the good in God and nature—even a child does that. You should love the terrible and the painful as well. A father loves the child, even when he is giving him trouble.

Shri Krishna was God, incarnated to save mankind. Gopi-lila (his disport with cowherd maids) is the acme of the religion of love in which individuality vanishes and there is communion. It is in this Lila that Shri Krishna shows what he preaches in the Gita: "Give up every other tie for me." Go and take shelter under Vrindavana-Lila to understand Bhakti. On this subject a great number of books is extant. It is the religion of India. The larger number of Hindus follow Shri Krishna.

Shri Krishna is the God of the poor, the beggar, the sinner, the son, the father, the wife, and of everyone. He enters intimately into all our human relations and makes everything holy and in the end brings us to salvation. He is the God who hides himself from the philosopher and the learned and reveals himself to the ignorant and the children. He is the God of faith and love and not of learning. With the Gopis, love and God were the same thing—they knew Him to be love incarnate.

In Dwaraka, Shri Krishna teaches duty; in Vrindavana, love. He allowed his sons to kill each other, they being wicked.

God, according to the Jewish and Mohammedan idea, is a big Session Judge. Our God is rigorous on the surface, but loving and merciful at heart.

There are some who do not understand Advaitism and make a travesty of its teachings. They say, "What is Shuddha and Ashuddha (pure and impure)—what is the difference between virtue and vice? It is all human superstition", and observe no moral restraint in their actions. It is downright roguery; and any amount of harm is done by the preaching of such things.

This body is made up of two sorts of Karma consisting of virtue and vice—injurious vice and non-injurious virtue. A thorn is pricking my body, and I take another thorn to take it out and then throw both away. A man desiring to be perfect takes a thorn of virtue and with it takes off the thorn of vice. He still lives, and virtue alone being left, the momentum of action left to him must be of virtue. A bit of holiness is left to the Jivanmukta, and he lives, but everything he does must be holy.

Virtue is that which tends to our improvement, and vice to our degeneration. Man is made up of three qualities—brutal, human, and godly. That which tends to increase the divinity in you is virtue, and that which tends to increase brutality in you is vice. You must kill the brutal nature and become human, that is, loving and charitable. You must transcend that too and become pure bliss, Sachchidananda, fire without burning, wonderfully loving, but without the weakness of human love, without the feeling of misery.

Bhakti is divided into Vaidhi and Raganuga Bhakti.

Vaidhi Bhakti is implicit belief in obedience to the teachings of the Vedas.

Raganuga Bhakti is of five kinds:

(1) Shanta as illustrated by the religion of Christ;

(2) Dasya as illustrated by that of Hanuman to Rama;

(3) Sakhya as illustrated by that of Arjuna to Shri Krishna;

(4) Vatsalya as illustrated by that of Vasudeva to Shri Krishna;

(5) Madhura (that of the husband and wife) in the lives of Shri Krishna and the Gopikas.

Keshab Chandra Sen compared society to an ellipse. God is the central sun. Society is sometimes in the aphelion and sometimes in the perihelion. An Avatar comes and takes it to the perihelion. Then it goes back again. Why should it be so? I cannot say. What necessity for an Avatara? What necessity was there to create? Why did He not create us all perfect? It is Lila (sport), we do not know.

Men can become Brahman but not God. If anybody becomes God, show me his creation. Vishvamitra's creation is his own imagination. It should have obeyed Vishvamitra's law. If anybody becomes a Creator, there would be an end of the world, on account of the conflict of laws. The balance is so nice that if you disturb the equilibrium of one atom, the whole world will come to an end.

There were great men—so great that no number nor human arithmetic could state the difference between them and us. But compared with God, they were geometrical points. In comparison with the Infinite, everything is nothing. Compared with God, what is Vishvamitra but a human moth?

Patanjali is the father of the theory of evolution, spiritual and physical.

Generally the organism is weaker than the environment. It is struggling to adjust itself. Sometimes it over-adjusts itself. Then the whole body changes into another species. Nandi was a man whose holiness was so great that the human body could not contain it. So those molecules changed into a god-body.

The tremendous engine of competition will destroy everything. If you are to live at all, you must adjust yourself to the times. If we are to live at all, we must be a scientific nation. Intellectual power is the force.

You must learn the power of organisation of the Europeans. You must become educated and must educate your women. You must abolish child marriage.

All these ideas are floating over society. You all know it, yet dare not act. Who is to bell the cat? In the fullness of time a wonderful man will come. Then all the rats will be made bold.

Whenever a great man comes, the circumstances are ready under his feet. He is the last straw to break the camel's back. He is the spark of the cannon. There is something in the talking—we are preparing for him.

Was Krishna cunning? No, he was not cunning. He tried his best to prevent war. It was Duryodhana who forced the war. But, when once in the thing, you should not recede—that is the man of duty. Do not run away, it is cowardice. When in the thing, you must do it. You should not budge an inch—of course not for a wrong thing; this was a righteous war.

The devil comes in many guises—anger in the form of justice—passion in the form of duty. When it first comes, the man knows and then he forgets. Just as your pleaders' conscience; at first they know it is all Badmashi (roguery), then it is duty to their clients; at last they get hardened.

Yogis live on the banks of the Narmada—the best place for them, because the climate is very even. Bhaktas live in Vrindavana.

Sipahis (sepoys) die soon—nature is full of defect—the athletes die soon. The gentlemen class are the strongest, while the poor are the hardiest. Fruit diet may agree with a costive man. Civilised man needs rest for intellectual work. For food he has to take spices and condiments. The savage walks forty or fifty miles a day. He relishes the blandest foods.

Our fruits are all artificial, and the natural mango is a poor affair. Wheat also is artificial.

Save the spiritual store in your body by observing continence.

The rule for a householder about the expenditure of his income is, one-fourth of the income for his family, one-fourth for charity, one-fourth to be saved, one-fourth for self.

Unity in variety is the plan of creation, individuality in universality.

Why deny the cause only? Deny the effect also. The cause must contain everything that is in the effect.

Christ's public life extended only over eighteen months, and for this he had silently been preparing himself for thirty-two years. Mohammed was forty years old before he came out.

***

It is true that the caste system becomes essential in the ordinary course of nature. Those that have aptitudes for a particular work form a class. But who is to settle the class of a particular individual? If a Brahmin thinks that he has a special aptitude for spiritual culture, why should he be afraid to meet a Shudra in an open field? Will a horse be afraid of running a race with a jade?

Refer to the life of the author of Krishna-karnamrita, Vilvamangala—a devotee who plucked his eyes out because he could not see God. His life illustrates the principle that even misdirected love leads in the end to love proper.

Too early religious advancement of the Hindus and that superfineness in everything which made them cling to higher alternatives, have reduced them to what they are. The Hindus have to learn a little bit of materialism from the West and teach them a little bit of spirituality.

Educate your women first and leave them to themselves; then they will tell you what reforms are necessary for them. In matters concerning them, who are you?

Who reduced the Bhangis and the Pariahs to their present degraded condition? Heartlessness in our behavior and at the same time preaching wonderful Advaitism—is it not adding insult to injury?

Form and formless are intertwined in this world. The formless can only be expressed in form and form can only be thought with the formless. The world is a form of our thoughts. The idol is the expression of religion.

In God all natures are possible. But we can see Him only through human nature. We can love Him as we love a man—as father, son. The strongest love in the world is that between man and woman, and that also when it is clandestine. This is typified in the love between Krishna and Radha.

Nowhere is it said in the Vedas that man is born a sinner. To say so is a great libel on human nature.

It is not an easy task to reach the state of seeing the Reality face to face. The other day one could not find the hidden cat in a whole picture, though it occupied the major portion of the picture.

***

You cannot injure anybody and sit quietly. It is a wonderful machinery—you cannot escape God's vengeance.

Kama (lust) is blind and leads to hell. Prema is love, it leads to heaven.

There is no idea of lust or sympathy in the love of Krishna and Radha. Radha says to Krishna, "If you place your feet on my heart, all lust will vanish."

When abstraction is reached lust dies and there is only love.

A poet loved a washerwoman. Hot Dal fell upon the feet of the woman and the feet of the poet were scalded.

Shiva is the sublime aspect of God, Krishna the beautiful aspect of God. Love crystallises into blueness. Blue colour is expressive of intense love. Solomon saw "Krishna". Here Krishna came to be seen by all.

Even now, when you get love, you see Radha. Become Radha and be saved. There is no other way, Christians do not understand Solomon's song. They call it prophecy symbolising Christ's love for the Church. They think it nonsense and father some story upon it.

Hindus believe Buddha to be an Avatara.

Hindus believe in God positively. Buddhism does not try to know whether He is or not.

Buddha came to whip us into practice. Be good, destroy the passions. Then you will know for yourself whether Dvaita or Advaita philosophy is true—whether there is one or there are more than one.

Buddha was a reformer of Hinduism.

In the same man the mother sees a son, while the wife at the same time sees differently with different results. The wicked see in God wickedness. The virtuous see in Him virtue. He admits of all forms. He can be moulded according to the imagination of each person. Water assumes various shapes in various vessels. But water is in all of them. Hence all religions are true.

God is cruel and not cruel. He is all being and not being at the same time. Hence He is all contradictions. Nature also is nothing but a mass of contradictions.

***

Freedom of the will—it is as you feel you are free to act. But this freedom is a species of necessity. There is one infinite link before, after, and between the thought and the action, but the latter takes the name of freedom—like a bird flitting through a bright room. We feel the freedom and feel it has no other cause. We cannot go beyond consciousness, therefore we feel we are free. We can trace it no further than consciousness. God alone feels the real freedom. Mahapurushas (saints) feel themselves identified with God; hence they also feel the real freedom.

You may stop the water flowing out of the fountain by closing that part of the stream and gathering it all in the fountain; you have no liberty beyond it. But the source remains unchanged. Everything is predestination—and a part of that predestination is that you shall have such feeling—the feeling of freedom. I am shaping my own action. Responsibility is the feeling of reaction. There is no absolute power. Power here is the conscious feeling of exercising any faculty which is created by necessity. Man has the feeling "I act"; what he means by power of freedom is the feeling. The power is attended with responsibility. Whatever may be done through us by predestination, we feel the reaction. A ball thrown by one, itself feels the reaction.

But this innate necessity which comes to us as our freedom does not affect also the conscious relations we form with our surroundings. The relativity is not changed. Either everybody is free or everybody is under necessity. That would not matter. The relations would be the same. Vice and virtue would be the same. If a thief pleads that he was under the necessity of stealing, the magistrate would say that he was under the necessity to punish. We are seated in a room, and the whole room is moving—the relation between us is unchanged. To get out of this infinite chain of causation is Mukti (freedom). Muktas (free souls) are not actuated by necessity, they are like god. They begin the chain of cause and effect. God is the only free being—the first source of their will—and is always experienced by them as such.

The feeling of want is the real prayer, not the words. But you must have patience to wait and see if your prayers are answered.

You should cultivate a noble nature by doing your duty. By doing our duty we get rid of the idea of duty; and then and then only we feel everything as done by God. We are but machines in His hand. This body is opaque, God is the lamp. Whatever is going out of the body is God's. You do not feel it. You feel "I". This is delusion. You must learn calm submission to the will of God. Duty is the best school for it. This duty is morality. Drill yourself to be thoroughly submissive. Get rid of the "I". No humbuggism. Then you can get rid of the idea of duty; for all is His. Then you go on naturally, forgiving, forgetting, etc.

Our religion always presents different gradations of duty and religion to different people.

Light is everywhere visible only in the men of holiness. A Mahapurusha is like crystal glass—full rays of God passing and repassing through. Why not worship a Jivanmukta?

Contact with holy men is good. If you go near holy men, you will find holiness overflowing unconsciously in everything there.

Resist not evil done to yourself, but you may resist evil done to others.

If you wish to become a saint, you should renounce all kinds of pleasures. Ordinarily, you may enjoy all, but pray to God for guidance, and He will lead you on.

The universe fills only a small portion of the heart which craves for something beyond and above the world.

Selfishness is the devil incarnate in every man. Every bit of self, bit by bit, is devil. Take off self by one side and God enters by the other. When the self is got rid of, only God remains. Light and darkness cannot remain together.

Forgetting the little "I" is a sign of healthy and pure mind. A healthy child forgets its body.

Sita—to say that she was pure is a blasphemy. She was purity itself embodied—the most beautiful character that ever lived on earth.

A Bhakta should be like Sita before Rama. He might be thrown into all kinds of difficulties. Sita did not mind her sufferings; she centreed herself in Rama.

***

Buddhism proves nothing about the Absolute Entity. In a stream the water is changing; we have no right to call the stream one. Buddhist deny the one, and say, it is many. We say it is one and deny the many. What they call Karma is what we call the soul. According to Buddhism, man is a series of waves. Every wave dies, but somehow the first wave causes the second. That the second wave is identical with the first is illusion. To get rid of illusion good Karma is necessary. Buddhists do not postulate anything beyond the world. We say, beyond the relative there is the Absolute. Buddhism accepts that there is misery, and sufficient it is that we can get rid of this Duhkha (misery); whether we get Sukha (happiness) or not, we do not know. Buddha preached not the soul preached by others. According to the Hindus, soul is an entity or substance, and God is absolute. Both agree in this, that they destroy the relative. But Buddhists do not give what is the effect of that destruction of the relative.

Present-day Hinduism and Buddhism were growths from the same branch. Buddhism degenerated, and Shankara lopped it off!

Buddha is said to have denied the Vedas because there is so much Himsa (killing) and other things. Every page of Buddhism is a fight with the Vedas (the ritualistic aspect). But he had no authority to do so.

Buddha is expressly agnostic about God; but God is everywhere preached in our religion. The Vedas teach God—both personal and impersonal. God is everywhere preached in the Gita. Hinduism is nothing without God. The Vedas are nothing without Him. That is the only way to salvation. Sannyasins have to repeat the following, several times: I, wishing for Mukti, take refuge in God, who created the world, who breathed out the Vedas.

Buddha, we may say now, ought to have understood the harmony of religions. He introduced sectarianism.

Modern Hinduism, modern Jainism, and Buddhism branched off at the same time. For some period, each seemed to have wanted to outdo the others in grotesqueness and humbuggism.

***

We cannot imagine anything which is not God. He is all that we can imagine with our five senses, and more. He is like a chameleon; each man, each nation, sees one face of Him and at different times, in different forms. Let each man see and take of God whatever is suitable to him. Compare each animal absorbing from nature whatever food is suitable to it.

The fault with all religions like Christianity is that they have one set of rules for all. But Hindu religion is suited to all grades of religious aspiration and progress. It contains all the ideals in their perfect form. For example, the ideal of Shanta or blessedness is to be found in Vasishtha; that of love in Krishna; that of duty in Rama and Sita; and that of intellect in Shukadeva. Study the characters of these and of other ideal men. Adopt one which suits you best.

Follow truth wherever it may lead you; carry ideas to their utmost logical conclusions. Do not be cowardly and hypocritical. You must have a great devotion to your ideal, devotion not of the moment, but calm, persevering, and steady devotion, like that of a Chataka (a kind of bird) which looks into the sky in the midst of thunder and lightening and would drink no water but from the clouds. Perish in the struggle to be holy; a thousand times welcome death. Be not disheartened. When good nectar is unattainable, it is no reason why we should eat poison. There is no escape. This world is as unknown as the other.

Charity never faileth; devotion to an ideal never fails in sympathy, never becomes weary of sympathising with others. Love to enemies is not possible for ordinary men: they drive out others in order to live themselves. Only a very few men lived in the world who practised both. King Janaka was one of them. Such a man is superior even to Sannyasins. Shukadeva, who was purity and renunciation embodied, made Janaka his Guru; and Janaka said to him, "You are a born Siddha; whatever you know and your father taught you, is true. I assure you of this."

***

Individuality in universality is the plan of creation. Each cell has its part in bringing about consciousness. Man is individual and at the same time universal. It is while realising our individual nature that we realise even our national and universal nature. Each is an infinite circle whose centre is everywhere and circumference nowhere. By practice one can feel universal Selfhood which is the essence of Hinduism. He who sees in every being his own Self is a Pandita (sage).

Rishis are discoverers of spiritual laws.

In Advaitism, there is no Jivatma; it is only a delusion. In Dvaitism, there is Jiva infinitely distinct from God. Both are true. One went to the fountain, another to the tank. Apparently we are all Dvaitists as far as our consciousness goes. But beyond? Beyond that we are Advaitists. In reality, this is the only truth. According to Advaitism, love every man as your own Self and not as your brother as in Christianity. Brotherhood should be superseded by universal Selfhood. Not universal brotherhood, but universal Selfhood is our motto. Advaitism may include also the "greatest happiness" theory.

So'ham—I am He. Repeat the idea constantly, voluntarily at first; then it becomes automatic in practice. It percolates to the nerves. So this idea, by rote, by repetition, should be driven even into the nerves.

Or, first begin with Dvaitism that is in your consciousness; second stage, Vishishtadvaitism—"I in you, you in me, and all is God." This is the teaching of Christ.

The highest Advaitism cannot be brought down to practical life. Advaitism made practical works from the plane of Vishishtadvaitism. Dvaitism—small circle different from the big circle, only connected by Bhakti; Vishishtadvaitism—small circle within big circle, motion regulated by the big circle; Advaitism—small circle expands and coincides with the big circle. In Advaitism "I" loses itself in God. God is here, God is there, God is "I".

***

One way for attaining Bhakti is by repeating the name of God a number of times. Mantras have effect—the mere repetition of words. Jalagiman Chetti's powers are due to the repetition of the Mantra—repetition of certain words with certain ceremonies. The powers of the Astras or Banas (missiles, arrows, etc.) of ancient war were due to Mantra. This is taken for granted throughout our Shastras. That we should take all these Shastras to be imagination is superstition.

To obtain Bhakti, seek the company of holy men who have Bhakti, and read books like the Gita and the Imitation of Christ; always think of the attributes of God.

The Vedas contain not only the means how to obtain Bhakti but also the means for obtaining any earthly good or evil. Take whatever you want.

Bengal is a land of Bhakti or Bhaktas. The stone on which Chaitanya used to stand in the temple of Jagannatha to see the image was worn by his tears of love and devotion. When he took Sannyasa, he showed his fitness for it to his Guru by keeping sugar on his tongue for some time without its being dissolved. He discovered Vrindavana by the power of insight he had acquired through devotion.

I will tell you something for your guidance in life. Everything that comes from India take as true, until you find congent reasons for disbelieving it. Everything that comes from Europe take as false, until you find congent reasons for believing it. Do not be carried away by European fooleries. Think for yourselves. Only one thing is lacking: you are slaves; you follow whatever Europeans do. That is simply an impotent state of mind. Society may take up materials from any quarter but should grow in its own way.

To be shocked by a new custom is the father of all superstition, the first road to hell. It leads to bigotry and fanaticism. Truth is heaven. Bigotry is hell.

Concentration

Concentration is the essence of all knowledge; nothing can be done without it. Ninety per cent of thought force is wasted by the ordinary human being, and therefore he is constantly committing blunders; the trained man or mind never makes a mistake. When the mind is concentrated and turned backward on itself, all within us will be our servants, not our masters. The Greeks applied their concentration to the external world, and the result was perfection in art, literature, etc. The Hindu concentrated on the internal world, upon the unseen realms in the Self, and developed the science of Yoga. Yoga is controlling the senses, will and mind. The benefit of its study is that we learn to control instead of being controlled. Mind seems to be layer on layer. Our real goal is to cross all these intervening strata of our being and find God. The end and aim of Yoga is to realise God. To do this we must go beyond relative knowledge, go beyond the sense-world. The world is awake to the senses, the children of the Lord are asleep on that plane. The world is asleep to the Eternal, the children of the Lord are awake in that realm. These are the sons of God. There is but one way to control the senses—to see Him who is the Reality in the universe. Then and only then can we really conquer our senses.

Concentration is restraining the mind into smaller and smaller limits. There are eight processes for thus restraining the mind. The first is Yama, controlling the mind by avoiding externals. All morality is included in this. Beget no evil. Injure no living creature. If you injure nothing for twelve years, then even lions and tigers will go down before you. Practise truthfulness. Twelve years of absolute truthfulness in thought, word, and deed gives a man what he wills. Be chaste in thought, word, and action. Chastity is the basis of all religions. Personal purity is imperative. Next in Niyama, not allowing the mind to wander in any direction. Then Asana, posture. There are eighty-four postures: but the best is that most natural to each one; that is, which can be kept longest with the greatest ease.

After this comes Pranayama, restraint of breath. Then Pratyahara, drawing in of the organs from their objects. Then Dharana, concentration. Then Dhyana, contemplation or meditation. (This is the kernel of the Yoga system.) And last, Samadhi, superconsciousness. The purer the body and mind, the quicker the desired result will be obtained. You must be perfectly pure. Do not think of evil things, such thoughts will surely drag you down. If you are perfectly pure and practise faithfully, your mind can finally be made a searchlight of infinite power. There is no limit to its scope. But there must be constant practice and non-attachment to the world. When a man reaches the superconscious state, all feeling of body melts away. Then alone does he become free and immortal. To all external appearances, unconsciousness and superconsciousness are the same; but they differ as a lump of clay from a lump of gold. The one whose whole soul is given up to God has reached the superconscious plane.

The Power Of The Mind

The cause becomes the effect. The cause is not one thing and the effect something else that exists as a result. The effect is always the cause worked out. Always, the cause becomes the effect. The popular idea is that the effect is the result of the operation of a cause which is something independent and aloof from the effect. This is not so. The effect is always the cause worked out into another condition.

The universe is really homogeneous. Heterogeneity is only in appearance. There seen to be different substances, different powers, etc. throughout nature. But take two different substances, say a piece of glass and a piece of wood, grind them up together fine enough, reduce them till there is nothing more to reduce, and the substance remaining appears homogeneous. All substances in the last analysis are one. Homogeneity is the substance, the reality; heterogeneity is the appearance of many things as though they were many substances. The One is homogeneity; the appearance of the One as many is heterogeneity.

Hearing, seeing, or tasting, etc. is the mind in different states of action.

The atmosphere of a room may be hypnotised so that everybody who enters it will see all sorts of things—men and objects flying through the air.

Everybody is hypnotised already. The work of attaining freedom, of realising one's real nature, consists in de-hypnotisation.

One thing to be remembered is that we are not gaining powers at all. We have them already. The whole process of growth is de-hypnotisation.

The purer the mind, the easier it is to control. Purity of the mind must be insisted upon if you would control it. Do not think covetously about mere mental powers. Let them go. One who seeks the powers of the mind succumbs to them. Almost all who desire powers become ensnared by them.

Perfect morality is the all in all of complete control over mind. The man who is perfectly moral has nothing more to do; he is free. The man who is perfectly moral cannot possibly hurt anything or anybody. Non-injuring has to be attained by him who would be free. No one is more powerful than he who has attained perfect non-injuring. No one could fight, no one could quarrel, in his presence. Yes, his very presence, and nothing else, means peace, means love wherever he may be. Nobody could be angry or fight in his presence. Even the animals, ferocious animals, would be peaceful before him.

I once knew a Yogi, a very old man, who lived in a hole in the ground all by himself[1]. All he had was a pan or two to cook his meals in. He ate very little, and wore scarcely anything, and spent most of his time meditating.

With him all people were alike. He had attained to non-injuring. What he saw in everything, in every person, in every animal, was the Soul, the Lord of the Universe. With him, every person and every animal was "my Lord". He never addressed any person or animal in any other way. Well, one day a thief came his way and stole one of his pans. He saw him and ran after him. The chase was a long one. At last the thief from exhaustion had to stop, and the Yogi, running up to him, fell on his knees before him and said, "My Lord, you do me a great honour to come my way. Do me the honour to accept the other pan. It is

---

1. Pavhari Baba of Ghazipur. (See Vol. IV. pp. 283-95).

also yours." This old man is dead now. He was full of love for everything in the world. He would have died for an ant. Wild animals instinctively knew this old man to be their friend. Snakes and ferocious animals would go into his hold and sleep with him. They all loved him and never fought in his presence.

Never talk about the faults of others, no matter how bad they may be. Nothing is ever gained by that. You never help one by talking about his fault; you do him an injury, and injure yourself as well.

All regulations in eating, practising, etc., are all right so long as they are complementary to a spiritual aspiration, but they are not ends in themselves; they are only helps.

Never quarrel about religion. All quarrels and disputation concerning religion simply show that spirituality is not present. Religious quarrels are always over the husks. When purity, when spirituality goes, leaving the soul dry, quarrels begin, and not before.

Lessons On Raja-Yoga[2]

Prana

The theory of creation is that matter is subject to five conditions: ether, luminous ether, gaseous, liquid, and solid. They are all evoked out of one primal element, which is very finest ether.

The name of the energy in the universe is Prana, which is the force residing in these elements. Mind is the great instrument for using the Prana. Mind is material. Behind the mind is Atman which takes hold of the Prana. Prana is the driving power of the world, and can be seen in every manifestation of life. The body is mortal and the mind is mortal; both, being compounds, must die. Behind all is the Atman which never dies. The Atman is pure intelligence controlling and directing Prana. But the intelligence we see around us is always imperfect. When intelligence is perfect, we get the Incarnation—the Christ. Intelligence is always trying to manifest itself, and in order to do this it is creating minds and bodies of different degrees of development. In reality, and at the back of

all things, every being is equal.

Mind is very fine matter; it is the instrument for manifesting Prana. Force requires matter for manifestation.

The next point is how to use this Prana. We all use it, but how sadly we waste it! The first doctrine in the preparatory stage is that all knowledge is the outcome of experience. Whatever is beyond the five senses must also be experienced in order to become true to us.

Our mind is acting on three planes: the subconscious, conscious, and superconscious. Of men, the Yogi alone is superconscious. The whole theory of Yoga is to go beyond the mind. These three planes can be understood by considering the vibrations of light or sound. There are certain vibrations of light too slow to become visible; then as they get faster, we see them as light; and then they get too fast for us to see them at all. The same with sound.

How to transcend the senses without disturbing the health is what we want to learn. The Western mind has stumbled into acquiring some of the psychic gifts which in them are abnormal and are frequently the sign of disease. The Hindu has studied and made perfect this subject of science, which all may now study without fear or danger.

Mental healing is a fine proof of the superconscious state; for the thought which heals is a sort of vibration in the Prana, and it does not go as a thought but as something higher for which we have no name.

Each thought has three states. First, the rising or beginning, of which we are unconscious; second, when the thought rises to the surface; and third, when it goes from us. Thought is like a bubble rising to the surface. When thought is joined to will, we call it power. That which strikes the sick person whom you are trying to help is not thought, but power. The self-man running through it all is called in Sanskrit Sutratma, the "Thread-self".

The last and highest manifestation of Prana is love. The moment you have succeeded in manufacturing love out of Prana, you are free. It is the hardest and the greatest thing to gain. You must not criticise others; you must criticise yourself. If you see a drunkard,

---

2. These lessons and those on Bhakti-Yoga that follow are made out of class notes preserved in England—Ed.

do not criticise him; remember he is you in another shape. He who has not darkness sees no darkness in others. What you have inside you is that you see in others. This is the surest way of reform. If the would-be reformers who criticise and see evil would themselves stop creating evil, the world would be better. Beat this idea into yourself.

The Practice of Yoga

The body must be properly taken care of. The people who torture their flesh are demoniacal. Always keep your mind joyful; if melancholy thoughts come, kick them out. A Yogi must not eat too much, but he also must not fast; he must not sleep too much, but he must not go without any sleep. In all things only the man who holds the golden mean can become a Yogi.

What is the best time for practice in Yoga? The junction time of dawn and twilight, when all nature becomes calm. Take help of nature. Take the easiest posture in sitting. Have the three parts straight—the ribs, the shoulders, and the head—leaving the spine free and straight, no leaning backwards or forwards. Then mentally hold the body as perfect, part by part. Then send a current of love to all the world; then pray for enlightenment. And lastly, join your mind to your breath and gradually attain the power of concentrating your attention on its movements. The reason for this will be apparent by degrees

The Ojas

The "Ojas" is that which makes the difference between man and man. The man who has much Ojas is the leader of men. It gives a tremendous power of attraction. Ojas is manufactured from the nerve-currents. It has this peculiarity: it is most easily made from that force which manifests itself in the sexual powers. If the powers of the sexual centres are not frittered away and their energies wasted (action is only thought in a grosser state), they can be manufactured into Ojas. The two great nerve currents of the body start from the brain, go down on each side of the spinal cord, but they cross in the shape of the figure 8 at the back of the head. Thus the left side of the body is governed by the right side of the head. At the lowest point of the circuit is the sexual centre, the Sacral Plexus. The energy conveyed by these two currents of nerves comes down, and a large amount is continually being stored in the Sacral Plexus. The last bone in the spine is over the Sacral Plexus and is described in symbolic language as a triangle; and as the energy is stored up beside it, this energy is symbolised by a serpent. Consciousness and subconsciousness work through these two nerve-currents. But superconsciousness takes off the nerve-current when it reaches the lower end of the circuit, and instead of allowing it to go up and complete the circuit, stops and forces it up the spinal cord as Ojas from the Sacral Plexus. The spinal cord is naturally closed, but it can be opened to form a passage for this Ojas. As the current travels from one centre of the spinal cord to another, you can travel from one plane of existence to another. This is why the human being is greater than others, because all planes, all experiences, are possible to the spirit in the human body. We do not need another; for man can, if he likes, finish in his body his probation and can after that become pure spirit. When the Ojas has gone from centre to centre and reaches the Pineal Gland (a part of the brain to which science can assign no function), man then becomes neither mind nor body, he is free from all bondage.

The great danger of psychic powers is that man stumbles, as it were, into them, and knows not how to use them rightly. He is without training and without knowledge of what has happened to him. The danger is that in using these psychic powers, the sexual feelings are abnormally roused as these powers are in fact manufactured out of the sexual centre. The best and safest way is to avoid psychic manifestations, for they play the most horrible pranks on their ignorant and untrained owners.

To go back to symbols. Because this movement of the Ojas up the spinal cord feels like a spiral one, it is called the "snake". The snake, therefore, or the serpent, rests on the bone or triangle. When it is roused, it travels up the spinal cord; and as it goes from centre to centre, a new natural world is opened inside us—the Kundalini is roused.

Pranayama

The practice of Pranayama is the training of the superconscious mind. The physical practice is divided into three parts and deals entirely with the breath. It consists of drawing in, holding, and throwing out the breath. The breath must be drawn in by one nostril whilst you count four, then held whilst you count sixteen, and thrown away by the other nostril whilst you count eight. Then reverse the process closing the other nostril while you breathe in. You will have to begin by holding one nostril with your thumb; but in time your breathing will obey your mind. Make four of these Pranayamas morning and evening.

Metagnosticism

"Repent, for the Kingdom of Heaven is at hand." The word "repent" is in Greek "metanoeite" ("meta" means behind, after, beyond) and means literally "go beyond knowledge"—the knowledge of the (five) senses—"and look within where you will find the kingdom of heaven".

Sir William Hamilton says at the end of a philosophical work, "Here philosophy ends, here religion begins". Religion is not, and never can be, in the field of intellect. Intellectual reasoning is based on facts evident to the senses. Now religion has nothing to do with the senses. The agnostics say they cannot know God, and rightly, for they have exhausted the limits of their senses and yet get no further in knowledge of God. Therefore in order to prove religion—that is, the existence of God, immortality, etc.—we have to go beyond the knowledge of the senses. All great prophets and seers claim to have "seen God", that is to say, they have had direct experience. There is no knowledge without experience, and man has to see God in his own soul. When man has come face to face with the one great fact in the universe, then alone will doubts vanish and crooked things become straight. This is "seeing God". Our business is to verify, not to swallow. Religion, like other sciences, requires you to gather facts, to see for yourself, and this is possible when you go beyond the knowledge which lies in the region of the five senses. Religious truths need verification by everyone. To see God is the one goal. Power is not the goal. Pure Existence-knowledge-and-love is the goal; and Love is God.

Thought, Imagination, and Meditation

The same faculty that we employ in dreams and thoughts, namely, imagination, will also be the means by which we arrive at Truth. When the imagination is very powerful, the object becomes visualised. Therefore by it we can bring our bodies to any state of health or disease. When we see a thing, the particles of the brain fall into a certain position like the mosaics of a kaleidoscope. Memory consists in getting back this combination and the same setting of the particles of the brain. The stronger the will, the greater will be the success in resetting these particles of the brain. There is only one power to cure the body, and that is in every man. Medicine only rouses this power. Disease is only the manifest struggle of that power to throw off the poison which has entered the body. Although the power to overthrow poison may be roused by medicine, it may be more permanently roused by the force of thought. Imagination must hold to the thought of health and strength in order that in case of illness the memory of the ideal of health may be roused and the particles re-arranged in the position into which they fell when healthy. The tendency of the body is then to follow the brain.

The next step is when this process can be arrived at by another's mind working on us. Instances of this may be seen every day. Words are only a mode of mind acting on mind. Good and evil thoughts are each a potent power, and they fill the universe. As vibration continues, so thought remains in the form of thought until translated into action. For example, force is latent in the man's arm until he strikes a blow, when he translates it into activity. We are the heirs of good and evil thought. If we make ourselves pure and the instruments of good thoughts, these will enter us. The good soul will not be receptive to evil thoughts. Evil thoughts find the best field in evil people; they are like microbes which germinate and increase only when they find a suitable soil. Mere thoughts are like little wavelets; fresh impulses to vibration come to them simultaneously, until at last one great wave seems to stand up and swallow up the rest. These universal thought-waves seem to recur every five hundred years, when invariably the great wave typifies and swallows up the others. It is this which constitutes a prophet. He focuses in his own mind the thought of the age in which he is living and gives it back to mankind in concrete form. Krishna, Buddha, Christ, Mohammed, and Luther may be instanced as the great waves that stood up above their fellows (with a probable lapse of five hundred years between them). Always the wave that is backed by the greatest purity and the noblest character is what breaks upon the world as movement of social reform. Once again in our day there is a vibration of the waves of thought and the central idea is that of the Immanent God, and this is everywhere cropping up in every form and every sect. In these waves, construction alternates with destruction; yet the construction always makes an end of the work of destruction. Now, as a man dives deeper to reach his spiritual nature, he feels no longer bound by superstition. The majority of sects will be transient, and last only as bubbles because the leaders are not usually men of character. Perfect love, the heart never reacting, this is what builds character. There is no allegiance possible where there is no character in the leader, and perfect purity ensures the most lasting allegiance and confidence.

Take up an idea, devote yourself to it, struggle on in patience, and the sun will rise for you.

***

To return to imagination:

We have to visualise the Kundalini. The symbol is the serpent coiled on the triangular bone.

Then practice the breathing as described before, and, while holding the breath, imagine that breath like the current which flows down the figure 8; when it reaches the lowest point, imagine that it strikes the serpent on the triangle and causes the serpent to mount up the channel within the spinal cord. Direct the breath in thought to this triangle.

We have now finished the physical process and from this point it becomes mental.

The first exercise is called the "gathering-in". The mind has to be gathered up or withdrawn from wandering.

After the physical process, let the mind run on and do not restrain it; but keep watch on your mind as a witness watching its action. This mind is thus divided into two—the player and the witness. Now strengthen the witnessing part and do not waste time in restraining your wanderings. The mind must think; but slowly and gradually, as the witness does its part, the player will come more and more under control, until at last you cease to play or wander. 2nd Exercise: Meditation—which may be divided into two. We are concrete in constitution and the mind must think in forms. Religion admits this necessity and gives the help of outward forms and ceremonies. You cannot meditate on God without some form. One will come to you, for thought and symbol are inseparable. Try to fix your mind on that form. 3rd Exercise: This is attained by practicing meditation and is really "one-pointedness". The mind usually works in a circle; make it remain on one point.

The last is the result. When the mind has reached this, all is gained—healing, clairvoyance, and all psychic gifts. In a moment you can direct this current of thought to anyone, as Jesus did, with instantaneous result.

People have stumbled upon these gifts without previous training, but I advise you to wait and practise all these steps slowly; then you will get everything under your control. You may practise healing a little if love is the motive, for that cannot hurt. Man is very short-sighted and impatient. All want power, but few will wait to gain it for themselves. He distributes but will not store up. It takes a long time to earn and but a short time to distribute. Therefore store up your powers as you acquire them and do not dissipate them.

Every wave of passion restrained is a balance in your favor. It is therefore good policy not to return anger for anger, as with all true morality. Christ said, "Resist not evil", and we do not understand it until we discover that it is not only moral but actually the best policy, for anger is loss of energy to the man who displays it. You should not allow your minds to come into those brain-combinations of anger and hatred.

When the primal element is discovered in chemical science, the work of the chemist will be finished. When unity is discovered, perfection in the science of religion is reached, and this was attained thousands of years ago. Perfect unity is reached when man says, "I and my Father are one".

Lessons On Bhakti-Yoga

The Yoga Through Devotion

We have been considering Raja-Yoga and the physical exercises. Now we shall consider Yoga through devotion. But you must remember that no one system is necessary (for all). I want to set before you many systems, many ideals, in order that you may find one that will suit you; if one does not, perhaps another may.

We want to become harmonious beings, with the psychical, spiritual, intellectual, and working (active) sides of our nature equally developed. Nations and individuals typify one of these sides or types and cannot understand more than that one. They get so built up into one ideal that they cannot see any other. The ideal is really that we should become many-sided. Indeed the cause of the misery of the world is that we are so one-sided that we cannot sympathise with one another. Consider a man looking at the sun from beneath the earth, up the shaft of a mine; he sees one aspect of the sun. Then another man sees the sun from the earth's level, another through mist and fog, another from the mountain top. To each the sun has a different appearance. So there are many appearances, but in reality there is only one sun. There is diversity of vision, but one object; and that is the sun.

Each man, according to his nature, has a peculiar tendency and takes to certain ideals and a certain path by which to reach them. But the goal is always the same to all. The Roman Catholic is deep and spiritual, but he has lost breadth. The Unitarian is wide, but he has lost spirituality and considers religion as of divided importance. What we want is the depth of the Roman Catholic and the breadth of the Unitarian. We must be as broad as the skies, as deep as the ocean; we must have the zeal of the fanatic, the depth of the mystic, and the width of the agnostic.

The word "toleration" has acquired an unpleasant association with the conceited man who, thinking himself in a high position, looks down on his fellow-creatures with pity. This is a horrible state of mind. We are all travelling the same way, towards the same goal, but by different paths made by the necessities of the case to suit diverse minds. We must become many-sided, indeed we must become protean in character, so as not only to tolerate, but to do what is much more difficult, to sympathise, to enter into another's path, and feel with him in his aspirations and seeking after God. There are two elements in every religion—a positive and a negative. In Christianity, for instance, when you speak of the Incarnation, of the Trinity, of salvation through Jesus Christ, I am with you. I say, "Very good, that I also hold true." But when you go on to say, "There is no other true religion, there is no other revelation of God", then I say, "Stop, I cannot go with you when you shut out, when you deny." Every religion has a message to deliver, something to teach man; but when it begins to protest, when it tries to disturb others, then it takes up a negative and therefore a dangerous position, and does not know where to begin or where to end.

Every force completes a circuit. The force we call man starts from the Infinite God and must return to Him. This return to God must be accomplished in one of two ways—either by slowly drifting back, going with nature, or by our own inward power, which causes us to stop on our course, which would, if left alone, carry us in a circuit back to God, and violently turn round and find God, as it were, by a short cut. This is what the Yogi does.

I have said that every man must choose his own ideal which is in accord with his nature. This ideal is called a man's Ishta. You must keep it sacred (and therefore secret) and when you worship God, worship according to your Ishta. How are we to find out the particular method? It is very difficult, but as you persevere in your worship, it will come of itself. Three things are the special gifts of God to man—the human body, the desire to be free, and the blessing of help from one who is already free. Now, we cannot have devotion without a Personal God. There must be the lover and the beloved. God is an infinitised human being. It is bound to be so, for so long as we are human, we must have a humanised God, we are forced to see a Personal God and Him only. Consider how all that we see in this world is not the object pure and simple, but the object plus our own mind. The chair plus the chair's reaction on your mind is the real chair. You must colour everything with your mind, and then alone you can see it. (Example: The white, square, shiny, hard box, seen by the man with three senses, then by the man with four senses, then by him with five senses. The last alone sees it with all the enumerated qualities, and each one before has seen an additional one to the previous man. Now suppose a man with six senses sees the same box, he would see still another quality added.)

Because I see love and knowledge, I know the universal cause is manifesting that love and knowledge. How can that be loveless which causes love in me? We cannot think of the universal cause without human qualities. To see God as separate from ourselves in the universe is necessary as a first step. There are three visions of God: the lowest vision, when God seems to have a body like ourselves (see Byzantine art); a higher vision when we invest God with human qualities; and then on and on, till we come to the highest vision, when we see God.

But remember that in *all* these steps we are seeing God and God alone; there is no illusion in it, no mistake. Just as when we saw the sun from different points, it was still the sun and not the moon or anything else.

We cannot help seeing God as we are—infinitised, but still as we are. Suppose we tried to conceive God as the

Absolute, we should have again to come back to the relative state in order to enjoy and love.

The devotion to God as seen in every religion is divided into two parts: the devotion which works through forms and ceremonies and through words, and that which works through love. In this world we are bound by laws, and we are always striving to break through these laws, we are always trying to disobey, to trample on nature. For instance, nature gives us no houses, we build them. Nature made us naked, we clothe ourselves. Man's goal is to be free, and just in so far as we are incompetent to break nature's laws shall we suffer. We only obey nature's law in order to be *outlawed*—beyond law. The whole struggle of life is *not* to obey. (That is why I sympathise with Christian Scientists, for they teach the liberty of man and the divinity of soul.) The soul is superior to all environment. "The universe is my father's kingdom; I am the heir-apparent"—that is the attitude for man to take. "My own soul can subdue all."

We must work through law before we come to liberty. External helps and methods, forms, ceremonies, creeds, doctrines, all have their right place and are meant to support and strengthen us until we become strong. Then they are no more necessary. They are our nurses, and as such indispensable in youth. Even books are nurses, medicines are nurses. But we must work to bring about the time when man shall recognise his mastery over his own body. Herbs and medicines have power over us as long as we allow them; when we become strong, these external methods are no more necessary.

Worships Through Words and Love

Body is only mind in a grosser form, mind being composed of finer layers and the body being the denser layers; and when man has perfect control over his mind, he will also have control over his body. Just as each mind has its own peculiar body, so to each word belongs a particular thought. We talk in double consonants when we are angry—"stupid", "fool", "idiot", etc.; in soft vowels when we are sad—"Ah me!" These are momentary feelings, of course; but there are eternal feelings, such as love, peace, calmness, joy, holiness; and these feelings have their word-expression in all religions, the word being only the embodiment of these, man's highest feelings. Now the thought has produced the word, and in their turn these words may produce the thoughts or feelings. This is where the help of words come in. Each of such words covers one ideal. These sacred mysterious words we all recognise and know, and yet if we merely read them in books, they have no effect on us. To be effective, they must be charged with spirit, touched and used by one who has himself been touched by the Spirit of God and who now *lives*. It is only he who can set the current in motion. The "laying on of hands" is the continuation of that current which was set in motion by Christ. The one who has the power of transmitting this current is called a Guru. With great teachers the use of words is not necessary—as with Jesus. But the "small fry" transmit this current through words.

Do not look on the faults of others. You cannot judge a man by his faults. (Example: Suppose we were to judge of an apple tree by the rotten, unripe, unformed apples we find on the ground. Even so do the faults of a man not show what the man's character is.) Remember, the wicked are always the same all over the world. The thief and the murderer are the same in Asia and Europe and America. They form a nation by themselves. It is only in the good and the pure and the strong that you find variety. Do not recognise wickedness in others. Wickedness is ignorance, weakness. What is the good of telling people they are weak?

Criticism and destruction are of no avail. We must give them something higher; tell them of their own glorious nature, their birthright. Why do not more people come to God? The reason is that so few people have any enjoyments outside their five senses. The majority *cannot* see with their eyes nor hear with their ears in the inner world.

We now come to *Worship through Love*.

It has been said, "It is good to be born in a church, but not to die in it." The tree receives support and shelter from the hedge that surrounds it when young; but unless the hedge is removed, the growth and strength of that tree will be hindered. Formal worship, as we have seen, is a necessary stage, but gradually by slow growth we outgrow it and come to a higher platform. When love to God becomes perfect, we think no more of the qualities of God—that He is omnipotent, omnipresent, and all those big adjectives. We do not want anything of God, so we do not care to notice these qualities. Just all we want is love of God. But anthropomorphism still follows us. We cannot get away from our humanity, we cannot jump out of our bodies; so we must love God as we love one another.

There are five steps in human love.

1. The lowest, most commonplace, "peaceful" love, when we look up to our Father for all we want—protection, food, etc.
2. The love which makes us want to serve. Man wants to serve God as his master, the longing to serve dominating every other feeling; and we are indifferent whether the master is good or bad, kind or unkind.
3. The love of a friend, the love of equals—companions, playmates. Man feels God to be his companion.
4. Motherly love. God is looked upon as a child. In India this is considered a higher love than the foregoing, because it has absolutely no element of fear.
5. The love of husband and wife; love for love's sake—god the perfect, beloved one.

It has been beautifully expressed: "Four eyes meet, a change begins to come into two souls; love comes in the middle between these two souls and makes them *one*."

When a man has this last and most perfect form of love, then all desires vanish, forms and doctrines and churches drop away, even the desire for freedom (the end and aim of all religions is freedom from birth and death and other things) is given up. The highest love is the love that is sexless, for it is perfect unity that is expressed in the highest love, and sex differentiates bodies. It is therefore only in spirit that union is possible. The less we have of the physical idea, the more perfect will be our love; at last all physical thought will be forgotten, and the two souls will become one. We love, love always. Love comes and penetrates through the forms and sees beyond. It has been said, "The lover sees Helen's beauty in an Ethiopian's brow." The Ethiopian is the suggestion and upon that suggestion the man throws his love. As the oyster throws over the irritants, it finds in its shell, the substance that turns the irritants into beautiful pearls, so man throws out love, and it is always man's highest ideal that he loves, and the highest ideal is always selfless; so man loves love. God is love, and we love God—or love love. We only see love, love cannot be expressed. "A dumb man eating butter" cannot tell you what butter is like. Butter is butter, and its qualities cannot be expressed to those who have not tasted it. Love for love's sake cannot be expressed to those who have not felt it.

Love may be symbolised by a triangle. The first angle is, love never begs, never asks for anything; the second, love knows no fear; the third and the apex, love for love's sake.

Through the power of love the senses become finer and higher. The perfect love is very rare in human relation, for human love is almost always interdependent and mutual. But God's love is a constant stream, nothing can hurt or disturb it. When man loves God as his highest ideal, as no beggar, wanting nothing, then is love carried to the extreme of evolution, and it becomes a great power in the universe. It takes a long time to get to these things, and we have to begin by that which is nearest to our nature; some are born to service, some to be mothers in love. Anyhow, the result is with God. We must take advantage of nature.

On Doing Good to the World

We are asked: What good is your Religion to society? Society is made a test of truth. Now this is very illogical. Society is only a stage of growth through which we are passing. We might just as well judge the good or utility of a scientific discovery by its use to the baby. It is simply monstrous. If the social state were permanent, it would be the same as if the baby remained a baby. There can be no perfect man-baby; the words are a contradiction in terms, so there can be no perfect society. Man must and will grow out of such early stages. Society is good at a certain stage, but it cannot be our ideal; it is a constant flux. The present mercantile civilisation must die, with all its pretensions and humbug—all a kind of "Lord Mayor's Show". What the world wants is thought-power through individuals. My Master used to say, "Why don't you help your own lotus flower to bloom? The bees will then come of themselves." The world needs people who are mad with love of God. You must believe in yourself, and then you will believe in God. The history of the world is that of six men of faith, six men of deep pure character. We need to have three things; the heart to feel, the brain to conceive, the hand to work. First we must go out of the world and make ourselves fit instruments. Make yourself a dynamo. *Feel* first for the world. At a time when all men are ready to work, where is the man of *feeling*? Where is the feeling that produced an Ignatius Loyola? Test your love and humility. That man is not humble or loving who is jealous. Jealousy is a terrible, horrible sin; it enters a man so mysteriously. Ask yourself, does your mind react in hatred or jealousy? Good works are continually being undone by the tons of hatred and anger which are being poured out on the world. If you are pure, if you are strong, *you*, *one* man, are equal to the whole world.

The brain to conceive the next condition of doing good works is only a dry Sahara after all; it cannot do anything alone unless it has the *feeling* behind it. Take love, which has never failed; and then the brain will conceive, and the hand will work righteousness. Sages have dreamed of and have *seen* the vision of God. "The pure in heart shall see God." All the great ones claim to have seen God. Thousands of years ago has the vision been seen, and the unity which lies beyond has been recognised; and now the only thing we can do is to fill in these glorious outlines.

Mother-Worship[1]

The two conjoint facts of perception we can never get rid of are happiness and unhappiness—things which bring us pain also bring pleasure. Our world is made up of these two. We cannot get rid of them; with every pulsation of life they are present. The world is busy trying to reconcile these opposites, sages trying to find solution of this commingling of the opposites. The burning heat of pain is intermitted by flashes of rest, the gleam of light breaking the darkness in intermittent flashes only to make the gloom deeper.

Children are born optimists, but the rest of life is a continuous disillusionment; not one ideal can be fully attained, not one thirst can be quenched. So on they go trying to solve the riddle, and religion has taken

---
1. Based on fragmentary notes of a class talk by Swami Vivekananda in New York.

up the task.

In religions of dualism, among the Persians, there was a God and a Satan. This through the Jews has gone all over Europe and America. It was a working hypothesis thousands of years ago; but now we know, that is not tenable. There is nothing absolutely good or evil; it is good to one and evil to another, evil today, good tomorrow, and vice versa. . . .

God was first of course a clan-god, then He became God of gods. With ancient Egyptians and Babylonians, this idea (of a dual God and Satan) was very practically carried out. Their Moloch became God of gods and the captured gods were forced to do homage in His temple.

Yet the riddle remains: Who presides over this Evil? Many are hoping against hope that all is good and that we do not understand. We are clutching at a straw, burying our heads in the sand. Yet we all follow morality and the gist of morality is sacrifice—not I but thou. Yet how it clashes with the great good God of the universe! He is so selfish, the most vengeful person that we know, with plagues, famines, war!

We all have to get experiences in this life. We may try to fly bitter experiences, but sooner or later they catch us. And I pity the man who does not face the whole.

Manu Deva of the Vedas, was transformed in Persia as Ahriman. So the mythological explanation of the question was dead; but the question remained, and there was no reply, no solution.

But there was the other idea in the old Vedic hymn to the Goddess: "I am the light. I am the light of the sun and moon; I am the air which animates all beings." This is the germ which afterwards develops into Mother-worship. By Mother-worship is not meant difference between father and mother. The first idea connoted by it is that of energy—I am the power that is in all beings.

The baby is a man of nerves. He goes on and on till he is a man of power. The idea of good and evil was not at first differentiated and developed. An advancing consciousness showed power as the primal idea. Resistance and struggle at every step is the law. We are the resultant of the two—energy and resistance, internal and external power. Every atom is working and resisting every thought in the mind. Everything we see and know is but the resultant of these two forces.

This idea of God is something new. In the Vedic hymns Varuna and Indra shower the choicest gifts and blessings on devotees, a very human idea, more human than man himself.

This is the new principle. There is one power behind all phenomena. Power is power everywhere, whether in the form of evil or as Saviour of the world. So this is the new idea; the old idea was man-god. Here is the first opening out of the idea of one universal power. "I stretch the bows of Rudra when He desires to destroy evil" (Rig-veda, X.125, *Devi-Sukta*).

Very soon in the Gita (IX.19, also X.4-5) we find, "O Arjuna, I am the Sat and I am the Asat, I am the good and I am the bad, I am the power of saints, I am the power of the wicked." But soon the speaker patches up truth, and the idea goes to sleep. I am power in good so long as it is doing good works.

In the religion of Persia, there was the idea of Satan, but in India, no conception of Satan. Later books began to realise this new idea. Evil exists, and there is no shirking the fact. The universe is a fact; and if a fact, it is a huge composition of good and evil. Whoever rules must rule over good and evil. If that power makes us live, the same makes us die. Laughter and tears are kin, and there are more tears than laughter in this world. Who made flowers, who made the Himalayas?—a very good God. Who made my sins and weaknesses?—karma, Satan, self. The result is a lame, one-legged universe, and naturally the God of the universe, a one-legged God.

The view of the absolute separation of good and evil, two cut and dried and separate existences, makes us brutes of unsympathetic hearts. The good woman jumps aside from the streetwalker. Why? She may be infinitely better than you in some respects. This view brings eternal jealousy and hatred in the world, eternal barrier between man and man, between the good man and the comparatively less good or evil man. Such brutal view is pure evil, more evil than evil itself. Good and evil are not separate existences, but there is an evolution of good, and what is less good we call evil.

Some are saints and some sinners. The sun shines on good and evil alike. Does he make any distinction?

The old idea of the fatherhood of God is connected with the sweet notion of God presiding over happiness. We want to deny facts. Evil is non-existent, is zero. The "I" is evil. And the "I" exists only too much. Am I zero? Every day I try to find myself so and fail.

All these ideas are attempts to fly evil. But we have to face it. Face the whole! Am I under contract to anyone to offer partial love to God only in happiness and good, not in misery and evil?

The lamp by the light of which one forges a name and another writes a cheque for a thousand dollars for famine, shines on both, knows no difference. Light knows no evil; you and I make it good or evil.

This idea must have a new name. It is called Mother, because in a literal sense it began long ago with a feminine writer elevated to a goddess. Then came Samkhya, and with it all energy is female. The magnet is still, the iron filings are active.

The highest of all feminine types in India is mother, higher than wife. Wife and children may desert a man, but his mother never. Mother is the same or loves her child perhaps a little more. Mother represents colourless love that knows no barter, love that never dies. Who can have such love?—only mother, not son, nor daughter, nor wife. "I am the Power that manifests everywhere", says the Mother—she who is bringing out this universe, and She who is bringing forth the following destruction. No need to say that destruction is only the beginning of creation. The top of a hill is only the beginning of a valley.

Be bold, face facts as facts. Do not be chased about the universe by evil. Evils are evils. What of that?

After all, it is only Mother's play. Nothing serious after all. What could move the Almighty? What made Mother create the universe? She could have no goal. Why? Because the goal is something that is not yet attained. What is this creation for? Just fun. We forget this and begin to quarrel and endure misery. We are the playmates of the Mother.

Look at the torture the mother bears in bringing up the baby. Does she enjoy it? Surely. Fasting and praying and watching. She loves it better than anything else. Why? Because there is no selfishness.

Pleasure will come—good: who forbids? Pain will come: welcome that too. A mosquito was sitting on a bull's horn; then his conscience troubled him and he said, "Mr. Bull, I have been sitting here a long time. Perhaps I annoy you. I am sorry, I will go away." But the bull replied, "Oh, no, not at all! Bring your whole family and live on my horn; what can you do to me?"

Why can we not say that to misery? To be brave is to have faith in the Mother! "I am Life, I am Death." She it is whose shadow is life and death. She is the pleasure in all pleasure. She is the misery in all misery. If life comes, it is the Mother; if death comes, it is the Mother. If heaven comes, She is. If hell comes, there is the Mother; plunge in. We have not faith, we have not patience to see this. We trust the man in the street; but there is one being in the universe we never trust and that is God. We trust Him when He works just our way. But the time will come when, getting blow after blow, the self-sufficient mind will die. In everything we do, the serpent ego is rising up. We are glad that there are so many thorns on the path. They strike the hood of the cobra.

Last of all will come self-surrender. Then we shall be able to give ourselves up to the Mother. If misery comes, welcome; if happiness comes, welcome. Then, when we come up to this love, all crooked things shall be straight. There will be the same sight for the Brahmin, the Pariah, and the dog. Until we love the universe with samesightedness, with impartial, undying love, we are missing again and again. But then all will have vanished, and we shall see in all the same infinite eternal Mother.

Narada-Bhakti-Sutras

A free translation dictated by Swamiji in America

Chapter I

1. Bhakti is intense love for God.
2. It is the nectar of love;
3. Getting which man becomes perfect, immortal, and satisfied for ever;
4. Getting which man desires no more, does not be-

come jealous of anything, does not take pleasure in vanities:

5. Knowing which man becomes filled with spirituality, becomes calm, and finds pleasure only in God.
6. It cannot be used to fill any desire, itself being the check to all desires.
7. Sannyasa is giving up both the popular and the scriptural forms of worship.
8. The Bhakti-sannyasin is the one whose whole soul goes unto God, and whatever militates against love to God, he rejects.
9. Giving up all other refuge, he takes refuge in God.
10. Scriptures are to be followed as long as one's life has not become firm;
11. Or else there is danger of doing evil in the name of liberty.
12. When love becomes established, even social forms are given up, except those which are necessary for the preservation of life.
13. There have been many definitions of love, but Narada gives these as the signs of love: When all thoughts, all words, and all deeds are given up unto the Lord, and the least forgetfulness of God makes one intensely miserable, then love has begun.
14. As the Gopis had it—
15. Because, although worshipping God as their lover, they never forgot his God-nature;
16. Otherwise they would have committed the sin of unchastity.
17. This is the highest form of love, because there is no desire of reciprocity, which desire is in all human love.

Chapter II

1. Bhakti is greater than Karma, greater than Jnana, greater than Yoga (Raja-Yoga), because Bhakti itself is its result, because Bhakti is both the means and the end (fruit).
2. As a man cannot satisfy his hunger by simple knowledge or sight of food, so a man cannot be satisfied by the knowledge or even the perception of God until love comes; therefore love is the highest.

Chapter III

1. These, however, the Masters have said about Bhakti:
2. One who wants this Bhakti must give up sense-enjoyments and even the company of people.
3. Day and night he must think about Bhakti and nothing else.
4. (He must) go where they sing or talk of God.
5. The principle cause of Bhakti is the mercy of a great (or free) soul.
6. Meeting with a great soul is hard to obtain, and never fails to save the soul.
7. Through the mercy of God we get such Gurus.
8. There is no difference between Him and His (own) ones.
9. Seek, therefore, for this.
10. Evil company is always to be shunned;
11. Because it leads to lust and anger, illusion, forgetfulness of the goal, destruction of the will (lack of perseverance), and destruction of everything.
12. These disturbances may at first be like ripples, but evil company at last makes them like the sea.
13. He gets across Maya who gives up all attachment, serves the great ones, lives alone, cuts the bondages of this world, goes beyond the qualities of nature, and depends upon the Lord for even his living.
14. He who gives up the fruits of work, he who
15. gives up all work and the dualism of joy and misery, who gives up even the scriptures, gets that unbroken love for God;
16. He crosses this river and helps others to cross it.

Chapter IV

1. The nature of love is inexpressible.

2. As the dumb man cannot express what he tastes, but his actions betray his feelings, so man cannot express this love in words, but his actions betray it.
3. In some rare persons it is expressed.
4. Beyond all qualities, all desires, ever increasing, unbroken, the finest perception is love.
5. When a man gets this love, he sees love everywhere, he hears love everywhere, he talks love everywhere, he thinks love everywhere.
6. According to the qualities or conditions, this love manifests itself differently.
7. The qualities are: Tamas (dullness, heaviness), Rajas (restlessness, activity), Sattva (serenity, purity); and the conditions are: Arta (afflicted), Artarthi (wanting something), Jijnasu (searching truth), Jnani (knower).
8. Of these the latter are higher than the preceding ones.
9. Bhakti is the easiest way of worship.
10. It is its own proof and does not require any other.
11. Its nature is peace and perfect bliss.
12. Bhakti never seeks to injure anyone or anything, not even the popular modes of worship.
13. Conversation about lust, or doubt of God or about one's enemies must not be listened to.
14. Egotism, pride, etc. must be given up.
15. If those passions cannot be controlled, place them upon God, and place all your actions on Him.
16. Merging the trinity of Love, Lover, and Beloved, worship God as His eternal servant, His eternal bride—thus love is to be made unto God.

Chapter V

1. That love is highest which is concentrated upon God.
2. When such speak of God, their voices stick in their throats, they cry and weep; and it is they who give holy places their holiness; they make good works, good books better, because they are permeated with God.
3. When a man loves God so much, his forefathers rejoice, the gods dance, and the earth gets a Master!
4. To such lovers there is no difference of caste, sex, knowledge, form, birth, or wealth;
5. Because they are all God's.
6. Arguments are to be avoided;
7. Because there is no end to them, and they lead to no satisfactory result.
8. Read books treating of this love, and do deeds which increase it.
9. Giving up all desires of pleasure and pain, gain and loss, worship God day and night. Not a moment is to be spent in vain.
10. Ahimsa (non-killing), truthfulness, purity, mercy, and godliness are always to be kept.
11. Giving up all other thoughts, the whole mind should day and night worship God. Thus being worshipped day and night, He reveals Himself and makes His worshippers feel Him.
12. In past, present, and future, Love is greatest!

Thus following the ancient sages, we have dared to preach the doctrine of Love, without fearing the jeers of the world.

WRITINGS: PROSE AND POEMS
(ORIGINAL AND TRANSLATED)

HISTORICAL EVOLUTION OF INDIA

OM TAT SAT

Om Namo Bhagavate Râmakrishnâya

नासतः सत् जायते — Existence cannot be produced by non-existence.

Non-existence can never be the cause of what exists. Something cannot come out of nothing. That the law of causation is omnipotent and knows no time or place when it did not exist is a doctrine as old as the Aryan race, sung by its ancient poet-seers, formulated by its philosophers, and made the corner-stone upon which the Hindu man even of today builds his whole scheme of life.

There was an inquisitiveness in the race to start with, which very soon developed into bold analysis, and though, in the first attempt, the work turned out might be like the attempts with shaky hands of the future master-sculptor, it very soon gave way to strict science, bold attempts, and startling results.

Its boldness made these men search every brick of their sacrificial altars; scan, cement, and pulverise every word of their scriptures; arrange, re-arrange, doubt, deny, or explain the ceremonies. It turned their gods inside out, and assigned only a secondary place to their omnipotent, omniscient, omnipresent Creator of the universe, their ancestral Father-in-heaven; or threw Him altogether overboard as useless, and started a world-religion without Him with even now the largest following of any religion. It evolved the science of geometry from the arrangements of bricks to build various altars, and startled the world with astronomical knowledge that arose from the attempts accurately to time their worship and oblations. It made their contribution to the science of mathematics the largest of any race, ancient or modern, and to their knowledge of chemistry, of metallic compounds in medicine, their scale of musical notes, their invention of the bow-instruments — (all) of great service in the building of modern European civilisation. It led them to invent the science of building up the child-mind through shining fables, of which every child in every civilised country learns in a nursery or a school and carries an impress through life.

Behind and before this analytical keenness, covering it as in a velvet sheath, was the other great mental peculiarity of the race — poetic insight. Its religion, its philosophy, its history, its ethics, its politics were all inlaid in a flower-bed of poetic imagery — the miracle of language which was called Sanskrit or "perfected", lending itself to expressing and manipulating them better than any other tongue. The aid of melodious numbers was invoked even to express the hard facts of mathematics.

This analytical power and the boldness of poetical visions which urged it onward are the two great internal causes in the make-up of the Hindu race. They together formed, as it were, the keynote to the national character. This combination is what is always making the race press onwards beyond the senses — the secret of those speculations which are like the steel blades the artisans used to manufacture — cutting through bars of iron, yet pliable enough to be easily bent into a circle.

They wrought poetry in silver and gold; the symphony of jewels, the maze of marble wonders, the music of colours, the fine fabrics which belong more to the fairyland of dreams than to the real — have back of them thousands of years of working of this national trait.

Arts and sciences, even the realities of domestic life, are covered with a mass of poetical conceptions, which are pressed forward till the sensuous touches the supersensuous and the real gets the rose-hue of the unreal.

The earliest glimpses we have of this race show it already in the possession of this characteristic, as an instrument of some use in its hands. Many forms of religion and society must have been left behind in the onward march, before we find the race as depicted in the scriptures, the Vedas.

An organised pantheon, elaborate ceremonials, divisions of society into hereditary classes necessitated by a variety of occupations, a great many necessaries and a good many luxuries of life are already there.

Most modern scholars are agreed that surroundings as to climate and conditions, purely Indian, were not yet working on the race.

Onwards through several centuries, we come to a multitude surrounded by the snows of Himalayas on the north and the heat of the south — vast plains, interminable forests, through which mighty rivers roll their tides. We catch a glimpse of different races — Dravidians, Tartars, and Aboriginals pouring in their quota of blood, of speech, of manners and religions. And at last a great nation emerges to our view — still keeping the type of the Aryan — stronger, broader, and more organised by the assimilation. We find the central assimilative core giving its type and character to the whole mass, clinging on with great pride to its name of "Aryan", and, though willing to give other races the benefits of its civilisation, it was by no means willing to admit them within the "Aryan" pale.

The Indian climate again gave a higher direction to the genius of the race. In a land where nature was propitious and yielded easy victories, the national mind started to grapple with and conquer the higher problems of life in the field of thought. Naturally the thinker, the priest, became the highest class in the Indian society, and not the man of the sword. The priests again, even at that dawn of history, put most of their energy in elaborating rituals; and when the nation began to find the load of ceremonies and lifeless rituals too heavy — came the first philosophical speculations, and the royal race was the first to break through the maze of killing rituals.

On the one hand, the majority of the priests impelled by economical considerations were bound to defend that form of religion which made their existence a necessity of society and assigned them the highest place in the scale of caste; on the other hand, the king-caste, whose strong right hand guarded and guided the nation and who now found itself as leading in the higher thoughts also, were loath to give up the first place to men who only knew how to conduct a ceremonial. There were then others, recruited from both the priests and king-castes, who ridiculed equally the ritualists and philosophers, declared spiritualism as fraud and priestcraft, and upheld the attainment of material comforts as the highest goal of life. The people, tired of ceremonials and wondering at the philosophers, joined in masses the materialists. This was the beginning of that caste question and that triangular fight in India between ceremonials, philosophy, and materialism which has come down unsolved to our own days.

The first solution of the difficulty attempted was by applying the eclecticism which from the earliest days had taught the people to see in differences the same truth in various garbs. The great leader of this school, Krishna — himself of royal race — and his sermon, the Gîtâ, have after various vicissitudes, brought about by the upheavals of the Jains, the Buddhists, and other sects, fairly established themselves as the "Prophet" of India and the truest philosophy of life. Though the tension was toned down for the time, it did not satisfy the social wants which were among the causes — the claim of the king-race to stand first in the scale of caste and the popular intolerance of priestly privilege. Krishna had opened the gates of spiritual knowledge and attainment to all irrespective of sex or caste, but he left undisturbed the same problem on the social side. This again has come down to our own days, in spite of the gigantic struggle of the Buddhists, Vaishnavas, etc. to attain social equality for all.

Modern India admits spiritual equality of all souls — but strictly keeps the social difference.

Thus we find the struggle renewed all along the line in the seventh century before the Christian era and finally in the sixth, overwhelming the ancient order of things under Shâkya Muni, the Buddha. In their reaction against the privileged priesthood, Buddhists swept off almost every bit of the old ritual of the Vedas, subordinated the gods of the Vedas to the position of servants to their own human saints, and declared the "Creator and Supreme Ruler" as an invention of priestcraft and superstition.

But the aim of Buddhism was reform of the Vedic religion by standing against ceremonials requiring offerings of animals, against hereditary caste and exclusive priesthood, and against belief in permanent souls. It never attempted to destroy that religion, or overturn the social order. It introduced a vigorous method by organising a class of Sannyâsins into a strong monastic brotherhood, and the Brahmavâdinis into a body of nuns — by introducing images of saints in the place of altar-fires.

It is probable that the reformers had for centuries the majority of the Indian people with them. The older forces were never entirely pacified, but they underwent a good deal of modification during the centuries of Buddhistic supremacy.

In ancient India the centres of national life were always the intellectual and spiritual and not political. Of old, as now, political and social power has been always subordinated to spiritual and intellectual. The outburst of national life was round colleges of sages and spiritual teachers. We thus find the Samitis of the Panchâlas, of the Kâshyas (of Varanasi), the Maithilas standing out as great centres of spiritual culture and philosophy, even in tile Upanishads. Again these centres in turn became the focus of political ambition of the various divisions of the Aryans.

The great epic Mahâbhârata tells us of the war of the Kurus and Panchalas for supremacy over the nation, in which they destroyed each other. The spiritual supremacy veered round and centred in the East among the Magadhas and Maithilas, and after the Kuru-Panchala war a sort of supremacy was obtained by the kings of Magadha.

The Buddhist reformation and its chief field of activity were also in the same eastern region; and when the Maurya kings, forced possibly by the bar sinister on their escutcheon, patronised and led the new movement, the new priest power joined hands with the political power of the empire of Pataliputra. The popularity of Buddhism and its fresh vigour made the Maurya kings the greatest emperors that India ever had. The power of the Maurya sovereigns made Buddhism that world-wide religion that we see even today.

The exclusiveness of the old form of Vedic religions debarred it from taking ready help from outside. At the same time it kept it pure and free from many debasing elements which Buddhism in its propagandist zeal was forced to assimilate.

This extreme adaptability in the long run made Indian Buddhism lose almost all its individuality, and extreme desire to be of the people made it unfit to cope with the intellectual forces of the mother religion in a few centuries. The Vedic party in the meanwhile got rid of a good deal of its most objectionable features, as animal sacrifice, and took lessons from the rival daughter in the judicious use of images, temple processions, and other impressive performances, and stood ready to take within her fold the whole empire of Indian Buddhism, already tottering to its fall.

And the crash came with the Scythian invasions and the total destruction of the empire of Pataliputra.

The invaders, already incensed at the invasion of their central Asiatic home by the preachers of Buddhism, found in the sun-worship of the Brahmins a great sympathy with their own solar religion — and when the Brahminist party were ready to adapt and spiritualise many of the customs of the new-comers, the invaders threw themselves heart and soul into the Brahminic cause.

Then there is a veil of darkness and shifting shadows; there are tumults of war, rumours of massacres; and the next scene rises upon a new phase of things.

The empire of Magadha was gone. Most of northern India was under the rule of petty chiefs always at war with one another. Buddhism was almost extinct except in some eastern and Himalayan provinces and in the extreme south and the nation after centuries of struggle against the power of a hereditary priesthood awoke to find itself in the clutches of a double priesthood of hereditary Brahmins and exclusive monks of the new regime, with all the powers of the Buddhistic organisation and without their sympathy for the people.

A renascent India, bought by the velour and blood of the heroic Rajputs, defined by the merciless intellect of a Brahmin from the same historical thought-centre of Mithila, led by a new philosophical impulse organised by Shankara and his bands of Sannyasins, and beautified by the arts and literature of the courts of Mâlavâ — arose on the ruins of the old.

The task before it was profound, problems vaster than any their ancestors had ever faced. A comparatively small and compact race of the same blood and speech and the same social and religious aspiration, trying to save its unity by unscalable walls around itself, grew huge by multiplication and addition during the Buddhistic supremacy; and (it) was divided by race, colour, speech, spiritual instinct, and social ambitions into hopelessly jarring factions. And this had to be unified and welded into one gigantic nation. This task Buddhism had also come to solve, and had taken it up when the proportions were not so vast.

So long it was a question of Aryanising the other types that were pressing for admission and thus, out of different elements, making a huge Aryan body. In spite of concessions and compromises, Buddhism was eminently successful and remained the national religion of India. But the time came when the allurements of sensual forms of worship, indiscriminately taken in along with various low races, were too dangerous for the central Aryan core, and a longer contact would certainly have destroyed the civilisation of the Aryans. Then came a natural reaction for self-preservation, and Buddhism and separate sect ceased to live in most parts of its land of birth.

The reaction-movement, led in close succession by Kumârila in the north, and Shankara and Râmânuja in the south, has become the last embodiment of that vast accumulation of sects and doctrines and rituals called Hinduism. For the last thousand years or more, its great task has been assimilation, with now and then an outburst of reformation. This reaction first wanted to revive the rituals of the Vedas — failing which, it made the Upanishads or the philosophic portions of the Vedas its basis. It brought Vyasa's system of Mimâmsâ philosophy and Krishna's sermon, the Gita, to the forefront; and all succeeding movements have followed the same. The movement of Shankara forced its way through its high intellectuality; but it could be of little service to the masses, because of its adherence to strict caste-laws, very small scope for ordinary emotion, and making Sanskrit the only vehicle of communication. Ramanuja on the other hand, with a most practical philosophy, a great appeal to the emotions, an entire denial of birthrights before spiritual attainments, and appeals through the popular tongue completely succeeded in bringing the masses back to the Vedic religion.

The northern reaction of ritualism was followed by the fitful glory of the Malava empire. With the destruction of that in a short time, northern India went to sleep as it were, for a long period, to be rudely awakened by the thundering onrush of Mohammedan cavalry across the passes of Afghanistan. In the south, however, the spiritual upheaval of Shankara and Ramanuja was followed by the usual Indian sequence of united races and powerful empires. It was the home of refuge of Indian religion and civilisation, when northern India from sea to sea lay bound at the feet of Central Asiatic conquerors. The Mohammedan tried for centuries to subjugate the south, but can scarcely be said to have got even a strong foothold; and when the strong and united empire of the Moguls was very near completing its conquest, the hills and plateaus of the south poured in their bands of fighting peasant horsemen, determined to die for the religion which Râmdâs preached and Tukâ sang; and in a short time the gigantic empire of the Moguls was only a name.

The movements in northern India during the Mohammedan period are characterised by their uniform attempt to hold the masses back from joining the religion of the conquerors — which brought in its train social and spiritual equality for all.

The friars of the orders founded by Râmânanda, Kabir, Dâdu, Chaitanya, or Nânak were all agreed in preaching the equality of man, however differing from each other in philosophy. Their energy was for the most part spent in checking the rapid conquest of Islam among the masses, and they had very little left to give birth to new thoughts and aspirations. Though evidently successful in their purpose of keeping the masses within the fold of the old religion, and tempering the fanaticism of the Mohammedans, they were mere apologists, struggling to obtain permission to live.

One great prophet, however, arose in the north, Govind Singh, the last Guru of the Sikhs, with creative genius; and the result of his spiritual work was followed by the well-known political organisation of the Sikhs. We have seen throughout the history of India, a spiritual upheaval is almost always succeeded by a political unity extending over more or less area of the continent, which in its turn helps to strengthen the spiritual aspiration that brings it to being. But the spiritual aspiration that preceded the rise of the Mahratta or the Sikh empire was entirely reactionary. We seek in vain to find in the court of Poona or Lahore even a ray of reflection of that intellectual glory which surrounded the courts of the Muguls, much less the brilliance of Malava or Vidyânagara. It was intellectually the darkest period of Indian history; and both these meteoric empires, representing the upheaval of mass-fanaticism and hating culture with all their hearts, lost all their motive power as soon as they had succeeded in destroying the rule of the hated Mohammedans.

Then there came again a period of confusion. Friends and foes, the Mogul empire and its destroyers, and the till then peaceful foreign traders, French and English, all joined in a mêlée of fight. For more than half a century there was nothing but war and pillage and destruction. And when the smoke and dust cleared, England was stalking victorious over the rest. There has been half a century of peace and law and order under the sway of Britain. Time alone will prove if it is the order of progress or not.

There have been a few religious movements amongst the Indian people during the British rule, following the same line that was taken up by northern Indian sects during the sway of the empire of Delhi. They are the voices of the dead or the dying — the feeble tones of a terrorised people, pleading for permission to live. They are ever eager to adjust their spiritual or social surroundings according to the tastes of the conquerors — if they are only left the right to live, especially the sects under the English domination, in which social differences with the conquering race are more glaring than the spiritual. The Hindu sects of the century seem to have set one ideal of truth before them — the approval of their English masters. No wonder that these sects have mushroom lives to live. The vast body of the Indian people religiously hold aloof from them, and the only popular recognition they get is the jubilation of the people when they die.

But possibly, for some time yet, it cannot be otherwise.

THE STORY OF THE BOY GOPALA

"O mother! I am so afraid to go to school through the woods alone; other boys have servants or somebody to bring them to school or take them home-why cannot I have someone to bring me home?"-thus said Gopâla, a little Brahmin boy, to his mother one winter afternoon when he was getting ready for school. The school hours were in the morning and afternoon. It was dark when the school closed in the afternoon, and the path lay through the woods.

Gopala's mother was a widow. His father who had lived as a Brahmin should-never caring for the goods of the world, studying and teaching, worshipping and helping others to worship—died when Gopala was a baby. And the poor widow retired entirely from the concerns of the world-even from that little she ever had-her soul given entirely to God, and waiting patiently with prayers, fasting, and discipline, for the great deliverer death, to meet in another life, him who was the eternal companion of her joys and sorrows, her partner in the good and evil of the beginningless chain of lives. She lived in her little cottage. A small rice-field her husband received as sacred gift to learning brought her sufficient rice; and the piece of land that surrounded her cottage, with its clumps of bamboos, a few cocoanut palms, a few mangoes, and lichis, with the help of the kindly village folk, brought forth sufficient vegetables all the year round. For the rest, she worked hard every day for hours at the spinning-wheel.

She was up long before the rosy dawn touched the tufted heads of the palms, long before the birds had begun to warble in their nests, and sitting on her bed-a mat on the ground covered with a blanket-repeated the sacred names of the holy women of the past, saluted the ancient sages, recited the sacred names of Nârâyana the Refuge of mankind, of Shiva the merciful, of Târâ the Saviour Mother; and above all, (she) prayed to Him whom her heart most loved, Krishna, who had taken the form of Gopala, a cowherd, to teach and save mankind, and rejoiced that by one day she was nearer to him who had gone ahead, and with him nearer by a day to Him, the Cowherd.

Before the light of the day, she had her bath in the neighbouring stream, praying that her mind might be made as clean by the mercy of Krishna, as her body by the water. Then she put on her fresh-washed whiter cotton garment, collected some flowers, rubbed a piece of sandalwood on a circular stone with a little water to make a fragrant paste, gathered a few sweet-scented Tulasi leaves, and retired into a little room in the cottage, kept apart for worship. In this room she kept her Baby Cowherd; on a small wooden throne under a small silk canopy; on a small velvet cushion, almost covered with flowers, was placed a bronze image of Krishna as a baby. Her mother's heart could only be satisfied by conceiving God as her baby. Many and many a time her learned husband had talked to her of Him who is preached in the Vedas, the formless, the infinite, the impersonal. She listened with all attention, and the conclusion was always the same-what is written in the Vedas must be true; but, oh! it was so immense, so far off, and she, only a weak, ignorant woman; and then, it was also written: "In whatsoever form one seeks Me, I reach him in that form, for all mankind are but following the paths I laid down for them"-and that was enough. She wanted to know no more. And there she was-all of the devotion, of faith, of love her heart was capable of, was there in Krishna, the Baby Cowherd, and all that heart entwined round the visible Cowherd, this little bronze image. Then again she had heard: "Serve Me as you would a being of flesh and blood, with love and purity, and I accept that all." So she served as she would a master, a beloved teacher, above all, as she would serve the apple of her eye, her only child, her son.

So she bathed and dressed the image, burned incense before it, and for offering?-oh, she was so poor!-but with tears in her eyes she remembered her husband reading from the books: "I accept with gladness even leaves and flowers, fruits and water, whatever is offered with love", and she offered: "Thou for whom the world of flowers bloom, accept my few common flowers. Thou who feedest the universe, accept my poor offerings of fruits. I am weak, I am ignorant. I do not know how to approach Thee, how to worship Thee, my God, my Cowherd, my child; let my worship be pure, my love for Thee selfless; and if there is any virtue in worship, let it be Thine, grant me only love, love that never asks for anything-'never seeks for anything but love'." Perchance the mendicant in his morning call was singing in the little yard:

>   Thy knowledge, man! I value not,
>   It is thy love I fear;
>   It is thy love that shakes My throne,
>   Brings God to human tear.

>   For love behold the Lord of all,
>   The formless, ever free,
>   Is made to take the human form
>   To play and live with thee.

>   What learning, they of Vrindâ's groves,
>   The herdsmen, ever got?
>   What science, girls that milked the kine?
>   They loved, and Me they bought.

Then, in the Divine, the mother-heart found her earthly son Gopala (lit. cowherd), named after the Divine Cowherd. And the soul which would almost mechanically move among its earthly surroundings-which, as it were, was constantly floating in a heavenly ether ready to drift away from contact of things material found its earthly moorings in her child. It was the only thing left to her to pile all her earthly joys and love on. Were not her movements, her thoughts, her pleasures, her very life for that little one that bound her to life?

For years she watched over the day-to-day unfolding of that baby life with all a mother's care; and now that he was old enough to go to school, how hard she worked for months to get the necessaries for the young scholar!

The necessaries however were few. In a land where men contentedly pass their lives poring over books in the the light of a mud lamp, with an ounce of oil in which is a thin cotton wick-a rush mat being the only furniture about them-the necessaries of a student are not many. Yet there were some, and even those cost many a day of hard work to the poor mother.

How for days she toiled over her wheel to buy Gopala a new cotton Dhoti and a piece of cotton Châdar, the under and upper coverings, the small mat in which Gopala was to put his bundle of palm leaves for writing and his reed pens, and which he was to carry rolled up under his arm to be used as his seat at school-and the inkstand. And what joy to her it was, when on a day of good omen Gopal attempted to write his first letters, only a mother's heart, a poor mother's, can know!

But today there is a dark shadow in her mind. Gopala is frightened to go alone through the wood. Never before had she felt her widowhood, her loneliness, her poverty so bitter. For a moment it was all dark, but she recalled to her mind what she had heard of the eternal promise: "Those that depend on Me giving up all other thoughts, to them I Myself carry whatever is necessary." And she was one of the souls who could believe.

So the mother wiped her tears and told her child that he need not fear. For in those woods lived another son of hers tending cattle, and also called Gopala; and if he was ever afraid passing through them, he had only to call on brother Gopala!

The child was that mother's son, and he believed.

That day, coming home from school through the wood, Gopala was frightened and called upon his brother Gopala, the cowherd: "Brother cowherd, are you here? Mother said you are, and I am to call on you: I am frightened being alone." And a voice came from behind the trees: "Don't be afraid, little brother, I am here; go home without fear."

Thus every day the boy called, and the voice answered. The mother heard of it with wonder and love; and she instructed her child to ask the brother of the wood to show himself the next time.

The next day the boy, when passing through the woods, called upon his brother. The voice came as usual, but the boy asked the brother in the woods to show himself to him. The voice replied, "I am busy today, brother, and cannot come." But the boy insisted, and out of the shade of the trees came the Cowherd of the woods, a boy dressed in the garb of cowherds, with a little crown on his head in which were peacock's feathers, and the cowherd's flute in his hands.

And they were so happy: they played together for hours in the woods, climbing trees, gathering fruits and flowers-the widow's Gopala and the Gopala of the woods, till it was almost late for school. Then the widow's Gopala went to school with a reluctant heart, and nearly forgot all his lesson, his mind eager to return to the woods and play with his brother.

Months passed this wise. The poor mother heard of it day by day and, in the joy of this Divine mercy, forgot her widowhood, her poverty, and blessed her miseries a thousand times.

Then there came some religious ceremonies which the teacher had to perform in honour of his ancestors. These village teachers, managing alone a number of boys and receiving no fixed fees from them, have to depend a great deal upon presents when the occasion requires them.

Each pupil brought in his share, in goods or money. And Gopala, the orphan, the widow's son!-the other boys smiled a smile of contempt on him when they talked of the presents they were bringing.

That night Gopala's heart was heavy, and he asked his mother for some present for the teacher, and the poor mother had nothing.

But she determined to do what she had been doing all her life, to depend on the Cowherd, and told her son to ask from his brother Gopala in the forests for some present for the teacher.

The next day, after Gopala had met the Cowherd boy in the woods as usual and after they had some games together, Gopala told his brother of the forest the grief that was in his mind and begged him to give him something to present his teacher with.

"Brother Gopala," said the cowherd, "I am only a cowherd you see, and have no money, but take this pot of cream as from a poor cowherd and present it to your teacher."

Gopala, quite glad that he now had something to

give his teacher, more so because it was a present from his brother in the forest, hastened to the home of the teacher and stood with an eager heart behind a crowd of boys handing over their presents to the teacher. Many and varied were the presents they had brought, and no one thought of looking even at the present of the orphan.

The neglect was quite disheartening; tears stood in the eyes of Gopala, when by a sudden stroke of fortune the teacher happened to take notice of him. He took the small pot of cream from Gopala's hand, and poured the cream into a big vessel, when to his wonder the pot filled up again! Again he emptied the contents into a bigger vessel, again it was full; and thus it went on, the small pot filling up quicker than he could empty it.

Then amazement took hold of everyone; and the teacher took the poor orphan in his arms and inquired about the pot of cream.

Gopala told his teacher all about his brother Cowherd in the forest, how he answered his call, how he played with him, and how at last he gave him the pot of cream.

The teacher asked Gopala to take him to the woods and show him his brother of the woods, and Gopala was only too glad to take his teacher there.

The boy called upon his brother to appear, but there was no voice even that day. He called again and again. No answer. And then the boy entreated his brother in the forest to speak, else the teacher would think he was not speaking the truth. Then came the voice as from a great distance:

"Gopala, thy mother's and thy love and faith brought Me to thee; but tell thy teacher, he will have to wait a long while yet."

MY PLAY IS DONE

Written in the Spring of 1895 in New York

Ever rising, ever falling with the waves of time,

still rolling on I go

From fleeting scene to scene ephemeral,

with life's currents' ebb and flow.

Oh! I am sick of this unending force;

these shows they please no more.

This ever running, never reaching,

nor e'en a distant glimpse of shore!

From life to life I'm waiting at the gates,

alas, they open not.

Dim are my eyes with vain attempt

to catch one ray long sought.

On little life's high, narrow bridge

I stand and see below

The struggling, crying, laughing throng.

For what? No one can know.

In front yon gates stand frowning dark,

and say: "No farther way,

This is the limit; tempt not Fate,

bear it as best you may;

Go, mix with them and drink this cup

and be as mad as they.

Who dares to know but comes to grief;

stop then, and with them stay."

Alas for me. I cannot rest.

This floating bubble, earth—

Its hollow form, its hollow name,
its hollow death and birth—
For me is nothing. How I long
to get beyond the crust
Of name and form! Ah! ope the gates;
to me they open must.
Open the gates of light, O Mother, to me Thy tired son. I long, oh, long to return home!
Mother, my play is done.
You sent me out in the dark to play,
and wore a frightful mask;
Then hope departed, terror came,
and play became a task.
Tossed to and fro, from wave to wave
in this seething, surging sea
Of passions strong and sorrows deep,
grief is, and joy to be,
Where life is living death, alas! and death—
who knows but 'tis
Another start, another round of this old wheel
of grief and bliss?
Where children dream bright, golden dreams,
too soon to find them dust,
And aye look back to hope long lost
and life a mass of rust!
Too late, the knowledge age cloth gain;
scarce from the wheel we're gone
When fresh, young lives put their strength
to the wheel, which thus goes on
From day to day and year to year.

'Tis but delusion's toy,
False hope its motor; desire, nave;
its spokes are grief and joy.
I go adrift and know not whither.
Save me from this fire!
Rescue me, merciful Mother, from floating with desire! Turn not to me Thy awful face,
'tis more than I can bear.
Be merciful and kind to me,
to chide my faults forbear.
Take me, O Mother, to those shores
where strifes for ever cease;
Beyond all sorrows, beyond tears,
beyond e'en earthly bliss;
Whose glory neither sun, nor moon,
nor stars that twinkle bright,
Nor flash of lightning can express.
They but reflect its light.
Let never more delusive dreams
veil off Thy face from me.
My play is done, O Mother,
break my chains and make me free!

THE CUP

This is your cup-the cup assigned
to you from the beginning.
Nay, My child, I know how much
of that dark drink is your own brew
Of fault and passion, ages long ago,
In the deep years of yesterday, I know.

This is your road-a painful road and drear.
I made the stones that never give you rest.
I set your friend in pleasant ways and clear,
And he shall come like you, unto My breast.
But you, My child, must travel here.

This is your task. It has no joy nor grace,
But it is not meant for any other hand,
And in My universe hath measured place,
Take it. I do not bid you understand.
I bid you close your eyes to see My face.

A BENEDICTION

Written to Sister Nivedita

The mother's heart, the hero's will,
The sweetness of the southern breeze,
The sacred charm and strength that dwell
On Aryan altars, flaming, free;
All these be yours, and many more
No ancient soul could dream before—
Be thou to India's future son
The mistress, servant, friend in one.

THE HYMN OF CREATION

A translation of the Nâsadiya-Sukta,
Rig-Veda, X. 129.

Existence was not then, nor non-existence,
The world was not, the sky beyond was neither.
What covered the mist? Of whom was that?
What was in the depths of darkness thick?

Death was not then, nor immortality,
The night was neither separate from day,
But motionless did That vibrate
Alone, with Its own glory one —
Beyond That nothing did exist.

At first in darkness hidden darkness lay,
Undistinguished as one mass of water,
Then That which lay in void thus covered
A glory did put forth by Tapah!

First desire rose, the primal seed of mind,
(The sages have seen all this in their hearts
Sifting existence from non-existence.)
Its rays above, below and sideways spread.

Creative then became the glory,
With self-sustaining principle below.
And Creative Energy above.

Who knew the way? Who there declared
Whence this arose? Projection whence?
For after this projection came the gods.
Who therefore knew indeed, came out this whence?

This projection whence arose,
Whether held or whether not,
He the ruler in the supreme sky, of this
He, O Sharman! knows, or knows not
He perchance!

ON THE SEA'S BOSOM

Swami Vivekananda composed this poem in Bengali during his return from his second trip to the West. At the time of writing it, he was probably crossing the eastern Mediterranean.)

In blue sky floats a multitude of clouds—
White, black, of snaky shades and thicknesses;
An orange sun, about to say farewell,
Touches the massed cloud-shapes with streaks of red.

The wind blows as it lists, a hurricane
Now carving shapes, now breaking them apart:
Fancies, colours, forms, inert creations—
A myriad scenes, though real, yet fantastic.

There light clouds spread, heaping up spun cotton;
See next a huge snake, then a strong lion;
Again, behold a couple locked in love.
All vanish, at last, in the vapoury sky.

Below, the sea sings a varied music,
But not grand, O India, nor ennobling:
Thy waters, widely praised, murmur serene
In soothing cadence, without a harsh roar.

HINDUISM AND SHRI RAMAKRISHNA

Translated from Bengali

By the word "Shastras" the Vedas without beginning or end are meant. In matters of religious duty the Vedas are the only capable authority.

The Puranas and other religious scriptures are all denoted by the word "Smriti". And their authority goes so far as they follow the Vedas and do not contradict them.

Truth is of two kinds: (1) that which is cognisable by the five ordinary senses of man, and by reasonings based thereon; (2) that which is cognisable by the subtle, supersensuous power of Yoga.

Knowledge acquired by the first means is called science; and knowledge acquired by the second is called the Vedas.

The whole body of supersensuous truths, having no beginning or end, and called by the name of the Vedas, is ever-existent. The Creator Himself is creating, preserving, and destroying the universe with the help of these truths.

The person in whom this supersensuous power is manifested is called a Rishi, and the supersensuous truths which he realises by this power are called the Vedas.

This Rishihood, this power of supersensuous perception of the Vedas, is real religion. And so long as this does not develop in the life of an initiate, so long is religion a mere empty word to him, and it is to be understood that he has not taken yet the first step in religion.

The authority of the Vedas extends to all ages, climes and persons; that is to say, their application is not confined to any particular place, time, and persons.

The Vedas are the only exponent of the universal religion.

Although the supersensuous vision of truths is to be met with in some measure in our Puranas and Itihasas and in the religious scriptures of other races, still the fourfold scripture known among the Aryan race as the Vedas being the first, the most complete, and the most undistorted collection of spiritual truths, deserve to occupy the highest place among all scriptures, command the respect of all nations of the earth, and furnish the rationale of all their respective scriptures.

With regard to the whole Vedic collection of truths discovered by the Aryan race, this also has to be understood that those portions alone which do not refer to purely secular matters and which do not merely record tradition or history, or merely provide incentives to duty, form the Vedas in the real sense.

The Vedas are divided into two portions, the Jnâna-kânda (knowledge-portion) and the Karma-kânda (ritual-portion). The ceremonies and the fruits of the Karma-kanda are confined within the limits of the world of Mâyâ, and therefore they have been undergoing and will undergo transformation according to the law of change which operates through time, space, and personality.

Social laws and customs likewise, being based on this Karma-kanda, have been changing and will continue to change hereafter. Minor social usages also will be recognised and accepted when they are compatible with the spirit of the true scriptures and the conduct and example of holy sages. But blind allegiance only to usages such as are repugnant to the spirit of the Shastras and the conduct of holy sages has been one of the main causes of the downfall of the Aryan race.

It is the Jnana-kanda or the Vedanta only that has for all time commanded recognition for leading men across Maya and bestowing salvation on them through the practice of Yoga, Bhakti, Jnana, or selfless work; and as its validity and authority remain unaffected by any limitations of time, place or persons, it is the only exponent of the universal and eternal religion for all mankind.

The Samhitas of Manu and other sages, following the lines laid down in the Karma-kanda, have mainly ordained rules of conduct conducive to social welfare, according to the exigencies of time, place, and persons. The Puranas etc. have taken up the truths imbedded in the Vedanta and have explained them in detail in the course of describing the exalted life and deeds of Avataras and others. They have each emphasised, besides, some out of the infinite aspects of the Divine Lord to teach men about them.

But when by the process of time, fallen from the true ideals and rules of conduct and devoid of the spirit of renunciation, addicted only to blind usages, and degraded in intellect, the descendants of the Aryans failed to appreciate even the spirit of these Puranas etc. which taught men of ordinary intelligence the abstruse truths of the Vedanta in concrete form and diffuse language and appeared antagonistic to one another on the surface, because of each inculcating with special emphasis only particular aspects of the spiritual ideal —

And when, as a consequence, they reduced India, the fair land of religion, to a scene of almost infernal confusion by breaking up piecemeal the one Eternal Religion of the Vedas (Sanâtana Dharma), the grand synthesis of all the aspects of the spiritual ideal, into conflicting sects and by seeking to sacrifice one another in the flames of sectarian hatred and intolerance —

Then it was that Shri Bhagavan Ramakrishna incarnated himself in India, to demonstrate what the true religion of the Aryan race is; to show where amidst all its many divisions and offshoots, scattered over the land in the course of its immemorial history, lies the true unity of the Hindu religion, which by its overwhelming number of sects discordant to superficial view, quarrelling constantly with each other and abounding in customs divergent in every way, has constituted itself a misleading enigma for our countrymen and the butt of contempt for foreigners; and above all, to hold up before men, for their lasting welfare, as a living embodiment of the Sanatana Dharma, his own wonderful life into which he infused the universal spirit and character of this Dharma, so long cast into oblivion by the process of time.

In order to show how the Vedic truths — eternally existent as the instrument with the Creator in His work of creation, preservation, and dissolution — reveal themselves spontaneously in the minds of the Rishis purified from all impressions of worldly attachment, and because such verification and confirmation of the scriptural truths will help the revival, reinstatement, and spread of religion — the Lord, though the very embodiment of the Vedas, in this His new incarnation has thoroughly discarded all external forms of learning.

That the Lord incarnates again and again in human form for the protection of the Vedas or the true religion, and of Brahminhood or the ministry of that religion — is a doctrine well established in the Puranas etc.

The waters of a river falling in a cataract acquire greater velocity, the rising wave after a hollow swells higher; so after every spell of decline, the Aryan society recovering from all the evils by the merciful dispensation of Providence has risen the more glorious and powerful — such is the testimony of history.

After rising from every fall, our revived society is expressing more and more its innate eternal perfection, and so also the omnipresent Lord in each successive incarnation is manifesting Himself more and more.

Again and again has our country fallen into a swoon, as it were, and again and again has India's Lord, by the manifestation of Himself, revivified her.

But greater than the present deep dismal night, now almost over, no pall of darkness had ever before enveloped this holy land of ours. And compared with the depth of this fall, all previous falls appear like little hoof-marks.

Therefore, before the effulgence of this new awakening' the glory of all past revivals in her history will pale like stars before the rising sun; and compared with this mighty manifestation of renewed strength, all the many past epochs of such restoration will be as child's play.

The various constituent ideals of the Religion Eternal, during its present state of decline, have been lying scattered here and there for want of competent men to realise them — some being preserved partially among small sects and some completely lost.

But strong in the strength of this new spiritual renaissance, men, after reorganising these scattered and disconnected spiritual ideals, will be able to comprehend and practice them in their own lives and also to recover from oblivion those that are lost. And as the sure pledge of this glorious future, the all-merciful Lord has manifested in the present age, as stated above, an incarnation which in point of completeness in revelation, its synthetic harmonising of all ideals, and its promoting of every sphere of spiritual culture, surpasses the manifestations of all past ages.

So at the very dawn of this momentous epoch, the reconciliation of all aspects and ideals of religious thought and worship is being proclaimed; this boundless, all embracing idea had been lying inherent, but so long concealed, in the Religion Eternal and its scriptures, and now rediscovered, it is being declared to humanity in a trumpet voice.

This epochal new dispensation is the harbinger of great good to the whole world, specially to India; and the inspirer of this dispensation, Shri Bhagavan Ramakrishna, is the reformed and remodelled manifestation of all the past great epoch-makers in religion. O man, have faith in this, and lay to heart.

The dead never return; the past night does not reappear; a spent-up tidal wave does not rise anew; neither does man inhabit the same body over again. So from the worship of the dead past, O man, we invite you to the worship of the living present; from the regretful brooding over bygones, we invite you to the activities of the present; from the waste of energy in retracing lost and demolished pathways, we call you back to broad new-laid highways lying very near. He that is wise, let him understand.

Of that power, which at the very first impulse has roused distant echoes from all the four quarters of the globe, conceive in your mind the manifestation in its fullness; and discarding all idle misgivings, weaknesses, and the jealousies characteristic of enslaved peoples, come and help in the turning of this mighty wheel of new dispensation!

With the conviction firmly rooted in your heart that you are the servants of the Lord, His children, helpers in the fulfilment of His purpose, enter the arena of work.

THE BENGALI LANGUAGE

Written for the "Udbodhan"

In our country, owing to all learning being in Sanskrit from the ancient times, there has arisen an immeasurable gulf between the learned and the common folk. All the great personages, from Buddha down to Chaitanya and Ramakrishna, who came for the well-being of the world, taught the common people in the language of the people themselves. Of course, scholarship is an excellent thing; but cannot scholarship be displayed through any other medium than a language that is stiff and unintelligible, that is unnatural and merely artificial? Is there no room for art in the spoken language? What is the use of creating an unnatural language to the exclusion of the natural one? Do you not think out your scholastic researches in the language which you are accustomed to speak at home? Why then do you introduce such a queer and unwieldy thing when you proceed to put them in black and white? The language in which you think out philosophy and science in your mind, and argue with others in public — is not that the language for writing philosophy and science? If it is not, how then do you reason out those truths within yourselves and in company of others in that very language? The language in which we naturally express ourselves, in which we communicate our anger, grief, or love, etc.— there cannot be a fitter language than that. We must stick to that idea, that manner of expression, that diction and all. No artificial language can ever have that force, and that brevity and expressiveness, or admit of being given any turn you please, as that spoken language. Language must be made like pure steel — turn and twist it any way you like, it is again the same — it cleaves a rock in twain at one stroke, without its edge being turned. Our language is becoming artificial by imitating the slow and pompous movement — and only that — of Sanskrit. And language is the chief means and index of a nation's progress.

If you say, "It is all right, but there are various kinds of dialects in different parts of Bengal — which of them to accept?" — the answer is: We must accept that which is gaining strength and spreading through natural laws, that is to say, the language of Calcutta. East or west, from wheresoever people may come, once they breathe in the air of Calcutta, they are found to speak the language in vogue there; so nature herself points out which language to write in. The more railroads and facilities of communication there are, the more will the difference of east and west disappear, and from Chittagong to Baidyanath there will be that one language, viz that of Calcutta. It is not the question which district possesses a language most approaching Sanskrit — you must see which language is triumphing. When it is evident that the language of Calcutta will soon become the language of the whole of Bengal, then, if one has to make the written and spoken language the same, one would, if one is intelligent enough certainly make the language of Calcutta one's foundation. Here local jealousies also should be thrown overboard. Where the welfare of the whole province is concerned, you must overlook the claims to superiority of your own district or village.

Language is the vehicle of ideas. It is the ideas that are of prime importance, language comes after. Does it look well to place a monkey on a horse that has trappings of diamonds and pearls? Just look at Sanskrit. Look at the Sanskrit of the Brâhmanas, at Shabara Swâmi's commentary on the Mimâmsâ philosophy, the Mahâbhâshya of Patanjali, and, finally, at the great Commentary of Achârya Shankara: and look also at the Sanskrit of comparatively recent times. You will at once understand that so long as a man is alive, he talks a living language, but when he is dead, he speaks a dead language. The nearer death approaches, the more does the power of original thinking wane, the more is there the attempt to bury one or two rotten ideas under a heap of flowers and scents. Great God! What a parade they make! After ten pages of big adjectives, all on a sudden you have — "There lived the King!" Oh, what an array of spun-out adjectives, and giant compounds, and skilful puns! They are symptoms of death. When the country began to decay, then all these signs became manifest. It was not merely in language — all the arts began to manifest them. A building now neither expressed any idea nor followed any style; the columns were turned and turned till they had all their strength taken out of them. The ornaments pierced the nose and the neck and converted the wearer into a veritable ogress; but oh, the profusion of leaves and foliage carved fantastically in them! Again, in music, nobody, not even the sage Bharata, the originator of dramatic performances, could understand whether it was singing, or weeping, or wrangling, and what meaning or purpose it sought to convey! And what an abundance of intricacies in that music! What labyrinths of flourishes — enough to strain all one's nerves! Over and above that, that music had its birth in the nasal tone uttered through the teeth compressed, in imitation of the Mohammedan musical experts! Nowadays there is an indication of correcting these; now will people gradually understand that a language, or art, or music that expresses no meaning and is lifeless is of no good. Now they will understand that the more strength is infused into the national life, the more will language art, and music, etc. become spontaneously instinct with ideas and life. The volume of meaning that a couple of words of everyday use will convey, you may search in vain in two thousand set epithets. Then every image of the Deity will inspire devotion, every girl decked in ornaments will appear to be a goddess, and every house and room and furniture will be animated with the vibration of life.

MATTER FOR SERIOUS THOUGHT

Translated from Bengali

A man presented himself to be blessed by a sight of the Deity. He had an access of joy and devotion at the sight; and perhaps to pay back the good he received, he burst out into a song. In one corner of the hall, reclining against a pillar, was Chobeji dozing. He was the priest in the temple, an athlete, a player on the guitar, was a good hand in swallowing two jugfuls of Bhâng (an intoxicating drink.), and had various other qualifications besides. All on a sudden, a dreadful noise assailing his tympanum, the fantastic universe conjured up under the influence of the inebriating liquor vanished for a moment from Chobeji's enormous chest of two and forty inches! And casting his crimson-tinged, languid eyes around in search of the cause of disturbance to his tranquil mind, Chobeji discovered that in front of the God was a man singing, overwhelmed with his own feelings, in a tune as touching as the scouring of cauldrons in a festive house, and, in so doing, he was subjecting the shades of the whole host of musical masters like Nârada, Bharata, Hanumân, Nâyaka, and the rest to ineffable anguish. The mortified Chobeji in a sharp reprimanding tone addressed the man who had been the direct obstacle to his enjoyment of that peculiar bliss of inebriation, "Hello, my friend, what are you shouting like that for, without caring for time or tune?" Quick came the response, "What need I care for time or tune? I am trying to win the Lord's heart." "Humph!" retorted Chobeji, "do you think the Lord is such a fool? You must be mad! You could not win my heart even — and has the Lord less brains than I?"

***

The Lord has declared unto Arjuna: "Take thou refuge in Me, thou hast nothing else to do. And I shall deliver thee." Bholâchand is mighty glad to hear this from some people; he now and then yells out in a trenchant note: "I have taken refuge in the Lord. I shall not have to do anything further." Bholachand is under the: impression that it is the height of devotion to bawl out those words repeatedly in the harshest tone possible. Moreover, he does not fail to make it known now and then in the aforesaid pitch that he is ever ready to lay down his life even, for the Lord's sake, and that if the Lord does not voluntarily surrender Himself to this tie of devotion, everything would be hollow and false. And a few foolish satellites of his also share the same opinion. But Bholachand is not prepared to give up a single piece of wickedness for the sake of the Lord. Well, is the Lord really such a fool? Why, this is not enough to hoodwink us even!

***

Bholâ Puri an out and out Vedantin — in everything he is careful to trumpet his Brahminhood. If all people are about to starve for food around Bhola Puri, it does not touch him even in the least; he expounds the unsubstantiality of pleasure and pain. If through disease, or affliction, or starvation people die by the thousand, what matters even that to him? He at once reflects on the immortality of the soul! If the strong overpower the weak and even kill them before his very eyes, Bhola Puri is lost in the profound depths of the meaning of the spiritual dictum, "The soul neither kills nor is killed." He is exceedingly averse to action of any kind. If hard pressed, he replies that he finished all actions in his previous births. But Bhola Puri's realisation of unity of the Self suffers a terrible check when he is hurt in one point. When there is some anomaly in the completeness of his Bhikshâ, or when the householder is unwilling to offer him worship according to his expectations, then, in the opinion of Puriji, there are no more despicable creatures on earth than householders, and he is at a loss to make out why the village that failed to offer adequate worship to him should, even for a moment add to the world's burden.

He, too, has evidently thought the Lord more foolish than ourselves.

***

"I say, Râm Charan, you have neither education nor the means to set up a trade, nor are you fit for physical labour. Besides, you cannot give up indulging in intoxications, nor do away with your wickednesses. Tell me, how do you manage to make your living?"

RAM CHARAN — "That is an easy job, sir; I preach unto all."

What has Ram Charan taken the Lord for?

***

The city of Lucknow is astir with the festivities of the Mohurrum. The gorgeous decorations and illumination in the principal mosque, the Imambara, know no bounds. Countless people have congregated. Hindus, Mohammedans, Christians, Jews — all sorts of people — men, women, and children of all races and creeds have crowded today to witness the Mohurrum. Lucknow is the capital of the Shias, and wailings in the name of the illustrious Hassan and Hossain rend the skies today. Who was there whose heart was not touched by the lamentation and beating of breasts that took place on this mournful occasion? The tale of the Kârbâlâ, now a thousand years old, has been renovated today.

Among this crowd of spectators were two Rajput gentlemen, who had come from a far-off village to see the festival. The Thakur Sahibs were — as is generally the case with village zemindârs (landlords) — innocent of learning. That Mohammedan culture, the shower of euphuistic phraseology with its nice and correct pronunciation, the varieties of fashionable dress — the loose-fitting cloaks and tight trousers and turbans, of a hundred different colours, to suit the taste of the townsfolk — all these had not yet found their way to such a remote village to convert the Thakur Sahibs. The Thakurs were, therefore, simple and straightforward, always fond of hunting, stalwart and hardy, and of exceedingly tough hearts.

The Thakurs had crossed the gate and were about to enter the mosque, when the guard interrupted them. Upon inquiring into the reasons, he answered, "Look here, this giant figure that you see standing by the doorway, you must give it five kicks first, and then you can go in." "Whose is the statue, pray?" "It is the statue of the nefarious Yejid who killed the illustrious Hassan and Hossain a thousand years ago. Therefore is this crying and this mourning." The guard thought that after this elaborate explanation the statue of Yejid was sure to merit ten kicks instead of five. But mysterious are the workings of Karma, and everything was sadly misunderstood. The Thakurs reverentially put their scarfs round their neck and prostrated and rolled themselves at the feet of the statue of Yeiid, praying with faltering accents: "What is the use of going in any more? What other gods need be seen? Bravo Yejid! Thou alone art the true God. Thou hast thrashed the rascals so well that they are weeping till now!"

***

There is the towering temple of the Eternal Hindu Religion, and how many ways of approaching it! And what can you not find there? From the Absolute Brahman of the Vedantin down to Brahma, Vishnu, Shiva, Shakti, Uncle Sun, (The Sun is popularly given this familiar appellation.) the rat-riding Ganesha, and the minor deities such as Shashthi and Mâkâl, and so forth — which is lacking there? And in the Vedas, in the Vedanta, and the Philosophies, in the Puranas and the Tantras, there are lots of materials, a single sentence of which is enough to break one's chain of transmigration for ever. And oh, the crowd! Millions and millions of people are rushing towards the temple. I, too, had a curiosity to see and join in the rush. But what was this that met my eyes when I reached the spot! Nobody was going inside the temple! By the side of the door, there was a standing figure, with fifty heads, a hundred arms, two hundred bellies, and five hundred legs, and everyone was rolling at the feet of that. I asked one for the reason and got the reply: "Those deities that you see in the interior, it is worship enough for them to make a short prostration, or throw in a few flowers from a distance. But the real worship must be offered to him who is at the gate; and those Vedas, the Vedanta, and the Philosophies, the Puranas and other scriptures that you see — there is no harm if you hear them read now and then; but you must obey the mandate of this one." Then I asked again, "Well, what is the name of this God of gods?" "He is named Popular Custom" — came the reply. I was reminded of the Thakur Sahibs, and exclaimed, "Bravo, Popular Custom! Thou hast thrashed them so well", etc.

***

Gurguré Krishnavyâl Bhattâchârya is a vastly learned man, who has the knowledge of the whole world at his finger-ends. His frame is a skeleton; his friends say it is through the rigours of his austerities, but his enemies ascribe it to want of food. The wicked, again, are of opinion that such a physique is but natural to one who has a dozen issues every year. However that may be, there is nothing on earth that Krishnavyal does not know; specially, he is omniscient about the flow of electric magnetic currents all over the human body, from the hair-tuft to its furthest nook and corner. And being possessed of this esoteric knowledge, he is incomparably the best authority for giving a scientific explanation all things — from a certain earth used in the worship of the goddess Durga down to the reasonable age of puberty of a girl being ten, and sundry inexplicable and mysterious rites pertaining to allied matters. And as for adducing precedents, well, he has made the thing so clear that even boys could understand it. There is forsooth no other land for religion than India, and within India itself none but the Brahmins have the qualification for understanding religion and among Brahmins, too, all others excepting the Krishnavyal family are as nothing and, of these latter again, Gurguré has the pre-eminent claim! Therefore whatever Gurguré Krishnavyal says is self-evident truth.

Learning is being cultivated to a considerable extent, and people are becoming a bit conscious and active, so that they want to understand anal taste everything; so Krishnavyal is assuring everybody: "Discard all fear! Whatever doubts are arising in your minds, I am giving scientific explanations for them. You remain just as you were. Sleep to your heart's content and never mind anything else. Only, don't forget my honorarium." The people exclaimed: "Oh, what a relief! What a great danger did really confront us! We should have had to sit up, and walk, and move — what a pest!" So they said, "Long live Krishnavyal", and turned on one side on the bed once more. The habit of a thousand years was not to go so soon. The body itself would resent it. The inveterate obtuseness of the mind of a thousand years was not to pass away at a moment's notice. And is it not for this that the Krishnavyal class are held in repute? "Bravo, Habit! Thou hast thrashed them so well", etc.

SHIVA'S DEMON

This incomplete story was found among Swamiji's papers after he had passed away. It is printed as the last article in the Bengali book Bhâbbâr Kathâ.

Baron K— lived in a district of Germany. Born in all aristocratic family, he inherited high rank, honour and wealth even in early youth; besides, he was highly cultured and endowed with many accomplishments. A good many charming, affluent, and young women of rank craved for his love. And which father or mother does not wish for a son-in-law of such parts, culture, handsomeness, social position, lineage, and youthful age? An aristocratic beauty had attracted Baron K— also, but the marriage was still far off. In spite of all rank and wealth, Baron K— had none to call his own, except a sister who was exquisitely beautiful and educated. The Baron had taken a vow that he would marry only after his sister had chosen her fiancé and the marriage celebrated with due éclat and rich dowries from him. She had been the apple of her parents' eyes. Baron K— did not want to enjoy a married life, before her wedding. Besides, the custom in this Western country is that the son does not live in his father's or in any relative's family after marriage; the couple live separately. It may be possible for the husband to live with his wife in his father-in-law's house but a wife will never live in her father-in-law's. So K— postponed his marriage till his sister's.

***

For some months K— had no news of his sister. Foregoing the life of ease, comfort, and happiness in a palace served by a big retinue, and snatching herself from the affection of her only brother, she had absconded. All search had been in vain. That brought K— untold sorrow. He had no more any relish for the pleasures of life; he was ever unhappy and dejected. His relatives now gave up all hope of the sister's return, and tried to make the Baron cheerful. They were very anxious about him, and his fiancée was ever full of apprehension.

***

It was the time of the Paris Exhibition. The elite of all countries assembled there. The art-treasures, and artistic products were brought to Paris from all quarters. Baron K—'s relatives advised him to go to Paris where his despondent heart would regain its normal health and buoyancy, once it was in contact with that active, invigorating current of joy. The Baron bowed down to their wishes and started for Paris with his friends.

EPISTLES - SECOND SERIES

1 — SIR[1]

Translated from Bengali

VRINDABAN,
12th Aug., 1888.

DEAR SIR,

Leaving Ayodhya I have reached the holy Vrindaban, and am putting up at Kâlâ Bâbu's Kunja. In the town the mind feels contracted. Places like Râdhâ-kunda, I have heard, are delightful; but they are at some distance from the town. I have a mind to proceed very shortly to Hardwar. In case you have any acquaintance there, you would be doing me a great favour if you would kindly write him an introduction for me. What about your visiting this place? Please reply early and oblige.

Yours etc.,
Vivekananda.

2 — SIR[2]

Translated from Bengali

VRINDABAN,
20th Aug., 1888.

DEAR SIR,

An aged brother-disciple of mine who has just come back to Vrindaban after visiting Kedarnath and Badrinath met Gangadhar. Twice did Gangadhar ascend up to Tibet and Bhutan. He is in great happiness and felt overwhelmed and wept at the meeting. He spent the winter at Kankhal. The Karoâ (waterpot) you gave him, he still keeps with him. He is coming back and is expected at Vrindaban this very month.

So in the hope of meeting him, I postpone my going to Hardwar for some days. Please convey my deepest respects to the Brahmin devotee of Shiva who is with you and accept the same yourself.

Yours etc.,
Vivekananda.

3 — SIR[3]

Translated from Bengali

Salutation to Bhagavan Ramakrishna!

THE BARANAGORE MATH,
19th Nov., 1888.

RESPECTED SIR,

I have received the two books sent by you and am filled with joy to read your wonderfully affectionate letter which betokens your broad, generous heart. No doubt, it is due to good merit of my previous births that you show, sir, so much kindness to a mendicant like me who lives on begging. By sending your gift of the "Vedanta", you have laid under lifelong obligation not only myself but the whole group of Shri Ramakrishna's Sannyasins. They all bow down to you in respect. It is not for my own sake alone that I asked of you the copy of Pânini's grammar; a good deal of study, in fact, is given to Sanskrit scriptures in this Math. The Vedas may well be said to have fallen quite out of vogue in Bengal. Many here in this Math are conversant with Sanskrit, and they have a mind to master the Samhitâ portions of the Vedas. They are of opinion that what has to be done must be done to a finish. So, believing that a full measure of proficiency in the Vedic language is impossible without first mastering Panini's grammar, which is the best available for the purpose, a copy of the latter was felt to be a necessity. The grammatical work Mugdhabodha, which we studied in our boyhood, is superior in many respects to Laghukaumudi. You are yourself, however, a deeply learned man and, therefore, the best judge we can have in this matter. So if you consider the

---

1. Letters 1—4, 6—14, 16—22, 24—26, 29, 31—33 and 124 are translated from Bengali letters written to Pramadadas Mitra of Varanasi, an orthodox Hindu, for whose profound erudition and piety Swamiji had the highest regard. These letters are most interesting being written (except the last) at a time when, after his Master's passing away, Swamiji was leading a wandering monk's life. In the early days he used to sign his name as Narendranath, though his now famous name, Vivekananda, is printed in all these pages for easy comprehension

2. See Note 1.

3. See Note 1.

Ashtâdhyâyi (Panini's) to be the most suitable in our case, you will lay us under a debt of lifelong gratitude by sending the same (provided you feel it convenient and feel so inclined). This Math is not wanting in men of perseverance, talent, and penetrative intellect. I may hope that by the grace of our Master, they will acquire in a short time Panini's system and then succeed in restoring the Vedas to Bengal. I beg to send you two photographs of my revered Master and two parts of some of his teachings as given in his homely style compiled, and published by a certain gentleman — hoping you will give us the pleasure of your acceptance. My health is now much improved, and I expect the blessings of meeting you within two or three months. . . .

Yours etc.,
Vivekananda.

4 — SIR[1]

Translated from Bengali

Victory to God!

BARANAGORE,
4th Feb., 1889.

DEAR SIR,

For some reason I had been feeling today agitated and cramped in my mind, when your letter of invitation to the heavenly city of Varanasi reached me. I accept it as the call of Vishveshvara. (The Lord of the Universe, or Shiva, as installed in the leading temple of Varanasi or Kashi.) I am going now on a pilgrimage to the place of my Master's nativity, and after a sojourn of a few days there, I shall present myself to you. He must be made of stone whose mind does not melt at the sigh of Kashi and its Lord! I feel now much improved in health. My regards to Jnanananda. I am coming as soon as I can. It all depends ultimately on Vishveshvara's will . . . . More when we meet.

Yours etc.,
Vivekananda.

---

1. See Note 1, p. 90.

5 — M—

AUNTPUR[2],
7th February, 1889.

DEAR M—,

Thanks a hundred thousand times, Master! You have hit Ramakrishna in the right point.

Few, alas, few understand him!

Yours etc.,
Vivekananda.

PS. My heart leaps with joy — and it is a wonder that I do not go mad when I find anybody thoroughly launched into the midst of the doctrine which is to shower peace on earth hereafter.

6 — SIR[3]

Translated from Bengali

Shri Durgâ be my Refuge!

BARANAGORE,
26th June, 1889.

DEAR SIR,

For sundry reasons I have been unable to write to you for long, for which please excuse me. I have now obtained news of Gangadhar. He met one of my brother disciples, and both are now staying in the Uttarakhanda (the sacred Himalayas). Four of us from here are in the Himalayas now, and with Gangadhar they are five. One brother-disciple named Shivananda came across Gangadhar at Srinagara on the way to holy Kedarnath, and Gangadhar has sent two letters here. During his first year in the Himalayas, he could not secure permission to enter Tibet, but he got it the next year. The Lamas love him much, and

---

2. A village in the Hooghly District, the birth-place of Swami Premananda. The letter was written to Master Mahashaya.

3. See Note 1, p. 90.

he had picked up the Tibetan language. He says the Lamas form ninety per cent of the population, but they mostly practice Tântrika forms of worship. The country is intensely cold — eatables there are scarcely any — only dried meat; and Gangadhar had to travel and live on that food. My health is passable, but the state of mind is terrible!

Yours etc.,
Vivekananda.

7 — SIR[4]

Translated from Bengali

Victory to God!

BAGHBAZAR, CALCUTTA,
4th July, 1889.

DEAR SIR,

It pleased me highly to know all the news in your letter yesterday. You have asked me to request Gangadhar to write to you, but I see no chance thereof, for though they are sending us letters, they do not stop anywhere for more than two or three days and therefore do not receive any of ours.

Some relative of my former life[5] has purchased a bungalow at Simultala (near Baidyanath). The place being credited with a healthy climate, I stayed there for some time. But the summer heat growing excessive, I had an attack of acute diarrhoea, and I have just fled away from the place.

Words fail to describe how strong is the desire in my mind to go to Varanasi and have my soul blessed by meeting you and sojourning with you in good converse, but everything rests on His will! I wonder what linking of heart existed between us, sir, from some previous incarnation that, receiving as I do the love and affection of not a few men of wealth and position in this city of Calcutta, I am apt to feel so much bored by their society, while only through one day's interview my heart felt charmed enough to accept you as a near relative and friend in spiritual life! One reason is that you are a favoured servant of God. Another perhaps is:

तच्चेतसा स्मरति नूनमबोधपूर्वं भावस्थिराणि जननान्तरसौहृदानि ।[6]

I am indebted to you for the advice which comes from you as the outcome of your experience and spiritual practice. It is very true, and I have also found it so very often, that one has to suffer at times for holding in one's brain novel views of all sorts.

But with me it is a different malady this time. I have not lost faith in a benign Providence—nor am I going ever to lose it—my faith in the scriptures is unshaken. But by the will of God, the last six or seven years of my life have been full of constant struggles with hindrances and obstacles of all sorts. I have been vouchsafed the ideal Shâstra; I have seen the ideal man; and yet fail myself to get on with anything to the end—this is my profound misery.

And particularly, I see no chance of success while remaining near Calcutta. In Calcutta live my mother and two brothers. I am the eldest; the second is preparing for the First Arts Examination, and the third is young.

They were quite well off before, but since my father's death, it is going very hard with them—they even have to go fasting at times! To crown all, some relatives, taking advantage of their helplessness, drove them away from the ancestral residence. Though a part of it is recovered through suing at the High Court, destitution is now upon them—a matter of course in litigation.

Living near Calcutta I have to witness their adversity, and the quality of Rajas prevailing, my egotism sometimes develops into the form of a desire that rises to plunge me into action; in such moments, a fierce fighting ensues in my mind, and so I wrote that the state of my mind was terrible. Now their lawsuit has come to an end. So bless me that after a stay here in Calcutta for a few days more to settle matters, I may

---

4. See Note 1, p. 90.

5. The life he has renounced.

6. Kalidasa's **Shakuntalam**, Act V: "It must be the memories, unwittingly recalled, of affinities firmly established in previous incarnations through depths of heart."

bid adieu to this place for ever.

आपूर्यमाणमचलप्रतिष्ठं समुद्रमापः प्रविशन्ति यद्वत् ।
तद्वत्कामा यं प्रविशन्ति सर्वे स शान्तिमाप्नोति न कामकामी ॥[1]

Bless me that my heart may wax strong with supreme strength Divine, and that all forms of Mâyâ may drop off from me for aye: "We have taken up the Cross, Thou hast laid it upon us and grant us strength that we bear it unto death. Amen!"—*Imitation of Christ*.

I am now staying in Calcutta. My address is: c/o Balaram Babu, 57 Ramkanta Bose's Street, Baghbazar, Calcutta.

Yours etc.,
Vivekananda.

8 — SIR[2]

Translated from Bengali

All Glory to God!

BARANAGORE, CALCUTTA,
7th Aug., 1889.

DEAR SIR,

It is more than a week since I received your letter, but having had another attack of fever, I could not send a reply all this time, for which please excuse me. For an interval of a month and a half I kept well, but I have suffered again for the last ten days; now I am doing well.

I have certain questions to put, and you, sir, have a wide knowledge of Sanskrit; so please favour me with answers to the following:

1. Does any narrative occur about Satyakâma, son of Jabâlâ, and about Jânashruti, anywhere else in the Vedas excepting the Upanishads[3]?

2. In most cases where Shankaracharya quotes Smriti in his commentary on the Vedânta-Sutras, he cites the authority of the Mahâbhârata. But seeing that we find clear proofs about caste being based on qualification both in the Bhishmaparva of the Mahabharata and in the stories there of the Ajagara and of Umâ and Maheshvara, has he made any mention in his writings of this fact?

3. The doctrine of caste in the *Purusha-Sukta* of the Vedas does not make it hereditary—so what are those instances in the Vedas where caste has been made a matter of hereditary transmission?

4. The Achârya could not adduce any proof from the Vedas to the effect that the Shudra should not study the Vedas. He only quotes "यज्ञेऽनवकॢप्तः"[4] (Tai. Samhita, VII. i. 1. 6) to maintain that when he is not entitled to perform Yajnas, he has neither any right to study the Upanishads and the like. But the same Acharya contends with reference to "अथातो ब्रह्मजिज्ञासा"[5], (*Vedânta-Sutras*, I. i. 1) that the word अथ (Ath) here does not mean "subsequent to the study of the Vedas", because it is contrary to proof that the study of the Upanishad is not permissible without the previous study of the Vedic Mantras and *Brâhmanas* and because there is no intrinsic sequence between the Vedic Karma-kânda and Vedic Janâna-kânda. It is evident, therefore, that one may attain to the knowledge of Brahman without having studied the ceremonial parts of the Vedas. So if there is no sequence between the sacrificial practices and Jnana, why does the Acharya contradict his own statement when it is a case of the Shudras, by inserting the clause "by force of the same logic"? Why should the Shudra not study the Upanishad?

I am mailing you, sir, a book named *Imitation of Christ* written by a Christian Sannyasin. It is a won-

---

1. The Gitâ, II.70: "Not he that lusteth after objects of desire but he alone obtaineth peace in whom desires lose themselves like river-water flowing into the ocean but leaving it unaffected and unmodified in spite of constant accession."

2. See Note 1, p. 90.

3. Shankarâchârya in his commentary on the **Vedanta-Sutras**, I. iii. 34-37, interprets the aphorisms to prove that Upanishadic wisdom was imparted to Janashruti and Satyakama, only because they were not Shudras, as borne out by actual texts. But as these texts are doubtful even after Shankaracharya's explanation, Swamiji wants to be referred to other similar Vedic texts.

4. "The Shudra is not conceived of as a performer of Yajna or Vedic sacrifices."

5. "Now then commences hence the inquiry about Brahman."

derful book. One is astonished to find that such renunciation, Vairâgya, and Dâsya-Bhakti have existed even among the Christians. Probably you may have read this book before; if not, it will give me the greatest pleasure if you will kindly read it.

Yours etc.,
Vivekananda.

9 — SIR[6]

Translated from Bengali

BARANAGORE,
17th Aug., 1889.

DEAR SIR,

You have expressed embarrassment in your last favour for being addressed reverentially. But the blame attaches not to me but to your own excellent qualities. I wrote in one letter before that from the way I feel attracted by your lofty virtues, it seems we had some affinity from previous births. I make no distinction as to householder or Sannyasin in this, that for all time my head shall bend low in reverence wherever I see greatness, broadness of heart, and holiness—Shântih! Shântih! Shântih! My prayer is that among the many people embracing Sannyâsa nowadays, greedy of honour, posing renunciation for the sake of a living, and fallen off from the ideal on both sides, may one in a lakh at least become high-souled like you! To you my Brahmin fellow-disciples who have heard of your noble virtues tender their best prostrations.

About one amongst my several questions to which you sent your replies, my wrong idea is corrected. For this I shall remain indebted to you for ever. Another of these questions was: Whether Acharya Shankara gives any conclusion regarding caste based on Gunas as mentioned in Puranâs like the Mahabharata. If he does, where is it to be found? I have no doubt that according to the ancient view in this country, caste was hereditary, and it cannot also be doubted that sometimes the Shudras used to be oppressed more than the helots among the Spartans and the negroes among the Americans! As for myself, I have no partiality for any party in this caste question, because I know it is a social law and is based on diversity of Guna and Karma. It also means grave harm if one bent on going beyond Guna and Karma cherishes in mind any caste distinctions. In these matters, I have got some settled ideas through the grace of my Guru but, if I come to know of your views, I may just confirm some points or rectify others in them. One doesn't have honey dripping unless one pokes at the hive—so I shall put you some more questions; and looking upon me as ignorant and as a boy, please give proper replies without taking any offence.

1. Is the Mukti, which the Vedanta-Sutras speaks of, one and the same with the Nirvana of the Avadhuta-Gitâ and other texts?

2. What is really meant by Nirvana if, according to the aphorism, "Without the function of creating etc."[7] (ibid., IV. iv. 7), none can attain to the fullest Godhead?

3. Chaitanya-deva is said to have told Sârvabhauma at Puri, "I understand the Sutras (aphorisms) of Vyasa, they are dualistic; but the commentator makes them, monistic, which I don't understand." Is this true? Tradition says, Chaitanya-deva had a dispute with Prakashananda Sarasvati on the point, and Chaitanya-deva won. One commentary by Chaitanya-deva was rumoured to have been existing in Prakashananda's Math.

4. In the Tantra, Acharya Shankara has been called a crypto-Buddhist; views expressed in Prajnâparamitâ, the Buddhist Mâhâyana book, perfectly tally

---

6. See Note 1, p. 90.

7. जगद्व्यापारवर्जं प्रकरणादसंनिहितत्वाच्च—"Having regard to the context which ascribes the threefold function relating to the universe only to God, and because the fact of their conscious mental distinction comes between that function and their liberated state, we have to conclude that the state of final liberation or Mukti in the case of men is devoid of the capacity to create, preserve, and dissolve the universe." So if this capacity is reserved only for God, what is meant, Swamiji asks, by saying that in Nirvana the human merges completely into the Divine? We must remember that many of the questions here reflect the intellectual stages through which Swamiji was reaching out in those days towards that plenitude of Vedantic wisdom which was his in future years. We also find a glimpse of those processes through which his intellect was growing towards a fuller understanding of our ancient scriptures and customs.

with the Vedantic views propounded by the Acharya. The author of Panchadashi also says, "What we call Brahman is the same truth as the Shunya of the Buddhist." What does all this mean?

5. Why has no foundation for the authority of the Vedas been adduced in the Vedanta-Satras? First, it has been said that the Vedas are the authority for the existence of God, and then it has been argued that the authority for the Vedas is the text: "It is the breath of God." Now, is this statement not vitiated by what in Western logic is called an argument in a circle?

6. The Vedanta requires of us faith, for conclusiveness cannot be reached by mere argumentation. Then why, has the slightest flaw, detected in the position of the schools of Sânkhya and Nyâya, been overwhelmed with a fusillade of dialectics? In whom, moreover, are we to put our faith? Everybody seems to be mad over establishing his own view; if, according to Vyasa, even the great Muni Kapila, "the greatest among perfected souls",[1] is himself deeply involved in error, then who would say that Vyasa may not be so involved in a greater measure? Did Kapila fail to understand the Vedas?

7. According to the Nyaya, "Shabda or Veda (the criterion of truth), is the word of those who have realised the highest"; so the Rishis as such are omniscient. Then how are they proved, according to the Surya-siddhânta, to be ignorant of such simple astronomical truths? How can we accept their intelligence as the refuge to ferry us across the ocean of transmigratory existence, seeing that they speak of the earth as triangular, of the serpent Vâsuki as the support of the earth and so on?

8. If in His acts of creation God is dependent on good and evil Karmas, then what does it avail us to worship Him? There is a fine song of Nareshchandra, where occurs the following: "If what lies in one's destiny is to happen anyhow, O Mother, then what good all this invoking by the holy name of Durgâ?"

9. True, it is improper to hold many texts on the same subject to be contradicted by one or two. But why then are the long-continued customs of Madhuparka[2] and the like repealed by one or two such texts as, "The horse sacrifice, the cow sacrifice, Sannyasa, meat-offerings in Shrâddha", etc.? If the Vedas are eternal, then what are the meaning and justification of such specifications as "this rule of Dharma is for the age of Dvâpara," "this for the age of Kali", and so forth?

10. The same God who gives out the Vedas becomes Buddha again to annul them; which of these dispensations is to be obeyed? Which of these remains authoritative, the earlier or the later one?

11. The Tantra says, in the Kali-Yuga the Veda-Mantras are futile. So which behest of God, the Shiva, is to be followed?

12. Vyasa makes out in the Vedanta-Sutras that it is wrong to worship the tetrad of divine manifestation, Vâsudeva, Sankarshana, etc., and again that very Vyasa expatiates on the great merits of that worship in the Bhâgavata! Is this Vyasa a madman?

I have many doubts besides these, and, hoping to have them dispelled from my mind through your kindness, I shall lay them before you in future. Such questions cannot be all set forth except in a personal interview; neither can as much satisfaction be obtained as one expects to. So I have a mind to lay before you all these facts when presenting myself to you, which I expect will be very soon, by the grace of the Guru.

I have heard it said that without inner progress in the practice of religion, no true conclusion can be reached concerning these matters, simply by means of reasoning; but satisfaction, at least to some extent, seems to be necessary at the outset.

Yours etc.,
Vivekananda.

---

1. Kapila is so spoken of in Shvetâshvatara Upanishad, V.2 In his commentary of **Vedanta-Sutras**, II. i. 1, Shankara doubts the identity of the Vedic Kapila with the Sankhyan Kapila.

2. Madhuparka was a Vedic ceremony, usually in honour of guest, in which a respectful offering was to be made consisting, among other dainties, of beef. The text which Swamiji partially quotes forbids such food. The full text means that in the Kali-Yuga the following five customs are to be forsaken: The horse sacrifice, cow-killing ceremonies, meat-offerings in Shraddha, Sannyasa, and maintaining the line of progeny through the husband's younger brother in case of failure through the husband.

10 — SIR[3]

Translated from Bengali

BAGHBAZAR, CALCUTTA,
2nd Sept., 1889.

DEAR SIR,

Some days ago I received your two kind letters. I am very much pleased to find in you a wonderful harmony of Jnana and Bhakti. Your advice to me to give up arguing and disputing is very true indeed, and that is really the goal of life for the individual — "Sundered are the knots of the heart, torn off are all his doubts, and the seeds of his Karma wear off, when the sight of the Transcendent One is gained." (Mundakonapanishad, II. ii. 8.) But then, as my Master used to say, when a pitcher is being filled (by immersion), it gurgles, but when full, it is noiseless; know my condition to be the same. Within two or three weeks perhaps, I shall be able to meet you — may God fulfil that wish!

Yours etc.,
Vivekananda.

11 — SIR[4]

Translated from Bengali

BAGHBAZAR,
3rd Dec., 1889.

DEAR SIR,

I have not heard from you for a long time, I hope you are doing well in body and mind. Two of my brother disciples are shortly leaving for Varanasi. One is Rakhal by name, the other is Subodh. The first-named was beloved of my Master and used to stay much with him. Please recommend them to some Satra (house of alms.) during their stay in the city, if you find it convenient. You will hear from them all my news.

With my best regards and greetings.

Yours etc.,
Vivekananda.

PS. Gangadhar is now proceeding to Kailas. The Tibetans wanted to slash him up on the way, taking him to be a spy of the foreigners. Eventually some Lamas kindly set him free. We obtain this news from a Tibet-going trader. Gangadhar's blood won't cool down before seeing Lhasa. The gain is that his physical endurance has grown immensely — one night he passed uncovered on a bed of snow, and that without much hardship.

12 — SIR[5]

Translated from Bengali

BARANAGORE, CALCUTTA,
13th Dec., 1889.

DEAR SIR,

I have all particulars from your letter; and from Rakhal's which followed, I came to know of your meeting. I have received the pamphlet written by you. A kind of scientific Advaitism has been spreading in Europe ever since the theory of the conservation of energy was discovered, but all that is Parinâmavâda, evolution by real modification. It is good you have shown the difference between this and Shankara's Vivartavâda (progressive manifestation by unreal superimposition). I can't appreciate your citing Spencer's parody on the German transcendentalists; he himself is fed much on their doles. It is doubtful whether your opponent Gough understands his Hegel sufficiently. Anyway, your rejoinder is very pointed and thrashing.

Yours etc.,
Vivekananda.

---

3. See Note 1, p. 90.
4. See Note 1, p. 90.
5. See Note 1, p. 90.

13 — SIR[1]

Translated from Bengali

BAIDYANATH,
26th Dec., 1889.

DEAR SIR,

After a long attempt, I think, I am now in a position to present myself before you. In a day or two I take myself to your feet at holy Kashi.

I have been putting up here for some days with a gentleman of Calcutta, but my mind is much longing for Varanasi. My idea is to remain there for some time, and to watch how Vishvanâtha and Annapurnâ[2] deal it out to my lot. And my resolve is something like "either to lay down my life or realise my ideal"[3]— so help me the Lord of Kashi.

Yours etc.,
Vivekananda.

14 — SIR[4]

Translated from Bengali

ALLAHABAD,
30th Dec., 1889.

DEAR SIR,

I wrote in a letter to you that I was to go to Varanasi in a day or two, but who can nullify the decree of Providence? News reached me that a brother-disciple, Yogen by name, had been attacked with smallpox after arriving here from a pilgrimage to Chitrakuta, Omkarnath, etc., and so I came to this place to nurse him. He has now completely recovered. Some Bengali gentlemen here are of a greatly pious and loving disposition. They are very lovingly taking care of me, and their importunate desire is that I should stay here during the month of Mâgha (Jan.-Feb.) keeping the Kalpa vow[5]. But my mind is very keenly harping on the name of Varanasi and is quite agog to see you. Yes, I am going to try my best to slip away and avoid their importunities in a day or two and betake myself to the holy realm of the Lord of Varanasi. If one of my monastic brother-disciples, Achyutananda Sarasvati by name, calls on you to enquire of me, please tell him I am soon coming to Varanasi. He is indeed a very good man and learned. I was obliged to leave him behind at Bankipore. Are Rakhal and Subodh still there in Varanasi? Please inquire and inform me whether the Kumbha fair this year is going to be held at Hardwar or not.

Many a man of wisdom, of piety, many a Sâdhu (holy man) and Pundit have I met in so many places, and I have been very much favoured by them, but "भिन्नरुचिर्हि लोकः— Men are of varying tastes" — Raghuvamsham. I know not what sort of soul-affinity there is between us, for nowhere else does it seem so pleasing and agreeable as with you. Let me see how the Lord of Kashi disposes.

Yours etc.,
Vivekananda.

My address is:
C/o Govinda Chandra Basu, Chauk, Allahabad.

15 — SIR

Salutation to Shri Ramakrishna!

ALLAHABAD,
5th January, 1890.

MY DEAR SIR, (Sj. Balaram Bose)

I am very sorry to hear of your illness from your kind note. The gist of the letter I wrote to you about your change to Baidyanath was that it would be impossible for a man of weak and extremely delicate

---

1. See Note 1, p. 90.
2. Shiva and His Divine Spouse as installed in Varanasi.
3. "शरीरं वा पातयामि मन्त्रं वा साधयामि।"
4. See Note 1, p. 90.
5. Special ablutions and worship regularly performed in that holy confluence—a very solemn and sacred practice.

physique like you to live in that place unless you spent a good deal of money. If change be really advisable for you, and if you have deferred it so long simply to select a cheaper place and that sort of thing, it is certainly a matter of regret. . . . Baidyanath is excellent so far as the air is concerned, but the water is not good, it upsets the stomach. I used to suffer from acidity every day. I have already written you a letter; have you got it, or finding it a bearing letter, have you left it to its fate? In my opinion, if you have to go away for a change, the sooner the better. But, pardon me, you have a tendency to expect that everything should fit in exactly with your requirements, but unfortunately, such a state of things is very rare in this world. "आत्मानं सततं रक्षेत्—One must save oneself under any circumstances." "Lord have mercy", is all right, but He helps him who helps himself. If you simply try to save your purse, will the Lord arrange the change for you by drawing on His ancestral capital? If you think you have so much reliance on the Lord, don't call in the doctor, please. . . . If that does not suit you, you should go to Varanasi. I would have already left this place, but the local gentlemen would not give me leave to depart! . . . But let me repeat once more, if change is actually decided upon, please do not hesitate out of miserliness. That would be suicide. And not even God can save a suicide. Please convey my compliments to Tulasi Babu and the rest.

With best regards,

Yours etc.,
Vivekananda.

16 — SIR[6]

Translated from Bengali

C/O BABU SATISH CHANDRA MUKHERJI,
GORABAZAR, GHAZIPUR,
21st Jan., 1890.

DEAR SIR,

I reached Ghazipur three days ago. Here I am putting up in the house of Babu Satish Chandra Mukherji, a friend of my early age. The place is very pleasant. Close by flows the Ganga, but bathing there is troublesome, for there is no regular path, and it is hard work wading through sands. Babu Ishan Chandra Mukherji, my friend's father, that noble-hearted man of whom I spoke to you, is here. Today he is leaving for Varanasi whence he will proceed to Calcutta. I again had a great mind to go over to Kashi, but the object of my coming here, namely, an interview with the Bâbâji (Pavhâri Bâbâ, the great saint.), has not yet been realised, and hence the delay of a few days becomes necessary. Everything here appears good. The people are all gentlemen, but very much Westernised; and it is a pity I am so thoroughly against every affectation of the Western idea. Only my friend very little affects such ideals. What a frippery civilisation is it indeed that the foreigners have brought over here! What a materialistic illusion have they created! May Vishvanâtha save these weak-hearted! After seeing Babaji, I shall send you a detailed account.

Yours etc.,
Vivekananda.

PS. Alas for the irony of our fate, that in this land of Bhagavân Shuka's birth, renunciation is looked down upon as madness and sin!

17 — SIR[7]

Translated from Bengali

GHAZIPUR,
31st Jan., 1890.

DEAR SIR,

It is so very difficult to meet the Babaji. He does not step out of his home; and, when willing to speak at all, he just comes near the door to speak from inside. I have come away with having just a view of his garden-house with chimneys tapering above and encircled by high walls — no means of admittance

6. See Note 1, p. 90.

7. See Note 1, p. 90.

within! People say there are cave-like rooms within where he dwells; and he only knows what he does there, for nobody has had a peep. I had to come away one day sorely used up with waiting and waiting, but shall take my chance again. On Sunday, I leave for holy Varanasi — only the Babus here won't let me off; otherwise all my fancy to see the Babaji has flattened down. I am prepared to be off today, but anyhow, I am leaving on Sunday. What of your plan of going to Hrishikesh?

Yours etc.,
Vivekananda.

PS. The redeeming feature is that the place seems healthy.

18 — SIR[1]

Translated from Bengali

GHAZIPUR,
4th Feb., 1890.

DEAR SIR,

Received your kind note, and through supreme good fortune, I have obtained an interview with Babaji. A great sage indeed! — It is all very wonderful, and in this atheistic age, a towering representation of marvellous power born of Bhakti and Yoga! I have sought refuge in his grace; and he has given me hope — a thing very few may be fortunate enough to obtain. It is Babaji's wish that I stay on for some days here, and he would do me some good. So following this saint's bidding I shall remain here for some time. No doubt, this will give you also much pleasure. I don't mention them in a letter, but the facts are very strange indeed — to be disclosed when we meet. Unless one is face to face with the life of such men, faith in the scriptures does not grow in all its real integrity.

Yours etc.,
Vivekananda.

---
1. See Note 1, p. 90.

19 — SIR[2]

Translated from Bengali

GHAZIPUR,
7th Feb., 1890.

DEAR SIR,

I feel very happy to hear from you just now. Apparently in his features, the Babaji is a Vaishnava the embodiment, so to speak, of Yoga, Bhakti, and humility. His dwelling has walls on all sides with a few doors in them. Inside these walls, there is one long underground burrow wherein he lays himself up in Samâdhi. He talks to others only when he comes out of the hole. Nobody knows what he eats, and so they call him Pavhâri (One living on air.) Bâbâ. Once he did not come out of the hole for five years, and people thought he had given up the body. But now again he is out. But this time he does not show himself to people and talks from behind the door. Such sweetness in speech I have never come across! He does not give a direct reply to questions but says, "What does this servant know?" But then fire comes out as the talking goes on. On my pressing him very much he said, "Favour me highly by staying here some days." But he never speaks in this way; so from this I understood he meant to reassure me and whenever I am importunate, he asks me to stay on. So I wait in hope. He is a learned man no doubt but nothing in the line betrays itself. He performs scriptural ceremonials, for from the full-moon day to the last day of the month, sacrificial oblations go on. So it is sure, he is not retiring into the hole during this period. How can I ask his permission, (Evidently for a proposed visit to the saint by the correspondent, Pramadadas Mitra of Varanasi.). for he never gives a direct reply; he goes on multiplying such expressions as "this servant", "my fortune", and so on. If you yourself have a mind, then come sharp on receipt of this note. Or after his passing away, the keenest regret will be left in your mind. In two days you may return after an interview — I mean a talk with him ab intra. My friend Satish Babu will receive you most warmly. So, do come up directly

---
2. See Note 1, p. 90.

you receive this; I shall meanwhile let Babaji know of you.

Yours etc.,
Vivekananda.

PS. Even though one can't have his company, no trouble taken for the sake of such a great soul can ever go unrewarded.

20 — SIR[3]

Translated from Bengali

GHAZIPUR,
13th Feb., 1890.

DEAR SIR,

I am in anxiety to hear of your illness. I am also having some sort of a pain in the loins which, being aggravated of late, gives much trouble. For two days I could not go out to meet Babaji, and so a man came from him to inquire about me. For this reason, I go today. I shall convey your countless compliments. "Fire comes out" that is, a wonderful devotion to Guru and resignation are revealed; and such amazing endurance and humility I have never seen. Whatever good things I may come by, sure, you have your share in them.

Yours etc.,
Vivekananda.

21 — SIR[4]

Translated from Bengali

GHAZIPUR,
14th Feb., 1890.

DEAR SIR,

In my note of yesterday I perhaps forgot to ask you to return brother Sharat's letter. Please send it. I have heard from brother Gangadhar. He is now in Rambag Samadhi, Srinagar, Kashmir. I am greatly suffering from lumbago.

Yours etc.,
Vivekananda.

PS. Rakhal and Subodh have come to Vrindaban after visiting Omkar, Girnar, Abu, Bombay, and Dwarka.

22 — SIR[5]

Translated from Bengali

Victory to the Lord!

GHAZIPUR,
19th Feb., 1890.

DEAR SIR,

I wrote a letter to brother Gangadhar asking him to stop his wandering and settle down somewhere and to send me an account of the various Sadhus he had come across in Tibet and their ways and customs. I enclose the reply that came from him. Brother Kali is having repeated attacks of fever at Hrishikesh. I have sent him a wire from this place. So if from the reply I find I am wanted by him, I shall be obliged to start direct for Hrishikesh from this place, otherwise I am coming to you in a day or two. Well, you may smile, sir, to see me weaving all this web of Mâyâ — and that is no doubt the fact. But then there is the chain of iron, and there is the chain of gold. Much good comes of the latter; and it drops off by itself when all the good is reaped. The sons of my Master are indeed the great objects of my service, and here alone I feel I have some duty left for me. Perhaps I shall send brother Kali down to Allahabad or somewhere else, as convenient. At your feet are laid a hundred and one faults of mine — "I am as thy son, so guide me who have taken refuge in thee." (An adaptation from the Gitâ, II. 7.)

Yours etc.,
Vivekananda.

---

3. See Note 1, p. 90.

4. See Note 1, p. 90.

5. See Note 1, p. 90.

23 — AKHANDANANDA

Salutation to Bhagavan Ramakrishna!

GHAZIPUR,
February, 1890.

BELOVED AKHANDANANDA,

Very glad to receive your letter. What you have written about Tibet is very promising, and I shall try to go there once. In Sanskrit Tibet is called the Uttarakuruvarsha, and is not a land of Mlechchhas. Being the highest tableland in the world, it is extremely cold, but by degrees one may become accustomed to it. About the manners and customs of the Tibetans you have written nothing. If they are so hospitable, why did they not allow you to go on? Please write everything in detail, in a long letter. I am sorry to learn that you will not be able to come, for I had a great longing to see you. It seems that I love you more than all others. However, I shall try to get rid of this Maya too.

The Tântrika rites among the Tibetans that you have spoken of arose in India itself, during the decline of Buddhism. It is my belief that the Tantras, in vogue amongst us, were the creation of the Buddhists themselves. Those Tantrika rites are even more dreadful than our doctrine of Vâmâchâra; for in them adultery got a free rein, and it was only when the Buddhists became demoralised through immorality that they were driven away by Kumârila Bhatta. As some Sannyasins speak of Shankara, or the Bâuls of Shri Chaitanya, that he was in secret an epicure, a drunkard, and one addicted to all sorts of abominable practices—so the modern Tantrika Buddhists speak of the Lord Buddha as a dire Vamâchâri and give an obscene interpretation to the many beautiful precepts of the *Prajnâpâramitâ*, such as the *Tattvagâthâ* and the like. The result of all this has been that the Buddhists are divided into two sects nowadays; the Burmese and the Sinhalese have generally set the Tantras at naught, have likewise banished the Hindu gods and goddesses, and at the same time have thrown overboard the Amitâbha Buddha held in regard among the Northern School of Buddhists. The long and the short of it is that the Amitabha Buddha and the other gods whom the Northern School worship are not mentioned in books like the *Prajnaparamita*, but a lot of gods and goddesses are recommended for worship. And the Southern people have wilfully transgressed the Shâstras and eschewed the gods and goddesses. The phase of Buddhism which declares "Everything for others", and which you find spread throughout Tibet, has greatly struck modern Europe. Concerning that phase, however, I have a good deal to say—which it is impossible to do in this letter. What Buddha did was to break wide open the gates of that very religion which was confined in the Upanishads to a particular caste. What special greatness does his theory of Nirvana confer on him? His greatness lies in his unrivalled sympathy. The high orders of Samadhi etc., that lend gravity to his religion are, almost all there in the Vedas; what are absent there are his intellect and heart, which have never since been paralleled throughout the history of the world.

The Vedic doctrine of Karma is the same as in Judaism and all other religions, that is to say, the purification of the mind through sacrifices and such other external means—and Buddha was the first man who stood against it. But the inner essence of the ideas remained as of old—look at that doctrine of mental exercises which he preached, and that mandate of his to believe in the Suttas instead of the Vedas. Caste also remained as of old (caste was not wholly obsolete at the time of Buddha), but it was now determined by personal qualifications; and those that were not believers in his religion were declared as heretics, all in the old style. "Heretic" was a very ancient word with the Buddhists, but then they never had recourse to the sword (good souls!) and had great toleration. Argument blew up the Vedas. But what is the proof of your religion? Well, put faith in it!—the same procedure as in all religions. It was however an imperative necessity of the times; and that was the reason of his having incarnated himself. His doctrine is like that of Kapila. But that of Shankara, how far more grand and rational! Buddha and Kapila are always saying the world is full of grief and nothing but that—flee from it—ay, for your life, do! Is happiness altogether absent here? It is a statement of the nature of what the

Brahmos say—the world is full of happiness! There is grief, forsooth, but what can be done? Perchance some will suggest that grief itself will appear as happiness when you become used to it by constant suffering. Shankara does not take this line of argument. He says: This world *is* and is *not—manifold* yet one; *I shall unravel its mystery—I shall know whether grief be there, or anything else*; I do not flee from it as from a bugbear. I will know all about it as to the infinite pain that attends its search, well, I am embracing it in its fullest measure. Am I a beast that you frighten me with happiness and misery, decay and death, which are but the outcome of the senses? I will know about it—will give up my life for it. There is nothing to know about in this world—therefore, if there be anything beyond this relative existence—what the Lord Buddha has designated as *Prajnâpâra*—the transcendental—if such there be, I want that alone. Whether happiness attends it or grief, I do not care. What a lofty idea! How grand! The religion of Buddha has reared itself on the Upanishads, and upon that also the philosophy of Shankara. Only, Shankara had not the slightest bit of Buddha's wonderful heart, dry intellect merely! For fear of the Tantras, for fear of the mob, in his attempt to cure a boil, he amputated the very arm itself[1]! One has to write a big volume if one has to write about them at all—but I have neither the learning nor the leisure for it.

The Lord Buddha is my Ishta—my God. He preached no theory about Godhead—he was himself God, I fully believe it. But no one has the power to put a limit to God's infinite glory. No, not even God Himself has the power to make Himself limited. The translation of the *Gandâra-Sutta* that you have made from the *Suttanipâta*, is excellent. In that book there is another *Sutta*—the *Dhaniya-Sutta*—which has got a similar idea. There are many passages in the Dhammapada too, with similar ideas. But that is at the last stage when one has got perfectly satisfied with knowledge and realisation, is the same under all circumstances and has gained mastery over his senses—"ज्ञानविज्ञानतृप्तात्मा कूटस्थो विजितिन्द्रियः" (Gita, VI. 8.). He who has not the least regard for his body as something to be taken care of—it is he who may roam about at pleasure like the mad elephant caring for naught. Whereas a puny creature like myself should practice devotion, sitting at one spot, till he attains realization; and then only should he behave like that; but it is a far-off question—very far indeed.

चिन्ताशून्यमदैन्यभैक्ष्यमशनं पानं सरिद्वारिषु
स्वातन्त्र्येण निरिक्षुशा स्थितिरभीर्नद्रा श्मशाने वने।
वस्त्रं क्षालनशोषणादिरहितं दिग्वास्तु शय्या मही
संचारो निगमान्तवीथिषु विदां क्रीडा परे ब्रह्मणि॥
विमानमालम्ब्य शरीरमेतद्
भुनक्त्यशेषान्विषयानुपस्थितान्।
परेच्छया बालवदात्मवेत्ता
योऽव्यक्तलिङ्गोऽननुषक्तबाह्यः॥
दिगम्बरो वापि च साम्बरो वा
त्वगम्बरो वापि चिदम्बरस्थः।
उन्मत्तवद्वापि च बालवद्वा
पिशाचवद्वापि चरत्यवन्याम्॥

(*Vivekachudmani*, 538-40)

—To a knower of Brahman food comes of itself, without effort—he drinks wherever he gets it. He roams at pleasure everywhere—he is fearless, sleeps sometimes in the forest, sometimes in a crematorium and, treads the Path which the Vedas have taken but whose end they have not seen. His body is like the sky; and he is guided, like a child, by others' wishes; he is sometimes naked, sometimes in gorgeous clothes, and at times has only Jnana as his clothing; he behaves sometimes like a child, sometimes like a madman, and at other times again like a ghoul, indifferent to cleanliness.

I pray to the holy feet of our Guru that you may have that state, and you may wander like the rhinoceros.

Yours etc.,
Vivekananda.

---

1. In his anxiety to defend the purity of the Vedic religion against the excesses of Tantrikism, which as capturing the rank and file of his countrymen, Shankara neglected the problem of the latter, stigmatised as Shudras by the Vedicists. This is perhaps the meaning of Swamiji. It seems he could never forgive Shankara for applying in his commentary on the Brahma-Sutras the old logic of forbidding Vedic rituals to the Shudras the more modern question of their right to higher modes of worship (Upâsanâ) and knowledge (Jnâna) of the Jnâna-kânda.

24 — SIR

Translated from Bengali

Victory to the Lord!

GHAZIPUR,
25th Feb., 1890.

DEAR SIR,

The lumbago is giving a good deal of trouble, or else I would have already sought to come to you. The mind does not find rest here any longer. It is three days since I came away from Babaji's place, but he inquires of me kindly almost every day. As soon as the lumbago is a little better, I bid good-bye to Babaji. Countless greetings to you.

Yours etc.,
Vivekananda.

25 — SIR

Translated from Bengali

Victory to the Lord!

GHAZIPUR,
3rd March, 1890.

DEAR SIR,

Your kind letter comes to hand just now. You know not, sir, I am a very soft-natured man in spite of the stern Vedantic views I hold. And this proves to be my undoing. At the slightest touch I give myself away; for howsoever I may try to think only of my own good, I slip off in spite of myself to think of other peoples' interests. This time it was with a very stern resolve that I set out to pursue my own good, but I had to run off at the news of the illness of a brother at Allahabad! And now comes this news from Hrishikesh, and my mind has run off with me there. I have wired to Sharat, hut no reply yet — a nice place indeed to delay even telegrams so much! The lumbago obstinately refuses to leave me, and the pain is very great. For the last few days I haven't been able to go to see Pavhariji, but out of his kindness he sends every day for my report. But now I see the whole matter is inverted in its bearings! While I myself have come, a beggar, at his door, he turns round and wants to learn of me! This saint perhaps is not yet perfected — too much of rites, vows, observances, and too much of self-concealment. The ocean in its fullness cannot be contained within its shores, I am sure. So it is not good, I have decided not to disturb this Sâdhu (holy man) for nothing, and very soon I shall ask leave of him to go. No help, you see; Providence has dealt me my death to make me so tender! Babaji does not let me off, and Gagan Babu (whom probably you know — an upright, pious, and kindhearted man) does not let me off. If the wire in reply requires my leaving this place, I go; if not, I am coming to you at Varanasi in a few days. I am not going to let you off — I must take you to Hrishikesh — no excuse or objections will do. What are you saying about difficulties there of keeping clean? Lack of water in the hills or lack of room!! Tirthas (places of pilgrimage) and Sannyasins of the Kali-Yuga — you know what they are. Spend money and the owners of temples will fling away the installed god to make room for you; so no anxiety about a resting-place! No trouble to face there, I say; the summer heat has set in there now, I believe, though not that degree of it as you find at Varanasi — so much the better. Always the nights are quite cool there, from which good sleep is almost a certainty.

Why do you get frightened so much? I stand guarantee that you shall return home safe and that you shall have no trouble anywhere. It is my experience that in this British realm no fakir or householder gets into any trouble.

Is it a mere idle fancy of mine that between us there some connection from previous birth? Just see how one letter from you sweeps away all my resolution and, I bend my steps towards Varanasi leaving all matters behind! . . .

I have written again to brother Gangadhar and have asked him this time to return to the Math. If he comes, he will meet you. How is the climate at Varanasi now? By my stay here I have been cured of all other symptoms of malaria, only the pain in the loins makes me frantic; day and night it is aching and chafes me very much. I know not how I shall climb up the hills. I find wonderful endurance in Babaji, and that's why I am begging something of him; but no inkling of the mood to give, only receiving and receiving! So I also fly off.

Yours etc.,
Vivekananda.

PS. To no big person am I going any longer —

"Remain, O mind, within yourself, go not to anybody else's door; whatever you seek, you shall obtain sitting at your ease, only seek for it in the privacy of your heart. There is the supreme Treasure, the philosophers' stone and He can give whatever you ask for; for countless gems, O mind, lie strewn about the portals of His abode. He is the wishing-stone that confers boons at the mere thought." Thus says the poet Kamalâkânta.

So now the great conclusion is that Ramakrishna has no peer; nowhere else in this world exists that unprecedented perfection, that wonderful kindness for all that does not stop to justify itself, that intense sympathy for man in bondage. Either he must be the Avatâra as he himself used to say, or else the ever-perfected divine man whom the Vedanta speaks of as the free one who assumes a body for the good of humanity. This is my conviction sure and certain; and the worship of such a divine man has been referred to by Patanjali in the aphorism: "Or the goal may be attained by meditating on a saint." (Patanjali's aphorism has "Ishvara" in place of "saint". Nârada has an aphorism which runs thus : Bhakti (Supreme Love) is attainable chiefly through the grace of a saint, or by a bit of Divine Grace.)

Never during his life did he refuse a single prayer of mine; millions of offences has he forgiven me; such great love even my parents never had for me. There is no poetry, no exaggeration in all this. It is the bare truth and every disciple of his knows it. In times of great danger, great temptation, I wept in extreme agony with the prayer, "O God, do save me," but no response came from anybody; but this wonderful saint, or Avatâra, or anything else he may be, came to know of all my affliction through his powers of insight into human hearts and lifted it off — in spite of my desire to the contrary — after getting me brought to his presence. If the soul be deathless, and so, if he still lives, I pray to trim again and again: "O Bhagavan Ramakrishna, thou infinite ocean of mercy and my only refuge, do graciously fulfil the desires of my esteemed friend, who is every inch a great man." May he impart to you all good, he whom alone I have found in this world to be like an ocean of unconditioned mercy! Shântih, Shântih, Shântih.

Please send a prompt reply.

Yours etc.,
Vivekananda.

26 — SIR

Translated from Bengali

Victory to God!

GHAZIPUR,
8th March, 1890.

DEAR SIR,

Your note duly reached met and so I too shall be off to Prayag. Please write to inform where you mean to put up while there.

PS. In case Abhedananda reaches your place in a day or two, I shall be much obliged if you will start him on his way to Calcutta.

Yours etc.,
Vivekananda.

27 — AKHANDANANDA

Translated from Bengali

Salutation to Bhagavan Ramakrishna!

GHAZIPUR,
March, 1890.

BELOVED AKHANDANANDA,

Very glad to receive your letter yesterday. I am at present staying with the wonderful Yogi and devotee of this place, called Pavhariji. He never comes out of his room and holds conversations with people from behind the door. Inside the room there is a pit in which he lives. It is rumoured that he remains in a state of Samadhi for months together. His fortitude is most wonderful. Our Bengal is the land of Bhakti and of Jnana, where Yoga is scarcely so much as talked of even. What little there is, is but the queer breathing exercises of the Hatha-Yoga — which is nothing but a kind of gymnastics. Therefore I am staying with this wonderful Raja-Yogi — and he has given me some hopes, too. There is a beautiful bungalow in a small garden belonging to a gentleman here; I mean to stay there. The garden is quite close to Babaji's cottage. A brother of the Babaji stays there to look after the comforts of the Sadhus, and I shall have my Bhikshâ at his place. Hence, with a view to seeing to the end of this fun, I give up for the present my plan of going to the hills. For the last two months I have had an attack of lumbago in the waist, which also makes it impossible to climb the hills now. Therefore let me wait and see what Babaji will give me.

My motto is to learn whatever good things I may come across anywhere. This leads many friends to think that it will take away from my devotion to the Guru. These ideas I count as those of lunatics and bigots. For all Gurus are one and are fragments and radiations of God, the Universal Guru.

If you come to Ghazipur, you have but to inquire at Satish Babu's or Gagan Babu's at Gorabazar, and you know my whereabouts. Or, Pavhari Baba is so well-known a person here that everyone will inform you about his Ashrama at the very mention of his name, and you have only to go there and inquire about the Paramahamsa, and they will tell you of me. Near Moghul Sarai there is a station named Dildarnagar, where you have to change to a short branch railway and get down at Tarighat, opposite Ghazipur; then you have to cross the Ganga to reach Ghazipur.

For the present, I stay at Ghazipur for some days, and wait and see what the Babaji does. If you come, we shall stay together at the said bungalow for some time, and then start for the hills, or for any other place we may decide upon. Don't, please, write to anyone at Baranagore that I am staying at Ghazipur.

With blessings and best wishes,

Ever yours,
Vivekananda.

28 — AKHANDANANDA

Translated from Bengali

Salutation to Bhagavan Ramakrishna!

GHAZIPUR,
March, 1890.

BELOVED AKHANDANANDA,

Received another letter of yours just now, and with great difficulty deciphered the scribblings. I have written everything in detail in my last letter. You start immediately on receipt of this. I know the route to Tibet via Nepal that you have spoken of. As they don't allow anyone to enter Tibet easily, so they don't allow anybody to go anywhere in Nepal, except Katmandu, its capital, and one or two places of pilgrimage. But a friend of mine is now a tutor to His Highness the Maharaja of Nepal, and a teacher in his school, from whom I have it that when the Nepal government send their subsidy to China, they send it via Lhasa. A Sadhu contrived in that way to go to Lhasa, China, Manchuria, and even to the holy seat of Târâ Devi in north China. We, too, can visit with dignity and respect Tibet, Lhasa, China, and all, if that friend of mine tries to arrange it. You therefore start immediately for Ghazipur. After a few days' stay here with the Babaji, I shall correspond with my friend, and, everything arranged, I shall certainly go to Tibet via Nepal.

You have to get down at Dildarnagar to come to Ghazipur. It is three or four stations from Moghul Sarai I would have sent you the passage if I could have collected it here; so you get it together and come. Gagan Babu with whom I am putting up, is an exceedingly courteous, noble, and generous-minded man. No sooner did he come to know of Kali's illness than he sent him the passage at Hrishikesh; he has besides spent much on my account. Under the circumstances it would be violating a Sannyasin's duty to tax him for the passage to Kashmir, and I desist from it. You collect the fare and start as soon as you receive this letter. Let the craze for visiting Amarnath be put back for the present.

Yours affectionately,
Vivekananda.

29 — SIR

Translated from Bengali

GHAZIPUR,
31st March, 1890.

DEAR SIR,

I haven't been here for the last few days and am again going away today. I have asked brother Gangadhar to come here; and if he comes, we go over to you together. For some special reasons, I shall continue to stay in secret in a village some distance from this place, and there's no facility for writing any letter from that place, owing to which I could not reply to your letter so long. Brother Gangadhar is very likely to come, otherwise the reply to my note would have reached me. Brother Abhedananda is putting up with Doctor Priya at Varanasi. Another brother of mine had been with me, but has left for Abhedananda's place. The news of his arrival has not yet been received, and, his health being bad, I am rather anxious for his sake. I have behaved very cruelly towards him — that is, I have harassed him much to make him leave my company. There's no help, you see; I am so very weak-hearted, so much overmastered by the distractions of love! Bless me that I may harden. What shall I say to you about the condition of my mind! Oh, it is as if the hell-fire is burning there day and night! Nothing, nothing could I do yet! And this life seems muddled away in vain; I feel quite helpless as to what to do! The Babaji throws out honeyed words and keeps me from leaving. Ah, what shall I say? I am committing hundreds of offenses against you — please excuse them as so many misdoings of a man driven mad with mental agonies. Abhedananda is suffering from dysentery. I shall be very much obliged if you will kindly inquire about his condition and send him down to our Math in case he wants to go there with our brother who has come from here. My Gurubhais must be thinking me very cruel and selfish. Oh, what can I do? Who will see deep down into my mind? Who will know how much I am suffering day and night? Bless me that I may have the most unflinching patience and perseverance.

PS. Abhedananda is staying in Doctor Priya's house at Sonarpura. My lumbago is as before.

Yours etc.,
Vivekananda.

30 — KALI

Translated from Bengali

GHAZIPUR,
2nd April, 1890.

MY DEAR KALI, (ABHEDANANDA)

Glad to receive your letter as well as Pramada Babu's and Baburam's (Premananda's). I am doing pretty well here. You have expressed a desire to see me. I too have a similar longing, and it is this that makes me afraid of going. Moreover, the Babaji forbids me to do so. I shall try to go on a few days' leave from him. But there is this fear that by so doing I shall be drawn up to the hills by the attraction I have for Hrishikesh, and it will be very difficult to shake it off, specially for one weak-minded, you see, like myself. The attack of lumbago, too, will not leave me on any account — a botheration! But then I am getting used to it. Please convey my countless salutations to Pramada Babu; his is a friendship which greatly benefits both my mind and body. And I am particularly indebted to him. Things will turn up some way, anyhow.

With best wishes,

Yours affectionately,
Vivekananda.

31 — SIR

Translated from Bengali

GHAZIPUR,
2nd April, 1890.

DEAR SIR,

Where shall I get that renunciation you speak of in your advice to me? It is for the sake of that very thing that I am out a tramp through the earth. If ever I get this true renunciation, I shall let you know; and if you get anything of the kind, please remember me as a partner thereof.

Yours,
Vivekananda.

32 — SIR

Translated from Bengali

Victory to Ramakrishna!

BARANAGORE,
10th May, 1890.

DEAR SIR,

I could not write to you because of various distractions and a relapse of fever. Glad to learn from Abhedananda's letter that you are doing well. Gangadhar (Akhandananda) has probably arrived at Varanasi by this time. King Death happens here to be casting into his jaws these days many of our friends and own people, hence I am very much taken up. Perhaps no letter for me has arrived there from Nepal. I know not how and when Vishvanâtha (the Lord of Kashi) would choose to vouchsafe some rest to me. Directly the hot weather relaxes a little, I am off from this place, but I am still at a loss where to go. Do please pray for me to Vishvanatha that He may grant me strength. You are a devotee, and I beseech you with the Lord's words coming to my mind, "Those who are the devoted ones to My devotees, are indeed considered the best of My devotees."

Yours etc.,
Vivekananda.

33 — SIR

Translated from Bengali

57, RAMAKANTA BOSE'S STREET,
BAGHBAZAR, CALCUTTA,
26th May, 1890.

DEAR SIR,

I write this to you while caught in a vortex of many untoward circumstances and great agitation of mind; with a prayer to Vishvanatha, please think of the propriety and possibility, or otherwise, of all that I set forth below and then oblige me greatly by a reply.

1. I already told you at the outset that I am Ramakrishna's slave, having laid my body at his feet "with Til and Tulasi leaves", I cannot disregard his behest. If it is in failure that that great sage laid down his life after having attained to superhuman heights of Jnana, Bhakti, Love, and powers, and after having practiced for forty years stern renunciation, non-attachment, holiness, and great austerities, then where is there anything for us to count on? So I am obliged to trust his words as the words of one identified with truth.

2. Now his behest to me was that I should devote myself to the service of the order of all-renouncing devotees founded by him, and in this I have to persevere, come what may, being ready to take heaven, hell, salvation, or anything that may happen to me.

3. His command was that his all-renouncing devotees should group themselves together, and I am entrusted with seeing to this. Of course, it matters not if any one of us goes out on visits to this place or that, but these shall be but visits, while his own opinion was that absolute homeless wandering suited him alone who was perfected to the highest point. Before that state, it is proper to settle somewhere to dive down into practice. When all the ideas of body and the like are dissolved of themselves, a person may then pursue whatever state comes to him. Otherwise, it is baneful for a practicing aspirant to be always wandering.

4. So in pursuance cf this his commandment, his group of Sannyasins are now assembled in a dilapidated house at Baranagore, and two of his lay disciples,

Babu Suresh Chandra Mitra and Babu Balaram Bose, so long provided for their food and house-rent.

5. For various reasons, the body of Bhagavan Ramakrishna had to be consigned to fire. There is no doubt that this act was very blamable. The remains of his ashes are now preserved, and if they be now properly enshrined somewhere on the banks of the Ganga, I presume we shall be able in some measure to expiate the sin lying on our head. These sacred remains, his seat, and his picture are every day worshipped in our Math in proper form; and it is known to you that a brother-disciple of mine, of Brahmin parentage, is occupied day and night with the task. The expenses of the worship used also to be borne by the two great souls mentioned above.

6. What greater regret can there be than this that no memorial could yet be raised in this land of Bengal in the very neighbourhood of the place where he lived his life of Sâdhanâ — he by whose birth the race of Bengalees has been sanctified, the land of Bengal has become hallowed, he who came on earth to save the Indians from the spell of the worldly glamour of Western culture and who therefore chose most of his all-renouncing disciples from university men?

7. The two gentlemen mentioned above had a strong desire to have some land purchased on the banks of the Ganga and see the sacred remains enshrined on it, with the disciples living there together; and Suresh Babu had offered a sum of Rs. 1,000 for the purpose, promising to give more, but for some inscrutable purpose of God he left this world yesternight! And the news of Balaram Babu's death is already known to you.

8. Now there is no knowing as to where his disciples will stand with his sacred remains and his seat (and you know well, people here in Bengal are profuse in their professions, but do not stir out an inch in practice). The disciples are Sannyasins and are ready forthwith to depart anywhere their way may lie. But I, their servant, am in an agony of sufferings, and my heart is breaking to think that a small piece of land could not be had in which to install the remains of Bhagavan Ramakrishna.

9. It is impossible with a sum of Rs. 1,000 to secure land and raise a temple near Calcutta. Some such land would at least cost about five to seven thousands.

10. You remain now the only friend and patron of Shri Ramakrishna's disciples. In the NorthWestern Province great indeed is your fame, your position, and your circle of acquaintance. I request you to consider, if you feel like it, the propriety of your getting the affair through by raising subscriptions from well-to-do pious men known to you in your province. If you deem it proper to have some shelter erected on the bangs of the Ganga in Bengal for Bhagavan Ramakrishna's sacred remains and for his disciples, I shall with your leave report myself to you, and I have not the slightest qualm to beg from door to door for this noble cause, for the sake of my Lord and his children. Please give this proposal your best thoughts with prayers to Vishvanatha. To my mind, if all these sincere, educated, youthful Sannyasins of good birth fail to dive up to the ideals of Shri Ramakrishna owing to want of an abode and help, then alas for our country!

11. If you ask, "You are a Sannyasin, so why do you trouble over these desires?" — I would then reply, I am Ramakrishna s servant, and I am willing even to steal and rob, if by doing so I can perpetuate his name in the land of his birth and Sâdhanâ (spiritual struggle) and help even a little his disciples to practice his great ideals. I know you to be my closest in kinship, and I lay my mind bare to you. I returned to Calcutta for this reason. I had told you this before I left, and now I leave it to you to do what you think best.

12. If you argue that it is better to have the plan carried out in some place like Kashi, my point is, as I have told you, it would be the greatest pity if the memorial shrine could not be raised in the land of his birth and Sadhana! The condition of Bengal is pitiable. The people here cannot even dream what renunciation truly means — luxury and sensuality have been so much eating into the vitals of the race! May God send renunciation and unworldliness into this land! They have here nothing to speak of, while the people of the North-Western Province, specially the rich there as I believe, have great zeal in noble causes like this. Please send me such reply as you think best. Gangadhar has not yet arrived today, and may do so tomorrow. I am so eager to see him again.

Please write to the address given above.

Yours etc.,
Vivekananda.

34 — SHARAT

BAGHBAZAR, CALCUTTA,
July 6, 1890.

DEAR SHARAT (SARADANANDA)
and KRIPANANDA,

Your letters have duly reached us. They say Almora is healthiest at this time of the year, yet you are taken ill! I hope it is nothing malarious. . .

I find Gangadhar the same pliant child with his turbulence moderated by his wanderings, and with a greater love for us and for our Lord. He is bold, brave, sincere, and steadfast. The only thing needed is a guiding mind to whom he would instinctively submit with reverence, and a fine man would be the result.

I had no wish to leave Ghazipur this time, and certainly not to come to Calcutta, but Kali's illness made me go to Varanasi, and Balaram's sudden death brought me to Calcutta. So Suresh Babu and Balaram Babu are both gone! G. C. Ghosh is supporting the Math. . . . I intend shortly, as soon as I can get my fare, to go up to Almora and thence to some place in Gharwal on the Ganga where I can settle down for a long meditation. Gangadhar is accompanying me. Indeed it was with this desire and intention that I brought him down from Kashmir.

I don't think you ought to be in any hurry about coming down to Calcutta. You have done with roving; that's good, but you have not yet attempted the one thing you should do, that is, be resolved to sit down and meditate. I don't think Jnana is a thing like rousing a maiden suddenly from sleep by saying, "Get up, dear girl, your marriage ceremony is waiting for you!" as we say. I am strongly of opinion that very few persons in any Yuga (age) attain Jnana, and therefore we should go on striving and striving even unto death. That's my old-fashioned way, you know. About the humbug of modern Sannyasins' Jnana I know too well. Peace be unto you and strength! Daksha, who is staying at Vrindaban with Rakhal (Brahmananda), has learnt to make gold and has become a pucca Jnani, so writes Rakhal. God bless him, and you may say, amen!

I am in fine health now, and the good I gained by my stay in Ghazipur will last, I am sure, for some time. I am longing for a flight to the Himalayas. This time I shall not go to Pavhari Baba or any other saint—they divert one from his highest purpose. Straight up!

How do you find the climate at Almora? Neither S— nor you need come down. What is the use of so many living together in one place and doing no good to one's soul? Don't be fools always wandering from place to place; that's all very good, but be heroes.

निर्मानमोहा जितसङ्गदोषा
अध्यात्मनित्या विनिवृत्तकामाः ।
द्वन्द्वैर्विमुक्ताः सुखदुःखसंज्ञै-
र्गच्छन्त्यमूढाः पदमव्ययं तत् ॥

—"Free from pride and delusion, with the evil of attachment conquered, ever dwelling in the Self, with desires completely receded, liberated from the pairs of opposites known as pleasure and pain, the undeluded reach that Goal Eternal" (Gita, XV. 5).

Who advises you to jump into fire? If you don't find the Himalayas a place for Sadhana, go somewhere else then. So many gushing inquiries simply betray a weak mind. Arise, ye mighty one, and be strong! Work on and on, struggle on and on! Nothing more to write.

Yours affectionately,
Vivekananda.

35 — GOVINDA SAHAY

AJMER,
14th April, 1891.

DEAR GOVINDA SAHAY,

... Try to be pure and unselfish — that is the whole of religion. ...

> Yours with love,
> Vivekananda.

36 — GOVINDA SAHAY

> MOUNT ABU,
> 30th April, 1891.

DEAR GOVINDA SAHAY,

Have you done the Upanayana of that Brahmin boy? Are you studying Sanskrit? How far have you advanced? I think you must have finished the first part. ... Are you diligent in your Shiva Pujâ? If not, try to be so. "Seek ye first the kingdom of God and all good things will be added unto you." Follow God and you shall have whatever you desire. ... To the two Commander Sahebs my best regards; they being men of high position were very kind to a poor fakir like me. My children, the secret of religion lies not in theories but in practice. To be good and to do good — that is the whole of religion. "Not he that crieth 'Lord', 'Lord', but he that doeth the will of the Father". You are a nice band of young men, you Alwaris, and I hope in no distant future many of you will be ornaments of the society and blessings to the country you are born in.

> Yours with blessings,
> V.

PS. Don't be ruffled if now and then you get a brush from the world; it will be over in no time, and everything will be all right.

37 — GOVINDA SAHAY

> MOUNT ABU,
> 1891.

DEAR GOVINDA SAHAY,

You must go on with your Japa whatever direction the mind takes. Tell Harbux that he is to begin with the Prânâyâma in the following way.

Try hard with your Sanskrit studies.

> Yours with love,
> Vivekananda.

38 — DOCTOR

> KHETRI,
> 27th April, 1893.

DEAR DOCTOR, (Dr. Nanjunda Rao, M.D.)

Your letter has just reached me. I am very much gratified by your love for my unworthy self. So, so sorry to learn that poor Bâlâji has lost his son. "The Lord gave and the Lord bath taken away; blessed be the name of the Lord." We only know that nothing is lost or can be lost. For us is only submission, calm and perfect. The soldier has no right to complain, nay murmur, if the general orders him into the cannon's mouth. May He comfort Balaji in his grief, and may it draw him closer and closer to the breast of the All-merciful Mother!

As to my taking ship from Madras, I do not think it feasible, as I have already made arrangements from Bombay. Tell Bhattacharya that the Raja (The Maharaja of Khetri, Rajputana.) or my Gurubhâis would be the last men to put any obstacles in my way. As for the Rajaji, his love for me is simply without limit.

May the Giver of all good bless you all here and hereafter, will be the constant prayer of

SACHCHIDANANDA.

(Swamiji uses to call himself such in those days.)

39 — MOTHER

> BOMBAY,
> 24th May, 1893.

DEAR MOTHER, (Shrimati Indumati Mitra)

Very glad to receive your letter and that of dear Haripada. Please do not be sorry that I could not write to you very often. I am always praying to the Lord for your welfare. I cannot go to Belgaum now as arrangements are all ready for my starting for America on the 31st next. The Lord willing, I shall see you on returning from my travels in America and Europe. Always resign yourselves to the Lord Shri Krishna. Always remember that we are but puppets in the Lord's hands. Remain pure always. Please be careful not to become impure even in thought, as also in speech and action; always try to do good to others as far as in you lies. And remember that the paramount duty of a woman is to serve her husband by thought, word, and deed. Please read the Gita every day to the best of your opportunity. Why have you signed yourself as. . . Dâsi (maidservant)? The Vaishya and the Shudra should sign as Dâsa and Dâsi, but the Brahmin and Kshatriya should write Deva and Devi (goddess). Moreover, these distinctions of caste and the like have been the invention of our modern sapient Brahmins. Who is a servant, and to whom? Everyone is a servant of the Lord Hari. Hence a woman should use her patronymic, that is, the surname of her husband. This is the ancient Vedic custom, as for example, such and such Mitra, or the like. It is needless to write much, dear mother; always know that I am constantly praying for your well-being. From America I shall now and then write you letters with descriptions of the wonderful things there. I am now at Bombay, and shall stay here up to the 31st. The private Secretary to the Maharaja of Khetri has come here to see me off.

With blessings,

Yours sincerely,
Vivekananda.

40 — MAHARAJA OF KHETRI

From a letter written to H. H. the Maharaja of Khetri.

AMERICA,
1894.

. . . "It is not the building that makes the home, but it is the wife that makes it,"[1] says a Sanskrit poet, and how true it is! The roof that affords you shelter from heat and cold and rain is not to be judged by the pillars that support it—the finest Corinthian columns though they be—but by the real spirit-pillar who is the centre, the real support of the home—the woman. Judged by that standard, the American home will not suffer in comparison with any home in the world.

I have heard many stories about the American home: of liberty running into licence, of unwomanly women smashing under their feet all the peace and happiness of home-life in their mad liberty-dance, and much nonsense of that type. And now after a year's experience of American homes, of American women, how utterly false and erroneous that sort of judgment appears! American women! A hundred lives would not be sufficient to pay my deep debt of gratitude to you! I have not words enough to express my gratitude to you. "The Oriental hyperbole" alone expresses the depth of Oriental gratitude—"If the Indian Ocean were an inkstand, the highest mountain of the Himalaya the pen, the earth the scroll and time itself the writer"[2] still it will not express my gratitude to you!

Last year I came to this country in summer, a wandering preacher of a far distant country, without name, fame, wealth, or learning to recommend me—friendless, helpless, almost in a state of destitution and American women befriended me, gave me shelter and food, took me to their homes and treated me as their own son, their own brother. They stood my friends even when their own priests were trying to persuade them to give up the "dangerous heathen"— even when day after day their best friends had told them not to stand by this "unknown foreigner, may be, of dangerous character". But they are better judges of character and soul—for it is the pure mirror that catches the reflection.

And how many beautiful homes I have seen, how many mothers whose purity of character, whose unselfish love for their children are beyond expression,

---
1. "न गृहं गृहमित्याहुर्गृहिणी गृहमुच्यते ।"
2. Adapted from the *Shiva-Mahimnah-Stotram*.

how many daughters and pure maidens, "pure as the icicle on Diana's temple", and withal with much culture, education, and spirituality in the highest sense! Is America then full of only wingless angels in the shape of women? There is good and bad everywhere, true—but a nation is not to be judged by its weaklings called the wicked, as they are only the weeds which lag behind, but by the good, the noble, and the pure who indicate the national life-current to be flowing clear and vigorous.

Do you judge of an apple tree and the taste of its fruits by the unripe, undeveloped, worm-eaten ones that strew the ground, large even though their number be sometimes? If there is one ripe developed fruit, that one would indicate the powers, the possibility and the purpose of the apple tree and not hundreds that could not grow.

And then the modern American women—I admire their broad and liberal minds. I have seen many liberal and broad-minded men too in this country, some even in the narrowest churches, but here is the difference—there is danger with the men to become broad at the cost of religion, at the cost of spirituality—women broaden out in sympathy to everything that is good everywhere, without dosing a bit of their own religion. They intuitively know that it is a question of positivity and not negativity, a question of addition and not subtraction. They are every day becoming aware of the fact that it is the affirmative and positive side of everything that shall be stored up, and that this very act of accumulating the affirmative and positive, and therefore soul-building forces of nature, is what destroys the negative and destructive elements in the world.

What a wonderful achievement was that World's Fair at Chicago! And that wonderful Parliament of Religions where voices from every corner of the earth expressed their religious ideas! I was also allowed to present my own ideas through the kindness of Dr. Barrows and Mr. Bonney. Mr. Bonney is such a wonderful man! Think of that mind that planned and carried out with great success that gigantic undertaking, and he, no clergyman, a lawyer, presiding over the dignitaries of all the churches—the sweet, learned, patient Mr. Bonney with all his soul speaking through his bright eyes. …

Yours etc.,
Vivekananda.

41 — SHASHI

Translated from Bengali

Salutation to Bhagavan Ramakrishna!

C/O GEORGE W. HALE, ESQ.,
541 DEARBORN AVENUE, CHICAGO,
19th March, 1894.

MY DEAR SHASHI (RAMAKRISHNANANDA),

I have not written to you since coming to this country. But Haridas Bhai's[3] letter gives me all the news. It is excellent that G. C. Ghosh[4] and all of you have treated him with due consideration.

I have no wants in this country, but mendicancy has no vogue here, and I have to labour, that is, lecture in places. It is as cold here as it is hot. The summer is not a bit less hot than in Calcutta. And how to describe the cold in winter! The whole country is covered with snow, three or four feet deep, nay, six or seven feet at places! In the southern parts there is no snow. Snow, however, is a thing of little consideration here. For it snows when the mercury stands at 32° F. In Calcutta it scarcely comes down to 60,° and it rarely approaches zero in England. But here, your mercury sinks to minus 4° or 5°. In Canada, in the north, mercury becomes condensed, when they have to use the alcohol thermometer. When it is too cold, that is, when the mercury stands even below 20°F, it does not snow. I used to think that it must be an exceedingly cold day on which the snow falls. But it is not so, it snows on comparatively warm days. Extreme cold produces a sort of intoxication. No carriages would run; only the sledge, which is without wheels, slides on the ground! Everything is frozen stiff—even an elephant can walk

---

3. Ex-Dewan of Junagarh. Shortly before Swamiji left India for America, he became intimately acquainted with this gentleman, and was introduced by him to many Indian princes.

4. Girish Chandra Ghosh, the great actor-dramatist of Bengal, and a staunch devotee of Shri Ramakrishna.

on rivers and canals and lakes. The massive falls of Niagara, of such tremendous velocity, are frozen to marble!! But I am doing nicely. I was a little afraid at first, but necessity makes me travel by rail to the borders of Canada one day, and the next day finds me lecturing in south U.S.A.! The carriages are kept quite warm, like your own room, by means of steam pipes, and all around are masses of snow, spotlessly white. Oh, the beauty of it!

I was mortally afraid that my nose and ears would fall off, but to this day they are all right. I have to go out, however, dressed in a heap of warm clothing surmounted by a fur-coat, with boots encased in a woollen jacket, and so on. No sooner do you breathe out than the breath freezes among the beard and moustache! Notwithstanding all this, the fun of it is that they won't drink water indoors without putting a lump of ice into it. This is because it is warm indoors. Every room and the staircase are kept warm by steam pipes. They are first and foremost in art and appliances, foremost in enjoyment and luxury, foremost in making money, and foremost in spending it. The daily wages of a coolie are six rupees, as also are those of a servant; you cannot hire a cab for less than three rupees, nor get a cigar for less than four annas. A decent pair of shoes costs twenty-four rupees, and a suit, five hundred rupees. As they earn, so they spend. A lecture fetches from two hundred up to three thousand rupees. I have got up to five hundred[1]. Of course now I am in the very heyday of fortune. They like me, and thousands of people come to hear me speak.

As it pleased the Lord, I met here Mr. Mazoomdar. He was very cordial at first, but when the whole Chicago population began to flock to me in overwhelming numbers, then grew the canker in his mind! . . . The priests tried their utmost to snub me. But the Guru (Teacher) is with me, what could anybody do? And the whole American nation loves and respects me, pays my expenses, and reveres me as a Guru. ... It was not in the power of your priests to do anything against me. Moreover, they are a nation of scholars. Here it would no longer do to say, "We marry our widows", "We do not worship idols", and things of that sort. What they want is philosophy, learning; and empty talk will no more do.

Dharmapala is a fine boy. He has not much of learning but is very gentle. He had a good deal of popularity in this country.

Brother, I have been brought to my senses. . . . ये नधिनन्ति निरर्थकं परहितं ते के न जानीमहे—We do not know what sort of people they are who for nothing hinder the welfare of others" (Bhartrihari). Brother, we can get rid of everything, but not of that cursed jealousy. . . . That is a national sin with us, speaking ill of others, and burning at heart at the greatness of others. Mine alone is the greatness, none else should rise to it!!

Nowhere in the world are women like those of this country. How pure, independent, self-relying, and kindhearted! It is the women who are the life and soul of this country. All learning and culture are centred in them. The saying, "या श्री: स्वयं सुकृतिनां भवनेषु—Who is the Goddess of Fortune Herself in the families of the meritorious" (Chandi)—holds good in this country, while that other, "अलक्ष्मीः पापात्मनां—The Goddess of ill luck in the homes of the sinful" (ibid.)—applies to ours. Just think on this. Great God! I am struck dumb with wonderment at seeing the women of America. "त्वं श्रीस्त्वमीश्वरी त्वं हरीः etc. — Thou art the Goddess of Fortune, Thou art the supreme Goddess, Thou art Modesty" (ibid.)," "या देवी सर्वभूतेषु शक्तिरूपेण संस्थिता—The Goddess who resides in all beings as Power" (ibid.)—all this holds good here. There are thousands of women here whose minds are as pure and white as the snow of this country. And look at our girls, becoming mothers below their teens!! Good Lord! I now see it all. Brother, "यत्र नार्यस्तु पूज्यन्ते रमन्ते तत्र देवताः—The gods are pleased where the women are held in esteem"—says the old Manu. We are horrible sinners, and our degradation is due to our calling women "despicable worms", "gateways to hell", and so forth. Goodness gracious! There is all the difference between heaven and hell!! "याथातथ्यतोऽर्थान् व्यदधात्—He adjudges gifts according to the merits of the case" (Isha, 8). Is the Lord to be hoodwinked by idle talk? The Lord has said, "त्वं स्त्री त्वं पुमानसि त्वं कुमार उत वा कुमारी—Thou art the woman, Thou

---

1. For some time after the Chicago addresses, Swamiji lectured on behalf of a lecture bureau. He soon gave it up as curtailing his independence, and devoted most of the money thus earned to various charitable works in the U.S.A. and India.

art the man, Thou art the boy and the girl as well." (Shvetâshvatara Upa.) And we on our part are crying, "दूरमपसर रे चण्डाल—Be off, thou outcast!" "केनेषा निर्मिता नारी मोहिनी etc.—Who has made the bewitching woman?" My brother, what experiences I have had in the South, of the upper classes torturing the lower! What Bacchanalian orgies within the temples! Is it a religion that fails to remove the misery of the poor and turn men into gods! Do you think our religion is worth the name? Ours is only Don't touchism, only "Touch me not", "Touch me not." Good heavens! A country, the big leaders of which have for the last two thousand years been only discussing whether to take food with the right hand or the left, whether to take water from the right-hand side or from the left, ... if such a country does not go to ruin, what other will? "कालः सुप्तेषु जागर्ति कालो हि दुरतिक्रमः—Time keeps wide awake when all else sleeps. Time is invincible indeed!" He knows it; who is there to throw dust in His eyes, my friend?

A country where millions of people live on flowers of the Mohuâ plant, and a million or two of Sadhus and a hundred million or so of Brahmins suck the blood out of these poor people, without even the least effort for their amelioration—is that a country or hell? Is that a religion, or the devil's dance? My brother, here is one thing for you to understand fully—I have travelled all over India, and seen this country too—can there be an effect without cause? Can there be punishment without sin?

सर्वशास्त्रपुराणेषु व्यासस्य वचनं ध्रुवम् ।
परोपकारः पुण्याय पापाय परपीडनम् ॥

—"Amidst all the scriptures and Purânas, know this statement of Vyâsa to be true, that doing good to others conduces to merit, and doing harm to them leads to sin."

Isn't it true?

My brother, in view of all this, specially of the poverty and ignorance, I had no sleep. At Cape Comorin sitting in Mother Kumari's temple, sitting on the last bit of Indian rock—I hit upon a plan: We are so many Sannyasins wandering about, and teaching the people metaphysics—it is all madness. Did not our Gurudeva use to say, "An empty stomach is no good for religion"? That those poor people are leading the life of brutes is simply due to ignorance. We have for all ages been sucking their blood and trampling them underfoot.

. . . Suppose some disinterested Sannyasins, bent on doing good to others, go from village to village, disseminating education and seeking in various ways to better the condition of all down to the Chandâla, through oral teaching, and by means of maps, cameras, globes, and such other accessories—can't that bring forth good in time? All these plans I cannot write out in this short letter. The long and the short of it is—if the mountain does not come to Mohammed, Mohammed must go to the mountain. The poor are too poor to come to schools and Pâthashâlâs, and they will gain nothing by reading poetry and all that sort of thing. We, as a nation, have lost our individuality, and that is the cause of all mischief in India. We have to give back to the nation its lost individuality and raise the masses. The Hindu, the Mohammedan, the Christian, all have trampled them underfoot. Again the force to raise them must come from inside, that is, from the orthodox Hindus. In every country the evils exist not with, but against, religion. Religion therefore is not to blame, but men.

To effect this, the first thing we need is men, and the next is funds. Through the grace of our Guru I was sure to get from ten to fifteen men in every town. I next travelled in search of funds, but do you think the people of India were going to spend money! . . . . Selfishness personified—are they to spend anything? Therefore I have come to America, to earn money myself, and then return to my country and devote the rest of my days to the realisation of this one aim of my life.

As our country is poor in social virtues, so this country is lacking in spirituality. I give them spirituality, and they give me money. I do not know how long I shall take to realise my end. ...These people are not hypocrites, and jealousy is altogether absent in them. I depend on no one in Hindusthan. I shall try to earn the wherewithal myself to the best of my might and carry out my plans, or die in the attempt. "सन्नमित्ते वरं त्यागो विनाशे नियते सति—When death is certain, it is best to sacrifice oneself for a good cause."

You may perhaps think what Utopian nonsense all this is! You little know what is in me. If any of you help me in my plans, all right, or Gurudeva will show me the way out. ... We cannot give up jealousy and rally together. That is our national sin!! It is not to be met with in this country, and this is what has made them so great.

Nowhere in the world have I come across such "frogs-in-the-well" as we are. Let anything new come from some foreign country, and America will be the first to accept it. But we?—oh, there are none like us in the world, we men of Aryan blood!! Where that heredity really expresses itself, I do not see. ...Yet they are descendants of the Aryans?

Ever yours,
Vivekananda.

42 — SIR

CHICAGO,
23rd June, 1894.

DEAR SIR, (Rao Bahadur Narasimhachariar.)

Your kindness to me makes me venture to take a little advantage of it. Mrs. Potter Palmer is the chief lady of the United States. She was the lady president of the World's Fair. She is much interested in raising the women of the world and is at the head of a big organisation for women. She is a particular friend of Lady Dufferin and has been entertained by the Royalties of Europe on account of her wealth and position. She has been very kind to me in this country. Now she is going to make a tour in China, Japan, Siam, and India. Of course she will be entertained by the Governors and other high people in India. But she is particularly anxious to see our society apart from English official aid. I have on many occasions told her about your noble efforts in raising the Indian women, of your wonderful College in Mysore. I think it is our duty to show a little hospitality to such personages from America in return for their kindness to our countrymen who came here. I hope she will find a warm reception at your hands and be helped to see a little of our women as they are. And I assure you she is no missionary, nor Christian even as to that. She wants to work apart from all religions to ameliorate the conditions of women all over the world. This would also be helping me a great deal in this country. May the Lord bless you!

Yours for ever and ever,

Affectionately,
Vivekananda.

43 — SISTERS

C/O GEORGE W. HALE, ESQ.,
541 DEARBORN AVENUE, CHICAGO,
26th June, 1894.

DEAR SISTERS, (Misses Mary and H. Hale.)

The great Hindi poet, Tulasidâsa, in his benediction to his translation of the Râmâyana, says, "I bow down to both the wicked and holy; but alas! for me, they are both equally torturers — the wicked begin to torture me as soon as they come in contact with me — the good, alas! take my life away when they leave me." I say amen to this. To me, for whom the only pleasure and love left in the world is to love the holy ones of God, it is a mortal torture to separate myself from them.

But these things must come. Thou Music of my Beloved's flute, lead on, I am following. It is impossible to express my pain, my anguish at being separated from you, noble and sweet and generous and holy ones. Oh! how I wish I had succeeded in becoming a Stoic! Hope you are enjoying the beautiful village scenery. "Where the world is awake, there the man of self-control is sleeping. Where the world sleeps, there he is waking." May even the dust of the world never touch you, for, after all the poets may say, it is only a piece of carrion covered over with garlands. Touch it not — if you can. Come up, young ones of the bird[6]* of Paradise, before your feet touch the cesspool of corruption, this world, and fly upwards.

"O those that are awake do not go to sleep again."

"Let the world love its many, we have but one Beloved — the Lord. We care not what they say; we are only afraid when they want to paint our Beloved and give Him all sorts of monstrous qualities. Let them do whatever they please — for us He is only the beloved — my love, my love, my love, and nothing more."

"Who cares to know how much power, how much quality He has — even that of doing good! We will say once for all: We love not for the long purse, we never sell our love, we want not, we give."

"You, philosopher, come to tell us of His essences His powers, His attributes — fool! We are here dying for a kiss of His lips."

"Take your nonsense back to your own home and send me a kiss of my Love — can you?"

"Fool! whom art thou bending thy tottering knees before, in awe and fear? I took my necklace and put it round His neck; and, tying a string to it as a collar, I am dragging Him along with me, for fear He may fly away even for a moment that necklace was the collar of love; that string the ecstasy of love. Fool! you know not the secret — the Infinite One comes within my fist under the bondage of love." "Knowest thou not that the Lord of the Universe is the bond slave of love?" "Knowest thou not that the Mover of the Universe used to dance to the music of the ringing bracelets of the shepherdesses of Vrindaban?"

Excuse my mad scribbling, excuse my foolery in trying to express the inexpressible. It is to be felt only.

Ever with blessings,

Your brother,
Vivekananda.

44 — SISTERS

GREENACRE INN,
ELLIOT, MAINE,
31st July, 1894.

DEAR SISTERS,

I have not written you long, and I have not much to write. This is a big inn and farm-house where the Christian Scientists are holding a session. Last spring in New York I was invited by the lady projector of the meeting to come here, and after all I am here. It is a beautiful and cool place, no doubt, and many of my old friends of Chicago are here. Mrs. Mills, Miss Stockham, and several other ladies and gentlemen live in tents which they have pitched on the open ground by the river. They have a lively time and sometimes all of them wear what you call your scientific dress the whole day. They have lectures almost every day. One Mr. Colville from Boston is here; he speaks every day, it is said, under spirit control. The Editor (?) of the Universal Truth has settled herself down here. She is conducting religious services and holding classes to heal all manner of diseases, and very soon I expect them to be giving eyes to the blind, and the like! After all, it is a queer gathering. They do not care much about social laws and are quite free and happy. Mrs. Mills is quite brilliant, and so are many other ladies. ... Another lady from Detroit — very cultured and with beautiful black eyes and long hair is going to take me to an island fifteen miles out at sea. I hope we shall have a nice time. ... I may go over to Annisquam from here, I suppose. This is a beautiful and nice place and the bathing is splendid. Cora Stockham has made a bathing dress for me, and I am having as good a time in the water as a duck this is delicious even for the denizens of mud Ville. I do not find anything more to write. Only I am so busy that I cannot find time enough to write to Mother Church separately. My love and respects to Miss Howe.

There is here Mr. Wood of Boston who is one of the great lights of your sect. But he objects to belong to the sect of Mrs. Whirlpool. So he calls himself a mental healer of metaphysico-chemico-physico-religiosio what not! Yesterday there was a tremendous cyclone which gave a good "treatment" to the tents. The big tent under which they had the lectures had developed so much spirituality, under the "treatment", that it entirely disappeared from mortal gaze, and about two hundred chairs were dancing about the grounds under spiritual ecstasy! Mrs. Figs of Mills company gives a class every morning; and Mrs. Mills is jumping all about the place; they are all in high spirits. I am especially glad for Cora, for they have suffered a good deal last winter and a little hilarity would do her good. You will be astounded with the liberty they enjoy in the camps, but they are very good and pure people there — a little erratic and that is all. I shall be here till Saturday next. ...

... The other night the camp people went to sleep beneath a pine tree under which I sit every morning a la Hindu and talk to them. Of course I went with them, and we had a nice night under the stars, sleeping on the lap of mother earth, and I enjoyed every bit of it. I cannot describe to you that night's glories — after a year of brutal life that I have led, to sleep on the ground, to meditate under the tree in the forest! The inn people are more or less well-to-do, and the camp people are healthy, young, sincere, and holy men and women. I teach them Shivo'ham, Shivo'ham, and they all repeat it, innocent and pure as they are and brave beyond all bounds. And so I am happy and glorified. Thank God for making me poor, thank God for making these children in the tents poor. The Dudes and Dudines are in the Hotel, but iron-bound nerves and souls of triple steel and spirits of fire are in the camp. If you had seen them yesterday, when the rain was falling in torrents and the cyclone was overturning everything, hanging by their tent strings to keep them from being blown down, and standing on the majesty of their souls — these brave ones — it would have done your hearts good. I will go a hundred miles to see the like of them. Lord bless them! I hope you are enjoying your nice village life. Never be anxious for a moment. I will be taken care of, and if not, I will know my time has come and shall pass out.

"Sweet One! Many people offer to You many things, I am poor — but I have the body, mind, and soul. I give them over to You. Deign to accept, Lord of the Universe, and refuse them not." — So have I given over my life and soul once for all. One thing — they are a dry sort of people here — and as to that very few in the whole world are there that are not. They do not understand "Mâdhava", the Sweet One. They are either intellectual or go after faith cure, table turning, witchcraft, etc., etc. Nowhere have I heard so much about "love, life, and liberty" as in this country, but nowhere is it less understood. Here God is either a terror or a healing power, vibration, and so forth. Lord bless their souls! And these parrots talk day and night of love and love and love!

Now, good dreams, good thoughts for you. You are good and noble. Instead of materialising the spirit, that is, dragging the spiritual to the material plane as these folks do, convert the matter into spirit, catch a glimpse at least, every day, of that world of infinite beauty and peace and purity — the spiritual, and try to live in it day and night. Seek not, touch not with your toes even, anything that is uncanny. Let your souls ascend day and night like an "unbroken string" unto the feet of the Beloved whose throne is in your own hearts and let the rest take care of themselves, that is the body and everything else. Life is evanescent, a fleeting dream; youth and beauty fade. Say day and night, "Thou art my father, my mother, my husband, my love, my lord, my God — I want nothing but Thee, nothing but Thee, nothing but Thee. Thou in me, I in Thee, I am Thee. Thou art me." Wealth goes, beauty vanishes, life flies, powers fly — but the Lord abideth for ever, love abideth for ever. If here is glory in keeping the machine in good trim, it is more glorious to withhold the soul from suffering with the body — that is the only demonstration of your being "not matter", by letting the matter alone.

Stick to God! Who cares what comes to the body or to anything else! Through the terrors of evil, say — my God, my love! Through the pangs of death, say — my God, my love! Through all the evils under the sun, say — my God, my love! Thou art here, I see Thee. Thou art with me, I feel Thee. I am Thine, take me. I am not of the world's but Thine, leave not then me. Do not go for glass beads leaving the mine of diamonds! This life is a great chance. What, seekest thou the pleasures of the world? — He is the fountain of all bliss. Seek for the highest, aim at that highest, and you shall reach the highest.

Yours with all blessings,
Vivekananda.

45 — BROTHERS

Translated from Bengali

Salutations to Bhagavan Shri Ramakrishna!

1894.

DEAR BROTHERS, (Brother-disciples of Swamiji.)

Before this I wrote to you a letter which for want of time was very incomplete. Rakhal (Brahmananda) and Hari (Turiyananda) wrote in a letter from Lucknow that Hindu newspapers were praising me, and that they were very glad that twenty thousand people had partaken of food at Shri Ramakrishna's anniversary. I could do much more work but for the Brahmos and missionaries who have been opposing me unceasingly, and the Hindus of India too did nothing for me. I mean, if the Hindus of Calcutta or Madras had held a meeting and passed a resolution recognising me as their representative, and thanking the American people for receiving me with kindness, things would have progressed appreciably. But it is over a year, and nothing done. Of course I never relied on the Bengalis, but the Madrasis couldn't do anything either. ...

There is no hope for our nation. Not one original idea crosses anyone's brains, all fighting over the same old, threadbare rug—that Ramakrishna Paramahamsa was such and such—and cock-and-bull stories—stories having neither head nor tail. My God! Won't you do something to show that you are in any way removed from the common run of men!—Only indulging in madness! ... Today you have your bell, tomorrow you add a horn, and follow suit with a chowry the day after; or you introduce a cot today, and tomorrow you have its legs silver-mounted, and people help themselves to a rice-porridge, and you spin out two thousand cock-and-bull stories—in short, nothing but external ceremonials. This is called in English imbecility. Those into whose heads nothing but that sort of silliness enters are called imbecile. Those whose heads have a tendency to be troubled day and night over such questions as whether the bell should ring on the right or on the left, whether the sandal-paste mark should be put on the head or anywhere else, whether the light should be waved twice or four times—simply deserve the name of wretches, and it is owing to that sort of notion that we are the outcasts of Fortune, kicked and spurned at, while the people of the West are masters of the whole world. ... There is an ocean of difference between idleness and renunciation.

If you want any good to come, just throw your ceremonials overboard and worship the Living God, the Man-God—every being that wears a human form—God in His universal as well as individual aspect. The universal aspect of God means this world, and worshipping it means serving it—this indeed is work, not indulging in ceremonials. Neither is it work to cogitate as to whether the rice-plate should be placed in front of the God for ten minutes or for half an hour—that is called lunacy. Millions of rupees have been spent only that the templedoors at Varanasi or Vrindaban may play at opening and shutting all day long! Now the Lord is having His toilet, now He is taking His meals, now He is busy on something else we know not what. ... And all this, while the Living God is dying for want of food, for want of education! The banias of Bombay are erecting hospitals for bugs—while they would do nothing for men even if they die! You have not the brain to understand this simple thing—that it is a plague with our country, and lunatic asylums are rife all over. ... Let some of you spread like fire, and preach this worship of the universal aspect of the Godhead—a thing that was never undertaken before in our country. No quarrelling with people, we must be friends with all. ...

Spread ideas—go from village to village, from door to door—then only there will be real work. Otherwise, lying complacently on the bed and ringing the bell now and then is a sort of disease, pure and simple. ... Be independent, learn to form independent judgments.—That such and such a chapter of such and such a Tantra has prescribed a standard length for the handle of a bell,—what matters it to me? Through the Lord's will, out of your lips shall come millions of Vedas and Tantras and Purânas. ... If now you can show this in practice, if you can make three or four hundred thousand disciples in India within a year, then only I may have some hope. ...

By the bye, you know the boy who had his head

shaven and went with Brother Tarak from Bombay to Rameswaram? He calls himself a disciple of Ramakrishna Paramahamsa! Let Brother Tarak initiate him. ... He had never even met Shri Ramakrishna in his life, and yet a disciple!—What impudence! Without an unbroken chain of discipleship—Guruparampara—nothing can be done. Is it a child's play? To have no connection whatsoever and call oneself a disciple! The idiot! If that boy refuses to go on in the right way, turn him out. Nothing, I say, can be done without the chain of discipleship, that is, the power that is transmitted from the Guru to the disciple, and from him to his disciple, and so on. Here he comes and proclaims himself a disciple of Ramakrishna—is it tomfoolery? Jagamohan told me of somebody calling himself a brother-disciple of mine. I have now a suspicion that it is that boy. To pose as a brother-disciple! He feels humiliated to call himself a disciple, I dare say, and would fain turn a Guru straightway! Turn him out if he does not follow the established procedure.

Talking of the restlessness of Tulasi (Nirmalananda) and Subodh (Subodhananda) it all means that they have got no work to do. ... Go from village to village, do good to humanity and to the world at large. Go to hell yourself to buy salvation for others. There is no Mukti on earth to call my own. Whenever you think of yourself, you are bound to feel restless. What business have you to do with peace, my boy? You have renounced everything. Come! Now is the turn for you to banish the desire for peace, and that for Mukti too! Don't worry in the least; heaven or hell, or Bhakti or Mukti—don't care for anything, but go, my boy, and spread the name of the Lord from door to door! It is only by doing good to others that one attains to one's own good, and it is by leading others to Bhakti and Mukti that one attains them oneself. Take that up, forget-your own self for it, be mad over the idea. As Shri Ramakrishna used to love you, as I love you, come, love the world like that. Bring all together. Where is Gunanidhi? You must have him with you. My infinite love to him. Where is Gupta (Sadananda)? Let him join if he likes. Call him in my name. Remember these few points:

1. We are Sannyasins, who have given up everything—Bhakti, and Mukti, and enjoyment, and all.

2. To do the highest good to the world, everyone down to the lowest—this is our vow. Welcome Mukti or hell, whichever comes of it.

3. Ramakrishna Paramahamsa came for the good of the world. Call him a man, or God, or an Incarnation, just as you please. Accept him each in your own light.

4. He who will bow before him will be converted into purest gold that very moment. Go with this message from door to door, if you can, my boy, and all your disquietude will be at an end. Never fear—where's the room for fear?—Caring for nothing whatsoever is a part of your life. You have so long spread his name and your character all around, well and good. Now spread them in an organised way. The Lord is with you. Take heart!

Whether I live or die, whether I go back to India or not, you go on spreading love, love that knows no bounds. Put Gupta too to this task. But remember one needs weapons to overcome others. "सन्नमित्ते वरं त्यागो विनाशे विनाशे नियते सति—When death is so certain, it is better to die for a good cause."

Yours affly.,

Vivekananda.

PS. Remember my previous letter—we want both men and women. There is no distinction of sex in the soul. It won't do merely to call Shri Ramakrishna an Incarnation, you must manifest power. Where are Gour-Mâ, Yogin-Mâ, and Golap-Mâ? Tell them to spread these ideas. We want thousands of men and thousands of women who will spread like wild fire from the Himalayas to Cape Comorin, from the North Pole to the South Pole—all over the world. It is no use indulging in child's play—neither is there time for it. Let those who have come for child's play be off now, while there is time, or they will surely come to grief. We want an organisation. Off with laziness. Spread! Spread! Run like fire to all places. Do not depend upon me. Whether I live or die, go on spreading, yourselves.

46 — MOTHER SARA

Translated from Bengali

Salutations to Bhagavan Shri Ramakrishna!

HOTEL BELLE VUE,
BEACON STREET, BOSTON,
19th September, '94.

DEAR MOTHER SARA, (Mrs. Ole Bull)

I did not forget you at all. You do not think I will be ever as ungrateful as that! You did not give me your address, still I have been getting news about you from Landsberg through Miss Phillips. Perhaps you have seen the memorial and address sent to me from Madras. I sent some to be sent to you at Landsberg's.

A Hindu son never lends to his mother, but the mother has every right over the son and so the son in the mother. I am very much offended at your offering to repay me the nasty few dollars. I can never repay my debts to you.

I am at present lecturing in several places in Boston. What I want is to get a place where I can sit down and write down my thoughts. I have had enough of speaking; now I want to write. I think I will have to go to New York for it. Mrs. Guernsey was so kind to me, and she is ever willing to help me. I think I will go to her and sit down and write my book.

Yours ever affectionately,
Vivekananda.

PS. Kindly write me whether the Guernseys have returned to town or are still in Fishkill. — V.

47 — BROTHER DISCIPLES

Translated from Bengali

NEW YORK,
25th September, 1894.

MY DEAR—, (Meant for his brother-disciples)

Glad to receive some letters from you. It gives me great pleasure to learn that Shashi and others are making a stir. We must create a stir, nothing short of this will do. You will be throwing the whole world into convulsion. Victory to the Guru! You know, "श्रेयांसि बहुविघ्नानि—Great undertakings are always fraught with many obstacles." It is these obstacles which knock and shape great characters. ... Is it in the power of missionaries and people of that sort to withstand this shock? ... Should a fool succeed where scholars have failed? It is no go, my boy, set your mind at ease about that. In every attempt there will be one set of men who will applaud, and another who will pick holes. Go on doing your own work, what need have you to reply to any party? "सत्यमेत्र जयते नानृतं सत्येन पन्था वितितो देवयानः—Truth alone triumphs, not falsehood. Through Truth lies Devayâna, the path of gods" (Mundaka, III. i. 6). Everything will come about by degrees.

Here in summer they go to the seaside: I also did the same. They have got almost a mania for boating and yachting. The yacht is a kind of light vessel which everyone, young and old, who has the means, possesses. They set sail in them every day to the sea, and return home, to eat and drink and dance—while music continues day and night. Pianos render it a botheration to stay indoors!

I shall now tell you something of the Hales to whose address you direct my letters. He and his wife are an old couple, having two daughters, two nieces, and a son. The son lives abroad where he earns a living. The daughters live at home. In this country, relationship is through the girls. The son marries and no longer belongs to the family, but the daughter's husband pays frequent visits to his father-in-law's house. They say,

"Son is son till he gets a wife;

The daughter is daughter all her life."

All the four are young and not yet married. Marriage is a very troublesome business here. In the first place, one must have a husband after one's heart. Secondly, he must be a moneyed man. ... They will probably live unmarried; besides, they are now full of renunciation through my contact and are busy with thoughts of Brahman!

The two daughters are blondes, that is, have golden hair, while the two nieces are brunettes, that is, of dark hair. They know all sorts of occupations. The nieces are not so rich, they conduct a kindergarten school; but the daughters do not earn. Many girls of this country earn their living. Nobody depends upon others. Even millionaires' sons earn their living; but they marry and have separate establishments of their own. The daughters call me brother; and I address their mother as mother. All my things are at their place; and they look after them, wherever I may go. Here the boys go in search of a living while quite young; and the girls are educated in the universities. So you will find that in a meeting there will be ninety-nine per cent of girls. The boys are nowhere in comparison with them.

There are a good many spiritualists in this country. The medium is one who induces the spirit. He goes behind a screen; and out of this come ghosts of all sizes and all colours. I have witnessed some cases; but they seemed to be a hoax. I shall test some more before I come to a final conclusion. Many of the spiritualists respect me.

Next comes Christian Science. They form the most influential party, nowadays, figuring everywhere. They are spreading by leaps and bounds, and causing heart-burn to the orthodox. They are Vedantins; I mean, they have picked up a few doctrines of the Advaita and grafted them upon the Bible. And they cure diseases by proclaiming "So'ham So'ham"—"I am He! I am He!"—through strength of mind. They all admire me highly.

Nowadays the orthodox section of this country are crying for help. "Devil worship"[1] is but a thing of the past. They are mortally afraid of me and exclaim, "What a pest? Thousands of men and women follow him! He is going to root out orthodoxy!" Well, the torch has been applied and the conflagration that has set in through the grace of the Guru will not be put out. In course of time the bigots will have their breath knocked out of them. ...

The Theosophists have not much power. But they, too, are dead set against the orthodox section.

The Christian Science is exactly like our Kartâbhajâ[2]

---

1. The Orthodox Christians brand Hindus and people of other religions with this name and look upon them with scorn.

2. An offshoot of degenerate Vaishnavism, calling God "Kartâ" or Master, and noted for efficiency in faith-cure.

sect: Say, "I have no disease", and you are whole; and say, "I am He"—"So'ham"—and you are quits—be at large. This is a thoroughly materialistic country. The people of this Christian land will recognise religion if only you can cure diseases, work miracles, and open up avenues to money; and they understand little of anything else. But there are honourable exceptions. ...

People here have found a new type of man in me. Even the orthodox are at their wit's end. And people are now looking up to me with an eye of reverence. Is there a greater strength than that of Brahmacharya—purity, my boy?

I am now busy writing a reply to the Madras Address, which was published in all the newspapers here and created a sensation. If it be cheap, I shall send it in print, but if dear, I shall send a type-written copy. To you also I shall send a copy; have it published in the Indian Mirror. The unmarried girls of this country are very good and have a good deal of self-respect. . . . These (the people) are come of Virochana's[3] race. To them ministering to the body is a great thing: they would trim and polish and give their whole attention to that. A thousand instruments for paring nails, ten thousand for hair-cutting, and who can count the varieties of dress and toilet and perfumery? . . . They are good-natured, kind, and truthful. All is right with them, but that enjoyment is their God. It is a country where money flows like a river, with beauty as its ripple and learning its waves, and which rolls in luxury.

कांक्षन्तः कर्मणां सिद्धिं यजन्त इह देवताः।
क्षिप्रं हि मानुषे लोके सिद्धिर्भवति कर्मजा॥

—"Longing for success in action, in this world, (men) worship the deities. For success is quickly attained through action in this world of Man." (Gita, IV.12)

Here you have a wonderful manifestation of grit and power—what strength, what practicality, and what manhood! Horses huge as elephants are drawing carriages that are as big as houses. You may take this as a specimen of the gigantic proportions in other things also. Here is a manifestation of tremendous energy. ...

---

3. The King of the Asuras and son of the saintly Prahlâda. He went to Brahma for Self-knowledge, but misunderstanding His teaching turned a materialist. (Chhândogya Upa., VIII).

They look with veneration upon women, who play a most prominent part in their lives. Here this form of worship has attained its perfection—that is the long and the short of it. But to come to the point. Well, I am almost at my wit's end to see the women of this country! They take me to the shops and everywhere, Is if I were a child. They do all sorts of work—I cannot do even a sixteenth part of what they do. They are like Lakshmi (the Goddess of Fortune) in beauty, and like Sarasvati (the Goddess of Learning) in virtues—they are the Divine Mother incarnate and worshipping them, one verily attains perfection in everything. Great God! Are we to be counted among men? If I can raise a thousand such Madonnas, Incarnations of the Divine Mother, in our country before I die, I shall die in peace. Then only will your countrymen become worthy of their name. . . .

I am really struck with wonder to see the women here. How gracious the Divine Mother is on them! Most wonderful women, these! They are about to corner the men, who have been nearly worsted in the competition. It is all through Thy grace, O Mother! ... I shall not rest till I root out this distinction of sex. Is there any sex-distinction in the Atman (Self)? Out with the differentiation between man and woman—all is Atman! Give up the identification with the body, and stand up! Say, "Asti, Asti"—"Everything is!"—cherish positive thoughts. By dwelling too much upon "Nâsti, Nâsti"—"It is not! It is not!" (negativism), the whole country is going to ruin! "So'ham, So'ham, Shivo'ham"—"I am He! I am He! I am Shiva!" What a botheration! In every soul is infinite strength; and should you turn yourselves into cats and dogs by harbouring negative thoughts? Who dares to preach negativism? Whom do you call weak and powerless? "Shivo'ham, Shivo'ham"—"I am Shiva! I am Shiva!" I feel as if a thunderbolt strikes me on the head when I hear people dwell on negative thoughts. That sort of self-depreciating attitude is another name for disease—do you call that humility? It is vanity in disguise! "न लिङ्गम् धर्मकारणं, समता सर्वभूतेषु एतन्मुक्तस्य लक्षणम्—The external badge does not confer spirituality. It is same-sightedness to all beings which is the test of a liberated soul." "अस्ति अस्ति" (It is, It is), "सोऽहं सोऽहं", "चिदानन्दरूपः शिवोऽहं शिवोऽहं"—"I am He!", "I am Shiva, of the essence of Knowledge and Bliss!" "निर्गच्छति जगज्जालात् पञ्जिरादिव केशरी—He frees himself from the meshes of this world as a lion from its cage!" "नायमात्मा बलहीनेन लभ्यः— This Atman is not accessible to the weak". . . . Hurl yourselves on the world like an avalanche—let the world crack in twain under your weight! Hara! Hara! Mahâdeva! उद्धरेदात्मनात्मानम्—One must save the self by one's own self"—by personal prowess.

. . . Will such a day come when this life will go for the sake of other's good? The world is not a child's play—and great men are those who build highways for others with their heart's blood. This has been taking place through eternity, that one builds a bridge by laying down his own body and thousands of others cross the river through its help. "एवमस्तु, एवमस्तु, शिवोऽहं शिवोऽहं— Be it so! Be it so! I am Shiva! I am Shiva!"

It is welcome news that Madras is in a stir.

Were you not going to start a paper or something of that sort, what about that? We must mix with all, and alienate none. All the powers of good against all the powers of evil—this is what we want. Do not insist upon everybody's believing in our Guru. . . . You shall have to edit a magazine, half Bengali and half Hindi—and if possible, another in English . . . . It won't do to be roaming aimlessly. Wherever you go, you must start a permanent preaching centre. Then only will people begin to change. I am writing a book. As soon as it is finished, I run for home! . . . Always remember that Shri Ramakrishna came for the good of the world—not for name or fame. Spread only what he came to teach. Never mind his flame—it will spread of itself. Directly you insist on everybody's accepting your Guru, you will be creating a sect, and everything will fall to the ground—so beware! Have a kind word for all—it spoils work to show temper. Let people say whatever they like, stick to your own convictions, and rest assured, the world will be at your feet. They say, "Have faith in this fellow or that fellow", but I say, "Have faith in yourself first", that's the way. Have faith in yourself—all power is in you—be conscious and bring it out. Say, "I can do everything." "Even the poison of a snake is powerless if you can firmly deny it." Beware! No saying "nay", no negative thoughts! Say, "Yea, Yea," "So'ham, So'ham"—"I am He! I am He!"

किंनाम रोदिषि सखे त्वयि सर्वशक्तिरामन्त्रयस्व भगवन् भगदं स्वरूपम्।
त्रैलोक्यमेतदखिलं तव पादमूले आत्मैव हि प्रभवते न जडं कदाचित्॥

—"What makes you weep, my friend? In you is all power. Summon up your all-powerful nature, O mighty one, and this whole universe will lie at your feet. It is the Self alone that predominates, and not matter."

To work, with undaunted energy! What fear! Who is powerful enough to thwart you!" कुर्मस्तारकचर्वणं तर्भुवनमुत्पाटयामो बलात्, किं भो न विज्ञानास्यस्मान् रामकृष्णदासा वयम्— We shall crush the stars to atoms, and unhinge the universe. Don't you know who we are? We are the servants of Shri Ramakrishna." Fear?

Whom to fear, forsooth?

क्षीणाः स्म दीनाः सकरुणा जल्पन्ति मूढा जना
नास्तिक्यन्तवदिन्तु अहह देहात्मवादातुराः।
प्रातः स्म वीरा गतभया अभयं प्रतिष्ठिता यदा
अस्तिक्यन्तवदिन्तु चनिमः रामकृष्णदासा वयम्॥
पीत्वा पीत्वा परममृतं वीतसंसाररागाः
हित्वा हित्वा सकलकलहप्रापणीं स्वार्थसिद्धिम्।
ध्यात्वा ध्यात्वा गुरुवरपदं सर्वकल्याणरूपम्
नत्वा नत्वा सकलभुवनं पातुमामन्त्रयामः॥
प्राप्तं यद्वै त्वनादिनिधनं वेदोदधिं मथित्वा
दत्तं यस्य प्रकरणे हरिहरब्रह्मादिदेवैर्बलम्।
पूर्णं यत्तु प्राणसारैर्भौमनारायणानां
रामकृष्णास्तनुं धत्ते तत्पूर्णपात्रमिदं भोः॥

—"It is those foolish people who identify themselves with their bodies, that piteously cry, 'We are weak, we are low.' All this is atheism. Now that we have attained the state beyond fear, we shall have no more fear and become heroes. This indeed is theism which we, the servants of Shri Ramakrishna, will choose.

"Giving up the attachment for the world and drinking constantly the supreme nectar of immortality, for ever discarding that self-seeking spirit which is the mother of all dissension, and ever meditating on the blessed feet of our Guru which are the embodiment of all well-being, with repeated salutations we invite the whole world to participate in drinking the nectar.

"That nectar which has been obtained by churning the infinite ocean of the Vedas, into which Brahmâ, Vishnu, Shiva, and the other gods have poured their strength, which is charged with the life-essence of the Avataras—Gods Incarnate on earth—Shri Ramakrishna holds that nectar in his person, in its fullest measure!"

We must work among the English educated young men. "त्यागेनैके अमृतत्वमानशुः—Through renunciation alone some (rare ones) attained immortality." Renunciation!—Renunciation!—you must preach this above everything else. There will be no spiritual strength unless one renounces the world....

Why are Baburam and Yogen suffering so much? It is owing to their negative, their self-abasing spirit. Tell them to brush aside their illness by mental strength, and in an hour it will disappear! I the Atman smitten with disease! Off with it! Tell them to meditate for an hour at a stretch, "I am the Atman, how can I be affected by disease!"—and everything will vanish. Think all of you that you are the infinitely powerful Atman, and see what strength comes out. . . . Self-depreciation! What is it for? I am the child of the Infinite, the all-powerful Divine Mother. What means disease, or fear, or want to me? Stamp out the negative spirit as if it were a pestilence, and it will conduce to your welfare in every way. No negative, all positive, affirmative. I am, God is, everything is in me. I will manifest health, purity, knowledge, whatever I want. Well, these foreign people could grasp my teachings, and you are suffering from illness owing to your negative spirit! Who says you are ill—what is disease to you? Brush it aside! वीर्यमसि वीर्य मयि धेहि, बलमसि बलं मयि धेहि, ओजोऽसि ओजो मयि धेहि, सहोऽसि सहो मयि धेहि—Thou art Energy, impart energy unto me. Thou art Strength, impart strength unto me. Thou art Spirituality, impart spirituality unto me. Thou art Fortitude, impart fortitude unto me!" The ceremony of steadying the seat (Âsana-pratishthâ) that you perform every day when you sit down to worship the Lord—"आत्मानमच्छिद्रं भावयेत्—One must think of oneself as strong and invulnerable," and so forth—what does it all mean? Say, "Everything is in me, and I can manifest it at will." Repeat to yourself that such and such are Atman, that they are infinite, and how can they have any disease? Repeat this an hour or so, on a few successive days, and all disease and trouble will vanish into nought.

Yours ever,
Vivekananda.

48 — MRS. BULL

Translated from Bengali

BOSTON,
26th Sept., 1894.

DEAR MRS. BULL,

I have received both of your kind notes. I will have to go back to Melrose on Saturday and remain there till Monday. On Tuesday I will come over to your place. But I have forgotten the exact location. If you kindly write me that, I cannot express my gratitude for your kindness. For that is exactly what I wanted, a quiet place to write. Of course, much less space will suffice me than what you have kindly proposed to put at my disposal, I can bundle myself up anywhere and feel quite comfortable.

Yours very sincerely,
Vivekananda.

49 — SWAMI RAMAKRISNANANDA

Translated from Bengali

BALTIMORE, U.S.A.,
22nd October, 1894.

DEAR—, (Swami Ramakrishnananda)

Glad to receive your letter and go through the contents. I received today a letter of Akshay Kumar Ghosh from London, which also gives me some information. . . .

Now you have come to know your own powers. Strike the iron while it is hot. Idleness won't do. Throw overboard all idea of jealousy and egotism, once for all. Come on to the practical field with tremendous energy; to work, in the fullness of strength! As to the rest, the Lord will point out the way. The whole world will be deluged by a tidal wave. Work, work, work — let this be your motto. I cannot see anything else. There is no end of work here — I am careering all over the country. Wherever the seed of his power will find its way, there it will fructify — आद्य वा अब्दशतान्ते वा—be it today, or in a hundred years." You must work in sympathy with all, then only it will lead to quick results . . . .

Our object is to do good to the world, and not the trumpeting of our own names. Why doesn't Niranjan (Niranjanananda) learn Pali in Ceylon, and study Buddhist books? I cannot make out what good will come of aimless rambling. Those that have come under his protection, have virtue, wealth, desires, and freedom lying at their feet. मा भैः मा भैः— Courage! Everything will come about by degrees. From all of you I want this that you must discard for ever self-aggrandisement, faction-mongering, and jealousy. You must be all-forbearing, like Mother Earth. If you can achieve this, the world will be at your feet. . . .

Try to give less of material food in the anniversary celebrations, and give some food for the brain instead. . . .

Yours affectionately,
Vivekananda.

50 — MRS. BULL

C/O MRS. E. TOTTEN,
1708, 1ST STREET, WASHINGTON, D.C.,
27th Oct., 1894.

DEAR MRS. BULL,

Many thanks for your kindness in sending me the introduction to Mr. Frederic Douglas. You need not be sorry on account of the ill-treatment I received at the hands of a low class hotel-keeper at Baltimore. It was the fault of the Vrooman brothers. Why should they take me to a low hotel?

And then the American women, as everywhere,

came to my rescue, and I had a very good time.

In Washington I am the guest of Mrs. E. Totten who is an influential lady here and a metaphysician. She is moreover the niece of one of my Chicago friends. So everything is going on all right. I also saw Mrs. Colville and Miss Young here.

With my eternal love and gratitude for you,

I remain,

Yours etc.,
Vivekananda.

51 — DEAR AND BELOVED

U.S.A.,
30th November, 1894.

DEAR AND BELOVED, (Dr. Nanjunda Rao)

Your beautiful letter just came to hand. I am so glad that you have come to know Shri Ramakrishna. I am very glad at the strength of your Vairâgya. It is the one primary necessity in reaching God. I had always great hopes for Madras, and still I have the firm belief that from Madras will come the spiritual wave that will deluge India. I can only say Godspeed to your good intentions; but here, my son, are the difficulties. In the first place, no man ought to take a hasty step. In the second place, you must have some respect for the feelings of your mother and wife. True, you may say that we, the disciples of Ramakrishna, had not always shown great deference to the opinions of our parents. I know, and know for sure, that great things are done only by great sacrifices. I know for certain that India requires the sacrifice of her highest and best, and I sincerely hope that it will be your good fortune to be one of them.

Throughout the history of the world you find great men make great sacrifices and the mass of mankind enjoy the benefit. If you want to give up everything for your own salvation, it is nothing. Do you want to forgo even your own salvation for the good of the world? You are God, think of that. My advice to you is to live the life of a Brahmacharin, i.e. giving up all sexual enjoyments for a certain time live in the house of your father; this is the "Kutichaka" stage. Try to bring your wife to consent to your great sacrifice for the good of the world. And if you have burning faith and all-conquering love and almighty purity, I do not doubt that you will shortly succeed. Give yourself body and soul to the work of spreading the teachings of Shri Ramakrishna, for work (Karma) is the first stage. Study Sanskrit diligently as well as practice devotion. For you are to be a great teacher of mankind, and my Guru Maharaja used to say, "A penknife is sufficient to commit suicide with, but to kill others one requires guns and swords." And in the fullness of time it will be given unto you when to go forth out of the world and preach His sacred name. Your determination is holy and good. Godspeed to you, but do not take any hasty step. First purify yourself by work and devotion India has suffered long, the Religion Eternal has suffered long. But the Lord is merciful. Once more He has come to help His children, once more the opportunity is given to rise to fallen India. India can only rise by sitting at the feet of Shri Ramakrishna. His life and his teachings are to be spread far and wide, are to be made to penetrate every pore of Hindu society. Who will do it? Who are to take up the flag of Ramakrishna and march for the salvation of the world? Who are to stem the tide of degeneration at the sacrifice of name and fame, wealth and enjoyment — nay of every hope of this or other worlds? A few young men have jumped in the breach, have sacrificed themselves. They are a few; we want a few thousands of such as they, and they will come. I am glad that our Lord has put it in your mind to be one of them Glory unto him on whom falls the Lord's choice. Your determination is good, your hopes are high, your aim is the noblest in the world — to bring millions sunk in darkness to the light of the Lord.

But, my son, here are the drawbacks. Nothing shall be done in haste. Purity, patience, and perseverance are the three essentials to success and, above all, love. All time is yours, there is no indecent haste. Everything will come right if you are pure and sincere. We want hundreds like you bursting upon society and bringing new life and vigour of the Spirit wherever they go. Godspeed to you.

Yours with all blessings,
Vivekananda.

52 — GOVINDA SAHAY

C/O G. W. HALE, ESQ.,
CHICAGO, U.S.A.,

DEAR GOVINDA SAHAY,

Do you keep any correspondence with my Gurubhâis of Calcutta? Are you progressing morally, spiritually, and in your worldly affairs? . . . Perhaps you have heard how for more than a year I have been preaching Hindu religion in America. I am doing very well here. Write to me as soon as you can and as often as you like.

Yours with love,
Vivekananda.

53 — GOVINDA SAHAY

U.S.A.,
1894.

DEAR GOVINDA SAHAY,

. . . Honesty is the best policy, and a virtuous man must gain in the end. . . . You must always bear in mind, my son, that however busy or however distant, or living with men however high in position I may be, I am always praying, blessing, and remembering everyone of my friends, even the humblest.

Yours, with blessings,
Vivekananda.

54 — SWAMI RAMAKRISHNANDA

Translated from Bengali

C/O GEORGE W. HALE, ESQ.,
541 DEARBORN AVENUE, CHICAGO,

(Beginning of?) 1894.

My Dear—, (Swami Ramakrishnananda)

Very glad to receive your letter. I am very sorry to hear of Mazoomdar's doings. One always behaves thus in trying to push oneself before all others. I am not much to blame. M— came here ten years ago, and got much reputation and honour; now I am in flying colours. Such is the will of the Guru, what shall I do? It is childishness on M—'s part to be annoyed at this. Never mind, उपेक्षितव्यं तद्वचनं भवत्सदृष्टानां महात्मनाम्। अपि कीटदंशनभीरुका वयं रामकृष्ण तनयस्तद्दृहृदयरुधिरपोषिताः। "अलोकसामान्यमचिन्त्यहेतुकं हनिन्दन्ति मन्दाश्चरितं महात्मनाम्" — Great men like you should pay no heed to what he says. Shall we, children of Shri Ramakrishna, nourished with his heart's blood, be afraid of worm-bites? "The wicked criticise the conduct of the magnanimous, which is extraordinary and whose motives are difficult to fathom" (Kalidasa's Kumârasambhavam.) — remember all this and forgive this fool. It is the will of the Lord that people of this land have their power of introspection roused, and does it lie in anybody to check His progress? I want no name — I want to be a voice without a form. I do not require anybody to defend me —

— who am I to check or to help the course of His march? And who are others also? Still, my heartfelt gratitude to them.

— "Established in which state a man is not moved even by great misfortune" (Gita) — that state he has not reached; think of this and look upon him with pity. Through the Lord's will, the desire for name and fame has not yet crept into my heart, and I dare say never will. I am an instrument, and He is the operator. Through this instrument He is rousing the religious instinct in thousands of hearts in this far-off country. Thousands of men and women here love and revere me. . . . "

the lame cross mountains." I am amazed at His grace. Whichever town I visit, it is in an uproar. They have named me "the cyclonic Hindu". Remember, it is His will — I am a voice without a form.

The Lord knows whether I shall go to England or any other blessed place. He will arrange everything. Here a cigar costs one rupee. Once you get into a cab, you have to pay three rupees, a coat costs a hundred rupees; the hotel charge is nine rupees a day. The Lord provides everything. . . . The Lord be praised, I know nothing. "— Truth alone triumphs, not falsehood. Through Truth alone lies the path of Devayâna." You must be fearless. It is the coward who fears and defends himself. Let no one amongst us come forward to defend me. I get all news of Madras and Rajputana from time to time. . . . There are eyes that can see at a distance of fourteen thousand miles. It is quite true. Keep quiet now, everything will see the light in time, as far as He wills it. Not one word of His proves untrue. My brother, do men grieve over the fight of cats and dogs? So the jealousy, envy, and elbowing of common men should make no impression on your mind. For the last six months I have been saying, the curtain is going up, the sun is rising. Yes, the curtain is lifting by degrees, slow but sure; you will come to know it in time. He knows. One cannot speak out one's mind. These are things not for writing. . . . Never let go your hold of the rudder, grasp it firm. We are steering all right, no mistaking that, but landing on the other shore is only a question of time. That's all. Can a leader be made my brother? A leader is born. Do you understand? And it is a very difficult task to take on the role of a leader. — One must be accommodate a thousand minds. There must not be a shade of jealousy or selfishness, then you are a leader. First, by birth, and secondly, unselfish — that's a leader. Everything is going all right, everything will come round. He casts the net all right, and winds it up likewise best instrument. Love conquers in the long run. It won't do to become impatient — wait, wait — patience is bound to give success. . . .

I tell you brother, let everything go on as it is, only take care that no form becomes necessary — unity in variety — see that universality be not hampered in the least. Everything must be sacrificed, if necessary, for that one sentiment, universality. Whether I live or die, whether I go back to India or not, remember this specially, that universality — perfect acceptance, not tolerance only — we preach and perform. Take care how you trample on the least rights of others. Many a huge ship has foundered in that whirlpool. Remember, perfect devotion minus its bigotry — this is what we have got to show. Through His grace everything will go all right. . . . Everybody wants to be a leader, but it is the failure to grasp that he is born, that causes all this mischief. ...

Our matrons are all hale and hearty, I hope? Where is Gour-Mâ? We want a thousand such Mothers with that noble stirring spirit. ... We want all. It is not at all necessary that all should have the same faith in our Lord as we have, but we want to unite all the powers of goodness against all the powers of evil. ... A besetting sin with Sannyasins is the taking pride in their monastic order. That may have its utility during the first stages, but when they are full-grown, they need it no more. One must make no distinction between householders and Sannyasins — then only one is a true Sannyasin. . . .

A movement which half a dozen penniless boys set on foot and which now bids fair to progress in such an accelerated motion — is it a humbug or the Lord's will? If it is, then let all give up party-spirit and jealousy, and unite in action. A universal religion cannot be set up through party faction. . . .

If all understand one day for one minute that one cannot become great by the mere wish, that he only rises whom He raises, and he falls whom He brings down then all trouble is at an end. But there is that egotism — hollow in itself, and without the power to move a finger: how ludicrous of it to say, "I won't let anyone rise!" That jealousy, that absence of conjoint action is the very nature of enslaved nations. But we must try to shake it off. The terrible jealousy is characteristic of us. . . . You will be convinced of this if you visit some other countries. Our fellows in this respect are the enfranchised negroes of this country — if but one amongst them rises to greatness, all the others would at once set themselves against him and try to level him down by making a common cause with the whites. . . .

At any cost, any price, any sacrifice, we must never allow that to creep in among ourselves. Whether we be ten or two, do not care, but those few must be perfect characters. . . . "It is not good to ask of one's father if the Lord keeps His promise (to look after His devotees)." And the Lord will do so, get your minds easy on that score. . . . We must spread his name in Rajputana, Punjab, U.P., Madras, and such other provinces — yes, in Rajputana, where still there are people who can say, "Such has ever been the custom with Raghu's line that they keep their word even at the cost of life."

A bird, in the course of its flight, reaches a spot whence it looks on the ground below with supreme calmness, Have you reached that spot? He who has not reached there has no right to teach others. Relax your limbs and float with the current, and you are sure to reach your destination.

Cold is making itself scarce by degrees, and I have been almost through the winter. Here in winter the whole body becomes charged with electricity. In shaking hands one feels a shock, accompanied by a sound. You can light the gas with your finger. And about the cold I have written to you already. I am coursing through the length and breadth of the country, but Chicago is my "Math" (monastery), where I always return after my wanderings. I am now making for the east. He knows where the bark will reach the shore. . . .

Has Dashu the same sort of love for you. Does he see you frequently? How is Bhavanath, and what is he doing. Do you visit him, and look upon him with an eye of regard? Yes, brother, the distinction between Sannyasin and layman is a fiction, etc. — "He makes the dumb fluent," etc. My friend it is difficult to judge what is in a particular individual. Shri Ramakrishna has spoken highly of him; and he deserves our respect. Fie upon you if you have no faith even after so much experience. Does he love you? Please convey to him my hearty love and esteem. My love to Kalikrishna Babu, he is a very noble soul. How is Ramlal (Nephew of Shri Ramakrishna.)? He has got a little faith and devotion? My love and greetings to him. Sanyal is moving all right with the mill, I suppose? Ask him to have patience, and the mill will go on all right.

My heart's love to all.

Ever yours in love,
Vivekananda.

55 — AKHANDANANDA

Translated from Bengali

Salutation to Bhagavan Ramakrishna!

(March or April?) 1894.

MY DEAR AKHANDANANDA,

I am very glad to receive your letter. It is a great pleasure to me to learn that you have regained your health to a great extent by your stay at Khetri.

Brother Tarak (Shivananda) has done a good deal of work in Madras. Very agreeable news indeed! I heard much praise of him from the people of Madras. . . .

Try to develop spirituality and philanthropy amongst the Thakurs in the different places of Rajputana. We must work, and this cannot be done by merely sitting idle. Make a trip now and then to Malsisar, Alsisar, and all the other "sars" that are there. And carefully learn Sanskrit and English. Gunanidhi is in the Punjab, I presume. Convey my special love to him and bring him to Khetri. Learn Sanskrit with his help, and teach him English. Let me have his address by all means. ...

Go from door to door amongst the poor and lower classes of the town of Khetri and teach them religion. Also, let them have oral lessons on geography and such other subjects. No good will come of sitting idle and having princely dishes, and saying "Ramakrishna, O Lord!" — unless you can do some good to the poor. Go to other villages from time to time, and teach the people the arts of life as well as religion. Work, worship, and Jnana (knowledge) — first work, and your mind will be purified; otherwise everything will be fruitless like pouring oblations on a pile of ashes instead of in the sacred fire. When Gunanidhi comes, move from door to door of the poor and the destitute in every village of Rajputana. If people object to the kind of food you take, give it up immediately. It is preferable to live on grass for the sake of doing good to others. The Gerua robe is not for enjoyment. It is the banner of heroic work. You must give your body, mind, and speech to "the welfare of the world". You have read— "मातृदेवो भव, पितृदेवो भव — Look upon your mother as God, look upon your father as God" — but I say "दरिद्रदेवो भव, मूर्खदेवो भव — The poor, the illiterate, the ignorant, the afflicted — let these be your God." Know that service to these alone is the highest religion.

Ever yours, with blessings,
Vivekananda.

56 — DEAR AND BELOVED

Translated from Bengali

Salutation to Bhagavan Ramakrishna!

(Summer?) 1894.

DEAR AND BELOVED, (The brother-disciples at Alambazar monastery)

Your letter gives me all the news over there. I am grieved to hear of the bereavement Balaram Babu's wife has sustained. Such is the Lord's will. This is a place for action, not enjoyment, and everyone will go home when his task is done — some earlier, and some later, that is all. Fakir has gone — well, such is the will of the Lord!

It is a welcome news that Shri Ramakrishna's festival has come off with great éclat; the more his name is spread, the better it is. But there is one thing to know: Great sages come with special messages for the world, and not for name; but their followers throw their teachings overboard and fight over their names — this is verily the history of the world. I do not take into any consideration whether people accept his name or not, but I am ready to lay down my life to help his teachings, his life, and his message spread all over the world. What I am most afraid of is the worship-room. It is not bad in itself, but there is a tendency in some to make this all in all and set up that old-fashioned nonsense over again — this is what makes me nervous. I know why they busy themselves with those old, effete ceremonials. Their spirit craves for work, but having no outlet they waste their energy in ringing bells and all that.

I am giving you a new idea. If you can work it out, then I shall know you are men and will be of service. . . . Make an organised plan. A few cameras, some maps, globes, and some chemicals, etc., are needed. The next thing you want is a big hut. Then you must get together a number of poor, indigent folk. Having done all this, show them pictures to teach them astronomy, geography, etc., and preach Shri Ramakrishna to them. Try to have their eyes opened as to what has taken place or is taking place in different countries, what this world is like and, so forth. You have got lots of poor and ignorant folk there. Go to their cottages, from door to door, in the evening, at noon, any time and open their eyes. Books etc., won't do — give them oral teaching. Then slowly extend your centres. Can you do all this? Or only bell-ringing?

I have heard everything about Brother Tarak from Madras. They are highly pleased with him. Dear Brother Tarak, if you go to Madras and live there for some time, a lot of work will be done. But before you go, start this work there first. Can't the lady devotees convert some widows; into disciples? And can't you put a bit of learning into their heads? And can't you then send them out to preach Sari Ramakrishna from door to door, and impart education along with it? . . .

Come! Apply yourselves heart and soul to it. The day of gossip and ceremonials is gone, my boy, you must work now. Now, let me see how far a Bengali's religion will go. Niranjan writes that Latu (Adbhutananda) wants some warm clothing. The people here import winter clothing from Europe and India. You will get a woollen wrap in Calcutta at one-fourth of the price at which I might buy it here. . . . I don't know when I shall go to Europe, everything is uncertain with me — I am getting on somehow in this country, that is all.

This is a very funny country. It is now summer; this morning it was as hot as April in Bengal, but now it is as cold as February at Allahabad! So much fluctuation within four hours! The hotels of this country beggar description. For instance there is a hotel in New York where a room can be hired for up to Rs. 5,000 a day, excluding boarding charges. Not even in Europe is there a country like this in point of luxury. It is indeed the richest country in the world, where money is drained off like water. I seldom live in hotels, but am mostly the guest of big people here. To them I am a widely known man. The whole country knows me now; so wherever I go they receive me with open arms into their homes. Mr. Hale's home is my centre in Chicago. I call his wife mother, and his daughters call me brother. I scarcely find a family so highly pure and kind. Or why should God shower His blessings on them in such abundance, my brother? Oh, how wonderfully kind they are! If they chance to learn that a poor man is in a strait at such and such a place, there they will go ladies and gentlemen, to give him food and clothing and find him some job! And what do we do!

In summer they leave their homes to go to foreign lands, or to the seaside. I, too, shall go somewhere, but have not yet fixed a place. In other points, they are just as you see Englishmen. They have got books and things of that sort, but very dear. You can have five times those things In Calcutta for the same price. In other words, these people will not let foreign goods be imported into the country. They set a heavy tax on them, and as a result, the market goes up enormously. Besides, they are not much in the way of manufacturing clothing etc. They construct tools and machinery, and grow wheat, rice, cotton, etc., which are fairly cheap.

By the bye, nowadays we have plenty of Hilsâ fish here. Eat your fill, but everything digests. There are many kinds of fruits; plantain, lemon, guava, apple, almond, raisin, and grape are in abundance; besides many other fruits come from California. There are plenty of pineapples but there are no mangoes or lichis, or things of that sort.

There is a kind of spinach, which, when cooked, tastes just like our Noté of Bengal, and another class, which they call asparagus, tastes exactly like the tender Dengo herb, but you can't have our Charchari made of it here. There is no Kalâi or any other pulse; they do not even know of them. There is rice, and bread, and numerous varieties of fish and meat, of all descriptions. Their menu is like that of the French. There is your milk, rarely curd, but plenty of whey. Cream is an article of everyday use. In tea and coffee and everything there is that cream — not the hardened crust of boiled milk, mind you — and there is your butter, too, and ice-water — no matter whether it is summer or winter, day or night, whether you have got a bad cold or fever — you have ice-water in abundance. These are scientific people and laugh when they are told that ice-water aggravates cold. The more you take, the better. And there is plenty of ice-cream, of all sorts of shapes. I have seen the Niagara Falls seven or eight times, the Lord be praised! Very grand no doubt, but not quite as you have heard them spoken of. One day, in winter, we had the aurora borealis.

. . . Only childish prattle! I have not much time to listen to that sort of thing in this life; it will be time enough to see if I can do that in the next. Yogen has completely rallied by this time, I hope? The vagabond spirit of Sarada (Trigunâtita) is not yet at an end, I see. What is wanted is a power of organisation — do you understand me? Have any of you got that much brain in your head? If you do, let your mind work. Brother Tarak, Sharat, and Hari will be able to do it. — has got very little originality, but is a very good workman and persevering — which is an essential necessity, and Shashi (Ramakrishnananda) is executive to a degree. ... We want some disciples — fiery young men — do you see? — intelligent and brave, who dare to go to the jaws of Death, and are ready to swim the ocean across. Do you follow me? We want hundreds like that, both men and women. Try your utmost for that end alone. Make converts right and left, and put them into our purity-drilling machine.

. . . What made you communicate to the Indian Mirror that Paramahamsa Deva used to call Narendra such and such, and all sorts of nonsense? — As if he had nothing else to do but that! Only thought-reading and nonsensical mystery-mongering! . . . It is excellent that Sanyal is visiting you often. Do you write letters to Gupta? Convey to him my love, and take kind care of him. Everything will come right by degrees. I don't find much time to write heaps of letters. As for lectures and so forth, I don't prepare them beforehand. Only one I wrote out, which you have printed. The rest I deliver off-hand, whatever comes to my lips — Gurudeva backs me up. I have nothing to do with pen and paper. Once at Detroit I held forth for three hours at a stretch. Sometimes I myself wonder at my own achievement — to think that there was such stuff in this pate! They ask me here to write a book. Well, I think I must do something that way, this time. But that's the botheration; who will take the trouble of putting things in black and white and all that! . . . We must electrify society, electrify the world. Idle gossip and barren ceremonials won't do. Ceremonials are meant for householders, your work is the distribution and propagation of thought-currents. If you can do that, then it is all right. . . .

Let character be formed and then I shall be in your midst. Do you see? We want two thousand Sannyasins, nay ten, or even twenty thousand — men and women, both. What are our matrons doing? We want converts at any risk. Go and tell them, and try yourselves, heart and soul. Not householder disciples, mind you, we want Sannyasins. Let each one of you have a hundred heads tonsured — young educated men, not fools. Then you are heroes. We must make a sensation. Give up your passive attitude, gird your loins and stand up. Let me see you make some electric circuits between Calcutta and Madras. Start centres at places, go on always making converts. Convert everyone into the monastic order whoever seeks for it, irrespective of sex, and then I shall be in your midst. A huge spiritual tidal wave is coming — he who is low shall become noble, and he who is ignorant shall become the teacher of great scholars — through HIS grace. "— Arise! Awake! and stop not till the goal is reached." Life is ever expanding, contraction is death. The self-seeking man who is looking after his personal comforts and leading a lazy life — there is no room for him even in hell. He alone is a child of Shri Ramakrishna who is moved to pity for all creatures and exerts himself for them even at the risk of incurring personal damnation, — others are vulgar people. Whoever, at this great spiritual juncture, will stand up with a courageous heart and go on spreading from door to door, from village to village, his message, is alone my brother, and a son of his. This is the test, he who is Ramakrishna's child does not seek his personal good. "the point of death." Those that care for their personal comforts and seek a lazy life, who are ready to sacrifice all before their personal whims, are none of us; let them pack off, while yet there is time. Propagate his character, his teaching, his religion. This is the only spiritual practice, the only worship, this verily is the means, and this the goal. Arise! Arise! A tidal wave is coming! Onward! Men and women, down to the Chandâla (Pariah) — all are pure in his eyes. Onward! Onward! There is no time to care for name, or fame, or Mukti, or Bhakti! We shall look to these some other time. Now in this life let us infinitely spread his lofty character, his sublime life, his infinite soul. This is the only work — there is nothing else to do. Wherever his name will reach, the veriest worm will attain divinity, nay, is actually attaining it; you have got eyes, and don't you see it? Is it a child's play? Is it silly prattle? Is it foolery?" back. I cannot write any more. — Onward! I only tell you this, that whoever reads this letter will imbibe my spirit! Have faith! Onward! Great Lord! . . . I feel as if somebody is moving my hand to write in this way. Onward! Great Lord! Everyone will be swept away! Take care, he is coming! Whoever will be ready to serve him — no, not him but his children — the poor and the downtrodden, the sinful and the afflicted, down to the very worm — who will be ready to serve these, in them he will manifest himself. Through their tongue the Goddess of Learning Herself will speak, and the Divine Mother — the Embodiment of all Power — will enthrone Herself in their hearts. Those that are atheists, unbelievers, worthless, and foppish, why do they call themselves as belonging to his fold. . . .

Yours affectionately,
Vivekananda.

PS. . . . The term organisation means division of labour. Each does his own part, and all the parts taken together express an ideal of harmony. . . .

57 — MRS. BULL

BROOKLYN,
28th Dec., 1894.

DEAR MRS. BULL,

I arrived safely in New York where Landsberg met me at the depot. I proceeded at once to Brooklyn where I arrived in time.

We had a nice evening. Several gentlemen belonging to the Ethical Culture Society came to see me.

Next Sunday we shall have a lecture. Dr. Janes was as usual very kind and good, and Mr. Higgins is as practical as ever. Here alone in New York I find more men interested in religion than in any other city, and do not know why here the interest is more amongst men than women. . . .

Herewith I send a copy of that pamphlet Mr. Higgins has published about me. Hope to send more in the future.

With my love to Miss Farmer and all the holy family,

I remain yours obediently,
Vivekananda.

58 — SARADA

Translated from Bengali

228 W.39, NEW YORK,
17th Jan., 1895.

DEAR SARADA,

Your two letters are to hand, as also the two of Ramdayal Babu. I have got the bill of lading; but it will be long before the goods arrive. Unless one arranges for the prompt despatch of goods they take about six months to come. It is four months since Haramohan wrote that the Rudrâksha beads and Kusha mats had been despatched, but there is no news of their whereabouts yet. The thing is, when the goods reach England, the agent of the company here gives me notice; and about a month later, the goods arrive. I received your bill of lading about three weeks ago, but no sign of the notice! Only the goods sent by Raja of Khetri arrive quickly. Most probably he spends a lot of money for them. However it is a matter of congratulation that goods do arrive without fail in this region of Pâtâla, at the other end of the globe. I shall let you know as soon as the goods come. Now keep quiet for at least three months.

Now is the time for you to apply yourself to start the magazine. Tell Ramdayal Babu that though the gentleman of whom he speaks be a competent person, I am not in a position to have anybody in America at present. . . . What about your article on Tibet? When it is published in the Mirror, send me a copy. . . . Come, here is a task for you, conduct that magazine. Thrust it on people and make them subscribe to it, and don't be afraid. What work do you expect from men of little hearts? — Nothing in the world! You must have an iron will if you would cross the ocean. You must be strong enough to pierce mountains. I am coming next winter. We shall set the world on fire — let those who will, join us and be blessed, and those that won't come, will lag behind for ever and ever; let them do so. You gird up your loins and keep yourself ready . . . . Never mind anything! In your lips and hands the Goddess of Learning will make Her seat; the Lord of infinite power will be seated on your chest; you will do works that will strike the world with wonder. By the bye, can't you shorten your name a bit, my boy? What a long, long name — a single name enough to fill a volume! Well, you hear people say that the Lord's name keeps away death! It is not the simple name Hari, mind you. It is those deep and sonorous names, such as (Destroyer of Agha, Bhaga, and Naraka) (Subduer of the pride of Tripura, demon of the "three cities"), and (Giver of infinite and endless blessings), and so forth — that put to rout King Death and his whole party. Won't it look nice if you simplify yours a little? But it is too late, I am afraid as it has already been abroad. But, believe me, it is a world-entrancing, death-defying name that you have got! (The full name which Swami Trigunatita, to whom this letter was addressed, bore at first was "Swami Trigunatitananda"— hence Swamiji's pleasantry about it.)

Yours affectionately,
Vivekananda.

PS. Throw the whole of Bengal and, for the matter of that, the whole of India into convulsion! Start centres at different places.

The Bhâgavata has reached me — a very nice edition indeed; but people of this country have not the least inclination for studying Sanskrit; hence there is very little hope for its sale. There may be a little in England, for there many are interested in the study of Sanskrit. Give my special thanks to the editor. I hope his noble attempt will meet with complete success. I shall try my best to push his book here. I have sent his prospectus to different places. Tell Ramdayal Babu that a flourishing trade can be set on foot with England and America in Mung Dâl, Arhar Dâl, etc. Dâl soup will have a go if properly introduced. There will be a good demand for these things if they be sent from house to house, in small packets, with directions for cooking on them and a depot started for storing a quantity of them. Similarly Badis (Pellets made of Dal, pounded and beaten.) too will have a good market. We want an enterprising spirit. Nothing is done by leading idle lives. If anyone forms a company and exports Indian goods here and into England, it will be a good trade. But they are a lazy set, enamoured of child marriage and nothing else.

59 — SANYAL

Translated from Bengali

54 W. 33rd ST., NEW YORK,
9th February, 1895.

DEAR SANYAL,

. . . Paramahamsa Deva was my Guru, and whatever I may think of him in point of greatness, why should the world think like me? And if you press the point hard, you will spoil everything. The idea of worshipping the Guru as God is nowhere to be met with outside Bengal, for other people are not yet ready to take up that ideal. . . . Many would fain associate my name with themselves — "I belong to them!" But when it comes to doing something I want, they are nowhere. So selfish is the whole world!

I shall consider myself absolved from a debt of obligation when I succeed in purchasing some land for Mother. I don't care for anything after that.

In this dire winter I have travelled across mountains and over snows at dead of night and collected a little fund; and I shall have peace of mind when a plot is secured for Mother.

Henceforth address my letters as above, which is to be my permanent seat from now. Try to send me an English translation of the Yogavâsishtha Râmâyana. . . . Don't forget those books I asked for before, viz Sanskrit Nârada and Shândilya Sutras.

"Hope is the greatest of miseries, the highest bliss lies in giving up hope."

Yours affectionately,
Vivekananda.

60 — MRS. BULL

54 W. 33rd ST., NEW YORK,
14th February, 1895.

DEAR MRS. BULL,

Accept my heartfelt gratitude for your motherly advice. I hope I will be able to carry out them in life.

How can I express my gratitude to you for what you have already done for me and my work, and my eternal gratitude to you for your offering to do something more this year. But I sincerely believe that you ought to turn all your help to Miss Farmer's Greenacre work this year. India can wait as she is waiting centuries and an immediate work at hand should always have the preference.

Again, according to Manu, collecting funds even for a good work is not good for a Sannyasin, and I have begun to feel that the old sages were right. "Hope is the greatest misery, despair is the greatest happiness." It appears like a hallucination. I am getting out of them. I was in these childish ideas of doing this and doing that.

"Give up all desire and be at peace. Have neither friends nor foes, and live alone. Thus shall we travel having neither friends nor foes, neither pleasure nor pain, neither desire nor jealousy, injuring no creatures, being the cause of injury to no creatures — from mountain to mountain, from village to village, preaching the name of the Lord."

"Seek no help from high or low, from above or below. Desire nothing — and look upon this vanishing panorama as a witness and let it pass."

Perhaps these mad desires were necessary to bring me over to this country. And I thank the Lord for the experience.

I am very happy now. Between Mr. Landsberg and me, we cook some rice and lentils or barley and quietly eat it, and write something or read or receive visits from poor people who want to learn something, and thus I feel I am more a Sannyasin now than I ever was in America.

"In wealth is the fear of poverty, in knowledge the fear of ignorance, in beauty the fear of age, in fame the fear of backbiters, in success the fear of jealousy, even in body is the fear of death. Everything in this earth is fraught with fear. He alone is fearless who has given up everything" (Vairâgya-Shatakam, 31).

I went to see Miss Corbin the other day, and Miss Farmer and Miss Thursby were also there. We had a nice half-hour and she wants me to hold some classes in her home from next Sunday.

I am no more seeking for these things. If they come, the Lord be blessed, if not, blessed more be He.

Again accept my eternal gratitude.

Your devoted son,
Vivekananda.

61 — MRS. BULL

54 W. 33rd ST., NEW YORK,
21st March, 1895.

DEAR MRS. BULL,

I am astonished to hear the scandals the Ramabai circles are indulging in about me. Don't you see, Mrs. Bull, that however a man may conduct himself, there will always be persons who invent the blackest lies about him? At Chicago I had such things every day against me. And these women are invariably the very Christian of Christians! . . . I am going to have a series of paid lectures in my rooms (downstairs), which will seat about a hundred persons, and that will cover the expenses. I am in no great hurry about the money to be sent to India. I will wait. Is Miss Farmer with you? Is Mrs. Peake at Chicago? Have you seen Josephine Locke? Miss Hamlin has been very kind to me and does all she can to help me.

My master used to say that these names, as Hindu, Christian, etc., stand as great bars to all brotherly feelings between man and man. We must try to break them down first. They have lost all their good powers and now only stand as baneful influences under whose black magic even the best of us behave like demons. Well, we will have to work hard and must succeed.

That is why I desire so much to have a centre. Organisation has its faults, no doubt, but without that nothing can be done. And here, I am afraid, I will have to differ from you — that no one ever succeeded in keeping society in good humour and at the same time did great works. One must work as the dictate comes from within, and then if it is light and good, society is bound to veer round, perhaps centuries after one is dead and gone. We must plunge heart and soul and body into the work. And until we be ready to sacrifice everything else to one Idea and to one alone, we never, never will see the light.

Those that want to help mankind must take their own pleasure and pain, name and fame, and all sorts of interests, and make a bundle of them and throw them into the sea, and then come to the Lord. This is what all the Masters said and did.

I went to Miss Corbin's last Saturday and told her that I should not be able to come to hold classes any more. Was it ever in the history of the world that any great work was done by the rich? It is the heart and the brain that do it ever and ever and not the purse.

My idea and all my life with it — and to God for help; to none else! This is the only secret of success. I am sure you are one with me here. My love to Mrs. Thursby and Mrs. Adams.

Ever yours in grateful affection,
Vivekananda.

62 — MRS. BULL

54 W. 33rd ST., NEW YORK,
11th April, 1895.

DEAR MRS. BULL,

. . . I am going away to the country tomorrow to see Mr. Leggett for a few days. A little fresh air will do me good, I hope.

I have given up the project of removing from this house just now, as it will be too expensive, and moreover it is not advisable to change just now. I am working it up slowly.

. . . I send you herewith the letter from H. H. the Maharaja of Khetri; also enclose the slip on Gurjan oil for leprosy. Miss Hamlin has been helping me a good deal. I am very grateful to her. She is very kind and, I hope, sincere. She wants me to be introduced to the "right kind of people". This is the second edition of the "Hold yourself steady" business, I am afraid. The only "right sort of people" are those whom the Lord sends — that is what I understand in my life's experience. They alone can and will help me. As for the rest, Lord help them in a mass and save me from them.

Every one of my friends thought it would end in nothing, this my getting up quarters all by myself, and that no ladies would ever come here. Miss Hamlin especially thought that "she" or "her right sort of people" were way up from such things as to go and listen to a man who lives by himself in a poor lodging. But the "right kind" came for all that, day and night, and she too. Lord! how hard it is for man to believe in Thee and Thy mercies! Shiva! Shiva! Where is the right kind and where is the bad, mother? It is all He! In the tiger and in the lamb, in the saint and sinner all He! In Him I have taken my refuge, body, soul, and Atman. Will He leave me now after carrying me in His arms all my life? Not a drop will be in the ocean, not a twig in the deepest forest, not a crumb in the house of the god of wealth, if the Lord is not merciful. Streams will be in the desert and the beggar will have plenty, if He wills it. He seeth the sparrow's fall. Are these but words, mother, or literal, actual life?

Truce to this "right sort of presentation". Thou art my right, Thou my wrong, my Shiva. Lord, since a child I have taken refuge in Thee. Thou wilt be with me in the tropics or at the poles, on the tops of mountains or in the depth of oceans. My stay — my guide in life — my refuge — my friend — my teacher — my God — my real Self, Thou wilt never leave me, never. I know it for sure. Sometimes I become weak, being alone and struggling against odds, my God; and I think of human help. Save Thou me for ever from these weaknesses, and may I never, never seek for help from any being but Thee. If a man puts his trust in another good man, he is never betrayed, never forsaken. Wilt Thou forsake me, Father of all good, Thou who knowest that all my life I am Thy servant and Thine alone? Wilt Thou give me over to be played upon by others, or dragged down by evil? He will never leave me, I am sure, mother.

Your ever obedient son,
Vivekananda.

63 — SHASHI

Translated from Bengali

U.S.A.,
11th April, 1895.

MY DEAR SHASHI,

. . . You write that you have recovered from your illness; but you must henceforth be very careful. Late dinners or unwholesome food, or living in a stinking place may bring on a relapse, and make it hard to escape the clutches of malaria. First of all you should hire a small garden-house — you may get one for thirty or forty rupees. Secondly, see that cooking and drinking water be filtered — a bamboo filter of a big size will do. Water is the cause of all sorts of disease. It is not the clearness or dirtiness of water, but its being full of disease germs, that causes disease. Let the water be boiled and filtered. You must all pay attention to your health first. A cook, a servant, clean beds, and timely meals — these are absolutely necessary. Please see that all these suggestions be carried out in toto. . . . The success of your undertakings depends wholly upon your mutual love. There is no good in store so long as malice and jealousy and egotism will prevail. ... Kali's pamphlet is very well written and has no exaggerations. Know that talking ill of others in private is a sin. You must wholly avoid it. Many things may occur to the mind, but it gradually makes a mountain of a molehill if you try to express them. Everything is ended if you forgive and forget. It is welcome news that Shri Ramakrishna's festival was celebrated with great éclat. You must try so that there is a muster of a hundred thousand people next year. Put your energies together to start a magazine. Shyness won't do any more.... He who has infinite patience and infinite energy at his back, will alone succeed. You must pay special attention to study. Do you understand? You must not huddle together too many fools. I shall be glad if you bring together a few real men. Why, I don't hear even a single one opening his lips. You distributed sweets at the festival, and there was singing by some parties, mostly idlers. True, but I don't hear what spiritual food you have given. So long as that nil admirari attitude is not gone, you will not be able to do anything, and none of you will have courage. Bullies are always cowards.

Take up everyone with sympathy, whether he believes in Shri Ramakrishna or not. If anybody comes to you for vain dispute, politely withdraw yourselves. ... You must express your sympathy with people of all sects. When these cardinal virtues will be manifested in you, then only you will be able to work with great energy. Otherwise, mere taking the name of the Guru will not do. However, there is no doubt that this year's festival has been a great success, and you deserve special thanks for it; but you must push forward, do you see? What is Sharat doing? Never shall you be able to know anything if you persist in pleading ignorance. ... We want something of a higher tone — that will appeal to the intellect of the learned. It won't do merely to get up musical parties and all that. Not only will this festival be his memorial, but also the central union of an intense propaganda of his doctrines. ... All will come in good time. But at times I fret and stamp like a leashed hound. Onward and forward, my old watchword. I am doing well. No use going back to India in a hurry. Summon all your energies and set yourselves to work heart and soul; that will really be heroic.

Yours affectionately,
Vivekananda.

64 — MRS. BULL

54 W. 33rd ST., NEW YORK,
25th April, 1895.

DEAR MRS. BULL,

The day before yesterday I received a kind note from Miss Farmer including a cheque for a hundred dollars for the Barbar House lectures. She is coming to New York next Saturday. I will of course tell her to put my name in her circulars; and what is more, I cannot go to Greenacre now; I have arranged to go to the Thousand Islands, wherever that may be. There is a cottage belonging to Miss Dutcher, one of my students, and a few of us will be there in rest and peace and seclusion. I want to manufacture a few "Yogis" out of the materials of the classes, and a busy farm like Greenacre is the last place for that, while the other is quite out of the way, and none of the curiosity-seekers will dare go there.

I am very glad that Miss Hamlin took down the names of the 130 persons who come to the Jnana-Yoga class. There are 50 more who come to the Wednesday Yoga class and about 50 more to the Monday class. Mr. Landsberg had all the names; and they will come anyhow, names or no names.... If they do not, others will, and so it will go on — the Lord be praised.

Taking down names and giving notices is a big task, no doubt, and I am very thankful to both of them for doing that for me. But I am thoroughly persuaded that it is laziness on my part, and therefore immoral, to depend on others, and always evil comes out of laziness. So henceforth I will do it all myself. ...

However, I will be only too glad to take in any one of Miss Hamlin's "right sort of persons", but unfortunately for me, not one such has as yet turned up. It is the duty of the teacher always to turn the "right sort" out of the most "unrighteous sort" of persons. After all, though I am very, very grateful to the young lady, Miss Hamlin, for the great hope and encouragement she gave tine of introducing me to the "right sort of New Yorkers" and for the practical help she has given me, I think I hard better do my little work with my own hands. . . .

I am only glad that you have such a great opinion about Miss Hamlin. I for one am glad to know that you will help her, for she requires it. But, mother, through the mercy of Ramakrishna, my instinct "sizes up" almost infallibly a human face as soon as I see it, and the result is this: you may do anything you please width my affairs, I will not even murmur; — I will be only too glad to take Miss Farmer's advice, in spite of ghosts and spooks. Behind the spooks I see a heart of immense love, only covered with a thin film of laudable ambition — even that is bound to vanish in a few years. Even I will allow Landsberg to "monkey" with my affairs from time to time; but here I put a full stop. Help from any other persons besides these frightens me. That is all I can say. Not only for the help you have given me, but from my instinct (or, as I call it, inspiration of my Master), I regard you as my mother and will always abide by any advice you may have for me — but only personally. When you select a medium, I will beg leave to exercise my choice. That is all.

Herewith I send the English gentleman's letter. I have made a few notes on the margin to explain Hindustani words.

Your obedient son,
Vivekananda.

65 — MRS. BULL

54 W. 33rd ST., NEW YORK,
7th May, 1895.

DEAR MRS. BULL,

...I had a newspaper from India with a publication in it of Dr. Barrows' short reply to the thanks sent over from India. Miss Thursby will send it to you. Yesterday I received another letter from India from the President of Madras meeting to thank the Americans and to send me an Address.... This gentleman is the chief citizen of Madras and a Judge of the Supreme Court, a very high position in India.

I am going to have two public lectures more in New York in the upper hall of the Mott's Memorial Building. The first one will be on Monday next, on the Science of Religion. The next, on the Rationale of Yoga.... Has Miss Hamlin sent you the book on the financial condition of India? I wish your brother will read it and then find out for himself what the English rule in India means.

Ever gratefully your son,
Vivekananda.

66 — MRS. BULL

54 W. 33rd ST., NEW YORK,
May, 1895, Thursday.

DEAR MRS. BULL,

The classes are going on; but I am sorry to say, though the attendance is large, it does not even pay enough to cover the rent. I will try this week and then give up.

I am going this summer to the Thousand Islands to Miss Dutcher's, one of my students. The different books on Vedanta are now being sent over to me from India. I expect to write a book in English on the Vedanta Philosophy in its three stages when I am at Thousand Islands, and I may go to Greenacre later on. Miss Farmer wants me to lecture there this summer.

I am rather busy just now in writing a promised article for the Press Association on Immortality.

Yours,
Vivekananda.

67 — MRS. BULL

PERCY, NEW HAMPSHIRE,
7th June, 1895.

DEAR MRS. BULL,

I am here at last with Mr. Leggett. This is one of the most beautiful spots I have ever seen. Imagine a lake, surrounded with hills covered with a huge forest, with nobody but ourselves. So lovely, so quiet, so restful! And you may imagine how glad I am to be here after the bustle of cities.

It gives me a new lease of life to be here. I go into the forest alone and read my Gita and am quite happy. I will leave this place in about ten days and go to the Thousand Island Park. I will meditate by the hour there and be all alone to myself. The very idea is ennobling.

Vivekananda.

68 — MRS. BULL

54 W. 33rd ST., NEW YORK
June, 1895.

DEAR MRS. BULL,

I have just arrived home. The trip did me good, and I enjoyed the country and the hills, and especially Mr. Leggett's country-house in New York State. Poor Landsberg has gone from this house. Neither has he left one his address. May the Lord bless Landsberg wherever he goes! He is one of the few sincere souls I have had the privilege in this life to come across.

All is for good. All conjunctions are for subsequent disjunction. I hope I shall be perfectly able to work alone. The less help from men, the more from the Lord! Just now I received a letter from an Englishman in London who had lived in India in the Himalayas with two of my brethren. He asks me to come to London.

Yours,
Vivekananda.

69 — SHASHI

Translated from Bengali

1895.

MY DEAR SHASHI,

. . . I am quite in agreement with what Sarada is doing, but it is not necessary to preach that Ramakrishna Paramahamsa was an Incarnation, and things of that sort. He came to do good to the world; not to trumpet his own name — you must always remember this. Disciples pay their whole attention to the preservation of their master's name and throw overboard his teachings; and sectarianism etc., are the result. Alasinga writes of Charu; but I do not recollect him. Write all about him and convey him my thanks. Write in detail about all; I have no time to spare for idle gossip .... Try to give up ceremonials. They are not meant for Sannyasins; and one must work only so long as one does not attain to illumination .... I have nothing to do with sectarianism. Or party-forming and playing the frog-in-the-well, whatever else I may do.... It is impossible to preach the catholic ideas of Ramakrishna Paramahamsa and form sects at the same time.... Only one kind of work I understand, and that is doing good to others; all else is doing evil. I therefore prostrate myself before the Lord Buddha.... I am a Vedantist; Sachchidananda — Existence-Knowledge-Bliss Absolute — is my God. I scarcely find any other God than the majestic form of my own Self. By the word "Incarnation" are meant those who have attained that Brahmanhood, in other words, the Jivanmuktas — those who have realised this freedom in this very life. I do not find any speciality in Incarnations: all beings from Brahmâ down to a clump of grass will attain to liberation-in-life in course of time, and our duty lies in helping all to reach that state. This help is called religion; the rest is irreligion. This help is work; the rest is evil-doing — I see nothing else. Other kinds of work, for example, the Vaidika or the Tântrika, may produce results; but resorting to them is simply waste of life, for that purity which is the goal of work is realisable only through doing good to others. Through works such as sacrifices etc., one may get enjoyments, but it is impossible to have the purity of soul.... Everything exists already in the Self of all beings. He who asserts he is free, shall be free. He who says he is bound, bound he shall remain. To me, the thought of oneself as low and humble is a sin and ignorance. "— This Atman is not to be attained by one who is weak."

— If you say Brahman is, existence will be the result; if you say Brahman is not, non existent It shall verily become." He who always thinks of himself as weak wild never become strong, but he who knows himself to be a lion,

— rushes out from the world's meshes, as a lion from its cage." Another point, it was no new truth that Ramakrishna Paramahamsa came to preach, though his advent brought the old truths to light. In other words, he was the embodiment of all the past religious thoughts of India. His life alone made me understand what the Shâstras really meant, and the whole plan and scope of the old Shastras.

Missionaries and others could not do much against me in this country. Through the Lord's grace the people here like me greatly and are not to be tricked by the opinions of any particular class. They appreciate my ideas in a manner my own countrymen cannot do, and are not selfish. I mean, when it comes to practical work they will give up jealousy and all those ideas of self-sufficiency. Then all of them agree and act under the direction of a capable man. That is what makes them so great. But then they are a nation of Mammon-worshippers. Money comes before everything. People of our country are very liberal in pecuniary matters, but not so much these people. Every home has a miser. It is almost a religion here. But they fall into the clutches of the priests when they do something bad, and then buy their passage to heaven with money. These things are the same in every country — priestcraft. I can say nothing as to whether I shall go back to India and when. There also I shall have to lead a wandering life as I do here; but here thousands of people listen to and understand my lectures, and these thousands are benefited. But can you say the same thing about India? . . . I am perfectly at one with what Sarada is doing. A thousand thanks to him.... In Madras and Bombay I have lots of men who are after my heart. They are learned and understand everything. Moreover they are kind-hearted and can therefore appreciate the philanthropic spirit.... I have printed neither books nor anything of the kind. I simply go on lecturing tours.... When I take a retrospective view of my past life, I feel no remorse. From country to country I have travelled teaching something, however little, to people, and in exchange for that have partaken of their slices of bread. If I had found I had done no work, but simply supported myself by imposing upon people, I would have committed suicide today. Why do those who think themselves unfit to teach their fellow-beings, wear the teacher's garb and earn their bread by cheating them? Is not that a deadly sin? ...

Yours etc.,
Vivekananda.

70 — ALBERTA

19 W. 38, NEW YORK,
8th July, 1895.

DEAR ALBERTA, (Miss Alberta Sturges.)

I am sure you are engrossed in your musical studies now. Hope you have found out all about the scales by this time. I will be so happy to take a lesson on the scales from you next time we meet.

We had such jolly good time up there at Percy with Mr. Leggett — isn't he a saint?

Hollister is also enjoying Germany greatly, I am sure, and I hope none of you have injured your tongues in trying to pronounce German words — especially those beginning with sch, tz, tsz, and other sweet things.

I read your letter to your mother from on board Most possibly I am going over to Europe next September. I have never been to Europe yet. It will not be very much different from the United States after all. And I am already well drilled in the manners and customs of this country.

We had a good deal of rowing at Percy and I learnt a point or two in rowing. Aunt Joe Joe had to pay for her sweetness, for the flies and mosquitoes would not leave her for a moment. They rather gave me a wide berth, I think because they were very orthodox sabbatarian flies and would not touch a heathen. Again, I think, I used to sing a good deal at Percy, and that must have frightened them away. We had such fine birch trees. I got up an idea of making books out of the bark, as was used to be done in ancient times in our country, and wrote Sanskrit verses for your mother and aunt.

I am sure, Alberta, you are going to be a tremendously learned lady very soon.

With love and blessings for both of you,

Ever your affectionate,
Swami Vivekananda.

71 — RAKHAL

Translated from Bengali

Salutation to Bhagavan Ramakrishna!

1895.

DEAR RAKHAL,

I have now got lots of newspapers etc., and you need not send any more. Let the movement now confine itself to India....

It isn't much use getting up a sensation every day. But avail yourselves of this stir that is rife all over the country, and scatter yourselves in all quarters. In other words, try to start branches at different places. Let it not be an empty sound merely. You must join the Madrasis and start associations etc., at different places. What about the magazine which I heard was going to be started? Why are you nervous about conducting it? ... Come? Do something heroic! Brother, what if you do not attain Mukti, what if you suffer damnation a few times? Is the saying untrue? —

— There are some saints who full of holiness in thought, word, and bleed, please the whole world by their numerous beneficent acts, and who develop their own hearts by magnifying an atom of virtue in others as if it were as great as a mountain" (Bhartrihari, Nitishataka).

What if you don't get Mukti? What childish prattle! Lord! They say even the venom of a snake loses its power by firmly denying it. Isn't it true? What queer humility is this to say, "I know nothing !" "I am nothing !" This is pseudo-renunciation and mock modesty, I tell you. Off with such a self-debasing spirit! "If I do not know, who on earth does!" What have you been doing so long if you now plead ignorance? These are the words of an atheist — the humility of a vagabond wretch. We can do everything, and will do everything! He who is fortunate enough will heroically join us, letting the worthless mew like cats from their corner. A saint writes, "Well, you have had enough of blazoning. Now come back home." I would have called him a man if he could build a house and call me. Ten years' experience of such things has made me wiser. I am no more to be duped by words. Let him who has courage in his mind and love in his heart come with me. I want none else. Through Mother's grace, single-handed I am worth a hundred thousand now and will be worth two millions.... There is no certainty about my going back to India. I shall have to lead a wandering life there also, as I am doing here. But here one lives in the company of scholars, and there one must live among fools — there is this difference as of the poles. People of this country organise and work, while our undertakings all come to dust clashing against laziness — miscalled "renunciation," — and jealousy, etc. — writes me big letters now and then, half of which I cannot decipher, which is a blessing to me. For a great part of the news is of the following description — that in such and such a place such and such a man was speaking ill of me, and that he, being unable to bear the same, had a quarrel with him, and so forth. Many thanks for his kind defence of me. But what seriously hinders me from listening to what particular people may be saying about me is —"

An organised society is wanted. Let Shashi look to the household management, Sanyal take charge of money matters and marketing, and Sharat act as secretary, that is, carry on correspondence etc. Make a permanent centre — it is no use making random efforts as you are doing now. Do you see my point? I have quite a heap of newspapers, now I want you to do something. If you can build a Math, I shall say you are heroes; otherwise you are nothing. Consult the Madras people when you work. They have a great capacity for work. Celebrate this year's Shri Ramakrishna festival with such éclat as to make it a record. The less the feeding propaganda is, the better. It is enough if you distribute Prasâda in earthen cups to the devotees standing in rows....

I am going to write a very short sketch of Shri Ramakrishna's life in English, which I shall send you. Have it printed and translated into Bengali and sell it at the festival — people do not read books that are distributed free. Fix some nominal price. Have the festival done with great pomp. . . .

You must have an all-sided intellect to do efficient work. In any towns or villages you may visit, start an association wherever you find a number of people revering Shri Ramakrishna. Have you travelled through so many villages all for nothing? We must slowly absorb the Hari Sabhâs and such other associations. Well, I cannot tell you all — if I could but get another demon like me! The Lord will supply me everything in time.... If one has got power, one must manifest it in action. ... Off with your ideas of Mukti and Bhakti! There is only one way in the world,

— "The good live for others alone", "The wise man should sacrifice himself for others". I can secure my own good only by doing you good. There is no other way, none whatsoever.... You are God, I am God, and man is God. It is this God manifested through humanity who is doing everything in this world. Is there a different God sitting high up somewhere? To work, therefore!

Bimala has sent me a book written by Shashi (Sanyal). ... From a perusal of that work Bimala has come to know that all the people of this world are impure and that they are by their very nature debarred from having a jot of religion; that only the handful of Brahmins that are in India have the sole right to it, and among these again, Shashi (Sanyal) and Bimala are the sun and moon, so to speak. Bravo! What a powerful religion indeed! In Bengal specially, that sort of religion is very easy to practice. There is no easier way than that. The whole truth about austerities and spiritual exercises is, in a nutshell, that I am pure and all the rest are impure! A beastly, demoniac, hellish religion this! If the American people are unfit for religion, if it is improper to preach religion here, why then ask their help? . . . What can remedy such a disease? Well, tell Shashi (Sanyal)to go to Malabar. The Raja there has taken his subjects' land and offered it at the feet of Brahmins. There are big monasteries in every village where sumptuous dinners are given, supplemented by presents in cash. ... There is no harm in touching the non-Brahmin classes when it serves one's purpose; and when you have done with it, you bathe, for the non-Brahmins are as a class unholy and must never be touched on other occasions! Monks and Sannyasins and Brahmins of a certain type have thrown the country into ruin. Intent all the while on theft and wickedness, these pose as preachers of religion! They will take gifts from the people and at the same time cry, "Don't touch me!" And what great things they have been doing! — "If a potato happens to touch a brinjal, how long will the universe last before it is deluged?" "If they do not apply earth a dozen times to clean their hands, will fourteen generations of ancestors go to hell, or twenty-four?" — For intricate problems like these they have been finding out scientific explanations for the last two thousand years — while one fourth of the people are starving. A girl of eight is married to a man of thirty, and the parents are jubilant over it.... And if anyone protests against it, the plea is put forward, "Our religion is being overturned." What sort of religion have they who want to see their girls becoming mothers before they attain puberty even and offer scientific explanations for it? Many, again, lay the blame at the door of the Mohammedans. They are to blame, indeed! Just read the Grihya-Sutras through and see what is given as the marriageable age of a girl. ... There it is expressly stated that a girl must be married before attaining puberty. The entire Grihya-Sutras enjoin this. And in the Vedic Ashvamedha sacrifice worse things would be done.... All the Brâhmanas mention them, and all the commentators admit them to be true. How can you deny them?

What I mean by mentioning all this is that there were many good things in the ancient times, but there were bad things too. The good things are to be retained, but the India that is to be, the future India, must be much greater than ancient India. From the day Shri Ramakrishna was born dates the growth of modern India and of the Golden Age. And you are the agents to bring about this Golden Age. To work, with this conviction at heart!

Hence, when you call Shri Ramakrishna an Incarnation and in the same breath plead your ignorance unhesitatingly, I say, "You are false to the backbone!" If Ramakrishna Paramahamsa be true, you also are true. But you must show it. ... In you all there is tremendous power. The atheist has nothing but rubbish in him. Those who are believers are heroes. They will manifest tremendous power. The world will be swept before them. "Sympathy and help to the poor"; "Man is God, he is Nârâyana"; "In Atman there is no distinction of male or female, of Brahmin or Kshatriya, and the like"; "All is Narayana from the Creator down to a clump of grass." The worm is less manifested, the Creator more manifested. Every action that helps a being manifest its divine nature more and more is good, every action that retards it is evil.

The only way of getting our divine nature manifested is by helping others to do the same.

If there is inequality in nature, still there must be equal chance for all — or if greater for some and for some less — the weaker should be given more chance than the strong.

In other words, a Brahmin is not so much in need of education as a Chandâla. If the son of a Brahmin needs one teacher, that of a Chandala needs ten. For greater help must be given to him whom nature has not endowed with an acute intellect from birth. It is a madman who carries coals to Newcastle. The poor, the downtrodden, the ignorant, let these be your God.

A dreadful slough is in front of you — take care; many fall into it and die. The slough is this, that the present religion of the Hindus is not in the Vedas, nor in the Puranas, nor in Bhakti, nor in Mukti — religion has entered into the cooking-pot. The present religion of the Hindus is neither the path of knowledge nor that of reason — it is "Don't-touchism". "Don't touch me!" "Don't touch me!" — that exhausts its description. See that you do not lose your lives in this dire irreligion of "Don't-touchism". Must the teaching, "— Looking upon all beings as your own self" — be confined to books alone? How will they grant salvation who cannot feed a hungry mouth with a crumb of bread? How will those who become impure at the mere breath of others purify others? Don't-touchism is a form of mental disease. Beware! All expansion is life, all contraction is death. All love is expansions all selfishness is contraction. Love is therefore the only law of life. He who loves lives, he who is selfish is dying. Therefore love for love's sake, because it is the only law of life, just as you breathe to live. This is the secret of selfless love, selfless action and the rest. ... Try to help Shashi (Sanyal) if you can, in any ways He is a very good and pious man, but of a narrow heart. It does not fall to the lot of all to feel for the misery of others. Good Lord! Of all Incarnations Lord Chaitanya was the greatest, but he was comparatively lacking in knowledge; in the Ramakrishna Incarnation there is knowledge, devotion and love — infinite knowledge, infinite love, infinite work, infinite compassion for all beings. You have not yet been able to understand him. "— Even after hearing about Him, most people do not understand Him." What the whole Hindu race has thought in ages, he lived in one life. His life is the living commentary to the Vedas of all nations. People will come to know him by degrees. My old watchword — struggle, struggle up to light! Onward!

Yours in service,
Vivekananda.

72 — AKHANDANANDA

Translated from Bengali

C/O E. T. STURDY, ESQ.,
HIGH VIEW, CAVERSHAM,
1895.

BELOVED AKHANDANANDA,

I am glad to go through the contents of your letter. Your idea is grand but our nation is totally lacking in the faculty of organisation. It is this one drawback which produces all sorts of evil. We are altogether averse to making a common cause for anything. The first requisite for organisation is obedience. I do a little bit of work when I feel so disposed, and then let it go to the dogs — this kind of work is of no avail. We must have plodding industry and perseverance. Keep a regular correspondence, I mean, make it a point to write to me every month, or twice a month, what work you are doing and what has been its outcome. We want here (in England) a Sannyasin well-versed in English and Sanskrit. I shall soon go to America again, and he is to work here in my absence. Except Sharat and Shashi — I find no one else for this task. I have sent money to Sharat and written to him to start at once. I have requested Rajaji that his Bombay agent may help Sharat in embarking. I forgot to write — but if you can take the trouble to do it, please send through Sharat a bag of Mung, gram, and Arhar Dâl, also a little of the spice called Methi. Please convey my love to Pundit Narayan Das, Mr. Shankar Lal, Ojhaji, Doctor, and all. Do you think you can get the medicine for Gopi's eyes here? — Everywhere you find patent medicines, which are all humbug. Please give my blessings to him and to the other boys. Yajneshwar has founded a certain society at Meerut and wants to work conjointly with us. By the bye, he has got a certain paper too; send Kali there, and let him start a Meerut centre, if he can and, try to have a paper in Hindi. I shall help a little now and then. I shall send some money when Kali goes to Meerut and reports to me exactly how matters stand. Try to open a centre at Ajmer. ... Pundit Agnihotri has started some society at Saharanpur. They wrote my a letter. Please keep in correspondence with them. Live on friendly terms with all. Work! Work! Go on opening centres in this way. We have them already in Calcutta and Madras, and it will be excellent if you can start new ones at Meerut and Ajmer. Go on slowly starting centres at different places like that. Here all my letters etc., are to be addressed in care of E. T. Sturdy, Esq., High View, Caversham, Reading, England, and those for America, C/o Miss Phillips, 19 W. 38 Street, New York. By degrees we must spread the world over. The first thing needed is obedience. You must be ready to plunge into fire — then will work be done. ... Form societies dike that at different villages in Rajputana. There you have a hint.

Yours affectionately,
Vivekananda.

73 — BROTHER DISCIPLES

Translated from Bengali

U.S.A.,
(Summer of?) 1895.

MY DEAR—, (Brother-disciples at the Math)

The books that Sanyal sent have arrived. I forgot to mention this. Please inform him about it.

Let me write down something for you all:

1. Know partiality to be the chief cause of all evil. That is to say, if you show towards any one more love than towards somebody else, rest assured, you will be sowing the seeds of future troubles.

2. If anybody comes to you to speak ill of any of his brothers, refuse to listen to him in toto. It is a great sin to listen even. In that lies the germ of future troubles.

3. Moreover, bear with everyone's shortcomings. Forgive offences by the million. And if you love all unselfishly, all will by degrees come to love one another. As soon as they fully understand that the interests of one depend upon those of others, everyone of them will give up jealousy. To do something conjointly is not in our very national character. Therefore you must try to inaugurate that spirit with the

utmost care, and wait patiently. To tell you the truth, I do not find among you any distinction of great or small: everyone has the capacity to manifest, in times of need, the highest energy. I see it. Look for instance how Shashi will remain always constant to his spot; his steadfastness is a great foundation-rock. How successfully Kali and Jogen brought about the Town Hall meeting; it was indeed a momentous task! Niranjan has done much work in Ceylon and elsewhere. How extensively has Sarada travelled and sown seeds of gigantic future works! Whenever I think of the wonderful renunciation of Hari, about his steadiness of intellect and forbearance, I get a new access of strength! In Tulasi, Gupta, Baburam, Sharat, to mention a few, in every one of you there is tremendous energy. If you still entertain any doubt as to Shri Ramakrishna's being a jewel-expert, what then is the difference between you and a madman! Behold, hundreds of men and women of this country are beginning to worship our Lord as the greatest of all Avataras! Steady! Every great work is done slowly. ...

He is at the helm, what fear! You are all of infinite strength — how long does it take you to keep off petty jealousy or egoistic ideas! The moment such propensity comes, resign yourselves to the Lord! Just make over your body and mind to His work, and all troubles will be at an end for ever.

There will not be room enough, I see, in the house where you are at present living. A commodious building is needed. That is to say, you need not huddle together in one room. If possible, not more than two should live in the same room. There should be a big hall, where the books may be kept.

Every morning there should be a little reading from the scriptures, which Kali and others may superintend by turns. In the evening there should be another class, with a little practice in meditation and Sankirtanas etc. You may divide the work, and set apart one day for Yoga, a day for Bhakti, another for Jnâna, and so forth: It will be excellent if you fix a routine like this, so that outside people also may join in the evening classes. And every Sunday, from ten in the morning up till night, there should be a continuous succession of classes and Sankirtanas etc. That is for the public. If you take the trouble to continue this kind of routine work for some time, it will gradually make itself easy and smooth. There should be no smoking in that hall, for which another place must be set apart. If you can take trouble to bring about this state of things by degrees, I shall think a great advance is made.

What about a certain magazine that Haramohan was trying to publish? If you can manage to start one, it will indeed be nice.

Yours affectionately,
Vivekananda.

74 — RAKHAL

Translated from Bengali

U.S.A.,
(End of?) 1895.

MY DEAR RAKHAL,

Just now I got your letter and was glad to go through it. No matter whether there is any work done in India or not, the real work lies here. I do not want anybody to come over now. On my return to India I shall train a few men, and after that there will be no danger for them in the West. Yes, it was of Gunanidhi that I wrote. Give my special love and blessings to Hari Singh and others. Never take part in quarrels and disputes. Who on earth possesses the power to put the Raja of Khetri down? — The Divine Mother is at his elbow! I have received Kali's letter too. It will be very good indeed if you can start a centre in Kashmir. Wherever you can, open a centre.... Now I have laid the foundations firm here and in England, and nobody has the power to shake them. New York is in a commotion this year. Next year will come the turn of London. Even big giants will give way, who counts your pigmies! Gird up your loins and set yourselves to work! We must throw the world into convulsions with our triumphal shouts. This is but the beginning, my boy. Do you think there are men in our country, it is a Golgotha! There is some chance if you can impart education to the masses. Is there a greater strength than that of Knowledge? Can you give them education? Name me the country where rich men ever helped anybody! In all countries it is the middle classes that do all great works. How long will it take to raise the money? Where are the men? Are there any in our country? Our countrymen are boys, and even must treat them as such.... There are some few religious and philosophical books left — the remnants of the mansion that has been burnt down; take them with you, quick and come over to this country. ...

Never fear! The Divine Mother is helping me! This year such work is going to be turned out that you will be struck dumb to hear of it!

What fear! Whom to fear! Steel your hearts and set yourselves to work!

Yours affectionately,
Vivekananda.

PS. Sarada is talking of bringing out a Bengali magazine. Help it with all your might. It is not a bad idea. You must not throw cold water on anybody's project. Give up criticism altogether. Help all as long as you find they are doing all right, and in cases where they seem to be going wrong, show them their mistakes gently. It is criticising each other that is at the root of all mischief. That is the chief factor in breaking down organizations. ...

75 — SHASHI

Translated from Bengali

(Beginning of?) 1895.

Yesterday I received a letter from you in which there was a smattering of news, but nothing in detail. I am much better now. Through the grace of the Lord I am proof against the severe cold for this year. Oh, the terrible cold! But these people keep all down through scientific knowledge. Every house has its cellar underground, in which there is a big boiler whence steam is made to course day and night through every room. This keeps all the rooms warm, but it has one defect, that while it is summer indoors, it is 30 to 40 degrees below zero outside! Most of the rich people of this country make for Europe during the winter, which is comparatively warm.

Now, let me give you some instructions. This letter is meant for you. Please go through these instructions once a day and act up to them. I have got Sarada's letter — he is doing good work — but now we want organization. To him, Brother Tarak, and others please give my special love and blessings. The reason why I give you these few instructions is that there is an organising power in you — the Lord has made this known to me — but it is not yet fully developed. Through His blessings it will soon be. That you never lose your centre of gravity is an evidence of this, but it must be both intensive and extensive.

1. All the Shâstras hold that the threefold misery that there is in this world is not natural, hence it is removable.

2. In the Buddha Incarnation the Lord says that the root of the Âdhibhautika misery or, misery arising from other terrestrial beings, is the formation of classes (Jâti); in other words, every form of class-distinction, whether based on birth, or acquirements, or wealth is at the bottom of this misery. In the Atman there is no distinction of sex, or Varna[7]* or Ashrama,[8]* or anything of the kind, and as mud cannot be washed away by mud, it is likewise impossible to bring about oneness by means of separative ideas.

3. In the Krishna Incarnation He says that the root of all sorts of misery is Avidyâ (Nescience) and that selfless work purifies the mind. But "what is no-work" (Gita).

4. Only that kind of work which develops our spirituality is work. Whatever fosters materiality is no-work.

5. Therefore work and no-work must be regulated by a person's aptitude, his country, and his age.

6. Works such as sacrifices were suited to the olden times but are not for the modern times.

7. From the date that the Ramakrishna Incarnation was born, has sprung the Satya-Yuga (Golden Age) . ...

8. In this Incarnation atheistic ideas ... will be destroyed by the sword of Jnana (knowledge), and the

whole world will be unified by means of Bhakti (devotion) and Prema (Divine Love). Moreover, in this Incarnation, Rajas, or the desire for name and fame etc., is altogether absent. In other words, blessed is he who acts up to His teachings; whether he accepts Him or not, does not matter.

9. The founders of different sects, in the ancient or modern times, have not been in the wrong. They have done well, but they must do better. Well — better — best.

10. Therefore we must take all up where they are, that is, we must lead them on to higher and higher ideals, without upsetting their own chosen attitude. As to social conditions, those that prevail now are good, but they shall be better — best.

11. There is no chance for the welfare of the world unless the condition of women is improved. It is not possible for a bird to fly on only one wing.

12. Hence, in the Ramakrishna Incarnation the acceptance of a woman as the Guru, hence His practicing in the woman's garb and frame of mind,[9]* hence too His preaching the motherhood of women as representations of the Divine Mother.

13. Hence it is that my first endeavour is to start a Math for women. This Math shall be the origin of Gârgis and Maitreyis, and women of even higher attainments than these. . . .

14. No great work can be achieved by humbug. It is through love, a passion for truth, and tremendous energy, that all undertakings are accomplished.

15. There is no need for quarrel or dispute with anybody. Give your message and leave others to their own thoughts. "— Truth alone triumphs, not falsehood." — Why then fight?

. . . Combine seriousness with childlike naïveté. Live in harmony with all. Give up all idea of egoism, and entertain no sectarian views. Useless wrangling is a great sin.

. . . From Sarada's letter I came to know that N— Ghosh has compared me with Jesus Christ, and the like. That kind of thing may pass muster in our country, but if you send such comments here in print, there is a chance of my being insulted! I mean, I do not like to hamper anybody's freedom of thought — am I a missionary? If Kali has not sent those papers to this country, tell him not to do it. Only the Address will do, I do not want the proceedings. Now many respectable ladies and gentlemen of this country hold me in reverence. The missionaries and others of that ilk have tried their utmost to put me down, but finding it useless have now become quiet. Every undertaking must pass through a lot of obstacles. Truth triumphs if only one pursues a peaceful course. I have no need to reply to what a Mr. Hudson has spoken against me. In the first place, it is Unnecessary, and secondly, I shall be bringing myself down to the level of people of Mr. Hudson's type. Are you mad? Shall I fight from here with one Mr. Hudson? Through the Lord's grace, people who are far above Mr. Hudson in rank listen to me with veneration. Please do not send any more papers. Let all that go on in India, it will do no harm. For the Lord's work at one time there was need for that kind of newspaper blazoning. When that is done, there is no more need for it. . . . It is one of the attendant evils of name and fame that you can't have anything private. . . . Before you begin any undertaking, pray to Shri Ramakrishna, and he will show you the right way. We want a big plot of land to begin with, then building and all will come. Slowly our Math is going to raise itself, don't worry abbot it. . . .

Kali and all others have done good work. Give my love and best wishes to all. Work in unison with the people of Madras, and let someone or other amongst you go there at intervals. Give up for ever the desire for name and fame and power. While I am on earth, Shri Ramakrishna is working through me. So long as you believe in this there is no danger of any evil for you.

The Ramakrishna Punthi (Life of Shri Ramakrishna in Bengali verse) that Akshaya has sent is very good, but there is no glorification of the Shakti at the opening which is a great defect. Tell him to remedy it in the second edition. Always bear this in mind that we are now standing before the gaze of the world, and that people are watching every one of our actions and utterances. Remember this and work.

. . . Be on the look-out for a site for our Math. .

. . . If it be at some little distance from Calcutta, no harm. Wherever we shall build our Math, there we shall have a stir made. Very glad to learn about Mahim Chakravarty. The Andes have turned into the holy Gaya, I see! Where is he? Please give him, Sj. Bijoy Goswami, and our other friends my cordial greetings. . . . To beat an opponent one needs a sword and buckler, so carefully learn English and Sanskrit. Kali's English is getting nicer every day, while that of Sarada is deteriorating. Tell Sarada to give up the flowery style. It is extremely difficult to write a flowery style in a foreign tongue. Please convey to him a hundred thousand bravos from me! There's a hero indeed. ... Well done, all of you! Bravo, lads! The beginning is excellent. Go on in that way. If the adder of jealousy foes not come in, there is no fear!

— Those who serve My devotees are My best devotees." Have all of you a little grave bearing. I am not writing any book on Hinduism at present. But I am jotting down my thoughts. Every religion is an expression, a language to express the same truth, and we must speak to each in his own language. That Sarada has grasped this, is all right. It will be time enough to look to Hinduism later on. Do you think people in this country would be much attracted if I talk of Hinduism? — The very name of narrowness in ideas will scare them away! The real thing is — the Religion taught by Shri Ramakrishna, let the Hindus call it Hinduism — and others call it in their own way. Only you must proceed slowly. "— One must make journeys slowly." Give my blessings to Dinanath, the new recruit. I have very little time to write — always lecture, lecture, lecture. Purity, Patience, Perseverance.... You must ask those numerous people who are now paying heed to Shri Ramakrishna's teachings, to help you pecuniarily to a certain extent. How can the Math be maintained unless they help you? You must not be shy of making this plain to all. ...

There is no gain in hastening my return from this country. In the first place, a little sound made here will resound there a great deal. Then, the people of this country are immensely rich and are bold enough to pay. While the people of our country have neither money nor the least bit of boldness.

You will know everything by degrees. Was Shri Ramakrishna the Saviour of India merely? It is this narrow idea that has brought about India's ruin, and her welfare is an impossibility so long as this is not rooted out. Had I the money I would send each one of you to travel all over the world. No great idea can have a place in the heart unless one steps out of his little corner. It will be verified in time. Every great achievement is done slowly. Such is the Lord's will. ...

Why didn't any of you write about Daksha and Harish? I shall be glad to know if you watch their whereabouts. That Sanyal is feeling miserable is because his mind is not yet pure like the water of the Ganga. It is not yet selfless, but will be in time. He will have no misery if he can give up the little crookedness and be straightforward. My special loving greetings to Rakhal and Hari. Take great care of them. ... Never forget that Rakhal was the special object of Shri Ramakrishna's love. Let nothing daunt you. Who on earth has the power to snub us so long as the Lord favours us? Even if you are at your last breath, be not afraid. Work on with the intrepidity of a lion but, at the same time with the tenderness of a flower. Let this year's Shri Ramakrishna festival be celebrated in great pomp. Let the feeding be quite ordinary — Prasâda being distributed in earthen plates among the devotees standing in rows. There should be readings from Shri Ramakrishna's Life. Place books like the Vedas and the Vedanta together and perform Ârati before them. . . . Avoid issuing invitation cards of the old style.

— With Bhagavan Shri Ramakrishna's blessings and our great esteem we have the pleasure to invite you." Write some such line, and then write that to defray the expenses of Shri Ramakrishna's Birthday Festival and those of the maintenance of the Math, you want his assistance. That if he likes, he may kindly send the money to such and such, at such and such address, and so on. Also add a page in English. The term "Lord Ramakrishna" has no meaning. You must give it up. Write "Bhagavan" in English characters, and add a line or two in English:

THE ANNIVERSARY OF BHAGAVAN SHRI RAMAKRISHNA

Sir, we have great pleasure in inviting you to join us in celebrating the ——th anniversary of Bhagavan Ramakrishna Paramahamsa. For the celebration of this great occasion and for the maintenance of the Alambazar Math funds are absolutely necessary. If you think that the cause is worthy of your sympathy, we shall be very grateful to receive your contribution to the great work.

Yours obediently,
(Name)

If you get more than enough money, spend only a little of it and keep the surplus as a reserve fund to defray your expenses. On the plea of offering the food to the Lord, do not make everybody wait till he is sick, to have a stale and unsavoury dinner. Have two filters made and use that filtered water for both cooking and drinking purposes. Boil the water before filtering. If you do this, you will never more hear of malaria. Keep a strict eye on everybody's health. If you can give up lying on the floor — in other words, if you can get the money to do it, it will be excellent indeed. Dirty clothes are the chief cause of disease. ... About the food offering, let me tell you that only a little Payasânna (milk-rice with sugar) will do. He used to love that alone. It is true that the worship-room is a help to many, but it is no use indulging in Râjasika and Tâmasika food. Let the ceremonials give place to a certain extent to a little study of the Gita or the Upanishads or other sacred books. What I mean is this — let there be as little materialism as possible, with the maximum of spirituality. ... Did Shri Ramakrishna come for this or that particular individual, or for the world at large? If the latter, then you must present him in such a light that the whole world may understand him. ... You must not identify yourselves with any life of his written by anybody nor give your sanction to any. There is no danger so long as such books do not come out associated with our name. ... "Say yea, yea, to all and stick to your own."

... A thousand thanks to Mahendra Babu for his kindly helping us. He is a very liberal-hearted man. ... About Sanyal, he will attain the highest good by doing his bit of work attentively, that is, by simply serving Shri Ramakrishna's children. ... Brother Tarak is doing very good work. Bravo! Well done! That is what we want. Let me see all of you shoot like so many meteors! What is Gangadhar doing? Some Zemindars in Rajputana respect him. Tell him to get some money from them as Bhikshâ; then he is a man. ...

Just now I read Akshaya's book. Give him a hundred thousand hearty embraces from me. Through his pen Shri Ramakrishna is manifesting himself. Blessed is Akshaya! Let him recite that Punthi before all. He must recite it before all in the Festival. If the work be too large, let him read extracts of it. Well, I do not find a single irrelevant word in it. I cannot tell in words the joy I have experienced by reading his book. Try all of you to give the book an extensive sale. Then ask Akshaya to go from village to village to preach. Well done Akshaya! He is doing his work. Go from village to village and proclaim to all Shri Ramakrishna's teachings, can there be a more blessed lot than this? I tell you, Akshaya's book and Akshaya himself must electrify the masses. Dear, dear, Akshaya, I bless you with all my heart, my dear brother. May the Lord sit in your tongue! Go and spread his teachings from door to door. There is no need whatever of your becoming a Sannyasin. ... Akshaya is the future apostle for the masses of Bengal. Take great care of Akshaya; his faith and devotion have borne fruit.

Ask Akshaya to write these few points in the third section of his book, "The Propagation of the Faith".

1. Whatever the Vedas, the Vedanta, and all other Incarnations have done in the past, Shri Ramakrishna lived to practice in the course of a single life.

2. One cannot understand the Vedas, the Vedanta, the Incarnations, and so forth, without understanding his life. For he was the explanation.

3. From the very date that he was born, has sprung the Satya-Yuga (Golden Age). Henceforth there is an end to all sorts of distinctions, and everyone down to the Chandâla will be a sharer in the Divine Love. The distinction between man and woman, between the rich and the poor, the literate and illiterate, Brahmins and Chandalas — he lived to root out all. And he was the harbinger of Peace — the separation be-

tween Hindus and Mohammedans, between Hindus and Christians, all are now things of the past. That fight about distinctions that there was, belonged to another era. In this Satya-Yuga the tidal wave of Shri Ramakrishna's Love has unified all.

Tell him to expand these ideas and write them in his own style.

Whoever — man or woman — will worship Shri Ramakrishna, be he or she ever so low, will be then and there converted into the very highest. Another thing, the Motherhood of God is prominent in this Incarnation. He used to dress himself as a woman — he was, as it were, our Mother — and we must likewise look upon all women as the reflections of the Mother. In India there are two great evils. Trampling on the women, and grinding the poor through caste restrictions. He was the Saviour of women, Saviour of the masses, Saviour of all, high and low. And let Akshaya introduce his worship in every home — Brahmin or Chandala, man or woman — everyone has the right to worship him. Whoever will worship him only with devotion shall be blessed for ever.

Tell him to write in this strain. Never mind anything — the Lord will be at his side.

Yours affectionately,
Vivekananda.

PS. ... Ask Sanyal to send me a copy each of the Nârada and Shândilya Sutras, and one of the Yogavâsishtha, that has been translated in Calcutta. I want the English translation of the last, not a Bengali edition....

76 — RAKHAL

Translated from Bengali

C/O E. T. STURDY, ESQ.,
READING, CAVERSHAM, ENGLAND,
1895.

DEAR RAKHAL,
Glad to receive your letters. There are two defects in the letters which you all write, specially in yours. The first is that very few of the important points I ask are answered. Secondly, there is unusual delay in replying. . . . I have to work day and night, and am always whirling from place to place besides.... These are countries where the people are most luxurious, fashionable folk, and nobody would touch a man who has but a speck of dirt on his body. ... I hoped that somebody would come while I was still here, but as yet nothing has been settled I see. ... Business is business, that is, you must do everything promptly; delay and shuffling won't do. By the end of next week I shall go to America, so there is no chance of my meeting him who is coming. . . . These are countries of gigantic scholars. Is it a joke to make disciples of such people? You are but children and talk like children. Only this much is needed that there should be someone to teach a little Sanskrit, or translate a bit in my absence, that's all. Why not let Girish Babu visit these lands? It is a good idea. It will cost him but 3000 rupees to visit England and America, and go back. The more people come to these countries, the better. But then it sets my nerves on edge to look at those who don hats and pose as Sahibs!

Black as chimney sweeps, and calling themselves Europeans! Why not wear one's country-dress, as befits gentlemen? — Instead of that, to add to that frightfulness of appearance! Good heavens! . . . Here, as in our country one has to spend from one's own pocket to give lectures, but one can make good the expenses if one lives long enough and makes a reputation. Another thing, my incessant lecturing tours are making my constitution very nervous, causing insomnia and other troubles. Over and above that, I have to work single-handed. It is no use depending on my countrymen. No one (in Bengal) has hitherto helped me with a penny, nor has a single soul stepped forward to my assistance. Everybody in this world seeks help, and the more you help him, the more he wants. And if you can do no further, he will call you a cheat.... I love — and trust him.... He will be free from disease through the Lord's grace. I take all his responsibility. . . .

Yours affectionately,
Vivekananda.

77 — SHASHI

Translated from Bengali

C/O E. T. STURDY, ESQ.,
READING, CAVERSHAM, ENGLAND,
1895.

DEAR SHASHI,

. . . I am in receipt of Rakhal's letter today. I am sorry to hear that — has suffered from gravel. Most probably it was due to indigestion. Gopal's debts have been cleared; now ask him to join the monastic order. The worldly-wise instinct is most difficult to root out. . . . Let him come and work in the Math. One is apt to imbibe a lot of mischievous ideas by concerning oneself too long in worldly affairs. If he refuses to take the monastic vow, please tell him to clear out. I don't want amphibious type of men who will be half monks and half householders. . . . Haramohan has coined a Lord Ramakrishna Paramahamsa, I see. What does he mean? English Lord, or Duke? Tell Rakhal, let people say whatever they will — "Men (who wrongly criticise) are to be treated as worms!" as Shri Ramakrishna used to say. Let there be no disparity between what you profess and what you do, also eschew the very name of Jesuitism. Was I ever an orthodox, Paurânika Hindu, an adherent of social usages? I do not pose as one. You will not have to say things that will be pleasant to any section of people. You must not so much as notice what the Bengalis say for or against us. . . . They could not do a penny-worth of service to him whose birth has sanctified their country where the primary laws of health and sanitation are trampled, and yet they would talk big! What matters is, my brother, what such men have got to say! . . . It is for you to go on doing your own work. Why look up to men for approbation, look up to God! I hope Sharat will be able to teach them the Gita and the Upanishads and their commentaries somehow, with the help of the dictionary. — Or, is it an empty Vairâgya that you have? The days of such Vairagya are gone! It is not for everyone, my boy, to become Ramakrishna Paramahamsa! I hope Sharat has started by this time. Please send a copy of the Panchadashi, a copy of the Gita (with as many commentaries as possible), a copy each of the Nârada and Shândilya Sutras (published in Varanasi), a translation (good, not worthless) of the Panchadashi — if it is available — and the translation by Kâlivara Vedântavâgisha of Shankara's Commentary. And if there be any translation, Bengali or English (by Shrish Babu of Allahabad), of Pânini's Sutras, or the Kâshikâ-Vritti, or the Phani-Bhâshya, please send a copy of each. ... Now, just tell your Bengalis to send me a copy of the Vâchaspatya Dictionary, and that will be a good test for those tall-talking people. In England, religious movements make very slow progress. These people here are either bigots or atheists. And the former again have only a bit of formal religion. They say, "Patriotism is our religion." That is all.

Send the books to America, c/o Miss Mary Phillips, 19 West 38th Street, New York, U.S.A. That is my American address. By the end of November I shall go to America. So send my books etc., there. If Sharat has started immediately on your receipt of my letter, then only I may meet him, otherwise not. Business is business, no child's play. Mr. Sturdy will see to him and accommodate him. This time I have come to England just to probe a little. Next summer I shall try to make some stir. The winter after that, I shall go to India. . . . Correspond regularly with those who are interested in us, so as to keep up their interest. Try to open centres in places all over Bengal.... This much for the present. In my next I shall give you more details. Mr. Sturdy is a very nice gentleman, a staunch Vedantist, and understands a smattering of Sanskrit. It is with a good deal of labour that you can do a little bit of work in these countries; a sheer uphill task, with cold and rain into the bargain. Moreover, here you must support yourself and do your labour of love. Englishmen won't spend a penny on lectures or things of that sort. If they do come to listen to you, well, thank your stars — as is the case in our country. Besides, the common people here do not even know of me now. In addition to all this, they will give you a wide berth if you preach God and such things to them. They think this must be another clergyman! Well, you just patiently do one thing — set about collecting everything that books, beginning with the Rig-Veda down to the most insignificant of Puranas and Tantras, have got to say about creation and annihilation of the universe, about race, heaven, and hell, the soul, consciousness, and intellect, etc., the sense-organs, Mukti, transmigration, and suchlike things. No child's play would do, I want real scholarly work. The most important thing is to collect the materials. My love to you all.

Yours affectionately,
Vivekananda.

78 — RAKHAL

Translated from Bengali

1895.

DEAR RAKHAL,

... Your suggestion to me to go back to India is no doubt right, but a seed has been sown in this country, and there is the possibility of its being nipped in the bud if I go away all on a sudden. Hence I have to wait some time. Moreover it will be possible to manage everything nicely from here. Everybody requests me to return to India. It is all right, but don't you see it is not wise to depend upon others. A wise man should stand firm on his own legs and act. Everything will come about slowly. For the present don't forget to be on the look-out for a site. We want a big plot — of about ten to twenty thousand rupees — it must be right on the Ganga. Though my capital is small, I am exceedingly bold. Have an eye on securing the land. At present we shall have to work three centres, one in New York, another in Calcutta and a third in Madras. Then, by degrees, as the Lord will arrange. ... You must keep a strict eye on your health; let everything else be subordinated to that. ...

Brother Tarak is eager for travel. Well, it is good, but these are very expensive countries; a preacher needs here at least a thousand rupees a month. But Brother Tarak has boldness, and it is God who provides every thing. Quite true, but he must have to improve his English a little. The thing is, one has to snatch one's bread from the jaws of the missionary scholars. That is, one must prevail over these people by dint of learning, or one will be blown off at a puff.

They understand neither Sâdhus nor your Sânnyasins, nor the spirit of renunciation. What they do understand is the vastness of learning, the display of eloquence and tremendous activity. Over and above that, the whole country will be searching for flaws, the clergy will day and night try to snub you, through force or guile. You must get rid of these obstructions to preach your doctrines. Through the mercy of the Divine Mother everything is possible. But in my opinion if Brother Tarak goes on starting some societies in the Punjab and Madras, and you become organised, it will be the best thing. It is indeed a great thing to discover a new path, but it is as difficult a task to cleanse that path and make it spacious and nice. If you live for some time in places where I have sown the seeds of our Master's ideals and succeed in developing the seeds into plants, you will be doing much greater work than I did. What will they who cannot manage some ready-made thing do with regard to things that are yet to come? If you cannot add a little salt to a dish almost done, how am I to believe that you will collect all the ingredients? Let Brother Tarak, as an alternative, start a Himalayan Math at Almora and have a library there, so that we may spend some of our spare time in a cool place and practice spiritual exercises. However, I have nothing to say against any particular course which any one may be led to adopt; on the contrary, God-speed —" bit. What's the good of being in a hurry? You shall all travel the whole world. Courage! Brother Tarak has a great capacity for work within him. Hence I expect much of him. . . . You remember, I suppose, how after Shri Ramakrishna's passing away, all forsook us as so many worthless, ragged boys. Only people like Balaram, Suresh, Master, and Chuni Babu were our friends at that hour of need. And we shall never be able to repay our debts to them. ... Tell Chuni Babu in private that he has nothing to fear, that those who are protected by the Lord must be above fear. I am a puny man, but the glories of the Lord are infinite. — Discard fear. Let not your faith be shaken. ...Has danger any power over one whom the Lord has taken into His fold?

Ever yours,
Vivekananda.

79 — MRS. BULL

C/O E. T. STURDY, ESQ.,
HIGH VIEW, CAVERSHAM,
READING, ENGLAND,
17th Sept., 1895.

DEAR MRS. BULL,

Mr. Sturdy and I want to get hold of a few of the best, say, strong and intelligent men in England to form a society, and therefore we must proceed slowly. We must take care not to be run over with "fads" from the first. This you will know has been my policy in America too. Mr. Sturdy has been in India living with our Sannyasins in their manner for some time. He is an exceedingly energetic man, educated and well versed in Sanskrit. ... So far so good. ... Purity, perseverance, and energy — these three I want, and if I get only half a dozen here, my work will go on. I have a great chance of such a few.

Yours with best wishes,
Vivekananda.

80 — MRS. BULL

READING, ENGLAND,
24th Sept., 1895.

DEAR MRS. BULL,

I have not done any visible work as yet except helping Mr. Sturdy in studying Sanskrit. ... Mr. Sturdy wants me to bring over a monk from India from amongst my brethren to help him when I am away in America. I have written to India for one. . . . So far it is all right. I am waiting for the next wave. "Avoid not and seek not — wait for what the Lord sends", is my motto. . . . I am a slow writer, but the heart is full of gratitude.

Yours with best wishes,
Vivekananda.

81 — MOTHER

C/O E. T. STURDY, ESQ.,
HIGH VIEW, CAVERSHAM,
READING, ENGLAND,
October, 1895.

DEAR MOTHER, (Mrs. F. H. Leggett)

You have not forgotten your son? Where are you now? And Tante and the babies? What about our saintly worshipper at your shrine? Joe Joe is not entering "Nirvana" so soon, but her deep silence almost seems to be a big "Samadhi".

Are you on the move? I am enjoying England very much. I am living with my friend on philosophy, leaving a little margin for eating and smoking. We are getting nothing else but Dualism and Monism and all the rest of them.

Hollister has become very manly, I suppose, in his long trousers; and Alberta is studying German.

The Englishmen here are very friendly. Except a few Anglo-Indians, they do not hate black men at all. Not even do they hoot at me in the streets. Sometimes I wonder whether my face has turned white, but the mirror tells the truth. Yet they are all so friendly here.

Again, the English men and women who love India are more Hindu than the Hindus themselves. I am getting plenty of vegetables cooked, you will be surprised to hear, à la Indienne perfectly. When an Englishman takes up a thing, he goes to its very depths. Yesterday I met a Prof. Fraser, a high official here. He has been half his life in India; and he has lived so much in ancient thought and wisdom that he does not care a fig for anything out of India!! You will be astonished to hear that many of the thoughtful English men and women think that the Hindu caste is the only solution of the social problem. With that idea in their head you may imagine how they hate the socialists and other social democrats!! Again, here the men — and the most highly educated — take the greatest interest in Indian thought, and very few women. The woman's sphere is narrower here than in America. So far everything is going very well with me. I shall let you know any further developments.

With my love to paterfamilias, to the Queen Mother, to Joe Joe (no title), and to the babies,

> Ever yours with love and blessings,
> Vivekananda.

82 — DEAR—

> READING, ENGLAND,
> 4th Oct., 1895.

DEAR—

. . . Purity, patience, and perseverance overcome all obstacles. All great things must of necessity be slow. . . .

> Yours with love,
> Vivekananda.

83 — RAKHAL

Translated from Bengali

> C/O E. T. STURDY,
> HIGH VIEW, CAVERSHAM, READING
> 4th October, 1895.

MY DEAR RAKHAL,

You know that I am now in England. I shall stay here for about a month and go back to America. Next summer I shall again come to England. At present there is not much prospect in England, but the Lord is omnipotent. Let us wait and see. . . .

It is impossible for — to come now. The thing is, the money belongs to Mr. Sturdy, and we must have the kind of man he likes. Mr. Sturdy has taken initiation from me, and is a very enterprising and good man.

In the first place we want a man who has a thorough mastery of English and Sanskrit. It is true that will be able to pick up English soon should he come here but I am as yet unable to bring men here to learn. We want them, first, who will be able to teach. In the second place, I trust those that will not desert me in prosperity and adversity alike. . . . The most trustworthy men are needed. Then, after the foundation is laid, let him who will, come and make a noise, there is no fear. — gave no proof of wisdom in being carried away by a hubbub and joining the party of those charlatans. Sir, granted that Ramakrishna Paramahamsa was a sham, granted that it has been a very serious mistake, indeed, to take refuge in him, but what is the way out now? What if one life is spent in vain, but shall a man eat his own words? Can there be such a thing as having a dozen husbands? Any of you may join any party you like, I have no objection, no, not in the least, but travelling this world over I find that save and except his circle alone, everywhere else thought and act are at variance. For those that belong to him, I have the utmost love, the utmost confidence. I have no alternative in the matter. Call me one-sided if you will, but there you have my bona fide avowal. If but a thorn pricks the foot of one who has surrendered himself to Shri Ramakrishna, it makes my bones ache. All others I love; you will find very few men so unsectarian as I am; but you must excuse me, I have that bit of bigotry. If I do not appeal to his name, whose else shall I? It will be time enough to seek for a big Guru in our next birth; but in this, it is that unlearned Brahmin who has bought this body of mine for ever.

I give you a bit of my mind; don't be angry, pray. I am your slave so long as you are his — step a hair's breadth outside that, and you and I are on a par. All the sects and societies that you see, the whole host of them, inside the country or out, he has already swallowed them all, my brother.

"— These have verily been killed by Myself long ago, be only the instrument, O Arjuna." Today or tomorrow they will be merged in your own body. O man of little faith! Through his grace, "— The whole universe becomes a hoof-mark of the cow." Be not traitors, that is a sin past atonement. Name, fame, good deeds, "— Whatever sacrifices you perform, whatever penances you undergo, whatever you eat" — surrender everything to his feet. What on earth do we want? He has given us refuge, what more do we want? Bhakti is verily its own reward — what else is needed? My brother, he who made men of us by feeding and clothing and imparting wisdom and knowledge, who opened the eyes of our self, whom day and night we found the living God — must we be traitors to him!!! And you forget the mercy of such a Lord! The lives of Buddha and Krishna and Jesus are matters of ancient history, and doubts are entertained about their historicity, and you in spite of seeing the greatness of Shri Ramakrishna's life in flesh and blood sometimes lose your head! Fie upon you! I have nothing to say. His likeness is being worshipped in and out of your country, by godless and heartless men, and you are stranded at times on disbelief!! In a breath he will create for himself hundreds of thousands of such as you are. Blessed is your birth, blessed your lineage, and blessed your country that you were allowed to take the dust of his feet. Well I can't help. He is protecting us, forsooth — I see it before my eyes. Insane that you are, is it through my own strength that beauty like that of fairies, and hundreds of thousands of rupees, lose their attraction and appear as nothing to me? Or is it he who is protecting me? He who has no faith in him and no reverence for the Holy Mother will be a downright loser, I tell you plainly.

. . . Haramohan has written about his troubled circumstances, and says he will be dislodged from his home soon. He has asked for some lectures; but I have none at present, but have still some money left in my purse, which I shall send him. So he need not be afraid. I could send him at once, but I suspect that the money I last sent was miscarried, therefore I postpone sending it. Secondly, I know, besides, of no address to send it to. I see the Madras people have failed to start the paper. Practical wisdom is altogether wanting in the Hindu race, I see. Whenever you promise to do any work, you must do it exactly at the appointed time, or people lose their faith in you. Money matters require a speedy reply. . . . If Master Mahashaya be willing, tell him to be my Calcutta agent, for I have an implicit faith in him, and he understands a good deal of these things; it is not for a childish and noisy rabble to do it. Tell him to fix upon a centre, an address that will not change every hour, and to which I shall direct all my Calcutta correspondence. . . . Business is business. . . .

Yours etc.,
Vivekananda.

84 — MRS. BULL

READING,
6th Oct., 1895.

DEAR MRS. BULL,

. . . I am translating a little book on Bhakti with Mr. Sturdy with copious commentaries, which is to be published soon. This month I am to give two lectures in London and one in Maidenhead. This will open up the way to some classes and parlour lectures. We do not wish to make any noise but to go quietly. . .

Yours with best wishes,
Vivekananda.

85 — AKHANDANANDA

Translated from Bengali

LONDON,
13th Nov., 1895.

MY DEAR AKHANDANANDA,

I am very glad to receive your letter. It is excellent work that you are doing. R— is very liberal and openhanded, but no advantage should be taken over him for that reason. About the raising of funds by Shrimân —, well, it is a fair enterprise; but my boy, this is a very queer world, where even the World-Gods Brahmâ and Vishnu find it difficult to evade the clutches of lust and gold. Wherever there is any the least concern with money, there is the chance for misunderstanding. Let therefore nobody undertake such work as raising money on behalf of the Math. ... Whenever you hear of any householder collecting funds in my or our name on the plea of erecting a Math, or some such thing, the first thing you should do is to distrust him, and never set your hand to it. The more so, as householders of poor means take to various tricks to supply their wants. Therefore, if ever a trusty devotee or a householder with a heart, being of affluent circumstances, undertakes such works as the founding of a Math, or if the funds raised be kept in the custody of a trusty householder of wealth —

well and good, otherwise never have a hand in it. On the contrary, you must dissuade others from such a thing. You are but a boy and are ignorant of the snare of gold. Opportunities will turn even a staunch moralist into a cheat. This is the way of the world.

It is not at all in our nature to do a work conjointly. It is to this that our miserable condition is due. He who knows how to obey knows how to command. Learn obedience first. Among these Western nations, with such a high spirit of independence, the spirit of obedience is equally strong. We are all of us self-important — which never produces any work. Great enterprise, boundless courage, tremendous energy, and, above all, perfect obedience — these are the only traits that lead to individual and national regeneration. These traits are altogether lacking in us.

Go on with the work as you are doing it, but then you must pay particular attention to study. J— Babu has sent a Hindi magazine, in which Pundit R— of Alwar has published a translation of my Chicago Address. Please convey my special indebtedness and thanks to both.

Let me now address myself to you — take particular care to start a centre in Rajputana. It must be in some central place like Jaipur or Ajmer. Then branches must be established in towns like Alwar and Khetri. You must mix with all, we do not want to quarrel with any. Give my loving embrace to Pundit N—; the man is very energetic, and will be a very practical man in time. Tender my loving regards to Mr. M— and —ji too. A Religious Association or something of the kind has been afoot at Ajmer — what is it? Let me know all about it. M— Babu writes that he and others have written me letters; but I have not received any up till now. . . . About Maths, or centres, or anything of the kind, it is no use starting them in Calcutta; Varanasi is the place for them. I have many plans like that, but all depends on funds. You will know of them by degrees. You might have noticed from the papers that our movement is steadily gaining ground in England. Every enterprise in this country takes some time to have a go. But once John Bull sets his hand to a thing, he will never let it go. The Americans are quick, but they are somewhat like straw on fire, ready to be extinguished. Do not preach to the public that Ramakrishna Paramahamsa was an Incarnation, and things of that sort. I have some followers at — look after them. . . . Infinite power will come unto you — never fear. Be pure, have faith, be obedient.

Teach against the marriage of boys. No scripture ever sanctions it. But for the present say nothing against little girls being married. Directly you stop the marriage of boys, that of girls will stop of itself. Girls surely are not going to marry among themselves! Write to the Secretary, Arya Samaj, Lahore, asking the whereabouts of a Sannyasin named Achyutananda who used to live with them. Make special inquiry of the man. . . . Never fear.

Yours affectionately,
Vivekananda.

86 — MRS. BULL

LONDON,
21st Nov., 1895.

DEAR MRS. BULL,

I sail by the Britannic on Wednesday, the 27th. My work so far has been very satisfactory here and I am sure to do splendid work here next summer. . . .

Yours with love,
Vivekananda.

87 — MRS. ALBERTA

R.M.S. "Britannic",
Thursday morning, Dec. 5, 1895.

DEAR ALBERTA,

Received your nice letter last evening. Very kind of you to remember me. I am going soon to see the "Heavenly Pair". Mr. Leggett is a saint as I have told you already, and your mother is a born empress, every inch of her, with a saint's heart inside.

I am so glad you are enjoying the Alps so much They must be wonderful. It is always in such places that the human soul aspires for freedom. Even if the nation is spiritually poor, it aspires for physical freedom. I met a young Swiss in London. He used to come to my classes. I was very successful in London, and though I did not care for the noisy city, I was very much pleased with the people. In your country, Alberta, the Vedantic thought was introduced in the beginning by ignorant "cranks", and one has to work his way through the difficulties created by such introductions. You may have noticed that only a few men or women of the upper classes ever joined my classes in America. Again in America the upper classes being the rich, their whole time is spent in enjoying their wealth and imitating (aping?) the Europeans. On the other hand in England the Vedantic ideas have been introduced by the most learned men in the country, and there are a large number among the upper classes in England who are very thoughtful. So you will be astonished to hear that I found my grounds all prepared, and I am convinced that my work will have more hold on England than America. Add to this the tremendous tenacity of the English character, and judge for yourself. By this you will find that I have changed a good deal of my opinion about England, and I am glad to confess it. I am perfectly sure that we will do still better in Germany. I am coming back to England next summer. In the meanwhile my work is in very able hands. Joe Joe has been the same kind good pure friend to me here as in America, and my debt to your family is simply immense. My love and blessings to Hollister and you. The steamer is standing at anchor on account of fog. The purser has very kindly given me a whole cabin by myself. Every Hindu is a Raja, they think, and are very polite — and the charm will break, of course, when they find that the Raja is penniless!!

Yours with love and blessings,
Vivekananda.

88 — MRS. BULL

228 WEST 39TH STREET, NEW YORK,
8th Dec., 1895.

DEAR MRS. BULL,

Many thanks for your kind note of welcome. I arrived last Friday after ten days of a very tedious voyage. It was awfully rough and for the first time in my life I was very badly seasick. . . . I have left some strong friends in England who will work in my absence expecting my arrival next summer. My plans are not settled yet about the work here. Only I have an idea to run to Detroit and Chicago meanwhile, and then come back to New York. The public lecture plan I intend to give up entirely, as I find the best thing for me to do is to step entirely out of the money question — either in public lectures or private classes. In the long run it does harm and sets a bad example.

In England I worked on this principle and refused even the voluntary collections they made. Mr. Sturdy, being a rich man, bore the major part of the expenses of lecturing in big halls — the rest I bore. It worked well. Again, to use rather a vulgar illustration, even in religion there is no use overstocking the market. The supply must follow the demand, and the demand alone. If people want me, they will get up lectures. I need not bother myself about these things. If you think after consultation with Mrs. Adams and Miss Locke that it would be practicable for me to come to Chicago for a course of lectures, write to me. Of course the money question should be left entirely out.

My idea is for autonomic, independent groups in different places. Let them work on their own account and do the best they can. As for myself, I do not want to entangle myself in any organisation. Hoping you are enjoying good health both physically and mentally,

I am yours, in the Lord,
Vivekananda.

89 — MRS. BULL

228 W. 39TH STREET, NEW YORK,
10th Dec., 1895.

DEAR MRS. BULL,

I have received the Secretary's letter and will be glad to lecture before the Harvard Philosophical Club as requested. The difficulty in the way is: I have begun to write in earnest, as I want to finish some text-books to form the basis of work when I am gone. I have to hurry through four little books before I go.

This month, notices are out for the four Sunday lectures. The lectures for the first week of February in Brooklyn are being arranged by Dr. Janes and others.

Yours, with best wishes,
Vivekananda.

90 — SISTER

NEW YORK,
29th Dec., 1895.

DEAR SISTER, (Miss S. Farmer)

In this universe where nothing is lost, where we live in the midst of death in life, every thought that is thought, in public or in private, in crowded thoroughfares or in the deep recesses of primeval forests, lives. They are continuously trying to become self-embodied, and until they have embodied themselves, they will struggle for expression, and any amount of repression cannot kill them. Nothing can be destroyed — those thoughts that caused evil in the past are also seeking embodiment, to be filtered through repeated expression and, at last, transfigured into perfect good.

As such, there is a mass of thought which is at the present time struggling to get expression. This new thought is telling us to give up our dreams of dualism, of good and evil in essence, and the still wilder dream of suppression. It teaches us that higher direction and not destruction is the law. It teaches us that it is not a world of bad and good, but good and better — and still better. It stops short of nothing but acceptance. It teaches that no situation is hopeless, and as such accepts every form of mental, moral, or spiritual thought where it already stands, and without a word of condemnation tells it that so far it has done good, now is the time to do better. What in old times was thought of as the elimination of bad, it teaches as the transfiguration of evil and the doing of better. It, above all, teaches that the kingdom of heaven is already in existence if we will have it, that perfection is already in man if he will see it.

The Greenacre meetings last summer were so wonderful, simply because you opened yourself fully to that thought which has found in you so competent a medium of expression, and because you took your stand on the highest teaching of this thought that the kingdom of heaven already exists.

You have been consecrated and chosen by the Lord as a channel for converting this thought into life, and every one that helps you in this wonderful work is serving the Lord.

Our scripture teaches that he who serves the servants of the Lord is His highest worshipper. You are a servant of the Lord, and as a disciple of Krishna I will always consider it a privilege and worship to render you any service in the carrying out of your inspired mission wherever I be.

Ever your affectionate brother,
Vivekananda.

91 — SARADA

Translated from Bengali

Jan., 1896.

DEAR SARADA,

. . .Your idea of the paper is very good indeed. Apply yourself to it heart and soul. . . . Never mind the funds. . . . There are many to preach Christianity and Mohammedanism — you just go through the preaching of your own country's religion. But then if you can get hold of a Mohammedan who is versed in Arabic and have old Arabic books translated, it will be a good plan. There is much of Indian history in the Persian language. If you can have the books translated bit by bit, it will be a good regular item. We want quite a number of writers, then there is the difficult task of getting subscribers. The way out is this: You lead a wandering life; wherever you find Bengali language spoken, thrust the paper on whomsoever you can lay your hands on. Enlist them by vehemence! — they would always turn tail the moment they have to spend something. Never mind anything! Push it on! Begin to contribute articles, all of you who can. It won't do merely to sit idle. You have done a heroic deed! Bravo! Those who falter and vacillate will lag behind, and you will jump straight on top of all! Those that are working for their own salvation will neither have their own nor that of others. Let the commotion that you make be such as to resound to the world's end. There are people who are ready to pick holes in everything, but when it comes to the question of work, not a scent of them can be had! To work! — as far as in you lies! Then I shall go to India and move the whole country. What fear! "Even a snake loses its venom if it is insisted that it has none." These people will go on the negative track, till they are actually reduced to nothing! . . .

Gangadhar has done right heroic work! Well done! Kali has joined him in work — thrice well done!! Let one go to Madras, and another to Bombay, let the world shake on its hinges! Oh, the grief! If I could get two or three like me, I could have left the world convulsed. As it is, I have to proceed gently. Move the world to its foundations! Send one to China, another to Japan! What will the poor householders do, with their little bits of life? It is for the Sannyasins, Shiva's demons, to rend the skies with their shouts of "Hara! Hara! Shambho!"

Yours affectionately,
Vivekananda.

92 — YOGEN

Translated from Bengali

228 W. 39, NEW YORK,
24th Jan., 1896.

DEAR YOGEN,

. . . I am very sorry to hear that your health is not yet all right. Can you go to a very cold climate where there is plenty of snowfall in the winter, Darjeeling, for instance? The severity of the cold will set your stomach right, as it has done in my case. And can you give up altogether the habit of using ghee and spices? Butter digests more quickly than ghee. ...

Three months more and I go to England, to try once more to make some stir; the following winter to India — and after that, it depends on the Lord.

Put forth all nerve for the magazine that Sarada is wanting to publish. Ask Shashi to look to it. One thing, neither Kali nor anybody else has any need of coming to England at present. I shall train them first when I go to India, and then they may go wherever they please.

We would do nothing ourselves and would scoff at others who try to do something — this is the bane that has brought about our downfall as a nation. Want of sympathy and lack of energy are at the root of all misery, and you must therefore give these two up. Who but the Lord knows what potentialities there are in particular individuals — let all have opportunities, and leave the rest to the Lord. It is indeed very difficult to have an equal love for all, but without it there is no Mukti.

Yours affectionately,
Vivekananda.

93 — MRS. BULL

NEW YORK,
25th Jan., 1896.

DEAR MRS. BULL,

Your letter to Sturdy has been sent over to me. It was very kind of you to write that note. This year, I am afraid, I am getting overworked, as I feel the strain. I want a rest badly. So it is very good, as you say, that the Boston work be taken up in the end of March. By the end of April I will start for England.

Land can be had in large plots in the Catskills for very little money. There is a plot of 101 acres for $200. The money I have ready, only I cannot buy the land in my name. You are the only friend in this country in whom I have perfect trust. If you consent, I will buy the land in your name. The students will go there in summer and build cottages or camps as they like and practice meditation. Later on, if they can collect funds, they may build something up. I am sorry, you cannot come just now. Tomorrow will be the last Sunday lecture of this month. The first Sunday of next month there will be a lecture in Brooklyn; the rest, three in New York, with which I will close this year's New York lectures.

I have worked my best. If there is any seed of truth in it, it will come to life. So I have no anxiety about anything. I am also getting tired of lecturing and having classes. After a few months' work in England I will go to India and hide myself absolutely for some years or for ever. I am satisfied in my conscience that I did not remain an idle Swami. I have a note-book which has travelled with me all over the world. I find these words written seven years ago — "Now to seek a corner and lay myself there to die!" Yet all this Karma remained. I hope I have worked it out. I hope the Lord will give me freedom from this preaching and adding good bondages.

"If you have known the Âtman as the one existence and that nothing else exists, for whom, for what desire, do you trouble yourself?" Through Maya all this doing good etc. came into my brain — now they are leaving me. I get more and more convinced that there is no other object in work except the purification of the soul — to make it fit for knowledge. This world with its good and evil will go on in various forms. Only the evil and good will take new names and new seats. My soul is hankering after peace and rest eternal undisturbed.

"Live alone, live alone. He who is alone never comes into conflict with others — never disturbs others, is never disturbed by others." I long, oh! I long for my rags, my shaven head, my sleep under the trees, and my food from begging! India is the only place where, with all its faults, the soul finds its freedom, its God. All this Western pomp is only vanity, only bondage of the soul. Never more in my life I realised more forcibly the vanity of the world. May the Lord break the bondage of all — may all come out of Maya — is the constant prayer of

Vivekananda.

94 — SARADA

Translated from Bengali

BOSTON,
2nd March, 1896.

DEAR SARADA,

Your letter informed me of everything; but I note that you do not so much as refer to the cable I sent about the celebration. The dictionary that Shashi sent a few months ago has not arrived so far. ... I am going to England soon. Sharat need not come now at all; for I am myself going to England. I do not want people who take such a long time to make up their minds. I did not invite him for a European tour, and I do not have the money either. So ask him not to come, and none else need.

On perusal of your letter on Tibet, I came to lose all regard for your common sense. In the first place, it is nonsense to say that Notovitch's book is genuine. Did you see any original copy, or bring it to India? Secondly, you say you saw in the Kailas Math the portrait of Jesus and the Samaritan Woman. How do you know that it was Jesus' portrait, and not that of a man in the street? Even taking it for granted, how do you know that it was not put up in the said Math by someone who was a Christian? And your opinions on the Tibetans too are unsound; you did not certainly see the heart of Tibet, but only a fringe of the trade route. In places like those only the dregs of a nation are to be met. If on seeing the Chinabazar and Barabazar quarters of Calcutta, anybody called every Bengali a liar, would that be correct?

Consult Shashi properly when writing any article. ... What you need is only obedience. ...

Yours affectionately,
Vivekananda.

95 — MRS. BULL

INDIANA AVE., CHICAGO, ILL.,
6th April, 1896.

DEAR MRS. BULL,

Your kind note was duly received. I had beautiful visits with my friends and have already held several classes. I shall have a few more and then start on Thursday.

Everything has been well arranged here, thanks to the kindness of Miss Adams. She is so, so good and kind.

I am suffering from slight fever the last two days; so I can't write a long letter.

My love to all in Boston.

Yours with kind regards,
Vivekananda.

96 — MRS. BULL

124 E. 44TH STREET, NEW YORK,
14th April, 1896.

DEAR MRS. BULL,

... Here is a curious person who comes to me with a letter from Bombay. He is a practical mechanic and his one idea is to see cutlery and other iron manufactories in this country.... I do not know anything about him, but even if he be a rogue, I like very much to foster this sort of adventurous spirit among my countrymen. He has money enough to pay his way.

Now, if with all caution testing of his genuineness of spirit, you feel satisfied, all he wants is to get some opportunities of seeing these manufactories. I hope he is true and that you can manage to help him in this.

Yours with kind regards,
Vivekananda.

97 — SARADA

Translated from Bengali

NEW YORK,
14th April, 1896.

DEAR SARADA,

Glad to hear everything in your letter. I have got news that Sharat arrived safe. I am in receipt of your letter and the copy of the Indian Mirror. Your contribution is good, go on writing regularly. ... It is very easy to search for faults, but the characteristic of a saint lies in looking for merits — never forget this. ... You need a little business faculty. ... Now what you want is organisation — that requires strict obedience and division of labour. I shall write out everything in every particular from England, for which I start tomorrow. I am determined to make you decent workers thoroughly organised. ...

The term "Friend" can be used with all. In the English language you have not that sort of cringing politeness common in Bengali, and such Bengali terms translated into English become ridiculous. That Ramakrishna Paramahamsa was God — and all that sort of thing — has no go in countries like this. M— has a tendency to put that stuff down everybody's throat, but that will make our movement a little sect. You keep aloof from such attempts; at the same time, if people worship him as God, no harm. Neither encourage nor discourage. The masses will always have the person, the higher ones the principle; we want both. But principles are universal, not persons. Therefore stick to the principles he taught, let people think whatever they like of his person. ... Truce to all quarrels and jealousies and bigotry! These will spoil everything. "But many that are first shall be last; and the last first." "devotees."

Yours affectionately,
Vivekananda.

98 — MRS. BULL

63 ST. GEORGE'S ROAD, LONDON,
30th May, 1896.

DEAR MRS. BULL,

. . . Day before yesterday I had a fine visit with Prof. Max Müller. He is a saintly man and looks like a young man in spite of his seventy years, and his face is without a wrinkle. I wish I had half his love for India and Vedanta. At the same time he is a friend of Yoga too and believes in it. Only he has no patience with humbugs.

Above all, his reverence for Ramakrishna Paramahamsa is extreme, and he has written an article on him for the Nineteenth Century. He asked me, "What are you doing to make him known to the world?" Ramakrishna has charmed him for years. Is it not good news? . . .

Things are going on here slowly but steadily. I am to begin from next Sunday my public lectures.

Yours ever in grateful affection,
Vivekananda.

99 — MRS. BULL

63 ST. GEORGE'S ROAD, LONDON S.W.,
5th June, 1896.

DEAR MRS. BULL,

The Raja-Yoga book is going on splendidly. Saradananda goes to the States soon.

I do not like any one whom I love to become a lawyer, although my father was one. My Master was against it, and I believe that that family is sure to come to grief where there are several lawyers. Our country is full of them; the universities turn them out by the hundreds. What my nation wants is pluck and scientific genius. So I want Mohin to be an electrician. Even if he fails in life, still I will have the satisfaction that he strove to become great and really useful to his country. ... In America alone there is that something in the air which brings out whatever is best in every one. ... I want him to be daring, bold, and to struggle to cut a new path for himself and his nation. An electrical engineer can make a living in India.

Yours with love,
Vivekananda.

PS. Goodwin is writing to you this mail with reference to a magazine in America. I think something of the sort is necessary to keep the work together, and shall of course do all that I can to help it on in the line he suggests. . . . I think it very probable that he will come over with Saradananda.

100 — SHASHI

Translated from Bengali

63 ST. GEORGE'S ROAD, LONDON S.W.,
24th June, 1896.

DEAR SHASHI,

Max Müller wants all the sayings of Shri Ramakrishna classified, that is, all on Karma in one place, on Vairagya in another place, so on Bhakti, Jnana, etc., etc. You must undertake to do this forthwith. ... We must take care to present only the universal aspect of his teachings. . . .

Sharat starts for America tomorrow. The work here is coming to a head. We have already got funds to start a London Centre. Next month I go to Switzerland to pass a month or two there, then I shall return to London. What will be the good of my going home? — This London is the hub of the world. The heart of India is here. How can I leave without laying a sure foundation here? Nonsense! For the present, I shall have Kali here, tell him to be ready. ...

We want great spirit, tremendous energy, and boundless enthusiasm, no womanishness will do. Try to go on exactly as I wrote to you in my last. We want organisation. Organisation is power, and the secret of this is obedience.

Yours affectionately,
Vivekananda.

101 — SHASHI

Translated from Bengali

HIGH VIEW, CAVERSHAM, READING,
3rd July, 1896.

DEAR SHASHI,

Send Kali to England as soon as you get this letter. . . . He will have to bring some books for me. I have only got Rig-Veda Samhitâ. Ask him to bring the Yajur-Veda, Sâma-Veda, Atharva-Samhita, as many of the Brâhmanas as he can get, beginning with the Shatapatha, some of the Sutras, and Yâska's Nirukta. . . .

Let there be no delay as in Sharat's case, but let Kali come at once. Sharat has gone to America, as he had no work to do here. That is to say, he was late by six months, and then when he came, I was here. . . .

Yours affectionately,
Vivekananda.

102 — FRANKINCENSE

63 ST. GEORGE'S ROAD, LONDON S.W.,
6th July, 1896.

DEAR FRANKINCENSE, (Mr. Francis H. Leggett whom Swamiji addressed thus)

. . . Things are going on with me very well on this side of the Atlantic.

The Sunday lectures were quite successful; so were the classes. The season has ended and I too am thoroughly exhausted. I am going to make a tour in Switzerland with Miss Müller. The Galsworthys have been very very kind. Joe (Miss Josephine MacLeod, also referred to as Joe Joe.) brought them round splendidly. I simply admire Joe in her tact and quiet way. She is a feminine statesman or woman. She can wield a kingdom. I have seldom seen such strong yet good common sense in a human being. I will return next autumn and take up the work in America.

The night before last I was at a party at Mrs. Martin's, about whom you must already know a good deal from Joe.

Well, the work is growing silently yet surely in England. Almost every other man or woman came to me and talked about the work. This British Empire with all its drawbacks is the greatest machine that ever existed for the dissemination of ideas. I mean to put my ideas in the centre of this machine, and they will spread all over the world. Of course, all great work is slow, and the difficulties are too many, especially as we Hindus are the conquered race. Yet, that is the very reason why it is bound to work, for spiritual ideals have always come from the downtrodden. Jews overwhelmed the Roman Empire with their spiritual ideals. You will be pleased to know that I am also learning my lessons every day in patience and, above all, in sympathy. I think I am beginning to see the Divine, even inside the high and mighty Anglo-Indians. I think I am slowly approaching to that state when I should be able to love the very "Devil" himself, if there were any.

At twenty years of age I was the most unsympathetic, uncompromising fanatic; I would not walk on the footpath on the theatre side of the streets in Calcutta. At thirty-three, I can live in the same house with prostitutes and never would think of saying a word of reproach to them. Is it degenerate? Or is it that I am broadening out into the Universal Love which is the Lord Himself? Again I have heard that if one does not sea the evil round him he cannot do good work — he lapses into a sort of fatalism. I do not see that. On the other hand, my power of work is immensely increasing and becoming immensely effective. Some days I get into a sort of ecstasy. I feel that I must bless every one, everything, love and embrace everything, and I do see that evil is a delusion. I am in one of these moods now, dear Francis, and am actually shedding tears of joy at the thought of you and Mrs. Leggett's love and kindness to me. I bless the day I was born. I have had so much of kindness and love here, and that Love Infinite that brought me into being has guarded every one of my actions, good or bad, (don't be frightened), for what am I, what was I ever, but a tool in His hands, for whose service I have given up everything, my beloved ones, my joys, my life? He is my playful darling, I am His playfellow. There is neither rhyme nor reason in the universe! What reason binds Him? He the playful one is playing these tears and laughters over all parts of the play! Great fun, great fun, as Joe says.

It is a funny world, and the funniest chap you ever saw is He — the Beloved Infinite! Fun, is it not? Brotherhood or playmatehood — a school of romping children let out to play in this playground of the world! Isn't it? Whom to praise, whom to blame, it is all His play. They want explanations, but how can you explain Him? He is brainless, nor has He any reason. He is fooling us with little brains and reason, but this time He won't find me napping.

I have learnt a thing or two: Beyond, beyond reason and learning and talking is the feeling, the "Love", the "Beloved". Ay, saké, fill up the cup and we will be mad.

Yours ever in madness,
Vivekananda.

103 — MRS. BULL

63 ST. GEORGE'S ROAD, LONDON S.W.,
8th July, 1896.

DEAR MRS. BULL,

The English people are very generous. In three minutes' time the other evening, my class raised £150 for the new quarters for next autumn's work. They would have given £500 on the spot if wanted, but we want to go slow, and not rush into expense. There will be many hands here to carry on the work, and they understand a bit of renunciation, here — the deep English character.

Yours with best wishes,
Vivekananda.

104 — MRS. BULL

SAAS-GRUND, SWITZERLAND,
25th July, 1896.

DEAR MRS. BULL,

I want to forget the world entirely at least for the next two months and practice hard. That is my rest. ... The mountains and snow have a beautifully quieting influence on me, and I am getting better sleep here than for a long time.

My love to all friends.

Yours etc.,
Vivekananda.

105 — SAHJI

C/O. E. T. STURDY, ESQ.,
High View, Caversham, Reading,
5th August, 1896.

DEAR SAHJI, (Lala Badri Sah. The letter was actually written from Switzerland)

Many thanks for your kind greetings. I have an inquiry to make; if you kindly forward me the information I seek, I would be much obliged.

I want to start a Math at Almora or near Almora rather. I have heard that there was a certain Mr. Ramsay who lived in a bungalow near Almora and that he had a garden round his bungalow. Can't it be bought? What is the price? If not to be bought, can it be rented?

Do you know of any suitable place near Almora where I can build my monastery with a garden etc.? I would rather like to have a hill all to myself.

Hoping to get an early reply, I remain, with blessings and love to you and all the rest of my friends in Almora.

Vivekananda.

106 — SHASHI

Translated from Bengali

LAKE LUCERNE, SWITZERLAND,
23rd August, 1896.

MY DEAR SHASHI,

Today I received a letter from Ramdayal Babu, in which he writes that many public women attend the Ramakrishna anniversary festival at Dakshineswar, which makes many less inclined to go there. Moreover, in his opinion one day should be appointed for men and another for women. My decision on the point is this:

1. If public women are not allowed to go to such a great place of pilgrimage as Dakshineswar, where else shall they go to? It is for the sinful that the Lord manifests Himself specially, not so much for the virtuous.

2. Let distinctions of sex, caste, wealth, learning, and the whole host of them, which are so many gateways to hell, be confined to the world alone. If such distinctions persist in holy places of pilgrimage, where then lies the difference between them and hell itself?

3. Ours is a gigantic City of Jagannâtha, where those who have sinned and those who have not, the saintly and the vicious, men and women and children irrespective of age, all have equal right. That for one day at least in the year thousand of men and women get rid of the sense of sin and ideas of distinction and sing and hear the name of the Lord, is in itself a supreme good.

4. If even in a place of pilgrimage people's tendency to evil be not curbed for one day, the fault lies with you, not them. Create such a huge tidal wave of spirituality that whatever people come near will be swept away.

5. Those who, even in a chapel, would think this is a public woman, that man is of a low caste, a third is poor, and yet another belongs to the masses — the less be the number of such people (that is, whom you call gentlemen) the better. Will they who look to the caste, sex, or profession of Bhaktas appreciate our Lord? I pray to the Lord that hundreds of public women may come and bow their heads at His feet; it does not matter if not one gentleman comes. Come public women, come drunkards, come thieves and all — His Gate is open to all. "It is easier for a camel to pass through the eye of a needle than for a rich man to enter the Kingdom of God." Never let such cruel, demoniacal ideas have a place in your mind.

6. But then some social vigilance is needed. How are we to do that? A few men (old men, preferably) should take charge as the warders for the day. They will make circuits round the scene of the festival, and in case they find any man or woman showing impropriety of speech or conduct, they will at once expel them from the garden. But so long as they behave like good men and women, they are Bhaktas and are to be respected — be they men or women, honest citizens or unchaste.

I am at present travelling in Switzerland, and shall soon go to Germany, to see Professor Deussen. I shall return to England from there about the 23rd or 24th September, and the next winter will find me back in my country.

My love to you and all.

Yours etc.,
Vivekananda.

107 — MRS. BULL

LUCERNE, SWITZERLAND,
23rd August, 1896.

DEAR MRS. BULL,

I received your last letter today. By this time you must have received my receipt for £5 you sent. I do not know what membership you mean. I have no objection to have my name to be put on the list of membership of any society. As for Sturdy, I do not know what his opinions are. I am now travelling in Switzerland; from hence I go to Germany, then to England, and next winter to India. I am very glad to hear that Saradananda and Goodwin are doing good work in the U.S. As for me, I do not lay any claim to that £500 for any work. I think I have worked enough. I am now going to retire. I have sent for another man from India who will join me next month. I have begun the work, let others work it out. So you see, to set the work going I had to touch money and property, for a time. Now I am sure my part of the work is done, and I have no more interest in Vedanta or any philosophy in the world or the work itself. I am getting ready to depart to return no more to this hell, this world. Even its religious utility is beginning to pall me. May Mother gather me soon to Herself never to come back any more! These works, and doing good, etc., are just a little exercise to cleanse the mind.

I had enough of it. This world will be world ever and always. What we are, so we see it. Who works? Whose work? There is no world. It is God Himself. In delusion we call it world. Neither I nor thou nor you — it is all He the Lord, all One. So I do not want anything to do about money matters from this time. It is your money. You spend what comes to you just as you like, and blessings follow you.

Yours in the Lord,
Vivekananda.

PS. I have entire sympathy with the work of Dr. Janes and have written him so. If Goodwin and Saradananda can speed the work in U.S., Godspeed to them. They are in no way bound to me or to Sturdy or to anybody else. It was an awful mistake in the Greenacre programme that it was printed that Saradananda was there by the kind permission (leave of absence from England) of Sturdy. Who is Sturdy or anybody else to permit a Sannyasin? Sturdy himself laughed at it and was sorry too. It was a piece of folly. Nothing short of that. It was an insult to Sturdy and would have proved serious for my work if it had reached India. Fortunately I tore all those notices to pieces and threw them into the gutter, and wondered whether it was the celebrated "Yankee" manners the English people delight in talking about. Even so, I am no master to any Sannyasin in this world. They do whatever it suits them, and if I can help them — that is all my connection with them. I have given up the bondage of iron, the family tie — I am not to take up the golden chain of religious brotherhood. I am free, must always be free. I wish everyone to be free — free as the air. If New York needs Vedanta, or Boston, or any other place in the U.S., it must receive them and keep them and provide for them. As for me, I am as good as retired. I have played my part in the world..

108 — SISTER

AIRLIE LODGE, RIDGEWAY GARDENS,
WIMBLEDON, ENGLAND,
17th Sept, 1896.

DEAR SISTER, (Miss Harriet Hale)

Your very welcome news reached me just now, on my return here from Switzerland. I am very, very happy to learn that at last you have thought it better to change your mind about the felicity of "Old Maids Home". You are perfectly right now — marriage is the truest goal for ninety-nine per cent of the human race, and they will live the happiest life as soon as they have learnt and are ready to abide by the eternal lesson — that we are bound to bear and forbear and that life to every one must be a compromise.

Believe me, dear Harriet, perfect life is a contradiction in terms. Therefore we must always expect to find things not up to our highest ideal. Knowing this, we are bound to make the best of everything. From what I know of you, you have the calm power which bears and forbears to a great degree, and therefore I am safe to prophesy that your married life will be very happy.

All blessings attend you and your fiancé and may the Lord make him always remember what good fortune was his in getting such a wife as you — good, intelligent, loving, and beautiful. I am afraid it is impossible for me to cross the Atlantic so soon. I wish I could, to see your marriage.

The best I can do in the circumstances is to quote from one of our books: "May you always enjoy the undivided love of your husband, helping him in attaining all that is desirable in this life, and when you have seen your children's children, and the drama of life is nearing its end, may you help each other in reaching that infinite ocean of Existence, Knowledge, and Bliss, at the touch of whose waters all distinctions melt away and we are all one!" (A reminiscence of Kalidasa's Shakuntalam, where Kanva gives his benedictions to Shakuntalâ on the eve of her departure to her husband's place.)

"May you be like Umâ, chaste and pure throughout life — may your husband be like Shiva, whose life was in Uma!"

Your loving brother,
Vivekananda.

109 — JOE JOE

C/O MISS MULLER,
AIRLIE LODGE, RIDGEWAY GARDENS,
WIMBLEDON, ENGLAND,
7th October, 1896.

DEAR SISTER, (Miss Harriet Hale)

Once more in London, dear Joe Joe, and the classes have begun already. Instinctively I looked about for one familiar face which never had a line of discouragement, never changed, but was always helpful, cheerful, and strengthening — and my mind conjured up that face before me, in spite of a few thousand miles of space. For what is space in the realm of spirit? Well, you are gone to your home of rest and peace. For me, ever-increasing mad work; yet I have your blessings with me always, have I not? My natural tendency is to go into a cave and be quiet, but a fate behind pushes me forward and I go. Whoever could resist fate?

Why did not Christ say in the Sermon on the Mount, "Blessed are they that are always cheerful and always hopeful for they have already the kingdom of heaven"? I am sure, He must have said it, He with the sorrows of a whole world in His heart, He who likened the saintly soul with the child — but it was not noted down; of a thousand things they noted down only one, I mean, remembered.

Most of our friends came — one of the Galsworthys too — i.e. the married daughter. Mrs. Galsworthy could not come today; it was very short notice. We have a hall now, a pretty big one holding about 200 or more. There is a big corner which will be fitted up as the Library. I have another man from India now to help me.

I enjoyed Switzerland immensely, also Germany. Prof. Deussen was very kind — we came together to London and had great fun here. Prof. Max Müller is very, very friendly too. In all, the English work is becoming solid — and respectable too, seeing that great scholars are sympathising. Probably I go to India this winter with some English friends. So far about my own sweet self.

Now what about the holy family? Everything is going on first-rate, I am sure. You must have heard of Fox by this time. I am afraid I rather made him dejected the day before he sailed by telling him that he could not marry Mabel, until he began to earn a good deal of money! Is Mabel with you now? Give her my love. Also give me your present address.

How is Mother? Frankincense, same solid sterling gold as ever, I am sure. Alberta, working at her music and languages, laughing a good deal and eating a good many apples as usual? By the by, I now live mostly on fruits and nuts. They seem to agree with me well. If ever the old doctor, with "land" up somewhere, comes to see you, you may confide to him this secret. I have lost a good deal of my fat. But on days I lecture, I have to go on solid food. How is Hollis? I never saw a sweeter boy — may all blessings ever attend him through life.

I hear your friend Cola is lecturing on Zoroastrian philosophy — surely the stars are not smiling on him. What about your Miss Andreas and our Yoganandla? What news about the brotherhood of the ZZZ's and our Mrs. (forgotten!)? I hear that half a shipload of Hindus and Buddhists and Mohammedans and Brotherhoods and what not have entered the U.S., and another cargo of Mahatma-seekers, evangelists etc. have entered India! Good. India and the U.S. seem to be two countries for religious enterprise. Have a care, Joe; the heathen corruption is dreadful. I met Madam Sterling in the street today. She does not come any more for my lectures, good for her. Too much of philosophy is not good. Do you remember that lady who used to come to every meeting too late to hear a word but button-holed me immediately after and kept me talking, till a battle of Waterloo would be raging in my internal economy through hunger? She came. They are all coming and more. That is cheering.

It is getting late in the night. So goodnight, Joe. (Is strict etiquette to be followed in New York too?) And Lord bless you ever and ever.

"Man's all-wise maker, wishing to create a faultless form whose matchless symmetry should far transcend creation's choicest works, did call together by his mighty will, and garner up in his eternal mind, a bright assemblage of all lovely things, and then, as in a picture, fashioned them into one perfect and ideal form. Such the divine, the wondrous prototype whence her fair shape was moulded into being." (Shakuntalam by Kalidasa, translated by Monier Williams).

That is you, Joe Joe; only I would add, the same the creator did with all purity and nobility and other qualities and then Joe was made.

Ever yours, with love and blessings,
Vivekananda.

PS. Mrs. & Mr. Sevier in whose house (flat) I am writing now, send their kindest regards.

110 — MISS S. E. WALDO

AIRLIE LODGE, RIDGEWAY GARDENS,
WIMBLEDON,
8th October, 1896.

DEAR, (MISS S. E. WALDO)

. . . I had a fine rest in Switzerland and made a great friend of Prof. Paul Deussen. My European work in fact is becoming more satisfactory to me than any other work, and it tells immensely on India. The London classes were resumed, and today is the opening lecture. I now have a hall to myself holding two hundred or more. ...

You know of course the steadiness of the English; they are the least jealous of each other of all nations, and that is why they dominate the world. They have solved the secret of obedience without slavish cringing — great freedom with great law-abidingness.

I know very little of the young man R—. He is a Bengali and can teach a little Sanskrit. You know my settled doctrine. I do not trust any one who has not conquered "lust and gold". You may try him in theoretical subjects, but keep him off from teaching Raja-Yoga — that is a dangerous game except for the regularly trained to play at. Of Saradananda, the blessing of the greatest Yogi of modern India is on him — and there is no danger. Why do you not begin to teach? . . . You have a thousand times more philosophy than this boy R—. Send notices to the class and hold regular talks and lectures.

I will be thousand times more pleased to see one of you start than any number of Hindus securing success in America — even one of my brethren. "Man wants Victory from everywhere, but defeat from his own children". . . . Make a blaze! Make a blaze!

With all love and blessings,
Vivekananda.

111 — MRS. BULL

WIMBLEDON,
8th October, 1896.

DEAR MRS. BULL,

. . . I met in Germany Prof. Deussen. I was his guest at Kiel and we travelled together to London and had some very pleasant meetings here. . . . Although I am in full sympathy with the various branches of religious and social work, I find that specification of work is absolutely necessary. Our special branch is to preach Vedanta. Helping in other work should be subservient to that one ideal. I hope you will inculcate this in the mind of Saradananda very strongly.

Did you read Max Müller's article on Ramakrishna? . . . Things are working very favourably here in England. The work is not only popular but appreciated.

Yours affly.,
Vivekananda.

112 — MARY

14 GREYCOAT GARDENS, WESTMINSTER,
LONDON, ENGLAND,
1st November, 1896.

MY DEAR MARY, (Miss Mary Hale)

"Silver and gold", my dear Mary, "have I none; but such as I have give I thee'" freely, and that is the knowledge that the goldness of gold, the silverness of silver, the manhood of man, the womanhood of woman, the reality of everything is the Lord — and that this Lord we are trying to realise from time without beginning in the objective, and in the attempt throwing up such "queer" creatures of our fancy as man, woman, child, body, mind, the earth, sun, moon, stars, the world, love, hate, property, wealth, etc.; also ghosts, devils, angels and gods, God etc.

The fact being that the Lord is in us, we are He, the eternal subject, the real ego, never to be objectified, and that all this objectifying process is mere waste of time and talent. When the soul becomes aware of this, it gives up objectifying and falls back more and more upon the subjective. This is the evolution, less and less in the body and more and more in the mind — man the highest form, meaning in Sanskrit manas, thought — the animal that thinks and not the animal that "senses" only. This is what in theology is called "renunciation". The formation of society, the institution of marriage, the love for children, our good works, morality, and ethics are all different forms of renunciation. All our lives in every society are the subjection of the will, the thirst, the desire. This surrender of the will or the fictitious self — or the desire to jump out of ourselves, as it were — the struggle still to objectify the subject — is the one phenomenon in this world of which all societies and social forms are various modes and stages. Love is the easiest and smoothest way towards the self-surrender or subjection of the will and hatred, the opposite.

People have been cajoled through various stories or superstitions of heavens and hells and Rulers above the sky, towards this one end of self-surrender. The philosopher does the same knowingly without superstition, by giving up desires.

An objective heaven or millennium therefore has existence only in the fancy — but a subjective one is already in existence. The musk-deer, after vain search for the cause of the scent of the musk, at last will have to find it in himself.

Objective society will always be a mixture of good and evil — objective life will always be followed by its shadow death, and the longer the life, the longer will also be the shadow. It is only when the sun is on our own head that there is no shadow. When God and good and everything else is in us, there is no evil. In objective life, however, every bullet has its billet — evil goes with every good as its shadow. Every improvement is coupled with an equal degradation. The reason being that good and evil are not two things but one, the difference being only in manifestation — one of degree, not kind.

Our very lives depend upon the death of others — plants or animals or bacilli! The other great mistake we often make is that good is taken as an ever-increasing item, whilst evil is a fixed quantity. From this it is argued that evil being diminished every day, there will come a time when good alone will remain. The fallacy lies in the assumption of a false premise. If good is increasing, so is evil. My desires have been much more than the desires of the masses among my race. My joys have been much greater than theirs — but my miseries a million times more intense The same constitution that makes you feel the least touch of good makes you feel the least of evil too. The same nerves that carry sensations of pleasure carry the sensations of pain too — and the same mind feels both. The progress of the world means more enjoyment and more misery too. This mixture of life and death, good and evil, knowledge and ignorance is what is called Maya — or the universal phenomenon. You may go on for eternity inside this net, seeking for happiness — you find much, and much evil too. To have good and no evil is childish nonsense. Two ways are left open — one by giving up all hope to take up the world as it is and bear the pangs and pains in the hope of a crumb of happiness now and then. The other, to give up the search for pleasure, knowing it to be pain in another form, and seek for truth — and those that dare try for truth succeed in finding that truth as ever present — present in themselves. Then we also discover how the same truth is manifesting itself both in our relative error and knowledge — we find also that the same truth is bliss which again is manifesting itself as good and evil, and with it also we find real existence which is manifesting itself as both death and life.

Thus we realise that all these phenomena are but the reflections, bifurcated or manifolded, of the one existence, truth-bliss-unity — my real Self and the reality of everything else. Then and then only is it possible to do good without evil, for such a soul has known and got the control of the material of which both good and evil are manufactured, and he alone can manifest one or the other as he likes, and we know he manifests only good. This is the Jivan-mukta — the living free — the goal of Vedanta as of all other philosophies.

Human society is in turn governed by the four castes — the priests, the soldiers, the traders, and the labourers. Each state has its glories as well as its defects. When the priest (Brahmin) rules, there is a tremendous exclusiveness on hereditary grounds; the persons of the priests and their descendants are hemmed in with all sorts of safeguards — none but they have any knowledge — none but they have the right to impart that knowledge. Its glory is that at this period is laid the foundation of sciences. The priests cultivate the mind, for through the mind they govern.

The military (Kshatriya) rule is tyrannical and cruel, but they are not exclusive; and during that period arts and social culture attain their height.

The commercial (Vaishya) rule comes next. It is awful in its silent crushing and blood-sucking power. Its advantage is, as the trader himself goes everywhere, he is a good disseminator of ideas collected during the two previous states. They are still less exclusive than the military, but culture begins to decay.

Last will come the labourer (Shudra) rule. Its advantages will be the distribution of physical comforts — its disadvantages, (perhaps) the lowering of culture. There will be a great distribution of ordinary education, but extraordinary geniuses will be less and less.

If it is possible to form a state in which the knowledge of the priest period, the culture of the military, the distributive spirit of the commercial, and the ideal of equality of the last can all be kept intact, minus their evils, it will be an deal state. But is it possible?

Yet the first three have had their day. Now is the time for the last — they must have it — none can resist it. I do not know all the difficulties about the gold or silver standards (nobody seems to know much as to that), but this much I see that the gold standard has been making the poor poorer, and the rich richer. Bryan was right when he said, "We refuse to be crucified on a cross of gold." The silver standard will give the poor a better chance in this unequal fight. I am a socialist not because I think it is a perfect system, but half a loaf is better than no bread.

The other systems have been tried and found wanting. Let this one be tried — if for nothing else, for the novelty of the thing. A redistribution of pain and pleasure is better than always the same persons having pains and pleasures. The sum total of good and evil in the world remains ever the same. The yoke will be lifted from shoulder to shoulder by new systems, that is all.

Let every dog have his day in this miserable world, so that after this experience of so-called happiness they may all come to the Lord and give up this vanity of a world and governments and all other botherations.

With love to you all,

Ever your faithful brother,
Vivekananda.

113 — MRS. BULL

GREYCOAT GARDENS,
WESTMINSTER, LONDON, S.W.,
13th November, 1896.

DEAR MRS. BULL,

... I am very soon starting for India, most probably on the 16th of December. As I am very desirous to see India once before I come again to America, and as I have arranged to take several friends from England with me to India, it is impossible for me to go to America on my way, however I might have liked it.

Dr. Janes is doing splendid work indeed. I can hardly express my gratitude for the many kindnesses and the help he has given me and my work. ... The work is progressing beautifully here.

You will be interested to know that the first edition of Raja-Yoga is sold out, and there is a standing order for several hundreds more.

Yours etc.,
Vivekananda.

114 — LALAJI

39 VICTORIA STREET,
LONDON S.W.,
21st November, 1896.

DEAR LALAJI, (Lala Badri Sah)

I reach Madras about the 7th of January; after a few days in the plains I intend to come up to Almora.

I have three English friends with me. Two of them, Mr. and Mrs. Sevier, are going to settle in Almora. They are my disciples, you know, and they are going to build the Goliath for me in the Himalayas. It was for that reason I asked you to look for some suitable site. We want a whole hill, with a view of the snow-range, all to ourselves. It would of course take time to fix on the site and complete the building. In the meanwhile will you kindly engage a small bungalow for my friends? The bungalow ought to accommodate three persons. I do not require a large one. A small one would do for the present. My friends will live in this bungalow in Almora and then go about looking for a site and building.

You need not reply to this letter, as before your reply will reach me, I shall be on my way to India. I will write to you from Madras as soon as I reach there.

With love and blessings to you all,

Yours,
Vivekananda.

115 — DEAR—

C/O E. T STURDY, ESQ.,
HIGH VIEW, CAVERSHAM, READING,
1896.

DEAR—,

. . . Can anything be done unless everybody exerts himself to his utmost? "Goddess of Wealth resorts to." No need of looking behind. FORWARD! We want infinite energy, infinite zeal, infinite courage, and infinite patience, then only will great things be achieved. . . .

With love and blessings to you all,

Yours affectionately,
Vivekananda.

116 — SISTERS

39 VICTORIA ST., LONDON S.W.,
28th Nov., 1896.

DEAR SISTERS, (Misses Mary and Harriet Hale)

. . . I feel impelled to write a few lines to you before my departure for India. The work in London has been a roaring success. The English are not so bright as the Americans, but once you touch their heart, it is yours for ever. Slowly have I gained, and it is strange that in six months' work altogether I would have a steady class of 120 persons apart from public lectures. Here every one means work — the practical Englishman. Capt. and Mrs. Sevier and Mr. Goodwin are going to India with me to work and spend their own money on it! There are scores here ready to do the same: men and women of position, ready to give up everything for the idea, once they feel convinced! And last though not the least, the help in the shape of money to start my "work" in India has come and more will follow. My ideas about the English have been revolutionized. I now understand why the Lord has blessed them above all other races. They are steady, sincere to the backbone, with great depths of feeling — only with a crust of stoicism on the surface; if that is broken, you have your man.

Now I am going to start a centre in Calcutta and another in the Himalayas. The Himalayan one will be an entire hill about 7,000 ft. high — cool in summer, cold in winter. Capt. and Mrs. Sevier will live there, and it will be the centre for European workers, as I do not want to kill them by forcing on them the Indian mode of living and the fiery plains. My plan is to send out numbers of Hindu boys to every civilised country to preach — get men and women from foreign countries to work in India. This would be a good exchange. After having established the centres, I go about up and down like the gentleman in the book of Job.

Here I must end to catch the mail. Things are opening for me. I am glad, and I know so you are. Now all blessings be yours and all happiness.

With eternal love,
Vivekananda.

PS. What about Dharmapala? What is he doing? Give him my love if you meet him.,

117 — ALBERTA

14 GREYCOAT GARDENS,
WESTMINSTER, LONDON S.W.,
3rd Dec., 1896.

DEAR ALBERTA,

Herewith I enclose a letter of Mabel to Joe Joe to you. I have enjoyed the news in it very much and so I am sure you will.

I am to start from here for India on the 16th and to take the steamer at Naples. I will, therefore, be in Italy for some days and in Rome for three or four days. I will be very happy to look in to say good-bye to you.

Capt. and Mrs. Sevier from England are going to India with me, and they will be with me in Italy of course. You saw them last summer.

I intend to return to the U.S. and to Europe thence in about a year.

With all love and blessings,
Vivekananda.

118 — MRS. BULL

39 VICTORIA STREET, LONDON,
9th Dec., 1896.

DEAR MRS. BULL,

It is needless to express my gratitude at your most generous offer. I don't want to encumber myself with a large amount of money at the first start, but as things progress on I will be very glad to find employment for that sum. My idea is to start on a very small scale. I do not know anything yet. I will know my bearings when on the spot in India. From India I will write to you more details about my plans and the practical way to realise them. I start on the 16th and after a few days in Italy take the steamer at Naples.

Kindly convey my love to Mrs. Vaughan and Saradananda and to the rest of my friends there. As for you, I have always regarded you as the best friend I have, and it will be the same all my life.

With all love and blessings,

Yours,
Vivekananda.

119 — FRANKINCENSE

13th Dec., 1896.

DEAR FRANKINCENSE,

So Gopâla has taken the female form! It is fit that it should be so — the time and the place considering. May all blessings follow her through life. She was keenly desired, prayed for, and she comes as a blessing to you and to your wife for life. I have not the least doubt.

I wish I could have come to America now if only to fulfil the form "the sages of the East bringing presents to the Western baby". But the heart is there with all prayers and blessings, and the mind is more powerful than the body.

I am starting on the 16th of this month and take the steamer at Naples. Will see Alberta in Rome surely. With all love to the holy family,

Yours ever in the Lord,
Vivekananda.

120 — ALBERTA

HOTEL MINERVA, FLORENCE,
20th Dec., 1896.

DEAR ALBERTA,

Tomorrow we reach Rome. I will most possibly come to see you day after tomorrow as it will be late in the night when we reach Rome. We stop at the Hotel Continental.

With all love and blessings,
Vivekananda.

121 — MARY

RAMNAD,
30th Jan., 1897.

MY DEAR MARY,

Things are turning out most curiously for me. From Colombo in Ceylon, where I landed, to Ramnad, the nearly southernmost point of the Indian continent where I am just now as the guest of the Raja of Ramnad, my journey has been a huge procession — crowds of people, illuminations, addresses, etc., etc. A monument forty feet high is being built on the spot where I landed. The Raja of Ramnad has presented his address to "His most Holiness" in a huge casket of solid gold beautifully worked. Madras and Calcutta are on the tiptoe of expectation as if the whole nation is rising to honour me. So you see, Mary, I am on the very height of my destiny, yet the mind turns to quietness and peace, to the days we had in Chicago, of rest, of peace, and love; and that is why I write just now, and may this find you all in health and peace! I wrote a letter to my people from London to receive Dr. Barrows kindly. They accorded him a big reception, but it was not my fault that he could not make any impression there. The Calcutta people are a hard-headed lot! Now Barrows thinks a world of me, I hear! Such is the world.

With all love to mother, father, and you all,

I remain, yours affly.,
Vivekananda.

122 — MRS. BULL

ALAMBAZAR MATH, CALCUTTA,
25th Feb., 1897.

DEAR MRS. BULL,

Saradananda sends £20 to be placed in the famine relief in India. But as there is famine in his own home, I thought it best to relieve that first, as the old proverb says. So it has been employed accordingly.

I have not a moment to die as they stay, what with processions and tomtomings and various other methods of reception all over the country; I am almost dead. As soon as the Birthday is over I will fly off to the hills. I received an address from the Cambridge Conference as well as one from the Brooklyn Ethical Association. One from the Vedanta Association of New York, as mentioned in Dr. Janes's letter, has not yet arrived.

Also there is a letter from Dr. Janes suggesting work along the line of your conference, here in India. It is almost impossible for me to pay any attention to these things. I am so, so tired. I do not know whether I would live even six months more or not, unless I have some rest.

Now I have to start two centres, one in Madras, the other in Calcutta. The Madras people are deeper and more sincere, and, I am sure, will be able to collect funds from Madras itself. The Calcutta people are mostly enthusiastic (I mean the aristocracy) through patriotism, and their sympathy would never materialise. On the other hand, the country is full of persons, jealous and pitiless, who would leave no stones unturned to pull my work to pieces.

But as you know well, the more the opposition, the more the demon in me is roused. My duty would not be complete if I die without starting the two places, one for the Sannyasins, the other for the women.

I have already £500 from England about, £500 from Mr. Sturdy, and if your money be added to it, I am sure I will be able to start the two. I think, therefore, you ought to send the money as soon as possible. The safest way is to put the money in a bank in America in your and my name jointly, so that either of us may draw it. In case I die before the money is employed, you will be able to draw it all and put it to the use I wanted. So that, in case of my death, none of my people would be able to meddle with it. The English money has been put in the bank in the same position in the joint names of Mr. Sturdy and myself.

With love to Saradananda and eternal love and gratitude to yourself,

Yours etc.,
Vivekananda.

123 — MARY

DARJEELING,
April 28, 1897.

DEAR MARY,

A few days ago I received your beautiful letter. Yesterday came the card announcing Harriet's marriage. Lord bless the happy pair!

The whole country here rose like one man to receive me. Hundreds of thousands of persons, shouting and cheering at every place, Rajas drawing my carriage, arches all over the streets of the capitals with blazing mottoes etc.,!!! The whole thing will soon come out in the form of a book, and you will have a copy soon. But unfortunately I was already exhausted by hard work in England; and this tremendous exertion in the heat of Southern India prostrated me completely. I had of course to give up the idea of visiting other parts of India and fly up to the nearest hill station, Darjeeling. Now I feel much better, and a month more in Almora would complete the cure. By the bye, I have just lost a chance of coming over to Europe. Raja Ajit Singh and several other Rajas start next Saturday for England. Of course, they wanted hard to get me to go over with them. But unfortunately the doctors would not hear of my undertaking any physical or mental labour just now. So with the greatest chagrin I had to give it up, reserving it for a near future.

Dr. Barrows has reached America by this time, I hope. Poor man! He came here to preach the most bigoted Christianity, with the usual result that nobody listened to him. Of course they received him very kindly; but it was my letter that did it. I could not put brains into him! Moreover, he seems to be a queer sort of man. I hear that he was mad at the national rejoicings over my coming home. You ought to have sent a brainier man anyway, for the Parliament of Religions has been made a farce of in the Hindu mind by Dr. Barrows. On metaphysical lines no nation on earth can hold a candle to the Hindus; and curiously all the fellows that come over here from Christian land have that one antiquated foolishness of an argument that because the Christians are powerful and rich and the Hindus are not, so Christianity must be better than Hinduism. To which the Hindus very aptly retort that, that is the very reason why Hinduism is a religion and Christianity is not; because, in this beastly world it is blackguardism and that alone which prospers, virtue always suffers. It seems, however advanced the Western nations are in scientific culture, they are mere babies in metaphysical and spiritual education. Material science can only give worldly prosperity, whilst spiritual science is for eternal life. If there be no eternal life, still the enjoyment of spiritual thoughts as ideals is keener and makes a man happier, whilst the foolery of materialism leads to competition and undue ambition and ultimate death, individual and national.

This Darjeeling is a beautiful spot with a view of the glorious Kanchenjanga (28,146 ft.) now and then when the clouds permit it, and from a near hilltop one can catch a glimpse of Gauri Shankar (29,000 ft?) now and then. Then, the people here too are so picturesque, the Tibetans and Nepalese and, above all, the beautiful Lepcha women. Do you know one Colston Turnbull of Chicago? He was here a few weeks before I reached India. He seems to have had a great liking for me, with the result that Hindu people all liked him very much. What about Joe, Mrs. Adams, Sister Josephine, and all the rest of our friends? Where are our beloved Mills? Grinding slow but sure? I wanted to send some nuptial presents to Harriet, but with your "terrible" duties I must reserve it for some near future. Maybe I shall meet them in Europe very soon. I would have been very glad, of course, if you could announce your engagement, and I would fulfil my promise by filling up half a dozen papers in one letter....

My hair is turning grey in bundles, and my face is getting wrinkled up all over; that losing of flesh has given me twenty years of age more. And now I am losing flesh rapidly, because I am made to live upon meat and meat alone — no bread, no rice, no potatoes, not even a lump of sugar in my coffee!! I am living with a Brahmin family who all dress in knickerbockers, women excepted of course! I am also in knickers. I would have given you a surprise if you had seen me bounding from rock to rock like a chamois, or galloping might and main up and down mountain roads.

I am very well here, for life in the plains has become a torture. I cannot put the tip of my nose out into the streets, but there is a curious crowd!! Fame is not all milk and honey!! I am going to train a big beard; now it is turning grey. It gives a venerable appearance and saves one from American scandal-mongers! O thou white hair, how much thou canst conceal, all glory unto thee, Hallelujah!

The mail time is nearly up, so I finish. Good dreams, good health, all blessings attend you.

With love to father and mother and you all,

Yours,
Vivekananda.

124 — SIR

Translated from Bengali

ALMORA,
30th May, 1897.

DEAR SIR,

I hear some unavoidable domestic grief has come upon you. To you, a man of wisdom, what can this misery do? Yet the amenities of friendly intercourse, incidental to relative existence in this world, require my making mention of it. Those moments of grief, however, very often bring out a better spiritual realisation. As if for a while the clouds withdraw and the sun of truth shines out. In the case of some, half of the bondage is loosened. Of all bandages the greatest is that of position — the fear of reputation is stronger than the fear of death; but even this bondage appears to relax a little. As if the mind sees for a moment that it is much better to listen to the indwelling Lord than to the opinions of men. But again the clouds close up, and this indeed is Mâyâ.

Though for a long time I had no direct correspondence with you, yet I have often been receiving from others almost all the news about you. Some time ago you kindly sent me to England a copy of a translation of the Gita. The cover only bore a line of your handwriting. The few words in acknowledgment of this gift, I am told, raised doubts in your mind about my old affection towards you.

Please know these doubts to be groundless. The reason of that laconic acknowledgment is that I was given to see, during four or five years, only that one line of your handwriting on the cover of an English Gita, from which fact I thought, if you had no leisure to write more, would you have leisure enough to read much? Secondly, I learnt, you were particularly the friend of white-skinned missionaries of the Hindu religion and the roguish black natives were repelling! There was apprehension on this score. Thirdly, I am a Mlechchha, Shudra, and so forth; I eat anything and everything, and with anybody and everybody — and that in public both abroad and here. In my views, besides, much perversion has supervened — one attributeless absolute Brahman, I see, I fairly understand, and I see in some particular individuals the special manifestations of that Brahman; if those individuals are called by the name of God, I can well follow — otherwise the mind does not feel inclined towards intellectual theorisings such as the postulated Creator and the like.

Such a God I have seen in my life, and his commands I live to follow. The Smritis and the Puranas are productions of men of limited intelligence and are full of fallacies, errors, the feelings of class and malice. Only parts of them breathing broadness of spirit and love are acceptable, the rest are to be rejected. The Upanishads and the Gita are the true scriptures; Rama, Krishna, Buddha, Chaitanya, Nanak, Kabir, and so on are the true Avatâras, for they had their hearts broad as the sky — and above all, Ramakrishna. Ramanuja, Shankara etc., seem to have been mere Pundits with much narrowness of heart. Where is that love, that weeping heart at the sorrow of others? — Dry pedantry of the Pundit — and the feeling of only oneself getting to salvation hurry-scurry! But is that going to be possible, sir? Was it ever likely or will it ever be so? Can anything be attained with any shred of "I" left anyhow?

Another great discrepancy: the conviction is daily gaining on my mind that the idea of caste is the greatest dividing factor and the root of Maya; all caste either on the principle of birth or of merit is bondage: Some friends advise, "True, lay all that at heart, but outside, in the world of relative experience, distinctions like caste must needs be maintained." ... The idea of oneness at heart (with a craven impotence of effort, that is to say), and outside, the hell-dance of demons — oppression and persecution — ay, the dealer of death to the poor, but if the Pariah be wealthy enough, "Oh, he is the protector of religion!"

Over and above, I come to see from my studies that the disciplines of religion are not for the Shudra; if he exercises any discrimination about food or about going out to foreign lands, it is all useless in his case, only so much labour lost. I am a Shudra, a Mlechchha, so I have nothing to do with all that botheration. To me what would Mlechchha's food matter or Pariah's? It is in the books written by priests that madnesses like that of caste are to be found, and not in books revealed from God. Let the priests enjoy the fruits of their ancestors' achievement, while I follow the word of God, for my good lies there.

Another truth I have realised is that altruistic service only is religion, the rest, such as ceremonial observances, are madness — even it is wrong to hanker after one's own salvation. Liberation is only for him who gives up everything for others, whereas others who tax their brains day and night harping on "my salvation", "my salvation", wander about with their true well-being ruined, both present and prospective; and this I have seen many a time with my own eyes. Reflecting on all these sundry matters, I had no heart for writing a letter to you. If notwithstanding all these discrepancies, you find your attachment for me intact, I shall feel it to be a very happy issue indeed.

Yours etc.,
Vivekananda

125 — SHUDDHANANDA

Translated from Bengali

ALMORA,
1st June, 1897.

DEAR SHUDDHANANDA,

Glad to know from your letter that all are doing well there, and to go through the news in detail. I too am in better health; the rest you will know from Dr. Shashi Bhushan. Let the teaching go on for the present in the method revised by Brahmananda, and if any changes ar needed in future, have them done. But it should never be lost sight of that this must be done with the consent of all.

I am now living in a garden belonging to a merchant situated a little to the north of Almora. Before me are the snow-peaks of the Himalayas looking, in the reflection of the sun, like a mass of silver, a delight to the heart. By taking free air, regular diet, and plenty of exercise, I have grown strong and healthy in body. But I hear the Yogananda is very ill. I am inviting him to come here But then, he fears the mountain air and water. I wrote to him today, saying, "Stay in this garden for some day' and if you find your illness shows no improvement, you may go to Calcutta." He will do as he pleases.

At Almora, every evening Achyutananda gathers the people together and reads to them the Gita and other Shâstras. Many residents of the town, as also soldiers from the cantonment, come there daily. I learn also that he is appreciated by all.

The Bengali interpretation that you have given of the Shloka interpretation in question is this: "When (the land) is flooded with water, what is the use of drinking water?" If the law of nature be such that when a land is flooded with water, drinking it is useless, that through certain air passages or through any other recondite way people's thirst may be allayed, then only can this novel interpretation be relevant, otherwise not. It is Shankara whom you should follow. Or you may explain it in this way: As, even when whole tracts are flooded with water, small pools are also of great use to the thirsty (that is to say, just a little water suffices him, and he says, as it were, "Let the vast sheet of water be, even a little of water will satisfy my object."), of identical use are the whole Vedas to a learned Brahmin. As even when the land is overflooded, one's concern lies in drinking the water and no more, so in all the Vedas illumination alone is the concern.

Here is another interpretation which hits better the meaning the author wishes to convey: Even when the land is overflooded, it is only that water which is drinkable and salutary, that people seek for, and no other kind. There are various kinds of water, which differ in quality and properties — even though the land be flooded over — according to the differences in property of their substratum, the soil. Likewise a skilful Brahmin, too, will, for the quenching of the worldly thirst, choose from that sea of words known as the Vedas, which is flooded over with diverse courses of knowledge, that which alone will be of potence to lead to liberation. And it is the knowledge of the Brahman which will do this.

With blessing and good wishes.

Yours,
Vivekananda.

126 — MISS NOBLE

ALMORA,
3rd June, 1897.

DEAR MISS NOBLE,

... As for myself I am quite content. I have roused a good many of our people, and that was all I wanted. Let things have their course and Karma its sway. I have no bonds here below. I have seen life, and it is all self — life is for self, love for self, honour for self, everything for self. I look back and scarcely find any action I have done for self — even my wicked deeds were not for self. So I am content; not that I feel I have done anything specially good or great, but the world is so little, life so mean a thing, existence so, so servile — that I wonder and smile that human beings, rational souls, should be running after this self — so mean and detestable a prize.

This is the truth. We are caught in a trap, and the sooner one gets out, the better for one. I have seen the truth — let the body float up or down, who cares?

It is a beautiful mountain park I am living in now. On the north, extending almost all along the horizon, are peak after peak of the snow-clad Himalayas — forests abounding. It is not cold here, neither very warm; the evenings and mornings are simply delicious. I should like to be here this summer, and when the rains set in, I go down to the plains to work.

I was born for the life of a scholar — retired, quiet, poring over my books. But the Mother dispenses otherwise — yet the tendency is there.

Yours etc.,
Vivekananda.

127 — RAKHAL

Translated from Bengali

ALMORA,
14th June, 1897.

DEAR RAKHAL,

I am wholly in sympathy with the subject-matter of the letter of Charu that you have sent me.

In the proposed Address to the Queen-Empress the following points should be noted:

1. That it must be free from exaggeration, in other words, statements to the effect that she is God's regent and so forth, which are so common to us natives.

2. That all religions having been protected during her reign, we have been able fearlessly to preach our Vedantic doctrines both in India and England.

3. Her kindness towards the Indian poor — as, for instance, her inspiring the English to unique acts of charity by contributing herself to the cause of famine-relief.

4. Prayer for her long life and for the continual growth of happiness and prosperity among the people of her dominions.

Have this written in correct English and send it to me at Almora, and I shall sign it and send it to Simla. Let me know to whom it should be addressed at Simla.

Yours etc.,
Vivekananda.

PS. Let Shuddhananda preserve a copy of the weekly letters that he writes to me from the Math.

128 — AKHANDANANDA

Translated from Bengali

ALMORA,
15th June, 1897.

MY DEAR AKHANDANANDA,

I am getting detailed reports of you and getting more and more delighted. It is that sort of work which can conquer the world. What do differences of sect and opinion matter? Bravo! Accept a hundred thousand embraces and blessings from me. Work, work, work — I care for nothing else. Work, work, work, even unto death! Those that are weak must make themselves great workers, great heroes — never mind money, it will drop from the heavens. Let them whose gifts you will accept, give in their own name if they like, no harm. Whose name, and what is it worth? Who cares for name? Off with it! If in the attempt to carry morsels of food to starving mouths, name and possession and all be doomed even — अहो भाग्यमहो भाग्यम् —thrice blessed art thou! It is the heart, the heart that conquers, not the brain. Books and learning, Yoga and meditation and illumination — all are but dust compared with love. It is love that gives you the supernatural powers, love that gives you Bhakti, love that gives illumination, and love, again, that reads to emancipation. This indeed is worship, worship of the Lord in the human tabernacle, "नेदं यदिदमुपासते — not this that people worship". (That is things other than God.) This is but the beginning, and unless we spread over the whole of India, nay, the whole earth, in that way, where lies the greatness of our Lord!

Let people see whether or not the touch of our Lord's feet confers divinity on man! It is this that is called liberation-in-life — when the last trace of egoism and selfishness is gone. Well done! Glory to the Lord! Gradually try to spread. If you can, go to Calcutta, and raise a fund with the help of another band of boys; set one or two of them to work at some place, and begin somewhere else. Spread in that way, and go on inspecting them. You will see that the work will gradually become permanent, and spread of religion and education will follow as a matter of course. I have given particular instructions to them in Calcutta. Do that kind of work, and I shall carry you on my shoulders — bravo! You will see that by degrees every district will become a centre — and that a permanent one. I am soon going down to the plains. I am a fighter, and shall die in the battlefield. Does it behave me to sit up here like a zenana lady?

Yours with all love,
Vivekananda.

129 — RAKHAL

Translated from Bengali

ALMORA,
20th June, 1897.

DEAR RAKHAL,

Glad to learn that you are better in health than before. Well, it is seldom that Brother Yogen reports the bare truths, so do not at all be anxious to hear them. I am all right now, with plenty of muscular strength, and no thirst. ... The liver, too, acts well. I am not certain as to what effects Shashi (Babu)'s medicine had. So I have stopped using it. I am having plenty of mangoes. I am getting exceptionally adept in riding, and do not feel the least pain or exhaustion even after a run of twenty or thirty miles at a stretch. Milk I have altogether stopped for fear of corpulence.

Yesterday I came to Almora, and shall not go any more to the garden. Henceforth I am to have three meals a day in the English fashion, as Miss Müller's guest. ...

Shuddhananda writes to say that they are going on with Ruddock's Practice of Medicine or something of that sort. What nonsense do you mean by having such things taught in the class? A set of common apparatus for physics and another for chemistry, an ordinary telescope and a microscope — all these can be had for Rupees 150 to 200. Shashi Babu may give a lecture on practical chemistry once a week, and Hariprasanna on physics etc. And buy all the good scientific books that you can have in Bengali, and have them read

Yours affectionately,
Vivekananda.

130 — RAKHAL

Translated from Bengali

Salutation to Bhagavan Ramakrishna!

ALMORA,
10th July, 1897.

DEAR RAKHAL,

Today I send back the proofs of the objects of our Association that you sent me, corrected. The rules and regulations portion (which the members of our Association had read) is full of mistakes. Correct it very carefully and reprint it, or people will laugh.

... The kind of work that is going on at Berhampore is exceedingly nice. It is those works that will triumph — can doctrines and dogmas touch the heart? Work, work — live the life; what do doctrines and opinions count? Philosophy and Yoga and penance — the worship-room — your sunned rice or vegetable offerings — all these constitute the religion of one man or one country; doing good to others is the one great, universal religion. Men and women, young and old, down to the Pariah, nay, the very animal — all can grasp this religion. Can a merely negative religion be of any avail? The stone is never unchaste, the cow never tells a lie, nor do trees commit theft or robbery, but what does it matter? Granted that you do not steal, nor tell a lie, nor lead an unchaste life, but meditate four hours a day and religiously ring the bell for twice as many hours — yet, what matters it after all? That work, little as it is, that you have done, has brought Berhampore to your feet for ever — now people will do whatever you wish them to. Now you will no longer have to argue to the people that "Ramakrishna is God." Without it what will mere lectures do? — Do fine words butter any parsnips? If you could do like that in ten districts, all the ten would become yours to have and hold. Therefore, like the intelligent boy that you are, lay your greatest stress, for the present, on that work department, and try heart and soul to augment the utility of that alone. Organise a number of boys to go from door to door, let them fetch, in the manner of the Alakhiâ Sâdhus, whatever they can get — money, or worn out clothes, or rice and eatables, or anything. Then distribute them. That is work, work indeed. After that people will have faith, and will then do what they are told.

Whatever is left over after defraying the expenses of the Calcutta meeting, remit for famine relief, or help with it the countless poor that live in the slums of Calcutta; let Memorial Halls and things of that kind go to the dogs. The Lord will do what He thinks best. I am at present in excellent health....

Why are you not collecting materials? — I shall go down and start the paper myself. Kindness and love can buy you the whole world; lectures and books and philosophy all stand lower than these.

Please write to Shashi to open a work department like this for the service of the poor.

... Curtail the expenses of worship to a rupee or two per mensem. The children of the Lord are dying of starvation.... Worship with water and Tulasi leaves alone, and let the allowance for His Bhoga (food offerings) be spent in offering food to the Living God who dwells in the persons of the poor — then will His grace descend on everything. Yogen felt unwell here; so today he started for Calcutta. I shall again go to Dewaldhar tomorrow. Please accept my love and tender it to all.

Yours affectionately,
Vivekananda.

131 — AKHANDANANDA

Translated from Bengali

Salutation to Bhagavan Ramakrishna!

ALMORA,
24th July, 1897.

MY DEAR AKHANDANANDA,

I am very glad to receive your letter and go through the contents. Your wishes about the orphanage are very good and Shri Maharaj (Shri Ramakrishna.) will not fail to fulfil them at an early date. Try your best to found a permanent centre. ... Never worry about money. Tomorrow I shall leave Almora for the plains; and wherever there will be made some stir, I shall open a subscription list for famine — set your mind easy on that score. When in every district there will be a Math on the model of our Math in Calcutta, then will my heart's desire be fulfilled. Let not the work of preaching, too, be at a standstill, and greater even than preaching, is the work of imparting education. By means of lectures and the like, the village people must be taught religion, history, and such other subjects — specially history. To help our educational work there is a Society in England, which, as I find from reports, is doing excellent work. In time we shall get help of this kind from everywhere, don't be frightened. They only do work who think that help will come, directly they are on the field of work.

All strength is in you, have faith in it. It will not go unmanifested. Accept my heartiest love and blessings, and convey them to the Brahmachârin. Write now and then fiery letters to the Math, so that all may take heart and work. Victory to the Guru!

Yours affectionately,
Vivekananda.

132 — AKHANDANANDA

Translated from Bengali

ALMORA,
30th July, 1897.

MY DEAR AKHANDANANDA,

According to your instructions, I write a letter to Mr. Levinge, the Dist. Magistrate. Besides, you will write a big letter to the Indian Mirror, describing in detail his method of work (having got the same revised by Dr. Shashi), and send a copy of it to the gentleman named above. Our fools only search for people's shortcomings. Let them see some virtues too.

I am leaving this place next Monday. ...

What do you talk of the difficulty in getting orphans? Better ask for four or five men from the Math, if you like; you can find some orphans in two days, if you seek from village to village.

Of course we must have a permanent centre. And can anything be done in this country unless the —— help? Do not mix in politics etc., nor have any connection with them. At the same time you need not have any quarrel with anybody. You must put your body, mind, and all you have to some one work. Here I gave a lecture to a European audience in English, and another to the Indian residents in Hindi. This was my maiden speech in Hindi, but everyone liked it for all that. Of course the Westerners, as is their wont, were in raptures over it, as coming from a "nigger"! "Oh, how wonderful!" and that sort of thing. Next Saturday there will be another lecture for the Europeans. A big Association has been set on foot here — let us wait and see how far it works in future. The object of the Association is to impart education and religion.

Monday next, trip to Bareilly then to Saharanpur, next to Ambala, thence, most probably, to Mussoorie with Captain Sevier, and as soon as it is a little cool, return to the plains and journey to Rajputana etc. Go on working at top speed. Never fear! I, too, have determined to work. The body must go, no mistake about that. Why then let it go in idleness? It is better to wear out than rust out. Don't be anxious even when I die, my very bones will work miracles. We must spread over the whole of India in ten years, short of this it is no good. To work like an athlete! Victory to the Guru! Money and all will come of themselves, we want men, not money. It is man that makes everything, what can money do? — Men we want, the more you get, the better. ... Here, for instance, was M—— who brought together a lot of money, but there was no man, and what good did he achieve?

Yours affectionately,
Vivekananda.

133 — MRS. BULL

THE MATH (The letter was actually written from Ambala.),
19th August, 1897.

DEAR MRS. BULL,

. . . My health is indifferent, and although I have some rest, I do not think I shall be able to regain my usual vigour till winter next. I had a letter from Joe saying that you are both coming to India. I, of course, will be very glad to see you in India, only you ought to know from the first that India is the dirtiest and unhealthiest hole in the world, with scarcely any European comforts except in the big capitals.

I learn from England that Mr. Sturdy is sending Abhedananda to New York. It seems that the English work is impossible without me. Only a magazine will be started and worked by Mr. Sturdy. I had arranged to come to England this season, but I was foolishly prevented by the doctors. In India the work is going on.

I do not think any European or American will be of any service here just now, and it will be hard for any Westerner to bear the climate. Annie Besant with her exceptional powers works only among the Theosophists, and thus she submits to all the indignities of isolation which a Mlechchha is made to undergo here. Even Goodwin smarts now and then and has to be called to order. Goodwin is doing good work, as he is a man and can mix with the people. Women have no place in men's society here, and she can do good only among her own sex in India. The English friends that came over to India have not been of any help as yet, and do not know whether they will be of any in the future. With all these, if anybody wants to try, she is welcome.

If Saradananda wants to come, he may, and I am sure he will be of very good service to me just now in organising the work, now that my health is broken. There is a young English woman, Miss Margaret Noble, very eager to come to India to learn the state of things, so that she may do some work when she is back home. I have written her to accompany you in case you come via London. The great difficulty is that you can never understand the situation here from a distance. The two types are so entirely different in all things that it is not possible to form any idea from America or England.

You ought to think that you are starting for the interior of Africa, and if you meet anything better, that will be unexpected.

Ever yours etc.,
Vivekananda.

134 — MOTHER

Translated from Bengali

1897.

DEAR MOTHER, (Shrimati Indumati Mitra)

Please be not anxious because I could not write to you and could not go to Belgaon. I was suffering very much from illness and it was impossible for me to go then. Now thanks to my travels in the Himalayas, I have greatly regained my health. I shall soon resume work. In two weeks I am going to the Punjab, and just after delivering a lecture or two at Lahore and Amritsar, I shall start via Karachi for Gujarat, Cutch, etc. I shall surely see you at Karachi.

This Kashmir is a veritable heaven on earth. Nowhere else in the world is such a country as this. Mountains and rivers, trees and plants, men and women, beasts and birds — all vie with one another for excellence. I feel a pang at heart not to have visited it so long. Please write to me in detail how you are doing, mentally and physically, and accept my special blessings. I am constantly hating your welfare at heart, know this for certain.

Yours sincerely,
Vivekananda.

135 — SARADA

Translated from Bengali

MURREE,
10th October, 1897.

DEAR SARADA,

I am sorry to learn from your letter that you are not doing well. If you can make an unpopular man popular, then I call you a clever fellow. There is no prospect of work there in the future; it would have been better had you gone rather to Dacca, or some other place. However, it is a good thing that the work will close in November. If you get very badly off in health, you should better come away. There is much field for work in the Central Provinces; and even without famine, there is no lack of poverty-stricken people in our country. Wherever it is, if you can choose a site with an eye to prospect, you are sure to turn out good work. However, be not sorry. What one does has no destruction — no, never. Who knows, at that very place the future may reap golden results.

I shall very soon begin my work in the plains. I have now no need of travelling over the mountains.

Keep watch over your health.

Yours affectionately,
Vivekananda.

136 — AKHANDANANDA

Translated from Bengali

MURREE,
10th October, 1897.

MY DEAR AKHANDANANDA,

I am very glad to receive your letter. You need not make a big plan for the present, but do only what is possible under existing circumstances. Gradually the way will open to you. We must certainly have the orphanage, no hesitating in that. We must not leave the girls in the lurch either. But then we must have a lady superintendent for an orphanage of girls. I believe Mother will be a very good hand for that. Or engage for this task some aged widow of the village who has no issue. And there must be separate places for the boys and girls. Captain Sevier is ready to send you money to help in this. Nedou's Hotel, Lahore — that is his address. If you write to him, write the words, "To wait arrival", on the letter. I am soon going to Rawalpindi, tomorrow or the day after; then I visit Lahore and other places via Jammu, and return to Rajputana via Karachi etc.

I am doing well.

Yours affectionately,
Vivekananda.

PS. You must admit Mohammedan boys, too, but never tamper with their religion. The only thing you will have to do is to make separate arrangements for their food etc., and teach them so that they may be moral, manly, and devoted to doing good to others. This indeed is religion.

Shelve your intricate philosophical speculations for the present. In our country we at present need manhood and kindness. "— The Lord is the Essence of unutterable love." But instead of saying" say, "— He is ever manifest as Love in all beings." What other God — the creation of your mind — are you then going to worship! Let the Vedas, the Koran, the Puranas, and all scriptural lumber rest now for some time — let there be worship of the visible God of Love and Compassion in the country. All idea of separation is bondage, that of non-differentiation is Mukti. Let not the words of people dead-drunk with worldliness terrify you. "— Be fearless" "Ignore the ordinary critics as worms!" Admit boys of all religions — Hindu, Mohammedan, Christian, or anything; but begin rather gently — I mean, see that they get their food and drink a little separately, and teach them only the universal side of religion.

Be mad over this, and strike others with this madness! This life has no other end. Preach His name, let His teachings penetrate the world to the very bone. Never forget. Repeat this Mantra in your heart of hearts unceasingly, as you go the round of your daily duties.

137 — RAKHAL

Translated from Bengali

MURREE,
10th October, 1897.

DEAR RAKHAL,

Reached Murree from Kashmir in the evening of the day before yesterday. Everybody had an enjoyable time of it, only Krishnalal (Dhirananda) and Gupta (Sadananda) suffered now and then from fever, which, however, was but slight. This Address is to be sent to the Raja of Khetri. Have it printed in gilt etc. The Raja is expected at Bombay about the 21st or 22nd of October. None of us is staying at Bombay at present — if there be any, send him a copy so that he may present the same to the Raja even on Board the ship, or somewhere in the city of Bombay. Send the superior copy to Khetri. Have this passed in a meeting and if any change is needed, no harm. Then sign it, all of you, only leaving a blank for my name, and I shall sign it on going to Khetri. Let no pains be spared in this.

. . . Captain Sevier says he is very anxious for a site. He wishes to have a spot near Mussoorie or in some other central place, as soon as possible. ... The thing is that we do not want a place which is too cold, at the same time it must not be too hot. Dehra Dun is unbearable in summer, but pleasant in winter; Mussoorie itself is, I dare say, not the right place for many in winter. Above or below it, that is, in British or Garhwal territory, some land is sure to be found. At the same time there must be a supply of water at the place throughout the year, for drinking purposes and for everyday use. My plan is this: With only Achyutananda and Gupta I go from Murree to Rawalpindi, thence to Jammu, thence to Lahore, and from Lahore straight to Karachi. ... Give my hearty love and blessings to Shashi Babu. I see that Master Mahashaya has buckled to work after such a long time. Alive him my special love and greetings. To see him, with his feminine retiringness, stirred to work, my courage has gone up by leaps and bounds. I am writing to him tomorrow even. Victory to the Lord! — To work! To work!

Yours affectionately,
Vivekananda.

138 — M—

C/O. LALA HANSRAJ,
RAWALPINDI,
Oct., 1897.

DEAR M—,

C'est bon, mon ami — now you are doing just the thing, Come out, man! No sleeping an life; time is flying. Bravo! That is the way.

Many thanks for your publication. Only, I am afraid it will not pay its way in a pamphlet form. . . . Never mind, pay or no pay — let it see the blaze of daylight. You will have many blessings on you and many more curses — but that is always the way of the world!

This is the time.

Yours in the Lord,
Vivekananda.

139 — MOTHER

Translated from Bengali

LAHORE,
15th November, 1897.

DEAR MOTHER, (Shrimati Indumati Mitra)

It is a matter of deep regret that in spite of my earnest wishes, I do not find it feasible to go to Karachi this time and see you. First, because Captain and Mrs. Sevier, who have come from England and are travelling with me for the last nine months nearly, are very anxious to buy some land at Dehra Dun and start an orphanage there. It is their special request that I should go and open the work. This makes it unavoidable to go to Dehra Dun.

Secondly, owing to my kidney troubles I cannot count upon a long life. Even now it is one of my desires to start a Math in Calcutta, towards which as yet I could do nothing. Moreover, the people of my country have withheld the little help that they used to give to our Math of late. They have got a notion that I have brought plenty of money from England! Over and above that, it is impossible to celebrate Shri Ramakrishna's festival this year, for the proprietors of

Rasmani's garden would not let me go there, as I am returned from the West! Hence my first duty lies in seeing the few friends we have in Rajputana and trying my best to have a centre in Calcutta. For these reasons I have been very sorry to postpone my tour to Sindh tat present. I shall try my best to go there via Rajputana and Kathiawar. Please do not be sorry. Never for a day do I forget you all. But duty must be done first. It will ease me of my anxiety when a Math is established in Calcutta. Then I can hope that the work for which I struggled all my life through all sorts of privation and suffering will not die out after I cease to live in this body. I start for Dehra Dun this very day. After a week's stay there, to Rajputana, thence to Kathiawar, and so on.

Yours sincerely,
Vivekananda.

140 — MOTHER

Translated from Bengali

DEHRA DUN,
24th November, 1897.

DEAR MOTHER, (Shrimati Indumati Mitra)

I have duly received your letter and that of dear Haripada. Of course you have ample reason to feel sorry for, but you see, I couldn't help it. And what took me here also became a fiasco; neither could I go to Sindh. It is the Lord's will. Now, I have an idea of proceeding to Calcutta through Rajputana, Kathiawar, and Sindh. But some difficulty may crop up on the way. If all goes well, I am certainly coming to Sindh. You must have undergone a lot of difficulty in coming to Hyderabad by arranging for leave etc. Any least trouble undergone, is bound to produce its excellent results. Friday next I shall leave this place, and have a mind to go via Saharanpur to Rajputana direct. I am doing well now, and trust you too are in health and peace of mind. . . .

With best love and blessings to yourself and Haripada,

Yours sincerely,
Vivekananda.

141 — MARGOT

ALMORA,
20th May, 1898.

DEAR MARGOT (Margaret E. Noble or Sister Nivedita)

. . . Duty has no end, and the world is extremely selfish.

Be of good cheer. "Never a worker of good came to grief." . . .

Ever yours etc.,
Vivekananda.

142 — FRIEND

ALMORA,
10th June, 1898.

MY DEAR FRIEND[1],

I appreciate your letter very much and am extremely happy to learn that the Lord is silently preparing wonderful things for our motherland.

Whether we call it Vedantism or any ism, the truth is that Advaitism is the last word of religion and thought and the only position from which one can look upon all religions and sects with love. I believe it is the religion of the future enlightened humanity. The Hindus may get the credit of arriving at it earlier than other races, they being an older race than either the Hebrew or the Arab; yet practical Advaitism, which looks upon and behaves to all mankind as one's own soul, was never developed among the Hindus universally.

On the other hand, my experience is that if ever any religion approached to this equality in an appreciable manner, it is Islam and Islam alone.

Therefore I am firmly persuaded that without the help of practical Islam, theories of Vedantism, however fine and wonderful they may be, are entirely valueless to the vast mass of mankind. We want to lead mankind to the place where there is neither the Vedas, nor the Bible, nor the Koran; yet this has to be done by harmonising the Vedas, the Bible and the Koran.

1. Written to Mohammed Sarfaraz Husain of Naini Tal.

Mankind ought to be taught that religions are but the varied expressions of THE RELIGION, which is Oneness, so that each may choose that path that suits him best.

For our own motherland a junction of the two great systems, Hinduism and Islam — Vedanta brain and Islam body — is the only hope.

I see in my mind's eye the future perfect India rising out of this chaos and strife, glorious and invincible, with Vedanta brain and Islam body.

Ever praying that the Lord may make of you a great instrument for the help of mankind, and especially of our poor, poor motherland.

Yours with love,
Vivekananda.

143 — MARGOT

KASHMIR,
25th Aug., 1898.

DEAR MARGOT (Margaret E. Noble or Sister Nivedita)

It is a lazy life I am leading for the last two months, floating leisurely in a boat, which is also my home, up and down the beautiful Jhelum, through the most gorgeous scenery God's world can afford, in nature's own park, where the earth, air, land, grass, plants, trees, mountains, snows, and the human form, all express, on the outside at least, the beauty of the Lord — with almost no possessions, scarcely a pen or an inkstand even, snatching up a meal whenever or wherever convenient, the very ideal of a Rip Van Winkle! . . .

Do not work yourself out. It is no use; always remember — "Duty is the midday sun whose fierce rays are burning the very vitals of humanity." It is necessary for a time as a discipline; beyond that, it is a morbid dream. Things go on all right whether we lend them our helping hands or not. We in delusion only break ourselves. There is a false sentiment which goes the extreme of unselfishness, only to injure others by its submission to every evil. We have no right to make others selfish by our unselfishness; have we? . . .

Yours etc.,
Vivekananda.

144 — DEAR

THE MATH, BELUR,
15th Dec., 1898.

DEAR—,

. . . The Mother is our guide and whatever happens or will happen is under Her ordination. . . .

Yours etc.,
Vivekananda.

145 — DHIRA MATA

BAIDYANATH, DEOGHAR,
29th Dec., 1898.

MY DEAR DHIRA MATA, (Mrs. Ole Bull)

You know already my inability to accompany you. I cannot gather strength enough to accompany you. The cold in the lungs continues, and that is just what makes me unfit for travel. On the whole I hope to improve here.

I find my cousin has been all these years cultivating her mind with a will, and she knows all that the Bengali literature can give her, and that is a good deal, especially of metaphysics. She has already learnt to sign her name in English and the Roman alphabet. It is now real brain work to teach her, and therefore I have desisted. I am trying simply to idle away my time and force myself to take rest.

Ere this I had only love for you, but recent development proves that you are appointed by the Mother to watch over my life; hence, faith has been added to love! As regards me and my work, I hold henceforth that you are inspired, and I will gladly shake off all responsibilities from my shoulder and abide by what the Mother ordains through you.

Hoping soon to join you in Europe or America, I remain,

Ever your loving son,
Vivekananda.

146 — DEAR

THE MATH,
11th April, 1899.

DEAR—,

. . . Two years of physical suffering have taken away twenty years of my life. Well, but the soul changeth not, does it? It is there, the same madcap Atman, mad upon one idea, intent and intense.

Yours etc.,
Vivekananda.

147 — MRS. BULL

RIDGELY,
4th Sept., 1899.

DEAR MRS. BULL,

. . .Mother knows best, that is all about me. . . .

Yours etc.,
Vivekananda.

148 — MARGOT

RIDGELY,
1st Nov., 1899.

DEAR MARGOT, (Margaret E. Noble or Sister Nivedita)

. . . It seems there is a gloom over your mind. Never mind, nothing is to last for ever. Anyhow life is not eternal. I am so, so thankful for it. Suffering is the lot of the world's best and bravest — yet, for aeons yet — till things are righted; if possible, here — at least it is a discipline which breaks the dream. In my sane moments I rejoice for my sufferings. Some one must suffer here; — I am glad it is I, amongst others of nature's sacrifices.

Yours etc.,
Vivekananda.

149 — MARGOT

NEW YORK,
15th Nov., 1899.

DEAR MARGOT, (Margaret E. Noble or Sister Nivedita)

. . . On the whole I don't think there is any cause for anxiety about my body. This sort of nervous body is just the instrument to play great music at times and at times to moan in darkness.

Yours etc.,
Vivekananda.

150 — MRS. BULL

12th Dec., 1899.

MY DEAR MRS. BULL,

You are perfectly right; I am brutal, very indeed. But about the tenderness etc., that is my fault. I wish I had less, much less of that — that is my weakness — and alas! all my sufferings have come from that. Well, the municipality is trying to tax us out — good; that is my fault as I did not make the Math public property by a deed of trust. I am very sorry I use harsh language to my boys, but they also know I love them more than anybody else on earth. I may have had Divine help — true; but oh, the pound of blood every bit of Divine help has been to me!! I would be gladder and a better man without that. The present looks very gloomy indeed; but I am a fighter and must die fighting, not give way — that is why I get crazy at the boys. I don't ask them to fight, but not to hinder my fight.

I don't grudge my fate. But oh! now I want a man, one of my boys, to stand by me and fight against all odds! Don't you vex yourself; if anything is to be done in India, my presence is necessary; and I am much better in health; possibly the sea will make me better. Anyway I did not do anything this time in America except bother my friends. Possibly Joe will help me out with the passage, and I have some money with Mr. Leggett. I have hopes of collecting some money in India yet. I did not see any of my friends in different parts of India. I have hope of collecting the fifteen thousand that will make up the fifty thousand, and a deed of trust will bring down the municipal taxes. If I cannot collect that — it is better to struggle and die for it than vegetate here in America. My mistakes have been great; but everyone of them was from too much love. How I hate love! Would I never had any Bhakti! Indeed, I wish I could be an Advaitist, calm and heartless. Well, this life is done. I will try in the next. I am sorry, especially now, that I have done more injury to my friends than there have been blessings on them. The peace, the quiet I am seeking, I never found.

I went years ago to the Himalayas, never to come back; and my sister committed suicide, the news reached me there, and that weak heart flung me off from that prospect of peace! It is the weak heart that has driven me out of India to seek some help for those I love, and here I am! Peace have I sought, but the heart, that seat of Bhakti, would not allow me to find it. Struggle and torture, torture and struggle. Well, be it then. since it is my fate, and the quicker it is over, the better. They say I am impulsive, but look at the circumstances!!! I am sorry I have been the cause of pain to you, to you above all, who love me so much, who have been so, so kind. But it is done — was a fact. I am now going to cut the knot or die in the attempt.

Ever your son,
Vivekananda.

PS. As Mother wants it, so let it be. I am going to beg of Joe a passage via San Francisco to India. If she gives it, I start immediately via Japan. It would take a month. In India, I think, I can raise some money to keep things straight or on a better footing — at least to leave things where I get them all muddled. The end is getting very dark and very much muddled; well, I expected it so. Don't think I give in in a moment. Lord bless you; if the Lord has made me His hack to work and die on the streets, let Him have it. I am more cheerful just now after your letter than I was for years — Wah Guru ki Fateh! Victory unto the Guru!! Yes, let the world come, the hells come, the gods come, let Mother come, I fight and do not give in. Râvana got his release in three births by fighting the Lord Himself! It is glorious to fight Mother.

All blessings on you and yours. You have done for me more, much more, than I deserved ever.

Love to Christine and Turiyananda.

151 — MARGOT

921, 21ST STREET, LOS ANGELES,
23rd December, 1899.

DEAR MARGOT, (Margaret E. Noble or Sister Nivedita)

Yes, I am really getting well under the manipulations of magnetic healing! At any rate I am all right. There was, never anything serious with my organs — it was nerves and dyspepsia.

Now I walk miles every day, at any time — before or after meals. I am perfectly well — and am going to remain so, I am sure.

The wheel is turning up, Mother is working it up. She cannot let me go before Her work is done — and that is the secret.

See, how England is working up. After this blood-letting, (Swamiji refers to the Boer war.) people will then have time of thinking better and higher things than "war", "war", "war". That is our opportunity. We run in quick, get hold of them by the dozens and then set the Indian work in full swing.

I pray that England will lose Cape Colony, so that she will be able to concentrate her energy on India. These capes and promontories never are of any use to England except in puffing up a false pride and costing her hordes in money and blood.

Things are looking up. So get ready. With all love to the four sisters and to you,

Yours etc.,
Vivekananda.

152 — MARGOT

LOS ANGELES, CALIFORNIA,
24th Jan., 1900.

DEAR MARGOT, (Margaret E. Noble or Sister Nivedita)

I am afraid that the rest and peace I seek for will never come. But Mother does good to others through me, at least some to my native land, and it is easier to be reconciled to one's fate as a sacrifice. We are all sacrifices — each in his own way. The great work is going on — no one can see its meaning except that it is a great sacrifice. Those that are willing escape a lot of pain. Those who resist are broken into submission and suffer more. I am now determined to be a willing one.

Yours etc.,
Vivekananda.

153 — NIVEDITA

C/O MISS MEAD,
447 DOUGLAS BUILDING,
LOS ANGELES, CALIFORNIA,
15th Feb., 1900.

MY DEAR NIVEDITA,

Yours of the — reached me today at Pasadena. I see Joe has missed you at Chicago — although I have not heard anything from them yet from New York.

There was a bundle of English newspapers from England with a line on the envelope expressing good wishes for me and signed, F.H.M. Nothing important was in those, however. I would have written a letter to Miss Müller, but I do not know the address; then I was afraid to frighten her.

In the meanwhile, Mrs. Leggett started a plan of a $100 subscription each a year for ten years to help me, and headed the list with her $100 for 1900, and got 2 others here to do the same. Then she went on writing letters to all my friends asking each to join in it. When she went on writing to Mrs. Miller I was rather shy — but she did it before I knew. A very polite but cold letter came to her in reply from Mrs. Hale, written by Mary, expressing their inability and assuring her of their love for me. I am afraid Mrs. Hale and Mary are displeased. But it was not my fault at all!!

I get news from Mrs. Sevier that Niranjan is seriously ill in Calcutta. I do not know if he has passed away. Well — but I am strong now, Margo, stronger than ever I was mentally. I was mentally getting a sort of ironing over my heart. I am getting nearer a Sannyasin's life now. I have not had any news from Saradananda for two weeks. I am glad you got the stories; rewrite them if you think so — get them published if you find anybody to do it and take the proceeds, if any, for your work. I do not want any I have got a few hundred dollars here. Going to San Francisco next week, and hope to do better there. Tell Mary when you see her next that I had nothing whatsoever to do with the proposal of $100 a year subscription to Mrs. Hale. I am so grateful to them.

Well, money will come for your school, never fear — it has got to come; if it does not come, who cares? One road is quite as good as the other. Mother knows best. I don't know whether I am very soon going to the East or not. If I have an opportunity, of course I will go to Indiana.

The international scheme is a good one and by all mean join it, and be the medium of getting some Indian women's clubs to join it through you, which is better. . . .

Things shall look up for us, never mind. As soon as the war is finished we go to England and try to do a big work there. What do you think? Shall I write to Mother Superior? If so, send her whereabouts. Has she written to you? Sturdies and "Shakies" will all come round — hold on.

You are learning your lessons — that is all I want. So am I; the moment we are fit, money and men must flow towards us. Between my nerves and your emotion we may make a mess of everything just now. So Mother is curing my nerves and drilling you into level-headedness — and then we go. This time good is coming in chunks, I am sure. We will make the foundations of the old land shake this time.

. . . I am getting cool as a cucumber — let anything come, I am ready. The next move — any blow shall tell — not one miss — such is the next chapter.

With all love,
Vivekananda.

154 — AKHANDANANDA

Translated from Bengali

CALIFORNIA,
21st February, 1900.

MY DEAR AKHANDANANDA,

I am very glad to receive your letter and go through the details of news. Learning and wisdom are superfluities, the surface glitter merely, but it is the heart that is the seat of all power. It is not in the brain but in the heart that the Atman, possessed of knowledge, power, and activity, has Its seat. "शतं चैका च हृदयस्य नाड्य: — The nerves of the heart are a hundred and one" etc. The chief nerve-centre near the heart, called the sympathetic ganglia, is where the Atman has Its citadel. The more heart you will be able to manifest, the greater will be the victory you achieve. It is only a few that understand the language of the brain, but everyone from the Creator down to a clump of grass, understands the language that comes from the heart. But then, in our country, it is a case of rousing men that are, as it were, dead. It will take time, but if you have infinite patience and perseverance, success is bound to come. No mistake in that.

How are the English officials to blame? Is the family, of whose unnatural cruelty you have written, an isolated one in India? Or, are there plenty of such? It is the same story all over the country. But then, it is not as a result of pure wickedness that the selfishness commonly met with in our country has come. This bestial selfishness is the outcome of centuries of failure and repression. It is not real selfishness, but deep-rooted despair. It will be cored at the first inkling of success. It is only this that the English officials are noticing all round, so how can they have faith at the very outset? But tell me, do they not sympathise with any real work that they meet with? . . .

In these days of dire famine, flood, disease, and pestilence, tell me where your Congressmen are. Will it do merely to say, "Hand the government of the country over to us"? And who is there to listen to them? If a man does work, has he to open his mouth to ask for anything? If there be two thousand people like you working in several districts, won't it be the turn of the English themselves to consult you in matters of political moment?" A— was not allowed to open a centre, but what of that! Has not Kishengarh allowed it?— Let him work on without ever opening his lips; there is no use of either telling anything to anybody, or quarrelling with any. Whoever will assist in this work of the Divine Mother of the universe, will have Her grace, and whoever will oppose it will not only be laying the axe to his own prospects. — all in good time. Many a little makes a mickle. When a great work is being done, when the foundations are laid or a road constructed, when superhuman energy is needed — it is one or two extraordinary men who silently and noiselessly work through a world of obstacles and difficulties. When thousands of people are benefited, there is a great tomtoming, and the whole country is loud in notes of praise. But then the machine has already been set agoing, and even a boy can work it, or a fool add to it some impetus. Grasp this that, that benefit done to a village or two, that orphanage with its twenty orphans, those ten or twenty workers — all these are enough; they form the nucleus, never to be destroyed. From these, hundreds of thousands of people will be benefited in time. Now we want half a dozen lions, then excellent work will be turned out by even hundreds of jackals. . .

If orphan girls happen to come to your hands for shelter, you must take them in above all else. Otherwise, Christian missionaries will take them, poor things, away! What matters it that you have no particular arrangements for them? Through the Divine Mother's will, they will be provided for. When you get a horse, never you worry about the whip. ... Get together whomsoever you can lay your hands on, no picking and choosing now — everything will be set right in course of time. In every attempt there are many obstacles to cope with, but gradually the path becomes smooth.

Convey to the European officer many thanks from me. Work on fearlessly — there is a hero! Bravo! Thrice well done! The starting of a centre at Bhagalpur that you have written about is no doubt a good idea — enlightening the schoolboys and things of that sort. But our mission is for the destitute, the poor, and the illiterate peasantry and labouring classes, and if, after everything has been done for them first, there is spare time, then only for the gentry. Those peasants and labouring people will be won over by love. Afterwards it will be they who will collect small sums and start missions at their own villages, and gradually, from among those very men, teachers will spring.

Teach some boys and girls of the peasant classes the rudiments of learning and infuse a number of ideas into their brains. Afterwards the peasants of each village will collect funds and have one of these in their village. "— this holds good in all spheres. We help them to help themselves. That they are supplying you with your daily bread is a real bit of work done. The moment they will come to understand their own condition and feel the necessity of help and improvement, know that your work is taking effect and is in the right direction, while the little good that the moneyed classes, out of pity, do to the poor, does not last, and ultimately it does nothing but harm to both parties. The peasants and labouring classes are in a moribund condition, so what is needed is that the moneyed people will only help them to regain their vitality, and nothing more. Then leave the peasants and labourers to look to their own problem, to grapple with and solve it. But then you must take care not to set up class-strife between the poor peasants, the labouring people, and wealthy classes. Make it a point not to abuse the moneyed classes. "— The wise man should achieve his own object."

Victory to the Guru! Victory to the Mother of the Universe! What fear! Opportunity, remedy, and its application will present themselves. I do not care about the result, well or ill. I shall be happy if only you do this much of work. Wordy warfares, texts and scriptures, doctrines and dogmas — all these I am coming to loathe as poison in this my advanced age. Know this for certain that he who will work will be the crown on my head. Useless bandying of words and making noise is taking away our time, is consuming our life-energy, without pushing the cause of humanitarianism a step further. — Away with fear! Bravo! There is a hero indeed! May the blessed Guru be enthroned in your heart, and the Divine Mother guide your hands.

Yours affectionately,
Vivekananda.

155 — NIVEDITA

SAN FRANCISCO,
4th March, 1900.

DEAR NIVEDITA,

I don't want to work. I want to be quiet and rest. I know the time and the place; but the fate or Karma, I think, drives me on — work, work. We are like cattle driven to the slaughter-house — hastily nibbling a bite of grass on the roadside as they are driven along under the whip. And all this is our work, our fear — fear, the beginning of misery, of disease, etc. By being nervous and fearful we injure others, by being so fearful to hurt we hurt more. By trying so much to avoid evil we fall into its jaws.

What a mass of namby-pamby nonsense we create round ourselves!! It does us no good, it leads us on to the very thing we try to avoid — misery. ...

Oh, to become fearless, to be daring, to be careless of everything! . . .

Yours etc.,
Vivekananda.

156 — NIVEDITA

SAN FRANCISCO,
25th March, 1900.

DEAR NIVEDITA,

I am much better and am growing very strong. I feel sometimes that freedom is near at hand, and the tortures of the last two years have been great lessons in many ways. Disease and misfortune come to do us good in the long run, although at the time we feel that we are submerged for ever.

I am the infinite blue sky; the clouds may gather over me, but I am the same infinite blue.

I am trying to get a taste of that peace which I know is my nature and everyone's nature. These tin pots of bodies and foolish dreams of happiness and misery —

what are they?

My dreams are breaking. Om Tat Sat!

Yours,
Vivekananda.

157 — MARGOT

1719 TURK STREET,
SAN FRANCISCO,
28th March, 1900.

MY DEAR MARGOT, (Margaret E. Noble or Sister Nivedita)

I am so glad at your good fortune. Things have got to come round if we are steady. I am sure you will get all the money you require here or in England.

I am working hard; and the harder I work, the better I feel. This ill health has done me a great good, sure. I am really understanding what non-attachment means. And I hope very soon to be perfectly non-attached.

We put all our energies to concentrate and get attached to one thing; but the other part, though equally difficult, we seldom pay any attention to — the faculty of detaching ourselves at a moment's notice from anything.

Both attachment and detachment perfectly developed make a man great and happy.

I am so glad at Mrs. Leggett's gift of $1,000. She is working up, wait. She has a great part to play in Ramakrishna's work, whether she knows it or not.

I enjoyed your accounts of Prof. Geddes, and Joe has a funny account of a clairvoyant. Things are just now beginning to turn. . . .

This letter, I think, Will reach you at Chicago. . . .

I had a nice letter from Max Gysic, the young Swiss who is a great friend of Miss Souter. Miss Souter also sends her love, and they ask to know the time when I come over to England. Many people are inquiring, they say.

Things have got to come round — the seed must die underground to come up as the tree. The last two years were the underground rotting. I never had a struggle in the jaws of death, but it meant a tremendous upheaval of the whole life. One such brought me to Ramakrishna, another sent me to the U.S., this has been the greatest of all. It is gone — I am so calm that it astonishes me sometimes!! I work every day morning and evening, eat anything any hour — and go to bed at 12 p.m. in the night — but such fine sleep!! I never had such power of sleeping before!

Yours with all love and blessings,
Vivekananda.

158 — JOE

ALAMEDA, CALIFORNIA,
18th April, 1900.

MY DEAR JOE,

Just now I received yours and Mrs. Bull's welcome letter. I direct this to London. I am so glad Mrs. Leggett is on the sure way to recovery.

I am so sorry Mr. Leggett resigned the presidentship.

Well, I keep quiet for fear of making further trouble.

You know my methods are extremely harsh and once roused I may rattle A— too much for his peace of mind.

I wrote to him only to tell him that his notions about Mrs. Bull are entirely wrong.

Work is always difficult; pray for me Joe that my works stop for ever, and my whole soul be absorbed in Mother. Her works, She knows.

You must be glad to be in London once more — the old friends, give them all my love and gratitude.

I am well, very well mentally. I feel the rest of the soul more shall that of the body. The battles are lost and won, I have bundled my things and am waiting for the great deliverer.

"Shiva, O Shiva, carry my boat to the other shore."

After all, Joe, I am only the boy who used to listen with rapt wonderment to the wonderful words of Ramakrishna under the Banyan at Dakshineswar. That is my true nature; works and activities, doing good and so forth are all superimpositions. Now I again hear his voice; the same old voice thrilling my soul. Bonds are breaking — love dying, work becoming tasteless — the glamour is off life. Only the voice of the Master calling. — "I come Lord, I come." "Let the dead bury the dead, follow thou Me." — "I come, my beloved Lord, I come."

Yes, I come. Nirvana is before me. I feel it at times — the same infinite ocean of peace, without a ripple, a breath.

I am glad I was born, glad I suffered so, glad I did make big blunders, glad to enter peace. I leave none bound, I take no bonds. Whether this body will fall and release me or I enter into freedom in the body, the old man is gone, gone for ever, never to come back again! The guide, the Guru, the leader, the teacher has passed away; the boy, the student, the servant is left behind.

You understand why I do not want to meddle with A—. Who am I to meddle with anyone, Joe? I have long given up my place as a leader — I have no right to raise my voice. Since the beginning of this year I have not dictated anything in India. You know that. Many thanks for what you and Mrs. Bull have been to me in the past. All blessings follow you ever! The sweetest moments of my life have been when I was drifting: I am drifting again — with the bright warm sun ahead and masses of vegetation around — and in the heat everything is so still, so calm — and I am drifting languidly — in the warm heart of the river! I dare not make a splash with my hands or feet — for fear of breaking the marvellous stillness, stillness that makes you feel sure it is an illusion!

Behind my work was ambition, behind my love was personality, behind my purity was fear, behind my guidance the thirst of power! Now they are vanishing, and I drift. I come! Mother, I come! In Thy warm bosom, floating wheresoever Thou takest me, in the voiceless, in the strange, in the wonderland, I come — a spectator, no more an actor.

Oh, it is so calm! My thoughts seem to come from a great, great distance in the interior of my own heart. They seem like rains, distant whispers, and peace is upon every thing, sweet, sweet peace — like that one feels for a few moments just before falling into sleep, when things are seen and felt like shadows — without fear, without love, without emotion. Peace that one feels alone, surrounded with statues and pictures — I come! Lord, I come!

The world is, but not beautiful nor ugly, but as sensations without exciting any emotion. Oh, Joe, the blessedness of it! Everything is good and beautiful; for things are all losing their relative proportions to me — my body among the first. Om That Existence!

I hope great things to come to you all in London and Paris. Fresh joy — fresh benefits to mind and body.

With love as ever to you and Mrs. Bull,

Yours faithfully,
Vivekananda.

159 — NIVEDITA

NEW YORK,
20th June, 1900.

DEAR NIVEDITA,

. . . Well, Mother seems to be kind again and the wheel is slowly rising up. . . .

Yours etc.,
Vivekananda.

160 — NIVEDITA

NEW YORK,
2nd July, 1900.

DEAR NIVEDITA,

. . . Mother knows, as I always say. Pray to Mother. It is hard work to be a leader — one must crush all one's own self under the feet of the community. . . .

Yours etc.,
Vivekananda.

161 — NIVEDITA

6 PLACE DES ETATS UNIS, PARIS,
25th Aug., 1900.

DEAR NIVEDITA,

Your letter reached me just now. Many thanks for the kind expressions.

I gave a chance to Mrs. Bull to draw her money out of the Math; and as she did not say anything about it, and the trust deeds were waiting here to be executed, I got them executed duly at the British Consulate; and they are on their way to India now.

Now I am free, as I have kept no power or authority or position for me in the work. I also have resigned the presidentship of the Ramakrishna Mission.

The Math etc., belong now to the immediate disciples of Ramakrishna except myself. The presidentship is now Brahmananda's — next it will fall on Premananda etc., etc., in turn.

I am so glad a whole load is off me, now I am happy. I have served Ramakrishna through mistakes and success for 20 years now. I retire for good and devote the rest of my life to myself.

I no longer represent anybody, nor am I responsible to anybody. As to my friends, I had a morbid sense of obligation. I have thought well and find I owe nothing to anybody; if anything, I have given my best energies, unto death almost, and received only hectoring and mischief-making and botheration. I am done with everyone here and in India.

Your letter indicates that I am jealous of your new friends. You must know once for all, I am born without jealousy, without avarice, without the desire to rule — whatever other vices I am born with.

I never directed you before; now, after I am nobody in the work, I have no direction whatever. I only know this much: So long as you serve "Mother" with a whole heart, She will be your guide.

I never had any jealousy about what friends you made. I never criticised my brethren for mixing up in anything. Only I do believe the Western people have the peculiarity of trying to force upon others whatever seems good to them, forgetting that what is good for you may not be good for others. As such, I am afraid you might try to force upon others whatever turn your mind might take in contact with new friends. That was the only reason I sometimes tried to stop any particular influence, and nothing else.

You are free, have your own choice, your own work.

...

Friends or foes, they are all instruments in Her hands to help us work out our own Karma, through pleasure or pain. As such "Mother" bless them all.

With all love and blessings,

Yours affectionately,
Vivekananda.

162 — NIVEDITA

PARIS,
28th August, 1900.

DEAR NIVEDITA,

Such is life — grind, grind; and yet what else are we to do? Grind, grind! Something will come — some way will be opened. If it does not, as it probably never will — then, then — what then? All our efforts are only to stave off, for a season, the great climax — death! Oh, what would the world do without you, Death! Thou great healer!

The world, as it is, is not real, is not eternal, thank the Lord!! How can the future be any better? That must be an effect of this one — at least like this, if not worse!

Dreams, oh dreams! Dream on! Dream, the magic of dream, is the cause of this life, it is also the remedy. Dream' dream; only dream! Kill dream by dream!

I am trying to learn French, talking to — here. Some are very appreciative already. Talk to all the world — of the eternal riddle, the eternal spool of fate, whose thread-end no one finds and everyone seems to find, at least to his own satisfaction, at least for a time — to fool himself a moment, isn't it?

Well, now great things are to be done! Who cares for great things? Why not do small things as well? One is as good as the other. The greatness of little things, that is what the Gita teaches — bless the old book!! . . .

I have not had much time to think of the body. So it must be well. Nothing is ever well here. We forget them at times, and that is being well and doing well. . . .

We play our parts here — good or bad. When the dream is finished and we have left the stage, we will have a hearty laugh at all this — of this only I am sure.

Yours etc.,
Vivekananda.

163 — MOTHER

6 PLACE DES ETATS UNIS, PARIS,
3rd Sept., 1900.

DEAR MOTHER, (Mrs. Francis Leggett)

We had a congress of cranks here in this house.

The representatives came from various countries, from India in the south, to Scotland in the north, with England and America buttressing the sides.

We were having great difficulty in electing the president, for though Dr. James (Professor William James) was there, he was more mindful of the blisters raised on him by Mrs. Melton (probably a magnetic healer) than solution of world problems.

I proposed Joe (Josephine MacLeod), but she refused on the ground of non-arrival of her new gown — and went to a corner to watch the scene, from a coign of vantage.

Mrs. (Ole) Bull was ready, but Margot (Sister Nivedita) objected to this meeting being reduced to a comparative philosophy class.

When we were thus in a fix — up sprung a short, square, almost round figure from the corner, and without any ceremony declared that all difficulties will be solved, not only of electing a president but of life itself, if we all took to worshipping the Sun God and Moon God. He delivered his speech in five minutes; but it took his disciple, who was present, fully three quarters of an hour to translate. In the meanwhile, the master began to draw the rugs in your parlour up in a heap, with the intention, as he said, of giving us an ocular demonstration of the power of "Fire God", then and there.

At this juncture Joe interposed and insisted that she did not want a fire sacrifice in her parlour; whereupon the Indian saint looked daggers at Joe, entirely disgusted at the behaviour of one he confidently believed to be a perfect convert to fire worship.

Then Dr. James snatched a minute from nursing his blisters and declared that he would have something very interesting to speak upon Fire God and his brethren, if he were not entirely occupied with the evolution of Meltonian blisters. Moreover his great Master, Herbert Spencer, not having investigated the subject before him, he would stick to golden silence.

"Chutney is the thing", said a voice near the door. We all looked back and saw Margot. "It is Chutney," she said, "Chutney and Kali, that will remove all difficulties of Life, and make it easy for us to swallow all evils, and relish what is good." But she stopped all of a sudden and vehemently asserted that she was not going to speak any further, as she has been obstructed by a certain male animal in the audience in her speech. She was sure one man in the audience had his head turned towards the window and was not paying the attention proper to a lady, and though as to herself she believed in the equality of the sexes, yet she wanted to know the reason of that disgusting man's want of due respect for women. Then one and all declared that they had been giving her the most undivided attention, and all above the equal right, her due, but to no purpose. Margot would have nothing to do with that horrible crowd and sat down.

Then Mrs. Bull of Boston took the floor and began to explain how all the difficulties of the world were from not understanding the true relation between the sexes. She said, "The only panacea was a right understanding of the proper persons, and then to find liberty in love and freedom in liberty and motherhood, brotherhood, fatherhood, Godhood, love in freedom and freedom in love, in the right holding up of the true ideal in sex."

To this the Scotch delegate vehemently objected

and said that as the hunter chased the goatherd, the goatherd the shepherd, the shepherd the peasant, and the peasant drove the fisher into the sea, now we wanted to fish out of the deep the fisher and let him fall upon the peasant, the peasant upon the shepherd, and so on; and the web of life will be completed and we will be all happy. He was not allowed to continue his driving businesss long. In a second everyone was on his feet, and we could only hear a confusion of voices — "Sun God and Moon God", "Chutney and Kali," "Freedom holdings up right understanding, sex, motherhood", "Never, the fisherman must go back to the shore", etc. Whereupon Joe declared that she was yearning to be the hunter for the time and chase them all out of the house if they did not stop their nonsense.

Then was peace and calm restored, and I hasten to write you about it.

Yours affectionately,
Vivekananda.

164 — ALBERTA

6 PLACE DES ETATS UNIS, PARIS,
10th September, 1900.

DEAR ALBERTA,

I am surely coming this evening and of course will be very glad to meet the princess (probably Princess Demidoff) and her brother. But if it be too late to find my way out here, you will have to find me a place to sleep in the house.

Yours with love and blessings,
Vivekananda.

165 — JOE

THE MATH, BELUR,
11th Dec., 1900.

DEAR JOE,

I arrived night before last. Alas! my hurrying was of no use.

Poor Captain Sevier passed away, a few days ago — thus two great Englishmen gave up their lives for us — us the Hindus. Thus is martyrdom if anything is. Mrs. Sevier I have written to just now, to know her decision.

I am well, things are well here — every way. Excuse this haste. I will write longer ere long.

Ever yours in truth,
Vivekananda.

166 — NIVEDITA

THE MATH, BELUR, HOWRAH,
19th Dec., 1900.

DEAR NIVEDITA,

Just a voice across the continents to say, how do you do? Are you not surprised? Verily I am a bird of passage. Gay and busy Paris, grim old Constantinople, sparkling little Athens, and pyramidal Cairo are left behind, and here I am writing in my room on the Ganga, in the Math. It is so quiet and still! The broad river is dancing in the bright sunshine, only now and then an occasional cargo boat breaking the silence with the splashing of the oars. It is the cold season here, but the middle of the day is warm and bright every day. But it is the winter of Southern California. Everything is green and gold, and the grass is like velvet; yet the air is cold and crisp and delightful.

Yours etc.,
Vivekananda.

167 — JOE

THE MATH, BELUR, HOWRAH,
26th Dec., 1900.

DEAR JOE,

This mail brought your letter including that of Mother and Alberta. What the learned friend of Alberta says about Russia is about the same I think myself. Only there is one difficulty of thought: Is it possible for the Hindu race to be Russianised?

Dear Mr. Sevier passed away before I could arrive. He was cremated on the banks of the river that flows by his Ashrama, à la Hindu, covered with garlands, the Brahmins carrying the body and boys chanting the Vedas.

The cause has already two martyrs. It makes me love dear old England and its heroic breed. The Mother is watering the plant of future India with the best blood of England. Glory unto Her!

Dear Mrs. Sevier is calm. A letter she wrote me to Paris comes back this mail. I am going up tomorrow to pay her a visit. Lord bless her, dear brave soul!

I am calm and strong. Occasion never found me low yet Mother will not make me now depressed.

It is very pleasant here, now the winter is on. The Himalayas will be still more beautiful with the uncovered snows.

The young man who started from New York, Mr. Johnston, has taken the vow of a Brahmachârin and is at Mayavati.

Send the money to Saradananda in the Math, as I will be away in the hills.

They have worked all right as far as they could; I am glad, and feel myself quite a fool on account of my nervous chagrin.

They are as good and as faithful as ever, and they are in good health. Write all this to Mrs. Bull and tell her she was always right and I was wrong, and I beg a hundred thousand pardons of her.

Oceans of love for her and for M—

I look behind and after

And find that all is right. In my deepest sorrows

There is a soul of light.

All love to M—, Mrs. C—, to Dear J.B.—, and to you, Dear Joe, Pranâms.

Vivekananda.

168 — NIVEDITA

THE MATH, BELUR,
7th Sept., 1901.

DEAR NIVEDITA,

We all work by bits, that is to say, in this cause. I try to keep down the spring, but something or other happens, and the spring goes whirr, and there you are — thinking, remembering, scribbling, scrawling, and all that!

Well, about the rains — they have come down now in right earnest, and it is a deluge, pouring, pouring, pouring night and day. The river is rising, flooding the banks; the ponds and tanks have overflowed. I have just now returned from lending a hand in cutting a deep drain to take off the water from the Math grounds. The rain-water stands at places some feet high. My huge stork is full of glee, and so are the ducks and geese. My tame antelope fled from the Math and gave us some days of anxiety in finding him out. One of my ducks unfortunately died yesterday. She had been gasping for breath more than a week. One of my waggish old monks says, "Sir, it is no use living in this Kali-Yuga when ducks catch cold from damp and rain, and frogs sneeze!"

One of the geese had her plumes falling off. Knowing no other method, I left her some minutes in a tub of water mixed with mild carbolic, so that it might either kill or heal; and she is all right now.

Yours etc.,
Vivekananda.

CONVERSATIONS AND DIALOGUES

I

The disciple is Sharatchandra Chakravarty, who published his records in a Bengali book, Swami-Shishya-Samvâda, in two parts. The present series of "Conversations and Dialogues" is a revised translation from this book. Five dialogues of this series have already appeared in the Vol. V.

Place: Calcutta, the house of the late Babu Priyanath Mukhopadhyaya, Baghbazar.

Year: 1897.

It is three or four days since Swamiji has set his foot in Calcutta (On February 20, 1897.) after his first return from the West. The joy of the devotees of Shri Ramakrishna knows no bounds at enjoying his holy presence after a long time. And the well-to-do among them are considering themselves blessed to cordially invite Swamiji to their own houses. This afternoon Swamiji had an invitation to the house of Srijut Priyanath Mukhopadhyaya, a devotee of Shri Ramakrishna, at Rajballabhpara in Baghbazar. Receiving this news, many devotees assembled today in his house.

The disciple also, informed of it through indirect sources, reached the house of Mr. Mukherjee at about 2-30 p.m. He had not yet made his acquaintance with Swamiji. So this was to be his first meeting with the Swami.

On the disciple's reaching there, Swami Turiyananda took him to Swamiji and introduced him. After his return to the Math, the Swami had already heard about him, having read a Hymn on Shri Ramakrishna composed by the disciple.

Swamiji also had come to know that the disciple used to visit Nâg Mahâshaya, a foremost devotee of Shri Ramakrishna[1].

When the disciple prostrated himself before him and took his seat, Swamiji addressed him in Sanskrit and asked him about Nag Mahashaya and his health, and while referring to his superhuman renunciation,

---

[1]. Durgacharan Nag, the great saint and perfected soul, living as a householder, who wonderfully reflected in his life—in many of its phases—the greatness of the Master, Shri Ramakrishna.

his unbounded love for God, and his humility, he said:

"वयं तत्त्वान्वेषात् हता मधुकर त्वं खलु कृती।"

(Words addressed by King Dushyanta to the bee which was teasing Shakuntalâ by darting at her lips—Kalidasa's Shâkuntalam.)

—"We are undone by our vain quest after reality; while, O bee, you are indeed blessed with success!" He then asked the disciple to send these words to Nag Mahashaya. Afterwards, finding it rather inconvenient to talk to the disciple in the crowd, he called him and Swami Turiyananda to a small room to the west and, addressing himself to the disciple, began to recite these words from the Vivekachudâmani (43):

मा भैष्ट विद्वंस्तव नास्त्युपायः
संसारसिन्धोस्तरणेऽस्त्युपायः।
येनैव याता यतयोऽस्य पारं
तमेव मार्गं तव निर्दिशामि॥

—"O wise one, fear not; you have not to perish. Means there are for crossing the ocean of this round of birth and death. I shall show you the same way by which holy men of renunciation have crossed this ocean." He then asked him to read Âchârya Shankara's work named Vivekachudâmani.

At these words, the disciple went on musing within himself. Was the Swami in this way hinting at the desirability of his own formal initiation? The disciple was at that time a staunch orthodox man in his ways, and a Vedantin. He had not yet settled his mind as regards the adoption of a Guru and was a devoted advocate of Varnâshrama or caste ordinances.

While various topics were going on, a man came in and announced that Mr. Narendranath Sen, the Editor of the Mirror, had come for an interview with Swamiji. Swamiji asked the bearer of this news to show him into that small room. Narendra Babu came and taking a seat there introduced various topics about England and America. In answer to his questions Swamiji said, "Nowhere in the world is to be found another nation like the Americans, so generous, broad-minded, hospitable, and so sincerely eager to accept new ideas." "Wherever work", he went on, "has been done in America has not been done through my power. The people of America have accepted the ideas of Vedanta, because they are so good-hearted." Referring to England he said, "There is no nation in the world so conservative as the English. They do not like so easily to accept any new idea, but if through perseverance they can be once made to understand any idea, they will never give it up by any means. Such firm determination you will find in no other nation. This is why they occupy the foremost position in the world in power and civilization."

Then declaring that if qualified preachers could be had, there was greater likelihood of the Vedanta work being permanently established in England than in America, he continued, "I have only laid the foundation of the work. If future preachers follow my path, a good deal of work may be done in time."

Narendra Babu asked, "What future prospect is there for us in preaching religion in this way?"

Swamiji said: "In our country there is only this religion of Vedanta. Compared with the Western civilisation, it may be said, we have hardly got anything else. But by the preaching of this universal religion of Vedanta, a religion which gives equal rights to acquire spirituality to men of all creeds and all paths of religious practice, the civilised West would come to know what a wonderful degree of spirituality once developed in India and how that is still existing. By the study of this religion, the Western nations will have increasing regard and sympathy for us. Already these have grown to some extent. In this way, if we have their real sympathy and regard, we would learn from them the sciences bearing on our material life, thereby qualifying ourselves better for the struggle for existence. On the other hand, by learning this Vedanta from us, they will be enabled to secure their own spiritual welfare."

Narendra Babu asked, "Is there any hope of our political progress in this kind of interchange?"

Swamiji said, "They (the Westerners) are the children of the great hero Virochana![1] Their power makes the five elements play like puppets in their hands. If you people believe that we shall in case of conflict with them gain freedom by applying those material forces, you are profoundly mistaken. Just as a little piece of stone figures before the Himalayas, so we differ from them in point of skill in the use of those forces. Do you know what my idea is? By preaching the profound secrets of the Vedanta religion in the Western world, we shall attract the sympathy and regard of these mighty nations, maintaining for ever the position of their teacher in spiritual matters, and they will remain our teachers in all material concerns. The day when, surrendering the spiritual into their hands, our countrymen would sit at the feet of the West to learn religion, that day indeed the nationality of this fallen nation will be dead and gone for good. Nothing will come of crying day and night before them, 'Give me this or give me that.' When there will grow a link of sympathy and regard between both nations by this give-and-take intercourse, there will be then no need for these noisy cries. They will do everything of their own accord. I believe that by this cultivation of religion and the wider diffusion of Vedanta, both this country and the West will gain enormously. To me the pursuit of politics is a secondary means in comparison with this. I will lay down my life to carry out this belief practically. If you believe in any other way of accomplishing the good of India, well, you may go on working your own way."

Narendra Babu shortly left, expressing his unqualified agreement with Swamiji's ideas. The disciple, hearing the above words from Swamiji, astonishingly contemplated his luminous features with steadfast gaze.

When Narendra Babu had departed, an enthusiastic preacher belonging to the society for the protection of cows came for an interview with Swamiji. He was dressed almost like a Sannyasin, if not fully so—with a Geruâ turban on the head; he was evidently an up-country Indian. At the announcement of this preacher of cow-protection Swamiji came out to the parlour room. The preacher saluted Swamiji and presented him with a picture of the mother-cow. Swamiji took that in his hand and, making it over to one standing by, commenced the following conversation with the preacher:

---

1. In ancient Indian tradition Virochana was the first great king of the Asuras, possessing supernatural powers. Recent investigations in Assyrian mythology prove the existence of a tradition in Assyrian history about such a king, called Berosus in certain ancient genealogies.

Swamiji: What is the object of your society?

Preacher: We protect the mother-cows of our country from the hands of the butcher. Cow-infirmaries have been founded in some places where the diseased, decrepit mother-cows or those bought from the butchers are provided for.

Swamiji: That is very good indeed. What is the source of your income?

Preacher: The work of the society is carried on only by gifts kindly made by great men like you.

Swamiji: What amount of money have you now laid by?

Preacher: The Marwari traders' community are the special supporters of this work. They have given a big amount for this good cause.

Swamiji: A terrible famine has now broken out in Central India. The Indian Government has published a death-roll of nine lakhs of starved people. Has your society done anything to render help in this time of famine?

Preacher: We do not help during famine or other distresses. This society has been established only for the protection of mother-cows.

Swamiji: During a famine when lakhs of people, your own brothers and sisters, have fallen into the jaws of death, you have not thought it your duty, though having the means, to help them in that terrible calamity with food!

Preacher: No. This famine broke out as a result of men's Karma, their sins. It is a case of "like Karma, like fruit".

Hearing the words of the preacher, sparks of fire, as it were, scintillated in Swamiji's large eyes; his face became flushed. But he suppressed his feeling and said: "Those associations which do not feel sympathy for men and, even seeing their own brothers dying from starvation, do not give them a handful of rice to save their lives, while giving away piles of food to save birds and beasts, I have not the least sympathy for, and I do not believe that society derives any good from them. If you make a plea of Karma by saying that men die through their Karma, then it becomes a settled fact that it is useless to try or struggle for anything in this world; and your work for the protection of animals is no exception. With regard to your cause also, it can be said—the mother-cows through their own Karma fall into the hands of the butchers and die, and we need not do anything in the matter."

The preacher was a little abashed and said: "Yes, what you say is true, but the Shâstras say that the cow is our mother."

Swamiji smilingly said, "Yes, that the cow is our mother, I understand: who else could give birth to such accomplished children?"

The up-country preacher did not speak further on the subject; perhaps he could not understand the point of Swamiji's poignant ridicule. He told Swamiji that he was begging something of him for the objects of the society.

Swamiji: I am a Sannyasin, a fakir. Where shall I find money enough to help you? But if ever I get money in my possession, I shall first spend that in the service of man. Man is first to be saved; he must be given food, education, and spirituality. If any money is left after doing all these, then only something would be given to your society.

At these words, the preacher went away after saluting Swamiji. Then Swamiji began to speak to us: "What words, these, forsooth! Says he that men are dying by reason of their Karma, so what avails doing any kindness to them! This is decisive proof that the country has gone to rack and ruin! Do you see how much abused the Karma theory of your Hinduism has been? Those who are men and yet have no feeling in the heart for man, well, are such to be counted as men at all?" While speaking these words, Swamiji's whole body seemed to shiver in anguish and grief.

Then, while smoking, Swamiji said to the disciple, "Well, see me again."

Disciple: Where will you be staying, sir? Perhaps you might put up in some rich man's house. Will he allow me there?

Swamiji: At present, I shall be living either at the Alambazar Math or at the garden-house of Gopal Lal Seal at Cossipore. You may come to either place.

Disciple: Sir, I very much wish to speak with you

in solitude.

Swamiji: All right. Come one night. We shall speak plenty of Vedanta.

Disciple: Sir, I have heard that some Europeans and Americans have come with you. Will they not get offended at my dress or my talk?

Swamiji: Why, they are also men, and moreover they are devoted to the Vedanta religion. They will be glad to converse with you.

Disciple: Sir, Vedanta speaks of some distinctive qualifications for its aspirants; how could these come out in your Western disciples? The Shastras say—he who has studied the Vedas and the Vedanta, who has formally expiated his sins, who has performed all the daily and occasional duties enjoined by the scriptures, who is self-restrained in his food and general conduct, and specially he who is accomplished in the four special Sâdhanâs (preliminary disciplines), he alone has a right to the practice of Vedanta. Your Western disciples are in the first place non-Brahmins, and then they are lax in point of proper food and dress; how could they understand the system of Vedanta?

Swamiji: When you speak with them, you will know at once whether they have understood Vedanta or not.

Swamiji, perhaps, could now see that the disciple was rigidly devoted to the external observances of orthodox Hinduism. Swamiji then, surrounded by some devotees of Shri Ramakrishna, went over to the house of Srijut Balaram Basu of Baghbazar. The disciple bought the book Vivekachudamani at Bat-tala and went towards his own home at Darjipara.

II

Translated from Bengali
From the Diary of a Disciple

The disciple is Sharatchandra Chakravarty, who published his records in a Bengali book, Swami-Shishya-Samvâda, in two parts. The present series of "Conversations and Dialogues" is a revised translation from this book.

Five dialogues of this series have already appeared in the Complete Works, Volume V.

Place: On the way from Calcutta to Cossipore and in the garden of the late Gopal Lal Seal.

Year: 1897.

Today Swamiji was taking rest at noon in the house of Srijut Girish Chandra Ghosh[1]. The disciple arriving there saluted him and found that Swamiji was just ready to go to the garden-house of Gopal Lal Seal. A carriage was waiting outside. He said to the disciple, "Well come with me." The disciple agreeing, Swamiji got up with him into the carriage and it started. When it drove up the Chitpur road, on seeing the Gangâ, Swamiji broke forth in a chant, self-involved: गङ्गातरङ्ग-रमणीय-जटा-कलापं etc.[2] The disciple listened in silent wonder to that wave of music, when after a short while, seeing a railway engine going towards the Chitpur hydraulic bridge, Swamiji said to the disciple, "Look how it goes majestically like a lion!" The disciple replied, "But that is inert matter. Behind it there is the intelligence of man working, and hence it moves. In moving thus, what credit is there for it?"

Swamiji: Well, say then, what is the sign of consciousness?

Disciple: Why, sir, that indeed is conscious which acts through intelligence.

Swamiji: Everything is conscious which rebels against nature: there, consciousness is manifested. Just try to kill a little ant, even it will once resist to save its life. Where there is struggle, where there is rebellion, there is the sign of life, there consciousness is manifested.

Disciple: Sir, can that test be applied also in the case of men and of nations?

Swamiji: Just read the history of the world and see whether it applies or not. You will find that excepting yours, it holds good in the case of all other nations. It is you only who are in this world lying prostrate today like inert matter. You have been hypnotised.

---

1. The famous actor and dramatist of Bengal and a foremost devotee of Shri Ramakrishna.

2. From Vyâsa's Hymn to Vishvanâtha, meaning "whose matted locks look charming with the waves of the Ganga playing among them".

From very old times, others have been telling you that you are weak, that you have no power, and you also, accepting that, have for about a thousand years gone on thinking, "We are wretched, we are good for nothing." (Pointing to his own body:) This body also is born of the soil of your country; but I never thought like that. And hence you see how, through His will, even those who always think us low and weak, have done and are still doing me divine honour. If you can think that infinite power, infinite knowledge and indomitable energy lie within you, and if you can bring out that power, you also can become like me.

Disciple: Where is the capacity in us for thinking that way, sir? Where is the teacher or preceptor who from our childhood will speak thus before us and make us understand? What we have heard and have learnt from all is that the object of having an education nowadays is to secure some good job.

Swamiji: For that reason is it that we have come forward with quite another precept and example. Learn that truth from us, understand it, and realise it and then spread that idea broadcast, in cities, in towns, and in villages. Go and preach to all, "Arise, awake, sleep no more; within each of you there is the power to remove all wants and all miseries. Believe this, and that power will be manifested." Teach this to all, and, with that, spread among the masses in plain language the central truths of science, philosophy, history, and geography. I have a plan to open a centre with the unmarried youths; first of all I shall teach them, and then carry on the work through them.

Disciple: But that requires a good deal of money. Where will you get this money?

Swamiji: What do you talk! Isn't it man that makes moneys Where did you ever hear of money making man? If you can make your thoughts and words perfectly at one, if you can, I say, make yourself one in speech and action, money will pour in at your feet of itself, like water.

Disciple: Well, sir, I take it for granted that money will come, and you will begin that good work. But what will that matter? Before this, also, many great men carried out many good deeds. But where are they now? To be sure, the same fate awaits the work which you are going to start. Then what is the good of such an endeavour?

Swamiji: He who always speculates as to what awaits him in future, accomplishes nothing whatsoever. What you have understood as true and good, just do that at once. What's the good of calculating what may or may not befall in future? The span of life is so, so short—and can anything be accomplished in it if you go on forecasting and computing results. God is the only dispenser of results; leave it to Him to do all that. What have you got to do with on working.

While he was thus going on, the cab reached the gardenhouse. Many people from Calcutta came to the garden that day to see Swamiji. Swamiji got down from the carriage, took his seat in the room, and began conversation with them all. Mr. Goodwin, a Western disciple of Swamiji, was standing near by, like the embodiment of service, as it were. The disciple had already made his acquaintance; so he came to Mr. Goodwin, and both engaged in a variety of talk about Swamiji.

In the evening Swamiji called the disciple and asked him, "Have you got the Katha Upanishad by heart?"

Disciple: No, sir, I have only read it with Shankara's commentary.

Swamiji: Among the Upanishads, one finds no other book so beautiful as this. I wish you would all get it by heart. What will it do only to read it? Rather try to bring into your life the faith, the courage, the discrimination, and the renunciation of Nachiketâ.

Disciple: Give your blessings, please, that I may realise these.

Swamiji: You have heard of Shri Ramakrishna's words, haven't you? He used to say, "The breeze of mercy is already blowing, do you only hoist the sail." Can anybody, my boy, thrust realization upon another? One's destiny is' in one's own hands—the Guru only makes this much understood. Through the power of the seed itself the tree grows, the air and water are only aids.

Disciple: There is, sir, the necessity also of extraneous help.

Swamiji: Yes, there is. But you should know that

if there be no substance within, no amount of outside help will avail anything. Yet there comes a time for everyone to realise the Self. For everyone is Brahman. The distinction of higher and lower is only in the degree of manifestation of that Brahman. In time, everyone will have perfect manifestation. Hence the Shâstras say, "कालेनात्मनि विन्दति"—In time, That is realised in one's self."

Disciples When, alas, will that happen, sir? From the Shastras we hear how many births we have had to pass in ignorance!

Swamiji: What's the fear? When you have come here this time, the goal shall be attained in this life. Liberation or Samâdhi—all this consists in simply doing away with the obstacles to the manifestation of Brahman. Otherwise the Self is always shining forth like the sun. The cloud of ignorance has only veiled it. Remove the cloud and the sun will manifest. Then you get into the state of "भिद्यते हृदयग्रन्थिः" ("the knot of the heart is broken") etc. The various paths that you find, all advise you to remove the obstacles on the way. The way by which one realises the Self, is the way which he preached to all. But the goal of all is the knowledge of the Self, the realization of this Self. To it all men, all beings have equal right. This is the view acceptable to all.

Disciple: Sir, when I read or hear these words of the Shastras, the thought that the Self has not yet been realised makes the heart very disconsolate.

Swamiji: This is what is called longing. The more it grows the more will the cloud of obstacles be dispelled, and stronger will faith be established. Gradually the Self will be realised like a fruit on the palm of one's hand. This realisation alone is the soul of religion. Everyone can go on abiding by some observances and formalities. Everyone can fulfil certain injunctions and prohibitions but how few have this longing for realization! This intense longing—becoming mad after realising God or getting the knowledge of the Self—is real spirituality. The irresistible madness which the Gopis had for the Lord, Shri Krishna, yea, it is intense longing like that which is necessary for the realization of the Self! Even in the Gopis' mind there was a slight distinction of man and woman. But in real Self-knowledge, there is not the slightest distinction of sex.

While speaking thus, Swamiji introduced the subject of Gita-Govindam (of Jayadeva) and continued saying:

Jayadeva was the last poet in Sanskrit literature though he often cared more for the jingling of words than for depth of sentiment. But just see how the poet has shown the culmination of love and longing in the Shloka "पतति पतत्रे" etc.[1] Such love indeed is necessary for Self-realisation. There must be fretting and pining within the heart. Now from His playful life at Vrindaban come to the Krishna of Kurukshetra, and see how that also is fascinating—how, amidst all that horrible din and uproar of fighting, Krishna remains calm, balanced, and peaceful. Ay, on the very battlefield, He is speaking the Gita to Arjuna and getting him on to fight, which is the Dharma of a Kshatriya! Himself an agent to bring about this terrible warfare, Shri Krishna remains unattached to action—He did not take up arms! To whichsoever phase of it you look, you will find the character of Shri Krishna perfect. As if He was the embodiment of knowledge, work, devotion, power of concentration, and everything! In the present age, this aspect of Shri Krishna should be specially studied. Only contemplating the Krishna of Vrindaban with His flute won't do nowadays—that will not bring salvation to humanity. Now is needed the worship of Shri Krishna uttering forth the lion-roar of the Gita, of Râma with His bow and arrows, of Mahâvira, of Mother Kâli. Then only will the people grow strong by going to work with great energy and will. I have considered the matter most carefully and come to the conclusion that of those who profess and talk of religion nowadays in this country, the majority are full of morbidity— crack-brained or fanatic. Without development of an abundance of Rajas, you have hopes neither in this world, nor in the next. The whole country is enveloped in intense Tamas; and naturally the result is—servitude in this

---

1.
"पतति पतत्रे विचलति पत्रे शङ्कितभवदुपयानम् ।
रचयति शयनं सचकितनयनं पश्यति तव पन्थानम् ॥"

— "At the flying of a bird or the stirring of a leaf, she fancies you are coming; she arranges your bed with eyes all alert looking towards the way you would come."

life and hell in the next.

Disciple: Do you expect in view of the Rajas in the Westerners that they will gradually become Sâttvika?

Swamiji: Certainly. Possessed of a plenitude of Rajas, they have now reached the culmination of Bhoga, or enjoyment. Do you think that it is not they, but you, who are going to achieve Yoga—you who hang about for the sake of your bellies? At the sight of their highly refined enjoyment, the delineation in Meghaduta—"विद्युद्वनतं ललितवसनाः" etc.[2] —comes to my mind. And your Bhoga consists in lying on a ragged bed in a muggy room, multiplying progeny every year like a hog!—Begetting a band of famished beggars and slaves! Hence do I say, let people be made energetic and active in nature by the stimulation of Rajas. Work, work, work; "नान्यः पन्था विद्यतेऽयनाय"—There is no other path of liberation but this."

Disciple: Sir, did our forefathers possess this kind of Rajas?

Swamiji: Why, did they not? Does not history tell us that they established colonies in many countries, and sent preachers of religion to Tibet, China, Sumatra, and even to far-off Japan? Do you think there is any other means of achieving progress except through Rajas?

As conversation thus went on, night approached; and meanwhile Miss Müller came there. She was an English lady, having great reverence for Swamiji. Swamiji introduced the disciple to her, and after a short talk Miss Müller went upstairs.

Swamiji: See, to what a heroic nation they belong! How far-off is her home, and she is the daughter of a rich man—yet how long a way has she come, only with the hope of realising the spiritual ideal!

Disciple: Yes, sir, but your works are stranger still! How so many Western ladies and gentlemen are always eager to serve you! For this age, it is very strange indeed!

Swamiji: If this body lasts, you will see many more things. If I can get some young men of heart and energy, I shall revolutionize the whole country. There are a few in Madras. But I have more hope in Bengal. Such clear brains are to be found scarcely in any other country. But they have no strength in their muscles. The brain and muscles must develop simultaneously. Iron nerves with an intelligent brain—and the whole world is at your feet.

Word was brought that supper was ready for Swamiji. He said to the disciple, "Come and have a look at my food." While going on with the supper, he said, "It is not good to take much fatty or oily substance. Roti is better than Luchi. Luchi is the food of the sick. Take fish and meat and fresh vegetables, but sweets sparingly." While thus talking, he inquired, "Well, how many Rotis have I taken? Am I to take more? He did not remember how much he took and did not feel even it he yet had any appetite. The sense of body faded away so much while he was talking!

He finished after taking a little more. The disciple also took leave and went back to Calcutta. Getting no cab for hire, he had to walk; and while walking, he thought over in his mind how soon again he could come the next day to see Swamiji.

III

Translated from Bengali
From the Diary of a Disciple

The disciple is Sharatchandra Chakravarty, who published his records in a Bengali book, Swami-Shishya-Samvâda, in two parts. The present series of "Conversations and Dialogues" is a revised translation from this book. Five dialogues of this series have already appeared in the Complete Works, Volume V.

2.
विद्युद्वनतं ललितवसनाः सेन्द्रचापं सचित्राः
सङ्गीताय प्रहतमुरजाः स्निग्धगम्भीरघोषम् ।
अन्तस्तोयं मणिमयभुवस्तुङ्गमभ्रंलिहाग्राः
प्रासादास्त्वां तुलयितुमलं यत्र तैस्तैर्विशेषैः ॥

— "The mansions of that city may well be compared with you, O cloud, there is correspondence in features: while flashes of lightning play within you, they have charmingly attired damsels moving within them; while you have the rainbow, they have their paintings; you have your deep, rolling rumble, they have their drums sounding forth music, you contain pellucid water within you, they have their interior bedecked with transparent gems; you soar so high, their roofs also kiss the sky" (Meghaduta, II. 1). Kalidasa thus introduces his description of the enjoyments of Alakâpuri. So the reference here is not only to the first verse quoted but also to the whole description which follows.

Place: Cossipore, at the garden of the late Gopal Lal Seal.
Year: 1897.

After his first return from the West, Swamiji resided for a few days at the garden of the late Gopal Lal Seal at Cossipore. Some well-known Pundits living at Barabazar, Calcutta, came to the garden one day with a view to holding a disputation with him. The disciple was present there on the occasion.

All the Pundits who came there could speak in Sanskrit fluently. They came and greeting Swamiji, who sat surrounded by a circle of visitors, began their conversation in Sanskrit. Swamiji also responded to them in melodious Sanskrit. The disciple cannot remember now the subject on which the Pundits argued with him that day. But this much he remembers that the Pundits, almost all in one strident voice, were rapping out to Swamiji in Sanskrit subtle questions of philosophy, and he, in a dignified serious mood, was giving out to them calmly his own well argued conclusions about those questions.

In the discussion with the Pundits Swamiji represented the side of the Siddhânta or conclusions to be established, while the Pundits represented that of the Purvapaksha or objections to be raised. The disciple remembers that, while arguing, Swamiji wrongly used in one place the word Asti instead of Svasti, which made the Pundits laugh out. At this, Swamiji at once submitted: "पण्डितानां दासोऽहं क्षन्तव्यमेतत् सखलनम्—I am but a servant of the Pundits, please excuse this mistake." The Pundits also were charmed at this humility of Swamiji. After a long dispute, the Pundits at last admitted that the conclusions of the Siddhanta side were adequate, and preparing to depart, they made their greetings to Swamiji.

After the Pundits had left, the disciple learnt from Swamiji that these Pundits who took the side of the Purvapaksha were well versed in the Purva-Mimâmsâ Shâstras, Swamiji advocated the philosophy of the Uttara-Mimâmsâ or Vedanta and proved to them the superiority of the path of knowledge, and they were obliged to accept his conclusions.

About the way the Pundits laughed at Swamiji, picking up one grammatical mistake, he said that this error of his was due to the fact of his not having spoken in Sanskrit for many years together. He did not blame the Pundits a bit for all that. But he pointed out in this connection that in the West it would imply a great incivility on the part of an opponent to point out any such slip in language, deviating from the real issue of dispute. A civilised society in such cases would accept the idea, taking no notice of the language. "But in your country, all the fighting is going on over the husk, nobody searches for the kernel within." So saying, Swamiji began to talk with the disciple in Sanskrit. The disciple also gave answers in broken Sanskrit. Yet Swamiji praised him for the sake of encouragement. From that day, at the request of Swamiji, the disciple used to speak with him in Sanskrit off and on.

In reply to the question, what is civilisation, Swamiji said that day: "The more advanced a society or nation is in spirituality, the more is that society or nation civilised. No nation can be said to have become civilised only because it has succeeded in increasing the comforts of material life by bringing into use lots of machinery and things of that sort. The present-day civilization of the West is multiplying day by day only the wants and distresses of men. On the other hand, the ancient Indian civilisation by showing people the way to spiritual advancement, doubtless succeeded, if not in removing once for all, at least in lessening, in a great measure, the material needs of men. In the present age, it is to bring into coalition both these civilisations that Bhagavan Shri Ramakrishna was born. In this age, as on the one hand people have to be intensely practical, so on the other hand they have to acquire deep spiritual knowledge." Swamiji made us clearly understand that day that from such interaction of the Indian civilization with that of the West would dawn on the world a new era. In the course of dilating upon this, he happened to remark in one place, "Well, another thing. People there in the West think that the more a man is religious, the more demure he must be in his outward bearing—no word about anything else from his lips! As the priests in the West would on the one hand be struck with wonder at my liberal religious discourses, they would be as much puzzled on the other hand when they found me, after such discourses, talking frivolities with my friends. Sometimes they would speak out to my face: 'Swami, you are a priest, you should not be joking and laughing in this way like ordinary men. Such levity does not look well in you.' To which I would reply, 'We are children of bliss, why should we look morose and sombre?' But I doubt if they could rightly catch the drift of my words."

That day Swamiji spoke many things about Bhâva Samâdhi and Nirvikalpa Samadhi as well. These are produced below as far as possible:

Suppose a man is cultivating that type of devotion to God which Hanumân represents. The more intense the attitude becomes, the more will the pose and demeanour of that aspirant, nay even his physical configuration, be cast in that would. It is in this way that transmutation of species takes place. Taking up any such emotional attitude, the worshipper becomes gradually shaped into the very form of his ideal. The ultimate stage of any such sentiment is called Bhava Samadhi. While the aspirant in the path of Jnana, pursuing the process of Neti, Neti, "not this, not this", such as "I am not the body, nor the mind, nor the intellect", and so on, attains to the Nirvikalpa Samadhi when he is established in absolute consciousness. It requires striving through many births to reach perfection or the ultimate stage with regard to a single one of these devotional attitudes. But Shri Ramakrishna, the king of the realm of spiritual sentiment, perfected himself in no less than eighteen different forms of devotion! He also used to say that his body would not have endured, had he not held himself on to this play of spiritual sentiment.

The disciple asked that day, "Sir, what sort of food did you use to take in the West?"

Swamiji: The same as they take there. We are Sannyasins and nothing can take away our caste!

On the subject of how he would work in future in this country, Swamiji said that day that starting two centres, one in Madras and another in Calcutta, he would rear up a new type of Sannyasins for the good of all men in all its phases. He further said that by a destructive method no progress either for the society or for the country could be achieved. In all ages and times progress has been effected by the constructive process, that is, by giving a new mould to old methods and customs. Every religious preacher in India, during the past ages, worked in that line. Only the religion of Bhagavan Buddha was destructive. Hence that religion has been extirpated from India.

The disciple remembers that while thus speaking on, he remarked, "If the Brahman is manifested in one man, thousands of men advance, finding their way out in that light. Only the knowers of Brahman are the spiritual teachers of mankind. This is corroborated by all scriptures and by reason too. It is only the selfish Brahmins who have introduced into this country the system of hereditary Gurus, which is against the Vedas and against the Shastras. Hence it is that even through their spiritual practice men do not now succeed in perfecting themselves or in realising Brahman. To remove all this corruption in religion, the Lord has incarnated Himself on earth in the present age in the person of Shri Ramakrishna. The universal teachings that he offered, if spread all over the world, will do good to humanity and the world. Not for many a century past has India produced so great, so wonderful, a teacher of religious synthesis."

A brother-disciple of Swamiji at that time asked him, "Why did you not publicly preach Shri Ramakrishna as an Avatâra in the West?"

Swamiji: They make much flourish and fuss over their science and philosophy. Hence, unless you first knock to pieces their intellectual conceit through reasoning, scientific argument, and philosophy, you cannot build anything there. Those who finding themselves off their moorings through their utmost intellectual reasoning would approach me in a real spirit of truth-seeking, to them alone, I would speak of Shri Ramakrishna. If, otherwise, I had forthwith spoken of the doctrine of incarnation, they might have said, "Oh, you do not say anything new—why, we have our Lord Jesus for all that!"

After thus spending some three or four delightful hours, the disciple came back to Calcutta that day along with the other visitors.

IV

Translated from Bengali
From the Diary of a Disciple

The disciple is Sharatchandra Chakravarty, who published his records in a Bengali book, Swami-Shishya-Samvâda, in two parts. The present series of "Conversations and Dialogues" is a revised translation from this book. Five dialogues of this series have already appeared in the Complete Works, Volume V.

Place: The Kali-temple at Dakshineswar and the Alambazar Math.

Year: 1897, March.

When Swamiji returned from England for the first time, the Ramakrishna Math was located at Alambazar. The birthday anniversary of Bhagavan Shri Ramakrishna was being celebrated this year at the Kali-temple of Rani Râsmani at Dakshineswar. Swamiji with some of his brother disciples reached there from the Alambazar Math at about 9 or 10 a.m. He was barefooted, with a yellow turban on his head. Crowds of people were waiting to see and hear him. In the temple of Mother Kali, Swamiji prostrated himself before the Mother of the Universe, and thousands of heads, following him, bent low. Then after prostrating himself before Râdhâkântaji he came into the room which Shri Ramakrishna used to occupy. There was not the least breathing space in the room.

Two European ladies who accompanied Swamiji to India attended the festival. Swamiji took them along with himself to show them the holy Panchavati and the Vilva tree.[1] Though the disciple was not yet quite familiar with Swamiji, he followed him, and presented him with the copy of a Sanskrit Ode about the Utsava (celebration) composed by himself. Swamiji read it while walking towards the Panchavati. And on the way he once looked aside towards the disciple and said, "Yes, it's done well. Attempt others like it."

The householder devotees of Shri Ramakrishna happened to be assembled on one side of the Panchavati, among whom was Babu Girish Chandra Ghosh. Swamiji, accompanied by a throng, came to Girish Babu and saluted him, saying, "Hello! here is Mr. Ghosh." Girish Babu returned his salutation with folded hands. Reminding Girish Babu of the old days, Swamiji said, "Think of it, Mr. Ghosh — from those days to these, what a transition!" Girish Babu endorsed Swamiji's sentiment and said, "Yes, that is true; but yet the mind longs to see more of it." After a short conversation, Swamiji proceeded towards the Vilva tree situated on the north-east of the Panchavati.

Now a huge crowd stood in keen expectancy to hear lecture from Swamiji. But though he tried his utmost, Swamiji could not speak louder than the noise and clamour of the people. Hence he had to give up attempting a lecture and left with the two European ladies to show them sites connected with Shri Ramakrishna's spiritual practices and introduce them to particular devotees and followers of the Master.

After 3 p.m. Swamiji said to the disciple, "Fetch me a cab, please; I must go to the Math now." The disciple brought one accordingly. Swamiji himself sat on one side and asked Swami Niranjanananda and the disciple to sit on the other and they drove towards the Alambazar Math. On the way, Swamiji said to the disciple, "It won't do to live on abstract ideas merely. These festivals and the like are also necessary; for then only, these ideas will spread gradually among the masses. You see, the Hindus have got their festivals throughout the year, and the secret of it is to infuse the great ideals of religion gradually into the minds of the people. It has also its drawback, though. For people in general miss their inner significance and become so much engrossed in externals that no sooner are these festivities over than they become their old selves again. Hence it is true that all these form the outer covering of religion, which in a way hide real spirituality and self-knowledge.

"But there are those who cannot at all understand in the abstract what 'religion' is or what the 'Self' is, and they try to realise spirituality gradually through these festivals and ceremonies. Just take this festival

---
1. Panchavati is a grove of five special trees arranged and grown to serve purposes of spiritual practice. The Vilva is also a holy tree of that sort.

celebrated today; those that attended it will at least once think of Shri Ramakrishna. The thought will occur to their mind as to who he was, in whose name such a great crowd assembled and why so many people came at all in his name. And those who will not feel that much even, will come once in a year to see all the devotional dancing and singing, or at least to partake of the sacred food-offerings, and will also have a look at the devotees of Shri Ramakrishna. This will rather benefit them than do any harm."

Disciple: But, sir, suppose somebody thinks these festivals and ceremonies to be the only thing essential, can he possibly advance any further? They will gradually come down to the level of commonplace observances, like the worship in our country of (the goddesses) Shashthi, Mangala-chandi, and the like. People are found to observe these rites till death; but where do we find even one among them rising through such observances to the knowledge of Brahman?

Swamiji: Why? In India so many spiritual heroes were born, and did they not make them the means of scaling the heights of greatness? When by persevering in practice through these props they gained a vision of the Self, they ceased to be keen on them. Yet, for the preservation of social balance even great men of the type of Incarnations follow these observances.

Disciple: Yes, they may observe these for appearance only. But when to a knower of the Self even this world itself becomes unreal like magic, is it possible for him to recognise these external observances as true?

Swamiji: Why not? Is not our idea of truth also a relative one, varying in relation to time, place, and person? Hence all observances have their utility, relatively to the varying qualifications in men. It is just as Shri Ramakrishna used to say, that the mother cooks Polâo and Kâlia (rich dishes) for one son, and sago for another.

Now the disciple understood at last and kept quiet. Meanwhile the carriage arrived at the Alambazar Math. The disciple followed Swamiji into the Math where Swamiji, being thirsty, drank some water. Then putting off his coat, he rested recumbent on the blanket spread on the floor. Swami Niranjanananda, seated by his side, said, "We never had such a great crowd in any year's Utsava before! As if the whole of Calcutta flocked there!"

Swamiji: It was quite natural; stranger things will happen hereafter.

Disciple: Sir, in every religious sect are found to exist external festivals of some kind or other. But there is no amity between one sect and another in this matter. Even in the case of such a liberal religion as that of Mohammed, I have found in Dacca that the Shiâs and Sunnis go to loggerheads with each other.

Swamiji: That is incidental more or less wherever you have sects. But do you know what the ruling sentiment amongst us is? — non-sectarianism. Our Lord was born to point that out. He would accept all forms, but would say withal that, looked at from the standpoint of the knowledge of Brahman, they were only like illusory Mâyâ.

Disciple: Sir, I can't understand your point. Sometimes it seems to me that, by thus celebrating these festivals, you are also inaugurating another sect round the name of Shri Ramakrishna. I have heard it from the lips of Nâg Mahâshaya that Shri Ramakrishna did not belong to any sect. He used to pay great respect to all creeds such as the Shâktas, the Vaishnavas, the Brahmos, the Mohammedans, and the Christians.

Swamiji: How do you know that we do not also hold in great esteem all the religious creeds?

So saying, Swamiji called out in evident amusement to Swami Niranjanananda: "Just think what this Bângâl[2] is saying!"

Disciple: Kindly make me understand, sir, what you mean.

Swamiji: Well, you have, to be sure, read my lectures. But where have I built on Shri Ramakrishna's name? It is only the pure Upanishadic religion that I have gone about preaching in the world.

Disciple: That's true, indeed. But what I find by being familiar with you is that you have surrendered yourself, body and soul, to Ramakrishna. If you have

---
2. This term as used of people hailing from East Bengal is too often supposed to have a ring of derision. But in the case of the disciple, it very easily and naturally grew to be a term of peculiar endearment. — Ed.

understood Shri Ramakrishna to be the Lord Himself, why not give it out to the people at large?

Swamiji: Well, I do preach what I have understood. And if you have found the Advaitic principles of Vedanta to be the truest religion, then why don't you go out and preach it to all men?

Disciple: But I must realise, before I can preach it to others. I have only studied Advaitism in books.

Swamiji: Good; realise first and then preach. Now, therefore, you have no right to say anything of the beliefs each man tries to live by. For you also proceed now by merely putting your faith on some such beliefs.

Disciple: True, I am also living now by believing in something; but I have the Shâstras for my authority. I do not accept any faith opposed to the Shastras.

Swamiji: What do you mean by the Shastras? If the Upanishads are authority, why not the Bible or the Zend-Avesta equally so?

Disciple: Granted these scriptures are also good authority, they are not, however, as old as the Vedas. And nowhere, moreover, is the theory of the Âtman better established than in the Vedas.

Swamiji: Supposing I admit that contention of yours, what right have you to maintain that truth can be found nowhere except in the Vedas?

Disciple: Yes, truth may also exist in all the scriptures other than the Vedas, and I don't say anything to the contrary. But as for me, I choose to abide by the teachings of the Upanishads, for I have very great faith in them.

Swamiji: Quite welcome to do that, but if somebody else has "very great" faith in any other set of doctrines, surely you should allow him to abide by that. You will discover that in the long run both he and yourself will arrive at the same goal. For haven't you read in the Mahimnah-stotram, "त्वमसि पयसामर्णव इव — Thou art as the ocean to the rivers falling into it?"

V

Translated from Bengali
From the Diary of a Disciple

The disciple is Sharatchandra Chakravarty, who published his records in a Bengali book, Swami-Shishya-Samvâda, in two parts. The present series of "Conversations and Dialogues" is a revised translation from this book. Five dialogues of this series have already appeared in the Complete Works, Volume V.

Place: Alambazar Math.

Year: 1897, May.

It was the 19th Vaishâkha (April-May) of the year 1303 B.S. Swamiji had agreed to initiate the disciple today. So, early in the morning, he reached the Alambazar Math. Seeing the disciple Swamiji jocosely said, "Well, you are to be 'sacrificed' today, are you not?"

After this remark to the disciple, Swamiji with a smile resumed his talk with others about American subjects. And in due relevancy came along such topics also as how one-pointed in devotion one has to be in order to build up a spiritual life, how firm faith and strong devotion to the Guru have to be kept up, how deep reliance has to be placed on the words of the Guru, and how even one's life has to be laid down for his sake. Then putting some questions to the disciple, Swamiji began to test his heart: "Well, are you ready to do my bidding to your utmost, whatever it be and whenever it may come? If I ask you to plunge into the Ganga or to jump from the roof of a house, meaning it all for your good, could you do even that without any hesitations Just think of it even now; otherwise don't rush forward on the spur of the moment to accept me as your Guru." And the disciple nodded assent to all questions of the kind.

Swamiji then continued: "The real Guru is he who leads you beyond this Mâyâ of endless birth and death — who graciously destroys all the griefs and maladies of the soul. The disciple of old used to repair to the hermitage of the Guru, fuel in hand; and the Guru, after ascertaining his competence, would teach him the Vedas after initiation, fastening round his waist the threefold filament of Munja, a kind of grass, as the emblem of his vow to keep his body, mind, and speech in control. With the help of this girdle, the disciples used to tie up their Kaupinas. Later on, the custom of wearing the sacred thread superseded this girdle of Munja grass."

Disciple: Would you, then, say, sir, that the use of the holy thread we have adopted is not really a Vedic custom?

Swamiji: Nowhere is there mention of thread being so used in the Vedas. The modern author of Smritis, Raghunandana Bhattacharya, also puts it thus: "At this stage,[1] the sacrificial girdle should be put on." Neither in Gobhila's Grihya-Sutras do we find any mention of the girdle made of thread. In the Shâstras, this first Vedic Samskâra (purification ceremony) before the Guru has been called the Upanayana; but see, to what a sad pass our country has been brought! Straying away from the true path of the Shastras, the country has been overwhelmed with usages and observances originating in particular localities, or popular opinion, or with the womenfolk! That's why I ask you to proceed along the path of the Shastras as in olden times. Have faith within yourselves and thereby bring it back into the country. Plant in your heart the faith of Nachiketâ. Even go up to the world of Yama like him. Yes, if to know the secrets of the Atman, to liberate your soul, to reach the true solution of the mystery of birth and death, you have to go to the very jaws of death and realise the truth thereby, well, go there with an undaunted heart. It is fear alone that is death. You have to go beyond all fear. So from this day be fearless. Off at once, to lay down your life for your own liberation and for the good of others. What good is it carrying along a load of bones and flesh! Initiated into the Mantra of extreme self-sacrifice for the sake of God, go, lay down for others this body of flesh and bones like the Muni Dadhichi! Those alone, say the Shastras, are the real Gurus, who have studied the Vedas and the Vedanta, who are knowers of the Brahman, who are able to lead others beyond to fearlessness; when such are at hand, get yourself initiated, "no speculation in such a case". Do you know what has become of this principle now? — "like the blind leading the blind"!

* * *

The initiation ceremony was duly gone through in the chapel. After this Swamiji spoke out: "Give me the Guru-dakshinâ."[2] The disciple replied, "Oh, what shall I give?" On this Swamiji suggested, "Well, fetch any fruit from the store-room." So the disciple ran to the store-room and came back into the chapel with ten or twelve lichis. These Swamiji took from his hand and ate them one by one, saying, "Now, your Guru-dakshina is made."

A member of the Math, Brahmachâri (now Swami) Shuddhananda, also had his initiation from Swamiji on this occasion.

Swamiji then had his dinner and went to take a short rest.

After the siesta, he came and sat in the hall of the upper storey. The disciple finding this opportunity asked, "Sir, how and whence came the ideas of virtue and vice?"

Swamiji: It is from the idea of the manifold that these have evolved. The more a man advances towards oneness, the more ideas of "I" and "you" subside, ideas from which all these pairs of opposites such as virtue and vice have originated. When the idea that So-and-so is different from me comes to the mind, all other ideas of distinction begin to manifest, while with the complete realisation of oneness, no more grief or illusion remains for man, "तत्र को मोहः कः शोकः एकमनुपश्यतः—For him who sees oneness, where is there any grief or any delusion?" Sin may be said to be the feeling of every kind of weakness. From this weakness spring jealousy, malice, and so forth. Hence weakness is sin. The Self within is always shining forth resplendent. Turning away from that people say "I", "I", "I", with their attention held up by this material body, this queer cage of flesh and bones. This is the root of all weakness. From that habit only, the relative outlook on life has emerged in this world. The

---

1. Referring, that is to say, to some steps in the Vedic ceremony of a Brahmin's initiation.

2. The special gift which a disciple has to make to his Guru as the symbol of the mutual relation being consummated.

absolute Truth lies beyond that duality.

Disciple: Well, is then all this relative experience not true?

Swamiji: As long as the idea of "I" remains, it is true. And the instant the realisation of "I" as the Atman comes, this world of relative existence becomes false. What people speak of as sin is the result of weakness — is but another form of the egoistic idea, "I am the body". When the mind gets steadfast in the truth, "I am the Self", then you go beyond merit and demerit, virtue and vice. Shri Ramakrishna used to say, "When the 'I' dies, all trouble is at an end."

Disciple: Sir, this "I" has a most tenacious life. It is very difficult to kill it.

Swamiji: Yes, in one sense, it is very difficult, but in another sense, it is quite easy. Can you tell me where this "I" exists? How can you speak of anything being killed, which never exists at all? Man only remains hypnotised with the false idea of an ego. When this ghost is off from us, all dreams vanish, and then it is found that the one Self only exists from the highest Being to a blade of grass. This will have to be known, to be realised. All practice or worship is only for taking off this veil. When that will go, you will find that the Sun of Absolute Knowledge is shining in Its own lustre. For the Atman only is self-luminous and has to be realised by Itself. How can that, which can be experienced only by itself be known with the help of any other thing? Hence the Shruti says, says, "विज्ञातारमरे केन विजानीयात्—Well, through what means is that to be known which is the Knower?" Whatever you know, you know through the instrumentality of your mind. But mind is something material. It is active only because there is the pure Self behind it. So, how can you know that Self through your mind? But this only becomes known, after all, that the mind cannot reach the pure Self, no, nor even the intellect. Our relative knowledge ends just there. Then, when the mind is free from activity or functioning, it vanishes, and the Self is revealed. This state has been described by the commentator Shankara as अपरोक्षानुभूतिः or supersensuous perception.

Disciple: But, sir, the mind itself is the "I". If that mind is gone, then the "I" also cannot remain.

Swamiji: Yes, the state that comes then is the real nature of the ego. The "I" that remains then is omnipresent, all-pervading, the Self of all. Just as the Ghatâkâsha, when the jar is broken, becomes the Mahâkâsha,[1] for with the destruction of the jar the enclosed space is not destroyed. The puny "I" which you were thinking of as confined in the body, becomes spread out and is thus realised in the form of the all pervading "I" or the Self. Hence what matters it to the real "I" or the Self, whether the mind remains or is destroyed? What I say you will realise in course of time. "कालेनात्मनि विन्दति—It is realised within oneself in due time." As you go on with Shravana and Manana (proper hearing and proper thinking), you will fully understand it in due time and then you will go beyond mind. Then there will be no room for any such question.

Hearing all this, the disciple remained quiet on his seat, and Swamiji, as he gently smoked, continued: "How many Shastras have been written to explain this simple thing, and yet men fail to understand it! How they are vesting this precious human life on the fleeting pleasures of some silver coins and the frail beauty of women! Wonderful is the influence of Mahâmâyâ (Divine Illusion)! Mother! Oh Mother!"

VI

Translated from Bengali

The disciple is Sharatchandra Chakravarty, who published his records in a Bengali book, Swami-Shishya-Samvâda, in two parts. The present series of "Conversations and Dialogues" is a revised translation from this book. Five dialogues of this series have already appeared in the Complete Works, Volume V.

Place: Baghbazar, Calcutta.

Year: 1897.

---

1. Ghatâkâsha and Mahâkâsha are technical terms in Vedanta, meaning the space enclosed by the jar and the omnipresent. The two are one and the same, only the former is limited by the Upâdhi (adjunct) of the Ghata or jar.

Swamiji has been staying for some days at the house of the late Balaram Babu. At his wish, a large number of devotees of Shri Ramakrishna have assembled at the house at 3 p.m. (on May 1, 1897). Swami Yogananda is amongst those present here. The object of Swamiji is to form an Association. When all present had taken their seats, Swamiji proceeded to speak as follows:

"The conviction has grown in my mind after all my travels in various lands that no great cause can succeed without an organisation. In a country like ours, however, it does not seem quite practicable to me to start an organisation at once with a democratic basis or work by general voting. People in the West are more educated in this respect, and less jealous of one another than ourselves. They have learnt to respect merit. Take for instance my case. I was just an insignificant man there, and yet see how cordially they received and entertained me. When with the spread of education the masses in our country grow more sympathetic and liberal, when they learn to have their thoughts expanded beyond the limits of sect or party, then it will be possible to work; on the democratic basis of organization. For this reason it is necessary to have a dictator for this Society. Everybody should obey him, and then in time we may work on the principle of general voting.

"Let this Association be named after him, in whose name indeed, we have embraced the monastic life, with whom as your Ideal in life you all toil on the field of work from your station in family life, within twenty years of whose passing away a wonderful diffusion of his holy name and extraordinary life has taken place both in the East and the West. We are the servants of the Lord. Be you all helpers In this cause."

When Srijut Girish Chandra Ghosh and all other householder disciples present had approved of the above proposal, the future programme of the Society of Shri Ramakrishna was taken up for discussion. The Society was named the Ramakrishna Mission.

Swamiji himself became the general president of the Mission and other office-bearers also were elected. The rule was laid down that the Association should hold meetings at the house of Balaram Babu every Sunday at 4 p.m. Needless to say that Swamiji used to attend these meetings whenever convenient.

When the meeting had broken up and the members departed, addressing Swami Yogananda, Swamiji said, "So the work is now begun this way; let us see how far it succeeds by the will of Shri Ramakrishna."

Swami Yogananda. You are doing these things with Western methods. Should you say Shri Ramakrishna left us any such instructions?

Swamiji: Well, how do you know that all this is not on Shri Ramakrishna's lines? He had an infinite breadth of feeling, and dare you shut him up within your own limited views of life. I will break down these limits and scatter broadcast over the earth his boundless inspiration. He never instructed me to introduce any rites of his own worship. We have to realise the teachings he has left us about religious practice and devotion, concentration and meditation, and such higher ideas and truths, and then preach these to all men. The infinite number of faiths are only so many paths. I haven't been born to found one more sect in a world already teeming with sects. We have been blessed with obtaining refuge at the feet of the Master, and we are born to carry his message to the dwellers of the three worlds.

Swami Yogananda uttered no word of dissent, and so Swamiji continued: Time and again have I received in this life marks of his grace. He stands behind and gets all this work done by me. When lying helpless under a tree in an agony of hunger, when I had not even a scrap of cloth for Kaupina, when I was resolved on travelling penniless round the world, even then help came in all ways by the grace of Shri Ramakrishna. And again when crowds jostled with one another in the streets of Chicago to have a sight of this Vivekananda, then also, just because I had his grace, I could digest without difficulty all that honour — a hundredth part of which would have been enough to turn mad any ordinary man; and by his will, victory followed everywhere. Now I must conclude by doing something in this country. So casting all doubt away, please help my work; and you will find everything fulfilled by his will.

Swami Yogananda: Yes, whatever you will, shall be

fulfilled; and are we not all ever obedient to you? Now and then I do clearly see how Shri Ramakrishna is getting all these things done through you. And yet, to speak plainly, some misgiving rises at intervals, for as we saw it, his was of doing things was different. So I question myself: "Are we sure that we are not going astray from Shri Ramakrishna's teachings?" And so I take the opposing attitude and warn you.

Swamiji: You see, the fact is that Shri Ramakrishna is not exactly what the ordinary followers have comprehended him to be. He had infinite moods and phases. Even if you might form an idea of the limits of Brahmajnâna, the knowledge of the Absolute, you could not have any idea of the unfathomable depths of his mind! Thousands of Vivekanandas may spring forth through one gracious glance of his eyes! But instead of doing that, he has chosen to get things done this time through me as his single instrument, and what can I do in this matter you see?

Saying this, Swamiji left to attend to something else waiting for him, and Swami Yogananda went on praising Swamiji's versatile gifts.

Meanwhile Swamiji returned and asked the disciple, "Do the people in your part of the country know much of Shri Ramakrishna?"

Disciple: Only one man, Nâg Mahâshaya, came to Shri Ramakrishna from our part of Bengal;[1] it is from him that many came to hear of him and had their curiosity excited to know more. But that Shri Ramakrishna was the Incarnation of God, the people there have not yet come to know and some would not believe it even if told so.

Swamiji: Do you think it is an easy matter to believe so? We who had actual dealings with him in every respect we who heard of that fact again and again from his own lips, we who lived and stayed with him for twenty-four hours of the day — even we off and on have doubts about it coming over us! So what to speak of others!

Disciple: Did Shri Ramakrishna, out of his own lips ever say that he was God, the all-perfect Brahman?

---

1. This is not quite correct, for at least two more disciples, viz Nityagopal Goswami and Pundit Kaliprasad Chakravarty are known to have come from Dacca. — Ed.

Swamiji: Yes, he did so many times. And he said this to all of us. One day while was staying at the Cossipore garden, his body in imminent danger of falling off for ever, by the side of his bed I was saying in my mind, "Well, now if you can declare that you are God, then only will I believe you are really God Himself." It was only two days before he passed away. Immediately, he looked up towards me all on a sudden and said, "He who was Rama, He who was Krishna, verily is He now Ramakrishna in this body. And that not merely from the standpoint of your Vedanta!"[2] At this I was struck dumb. Even we haven't had yet the perfect faith, after hearing it again and again from the holy lips of our Lord himself — our minds still get disturbed now and then with doubt and despair — and so, what shall we speak of others being slow to believe? It is indeed a very difficult matter to be able to declare and believe a man with a body like ours to be God Himself. We may just go to the length of declaring him to be a "perfected one", or a "knower of Brahman". Well, it matters nothing, whatever you may call him or think of him, a saint, or a knower of Brahman, or anything. But take it from me, never did come to this earth such an all-perfect man as Shri Ramakrishna! In the utter darkness of the world, this great man is like the shining pillar of illumination in this age! And by his light alone will man now cross the ocean of Samsâra!

Disciple: To me it seems, sir, that true faith comes only after actually seeing or hearing something. Mathur[3] Babu, I have heard, actually saw so many things about Shri Ramakrishna, and thus he had that wonderful faith in him.

Swamiji: He who believes not, believes not even after seeing, and thinks that it is all hallucination, or dream and so on. The great transfiguration of Krishna — the Vishvarupa (form universal) — was seen alike by Duryodhana and by Arjuna. But only Arjuna believed, while Duryodhana took it to be magic! Unless He makes us understand, nothing can be stated or understood. Somebody comes to the fullest faith

---

2. In the sense that a knower of Brahman may declare his identity with any being, such as Manu and so forth. Vide the Vedanta-Sutras I. i. 30.

3. Mathura Nath Biswas, son-in-law of Rani Rasmani, the foundress of the temple at Dakshineswar.

even without seeing or hearing, while somebody else remains plunged in doubt even after witnessing with his own eyes various extraordinary powers for twelve years! The secret of it all is His grace! But then one must persevere, so that the grace may be received.

Disciple: Is there, sir, any law of graces

Swamiji: Yes and no.

Disciple: How is that?

Swamiji: Those who are pure always in body, mind, and speech, who have strong devotion, who discriminate between the real and the unreal, who persevere in meditation and contemplation — upon them alone the grace of the Lord descends. The Lord, however, is beyond all natural laws — is not under any rules and regulations, or just as Shri Ramakrishna used to say, He has the child's nature — and that's why we find some failing to get any response even after calling on Him for millions of births, while some one else whom we regard as a sinful or penitent man or a disbeliever, would have Illumination in a flash! — On the latter the Lord perhaps lavishes His grace quite unsolicited! You may argue that this man had good merits stored up from previous life, but the mystery is really difficult to understand. Shri Ramakrishna used to say sometimes, "Do rely on Him; be like the dry leaf at the mercy of the wind"; and again he would say, "The wind of His grace is always blowing, what you need to do is to unfurl your sail."

Disciple: But, sir, this is a most tremendous statement. No reasoning, I see, can stand here.

Swamiji: Ah, all reasoning and arguing is within the limit of the realm of Maya; it lies within the categories of space, time, and causation. But He is beyond these categories. We speak of His law, still He is beyond all law. He creates, or becomes, all that we speak of as laws of nature, and yet He is outside of them all. He on whom His grace descends, in a moment goes beyond all law. For this reason there is no condition in grace. It is as His play or sport. And this creation of the universe is like His play — "लोकवत् लीलाकैवल्यम् — It is the pure delight of sport, as in the case of men" (Vedanta-Sutras, II. i. 33). Is it not possible for Him who creates and destroys the universe as if in play to grant salvation by grace to the greatest sinner?

But then it is just His pleasure, His play, to get somebody through the practice of spiritual discipline and somebody else without it.

Disciple: Sir, I can't understand this.

Swamiji: And you needn't. Only get your mind to cling to Him as far as you can. For then only the great magic of this world will break of itself. But then, you must persevere. You must take off your mind from lust and lucre, must discriminate always between the real and the unreal — must settle down into the mood of bodilessness with the brooding thought that you are not this body, and must always have the realisation that you are the all-pervading Atman. This persevering practice is called Purushakâra (self-exertion — as distinguished from grace). By such self-exertion will come true reliance on Him, and that is the goal of human achievement.

After a pause Swamiji resumed: Had you not been receiving His grace, why else would you come here at all? Shri Ramakrishna used to say, "Those who have had the grace of God cannot but come here. Wherever they might be, whatever they might be doing, they are sure to be affected by words or sentiments uttered from here."[4] Just take your own case — do you think it is possible without the grace of God to have the blessed company of Nag Mahashaya, a man who rose to spiritual perfection through the strength of divine grace and came to know fully what this grace really means? "अनेकजन्मसंसिद्धस्ततो याति परां गतिम् — One attains the highest stage after being perfected by the practice of repeated births" (Gita, VI. 45). It is only by virtue of great religious merit acquired through many births that one comes across a great soul like him. All the characteristics of the highest type of Bhakti, spoken of in the scriptures, have manifested themselves in Nag Mahashaya. It is only in him that we actually see fulfilled the widely quoted text, "तृणादपि सुनीचेन". ("Lowlier than the lowly stalk of grass.") Blessed indeed is your East Bengal to have been hallowed by the touch of Nag Mahashaya's feet!

While speaking thus, Swamiji rose to pay a visit to

---

4. With his egoism perfectly merged in the consciousness of the Mother, the use of to word "here" by Shri Ramakrishna would often stand for the ordinary reference to self. By "here" is evidently meant the centre of the Mother's self-revelation.

the great poet, Babu Girish Chandra Ghosh. Swami Yogananda and the disciple followed him. Reaching Girish Babu's place, Swamiji seated himself and said "You see, G. C., the impulse is constantly coming nowadays to my mind to do this and to do that, to scatter broadcast on earth the message of Shri Ramakrishna and so on. But I pause again to reflect, lest all this give rise to another sect in India. So I have to work with a good deal of caution. Sometimes I think, what if a sect does grow up. But then again the thought comes! 'No. Shri Ramakrishna never disturbed anybody's own spiritual outlook; he always looked at the inner sameness.' Often do I restrain myself with this thought. Now, what do you say?"

Girish Babu: What can I say to this? You are the instrument in his hand. You have to do just what he would have you do. I don't trouble myself over the detail. But I see that the power of the Lord is getting things done by you, I see it clear as daylight.

Swamiji: But I think we do things according to our own will. Yet, that in misfortunes and adversities, in times of want and poverty, he reveals himself to us and guides us along the true path — this I have been able to realise. But alas, I still fail to comprehend in any way the greatness of his power.

Girish Babu: Yes, he said, "If you understand it to the full, everything will at once vanish. Who will work then or who will be made to work?"

After this the talk drifted on to America. And Swamiji grew warm on his subject and went on describing the wonderful wealth of the country, the virtues and defects of men and women there, their luxury and so on.

VII

Translated from Bengali
From the Diary of a Disciple

The disciple is Sharatchandra Chakravarty, who published his records in a Bengali book, Swami-Shishya-Samvâda, in two parts. The present series of "Conversations and Dialogues" is a revised translation from this book. Five dialogues of this series have already appeared in the Complete Works, Volume V.

Place: Calcutta.

Year: 1897.

For some days past, Swamiji has been staying at Balaram Bose's house, Baghbazar. There will be a total eclipse of the sun today. The disciple is to cook for Swamiji this morning, and on his presenting himself, Swamiji said, "Well, the cooking must be in the East Bengal style; and we must finish our dinner before the eclipse starts."

The inner apartments of the house were all unoccupied now. So the disciple went inside into the kitchen and started his cooking. Swamiji also was looking in now and then with a word of encouragement and sometimes with a joke, as, "Take care, the soup[1] must be after the East Bengal fashion."

The cooking had been almost completed, when Swamiji came in after his bath and sat down for dinner, putting up his own seat and plate. "Do bring in anything finished, quick," he said, "I can't wait, I'm burning with hunger!" While eating, Swamiji was pleased with the curry with bitters and remarked, "Never have I enjoyed such a nice thing! But none of the things is so hot as your soup." "It's just after the style of the Burdwan District", said Swamiji tasting the sour preparation. He then brought his dinner to a close and after washing sat on the bedstead inside the room. While having his after-dinner smoke, Swamiji remarked to the disciple, "Whoever cannot cook well cannot become a good Sâdhu; unless the mind is pure, good tasteful cooking is not possible. "

Soon after this, the sound of bells and conch-shells, etc., rose from all quarters, when Swamiji said, "Now that the eclipse has begun, let me sleep, and you please massage my feet!" Gradually the eclipse covered the whole of the sun's disc and all around fell the darkness of dusk.

While there were fifteen or twenty minutes left for the eclipse to pass off, Swamiji rose from his siesta,

---
1. The Bengali expression has a peculiar pronunciation in East Bengal which gives the point of the joke.

and after washing, jocosely said while taking a smoke, "Well, people say that whatever one does during an eclipse, one gets that millionfold in future; so I thought that the Mother, Mahâmâyâ, did not ordain that this body might have good sleep, and if I could get some sleep during the eclipse, I might have plenty of it in future. But it all failed, for I slept only for fifteen minutes a. the most."

After this, at the behest of Swamiji some short speeches were made. There was yet an hour left before dusk. When all had assembled in the parlour, Swamiji told them to put him any question they liked.

Swami Shuddhananda asked, "What is the real nature of meditation, sir?"

Swamiji: Meditation is the focusing of the mind on some object. If the mind acquires concentration on one object, it can be so concentrated on any object whatsoever.

Disciple: Mention is made in the scriptures of two kinds of meditation — one having some object and the other objectless. What is meant by all that, and which of the two is the higher one?

Swamiji: First, the practice of meditation has to proceed with some one object before the mind. Once I used to concentrate my mind on some black point. Ultimately, during those days, I could not see the point any more, nor notice that the point was before me at all — the mind used to be no more — no wave of functioning would rise, as if it were all an ocean without any breath of air. In that state I used to experience glimpses of supersensuous truth. So I think, the practice of meditation even with some trifling external object leads to mental concentration. But it is true that the mind very easily attains calmness when one practices meditation with anything on which one's mind is most apt to settle down. This is the reason why we have in this country so much worship of the images of gods and goddesses. And what wonderful art developed from such worship! But no more of that now. The fact, however, is that the objects of meditation can never be the same in the case of all men. People have proclaimed and preached to others only those external objects to which they held on to become perfected in meditation. Oblivious of the fact, later on, that these objects are aids to the attainment of perfect mental calmness, men have extolled them beyond everything else. They have wholly concerned themselves with the means, getting comparatively unmindful of the end. The real aim is to make the mind functionless, but this cannot be got at unless one becomes absorbed in some object.

Disciple: But if the mind becomes completely engrossed and identified with some object, how can it give us the consciousness of Brahman?

Swamiji: Yes, though the mind at first assumes the form of the object, yet later on the consciousness of that object vanishes. Then only the experience of pure "isness" remains.

Disciple: Well, sir, how is it that desires rise even after mental concentration is acquired?

Swamiji: Those are the outcome of previous Samskâras (deep-rooted impressions or tendencies). When Buddha was on the point of merging in Samadhi (superconsciousness), Mâra made his appearance. There was really no Mara extraneous to the mind; it was only the external reflection of the mind's previous Samskaras.

Disciple: But one hears of various fearful experiences prior to the attainment of perfection. Are they all mental projections?

Swamiji: What else but that? The aspiring soul, of course, does not make out at that time that all these are external manifestations of his own mind. But all the same, there is nothing outside of it. Even what you see as this world does not exist outside. It is all a mental projection. When the mind becomes functionless, it reflects the Brahman-consciousness. Then the vision of all spheres of existence may supervene, "यं यं लोकं मनसा संविभाति— Whatsoever sphere one may call up in mind" (Mundaka, III. i. 10). Whatsoever is resolved on becomes realised at once. He who, even on attaining this state of unfalsified self-determination, preserves his watchfulness and is free from the bondage of desire, verily attains to the knowledge of Brahman. But he who loses his balance after reaching this state gets the manifold powers, but falls off from the Supreme goal.

So saying, Swamiji began to repeat "Shiva, Shiva",

and then continued: There is no way, none whatsoever, to the solution of the profound mystery of this life except through renunciation. Renunciation, renunciation and renunciation — let this be the one motto of your lives. "सर्वं वस्तु भयान्वितं भुवि नृणां वैराग्यमेवाभयम् — For men, all things on earth are infected with fear, Vairâgya (renunciation) alone constitutes fearlessness" (Vairâgya-Shatakam).

VIII

Translated from Bengali
From the Diary of a Disciple

The disciple is Sharatchandra Chakravarty, who published his records in a Bengali book, Swami-Shishya-Samvâda, in two parts. The present series of "Conversations and Dialogues" is a revised translation from this book. Five dialogues of this series have already appeared in the Complete Works, Volume V.

Place: Calcutta.

Year: 1897, March or April.

Today the disciple came to meet Swamiji at Baghbazar, but found him ready for a visiting engagement. "Well, come along with me", were the words with which Swamiji accosted him as he went downstairs, and the disciple followed. They then put themselves into a hired cab which proceeded southwards.

Disciple: Sir, where are you going to visit, please?

Swamiji: Well, come with me and you will see.

Thus keeping back the destination from the disciple, Swamiji opened the following conversation as the carriage reached the Beadon Street: One does not find any real endeavour in your country to get the women educated. You, the men are educating yourselves to develop your manhood, but what are you doing to educate and advance those who share all your happiness and misery, who lay down their lives to serve you in your homes?

Disciple: Why, sir, just see how many schools and colleges hare sprung up nowadays for our women, and how many of them are getting degrees of B.A. and M.A.

Swamiji: But all that is in the Western style. How many schools have been started on your own national lines, in the spirit of your own religious ordinances? But alas, such a system does not obtain even among the men of your country, what to speak of women! It is seen from the official statistics that only three or four per cent of the people in India are educated, and not even one per cent of the women.

Otherwise, how could the country come to such a fallen condition? How can there be any progress of the country without the spread of education, the dawning of knowledge? Even no real effort or exertion in the cause is visible among the few in your country who are the promise of the future, you who have received the blessings of education. But know for certain that absolutely nothing can be done to improve the state of things, unless there is spread of education first among the women and the masses. And so I have it in my mind to train up some Brahmachârins and Brahmachârinis, the former of whom will eventually take the vow of Sannyâsa and try to carry the light of education among the masses, from village to village, throughout the country, while the latter will do the same among women. But the whole work must be done in the style of our own country. Just as centres have to be started for men, so also centres have to be started for teaching women. Brahmacharinis of education and character should take up the task of teaching at these different centres. History and the Purânas, housekeeping and the arts, the duties of home-life and principles that make for the development of an ideal character have to be taught with the help of modern science, and the women students must be trained up in ethical and spiritual life. We must see to their growing up as ideal matrons of home in time. The children of such mothers will make further progress in the virtues that distinguish the mothers. It is only in the homes of educated and pious mothers that great men are born. And you have reduced your women to something like manufacturing machines; alas, for heaven's sake, is this the outcome of your education? The uplift of the women, the awakening of the masses must come first, and then only can any real good come about for the country, for India.

Near Chorebagan Swamiji gave it out to the disciple that the foundress of the Mahâkali Pâthashâlâ, the Tapasvini Mâtâji (ascetic mother), had invited him to visit her institution. When our carriage stopped at its destination, three or four gentlemen greeted Swamiji and showed him up to the first door. There the Tapasvini mother received him standing. Presently she escorted him into one of the classes, where all the maidens stood up in greeting. At a word from Mataji all of them commenced reciting the Sanskrit meditation of Lord Shiva with proper intonation. Then they demonstrated at the instance of the Mother how they were taught the ceremonies of worship in their school. After watching all this with much delight and interest, Swamiji proceeded to visit the other classes. After this, Mataji sent for some particular girl and asked her to explain before Swamiji the first verse of the third canto of Kalidasa's Raghavamsham, which she did in Sanskrit. Swamiji expressed his great appreciation of the measure of success Mataji had attained by her perseverance and application in the cause of diffusing education among women. In reply, she said with much humility, "In my service to my students, I look upon them as the Divine Mother; well, in starting the school I have neither fame nor any other object in view."

Being asked by Mataji, Swamiji recorded his opinion about the institution in the Visitors' Book, the last line of which was: "The movement is in the right direction."

After saluting Mataji, Swamiji went back to his carriage, which then proceeded towards Baghbazar, while the following conversation took place between Swamiji and the disciple.

Swamiji: How far is the birthplace of this venerable lady! She has renounced everything of her worldly life, and yet how diligent in the service of humanity! Had she not been a woman, could she ever have undertaken the teaching of women in the way she is doing? What I saw here was all good, but that some male householders should be pitchforked as teachers is a thing I cannot approve of. The duty of teaching in the school ought to devolve in every respect on educated widows and Brahmacharinis. It is good to avoid in this country any association of men with women's schools.

Disciple: But, sir, how would you get now in thin country learned and virtuous women like Gârgi, Khanâ or Lilâvati?

Swamiji: Do you think women of the type don't exist now in the country? Still on this sacred soil of India, this land of Sitâ and Sâvitri, among women may be found such character, such spirit of service, such affection, compassion, contentment, and reverence, as I could not find anywhere else in the world! In the West, the women did not very often seem to me to be women at all, they appeared to be quite the replicas of men! Driving vehicles, drudging in offices, attending schools, doing professional duties! In India alone the sight of feminine modesty and reserve soothes the eye! With such materials of great promise, you could not, alas, work out their uplift! You did not try to infuse the light of knowledge into them. If they get the right sort of education, they may well turn out to be the ideal women in the world.

Disciple: Do you think, sir, the same consummation would be reached through the way Mataji is educating her students? These students would soon grow up and get married and would presently shade into the likeness of all other women of the common run. So I think, if these girls might be made to adopt Brahmacharya, then only could they devote their lives to the cause of the country's progress and attain to the high ideals preached in our sacred books.

Swamiji: Yes, everything will come about in time. Such educated men are not yet born in this country, who can keep their girls unmarried without fear of social punishment. Just see how before the girls exceed the age of twelve or thirteen, people hasten to give them away in marriage out of this fear of their social equals. Only the other day, when the Age of Consent Bill was being passed, the leaders of society massed together millions of men to send up the cry "We don't want the Bill." Had this been in any other country, far from getting up meetings to send forth a cry like that, people would have hidden their heads under their roofs in shame, that such a calumny could yet stain their society.

Disciple: But, sir, I don't think the ancient law-givers supported this custom of early marriage without any rhyme or reason. There must have been some secret meaning in this attitude of theirs.

Swamiji: Well, what might have been this secret meaning, please?

Disciple: Take it, for instance, in the first place that if the girls are married at an early age, they may come over to their husbands' home to learn the particular ways and usages of the family from the early years of their life. They may acquire adequate skill in the duties of the household under the guidance of their parents-in-law. In the homes of their own parents, on the other hand, there is the likelihood of grown-up daughters going astray. But married early, they have no chance of thus going wrong, and over and above this, such feminine virtues as modesty, reserve, fortitude, and diligence are apt to develop in them.

Swamiji: In favour of the other side of the question, again, it may be argued that early marriage leads to premature child-bearing, which accounts for most of our women dying early; their progeny also, being of low vitality, go to swell the ranks of our country's beggars! For if the physique of the parents be not strong and healthy, how can strong and healthy children be born at all? Married a little later and bred in culture, our mothers will give birth to children who would be able to achieve the real good of the country. The reason why you have so many widows in every home lies here, in this custom of early marriage. If the number of early marriages declines, that of widows is bound to follow suit.

Disciple: But, sir, it seems to me, if our women are married late in life, they are apt to be less mindful of their household duties. I have heard that the mothers-in-law in Calcutta very often do all the cooking, while the educated daughters-in-law sit idle with red paint round their feet! But in our East Bengal such a thing is never allowed to take place.

Swamiji: But everywhere under the sun you find the same blending of the good and the bad. In my opinion society in every country shapes itself out of its own initiative. So we need not trouble our heads prematurely about such reforms as the abolition of early marriage, the remarriage of widows, and so on. Our part of the duty lies in imparting true education to all men and women in society. As an outcome of that education, they will of themselves be able to know what is good for them and what is bad, and will spontaneously eschew the latter. It will not be then necessary to pull down or set up anything in society by coercion.

Disciple: What sort of education, do you think, is suited to our women?

Swamiji: Religion, arts, science, housekeeping, cooking, sewing, hygiene — the simple essential points in these subjects ought to be taught to our women. It is not good to let them touch novels and fiction. The Mahakali Pathashala is to a great extent moving in the right direction. But only teaching rites of worship won't do; their education must be an eye-opener in all matters. Ideal characters must always be presented before the view of the girls to imbue them with a devotion to lofty principles of selflessness. The noble examples of Sita, Savitri, Damavanti, Lilavati, Khana, and Mirâ should be brought home to their minds and they should be inspired to mould their own lives in the light of these.

Our cab now reached the house of the late Babu Balaram Bose at Baghbazar. Swamiji alighted from it and went upstairs. There he recounted the whole of his experience at the Mahakali Pathashala to those who had assembled there to see him.

Then while discussing what the members of the newly formed Ramakrishna Mission should do, Swamiji proceeded to establish by various arguments the supreme importance of the 'gift of learning" and the "gift of knowledge".[1] Turning to the disciple he said, "Educate, educate, 'नान्यः पन्था विद्यतेऽयनाय — Than this there is no other way'." And referring in banter to the party who do not favour educational propaganda, he said, "Well, don't go into the party of Prahlâdas!" Asked as to the meaning of the expression he replied, "Oh, haven't you heard? Tears rushed out of the eyes

---

1. The allusion here is to the classification of various gifts, mentioned by Manu.

of Prahlada at the very sight of the first letter 'Ka' of the alphabet as it reminded him Of Krishna; so how could any studies be proceeded with? But then the tears in Prahlada's eyes were tears of love, while your fools affect tears in fright! Many of the devotees are also like that." All of those present burst out laughing on hearing this, and Swami Yogananda said to Swamiji, "Well, once you have the urge within towards anything to be done, you won't have any peace until you see the utmost done about it. Now what you have a mind to have done shall be done no doubt."

IX

*Translated from Bengali
From the Diary of a Disciple*

The disciple is Sharatchandra Chakravarty, who published his records in a Bengali book, Swami-Shishya-Samvâda, in two parts. The present series of "Conversations and Dialogues" is a revised translation from this book. Five dialogues of this series have already appeared in the Complete Works, Volume V.

Place: Calcutta.

Year: 1897.

For the last ten days, the disciple had been studying Sâyana's commentary on the Rig-Veda with Swamiji, who was staying then at the house of the late Babu Balaram Bose at Baghbazar. Max Müller's volumes on the Rig-Veda had been brought from a wealthy friend's private library. Swamiji was correcting the disciple every now and then and giving him the true pronunciation or construction as necessary. Sometimes while explaining the arguments of Sayana to establish the eternity of the Vedas, Swamiji was praising very highly the commentator's wonderful ingenuity; sometimes again while arguing out the deeper significance of the doctrine, he was putting forward a difference in view and indulging in an innocent squib at Sayana.

While our study had proceeded thus for a while, Swamiji raised the topic about Max Müller and continued thus: Well, do you know, my impression is that it is Sayana who is born again as Max Müller to revive his own commentary on the Vedas? I have had this notion for long. It became confirmed in my mind, it seems, after I had seen Max Müller. Even here in this country, you don't find a scholar so persevering, and so firmly grounded in the Vedas and the Vedanta. Over and above this, what a deep, unfathomable respect for Sri Ramakrishna! Do you know, he believes in his Divine Incarnation! And what great hospitality towards me when I was his guest! Seeing the old man and his lady, it seemed to me that they were living their home-life like another Vasishtha and Arundhati! At the time of parting with me, tears came into the eyes of the old man.

Disciple: But, sir, if Sayana himself became Max Müller, then why was he born as a Mlechchha instead of being born in the sacred land of India?

Swamiji: The feeling and the distinction that I am an Aryan and the other is a Mlechchha come from ignorance. But what are Varnâshrama and caste divisions to one who is the commentator of the Vedas, the shining embodiment of knowledge? To him they are wholly meaningless, and he can assume human birth wherever he likes for doing good to mankind. Specially, if he did not choose to be born in a land which excelled both in learning and wealth, where would he secure the large expenses for publishing such stupendous volumes? Didn't you hear that the East India Company paid nine lakhs of rupees in cash to have the Rig-Veda published? Even this money was not enough. Hundreds of Vedic Pundits had to be employed in this country on monthly stipends. Has anybody seen in this age, here in this country, such profound yearning for knowledge, such prodigious investment of money for the sake of light and learning? Max Müller himself has written it in his preface, that for twenty-five years he prepared only the manuscripts. Then the printing took another twenty years! It is not possible for an ordinary man to drudge for fortyfive years of his life with one publication. Just think of it! Is it an idle fancy of mine to say he is Sayana himself?

After this talk about Max Müller the leading of the

Vedas was resumed. Now Swamiji began variously to support the view of Sayana that creation proceeded out of the Vedas. He said: Veda means the sum total of eternal truths; the Vedic Rishis experienced those truths; they can be experienced only by seers of the supersensuous and not by common men like us. That is why in the Vedas the term Rishi means "the seer of the truth of the Mantras", and not any Brahmin with the holy thread hanging down the neck. The division of society into castes came about later on. Veda is of the nature of Shabda or of idea. It is but the sum total of ideas. Shabda, according to the old Vedic meaning of the term, is the subtle idea, which reveals itself by taking the gross form later on. So owing to the dissolution of the creation the subtle seeds of the future creation become involved in the Veda. Accordingly, in the Puranas you find that during the first Divine Incarnation, the Minâvatâra, the Veda is first made manifest. The Vedas having been first revealed in this Incarnation, the other creative manifestations followed. Or in other words, all the created objects began to take concrete shape out of the Shabdas or ideas in the Veda. For in Shabda or idea, all gross objects have their subtle forms. Creation had proceeded in the same way in all previous cycles or Kalpas. This you find in the Sandhyâ Mantra of the Vedas:

"सूर्याचन्द्रमसौ धाता यथापूर्वमकल्पयत् पृथिवीं दिवं चान्तरीक्षमथो स्वः — The Creator projected the sun, the moon, the earth, the atmosphere, the heaven, and the upper spheres in the same manner and process as in previous cycles." Do you understand?

Disciple: But, sir, how in the absence of an actual concrete object can the Shabda or idea be applied and for what? And how can the names too be given at all?

Swamiji: Yes. that is what on first thought seems to be the difficulty. But just think of this. Supposing this jug breaks into pieces; does the idea of a jug become null and void? No. Because, the jug is the gross effect, while the idea, "jug", is the subtle state or the Shabda-state of the jug. In the same way, the Shabda-state of every object is its subtle state, and the things we see, hear, touch, or perceive in any manner are the gross manifestations of entities in the subtle or Shabda-state. Just as we may speak of the effect and its cause. Even when the whole creation is annihilated, the Shabda, as the consciousness of the universe or the subtle reality of all concrete things, exists in Brahman as the cause. At the point of creative manifestation, this sum total of causal entities vibrates into activity, as it were, and as being the sonant, material substance of it all, the eternal, primal sound of "Om" continues to come out of itself. And then from the causal totality comes out first the subtle image or Shabda-form of each particular thing and then its gross manifestation. Now that causal Shabda, or word-consciousness, is Brahman, and it is the Veda. This is the purport of Sayana. Do you now understand?

Disciple: No, sir, I can't clearly comprehend it.

Swamiji: Well, you understand, I suppose, that even if all the jugs in the universe were to be destroyed, the idea or Shabda, "jug", would still exist. So if the universe be destroyed — I mean if all the things making up the universe be smashed to atoms — why should not the ideas or Shabdas representing all of them in consciousness, be still existing; And why cannot a second creation be supposed to come out of them in time?

Disciple: But, sir, if one cries out "jug", "jug", that does not cause any jug to be produced!

Swamiji: No, nothing is produced if you or I cry out like that; but a jug must be revealed if the idea of it rises in Brahman which is perfect in Its creative determinations. When we see even those established in the practice of religion (Sâdhakas) bring about by will-power things otherwise impossible to happen, what to speak of Brahman with perfect creativeness of will? At the point of creation Brahman becomes manifest as Shabda (Idea), and then assumes the form of "Nâda" or "Om". At the next stage, the particular Shabdas or ideas, that variously existed in former cycles, such as Bhuh, Bhuvah, Svah, cow, man, etc., begin to come out of the "Om". As soon as these ideas appear in Brahman endowed with perfect will, the corresponding concrete things also appear, and gradually the diversified universe becomes manifest. Do you now understand how Shabda is the source of creation?

Disciple: Yes, I just form some idea of it, but there is no clear comprehension in the mind.

Swamiji: Well, clear comprehension, inward realisation, is no small matter, my son. When the mind proceeds towards self-absorption in Brahman, it passes through all these stages one by one to reach the absolute (Nirvikalpa) state at last. In the process of entering into Samadhi, first the universe appears as one mass of ideas; then the whole thing loses itself in a profound "Om". Then even that melts away, even that seems to be between being and non-being. That is the experience of the eternal Nada. And then the mind becomes lost in the Reality of Brahman, and then it is done! All is peace!

The disciple sat mute, thinking that none could express and explain it in the way Swamiji was doing, unless the whole thing were a matter of one's own experience!

Swamiji then resumed the subject: Great men like Avatâras, in coming back from Samadhi to the realm of "I" and "mine", first experience the unmanifest Nada, which by degrees grows distinct and appears as Om, and then from Omkâra, the subtle form of the universe as a mass of ideas becomes experienced, and last, the material universe comes into perception. But ordinary Sadhakas somehow reach beyond Nada through immense practice, and when once they attain to the direct realisation of Brahman, they cannot again come back to the lower plane of material perception. They melt away in Brahman, "क्षीरे नीरवत्—Like water in milk".

When all this talk on the theory of creation was going on, the great dramatist, Babu Girish Chandra Ghosh, appeared on the scene. Swamiji gave him his courteous greetings and continued his lessons to the disciple.

Shabdas are again divided into two classes, the Vedic Shabdas and those in common human use. I found this position in the Nyâya book called Shabdashaktiprakâshikâ. There the arguments no doubt indicate great power of thought; but, oh, the terminology confounds the brain!

Now turning to Girish Babu Swamiji said: What do you say, G. C.? Well, you do not care to study all this, you pass your days with your adoration of this and that god, eh?

Girish Babu: What shall I study, brother? I have neither time nor understanding enough to pry into all that. But this time, with Shri Ramakrishna's grace, I shall pass by with greetings to your Vedas and Vedanta, and take one leap to the far beyond! He gets you through all these studies, because he wants to get many a thing done by you. But we have no need of them. Saying this, Girish Babu again and again touched the big Rig-Veda volumes with his head, uttering, "All Victory to Ramakrishna in the form of Veda!"

Swamiji was now in a sort of deep reverie, when Girish Babu suddenly called out to him and said: Well, hear me, please. A good deal of study you have made in the Vedas and Vedanta, but say, did you find anywhere in them any way for us out of all these profound miseries in the country, all these wailings of grief, all this starvation, all these crimes of adultery, and the many horrible sins?

Saying this he painted over and over again the horrid pictures of society. Swamiji remained perfectly quiet and speechless, while at the thought of the sorrows and miseries of his fellow men, tears began to flow out of his eyes, and seemingly to hide his feelings from us, he rose and left the room.

Meanwhile, addressing the disciple, Girish Babu said: Did you see, Bângâl? What a great loving heart! I don't honour your Swamiji simply for being a Pundit versed in the Vedas; but I honour him for that great heart of his which just made him retire weeping at the sorrows of his fellow beings.

The disciple and Girish Babu then went on conversing with each other, the latter proving that knowledge and love were ultimately the same.

In the meantime, Swamiji returned and asked the disciple, "Well, what was all this talk going on between you?" The disciple said, "Sir, we are talking about the Vedas, and the wonder of it is that our Girish Babu has not studied these books but has grasped the ultimate truths with clean precision!"

Swamiji: All truths reveal themselves to him who has got real devotion to the Guru; he has hardly any need of studies. But such devotion and faith are very rare in this world. He who possesses those in the measure of our friend here need not study the Shastras. But he who rushes forward to imitate him will only bring about his own ruin. Always follow his advice, but never attempt to imitate his ways.

Disciple: Yes, sir,

Swamiji: No saying ditto merely! Do grasp dearly the words I say. Don't nod assent like a fool to everything said. Don't put implicit faith, even if I declare something. First clearly grasp and then accept. Shri Ramakrishna always used to insist on my accepting every word of his only after dear comprehension of it. Walk on your path, only with what sound principle, clear reasoning, and scripture all declare as true. Thus by constant reflection, the intellect will become dear, and then only can Brahman be reflected therein. Do you understand?

Disciple: Yes, sir, I do. But the brain gets puzzled with the different views of different men. This very moment I was being told by Girish Babu, "What will you do with all this studying?" And then you come and say, "Reflect on what you hear and read about." So what exactly am I to do?

Swamiji: Both what he and I have advised you are true. The only difference is that the advice of both has been given from different standpoints. There is a stage of spiritual life where all reasonings are hushed; "मूकास्वादनवत् — Like some delicious taste enjoyed by the dumb". And there is another mode of spiritual life in which one has to realise the Truth through the pursuit of scriptural learning, through studying and teaching. You have to proceed through studies and reflection, that is your way to realisation. Do you see?

Receiving such a mandate from Swamiji, the disciple in his folly took it to imply Girish Babu's discomfiture, and so turning towards him said: "Do you hear, sir? Swamiji's advice to me plainly is just to study and reflect on the Vedas and Vedanta."

Girish Babu: Well, you go on doing so; with Swamiji's blessings, you will, indeed, succeed in that way.

Swami Sadananda arrived there at that moment, and seeing him, Swamiji at once said, "Do you know, my heart is sorely troubled by the picture of our country's miseries G. C. was depicting just now; well, can you do anything for our country?"

Sadananda: Mahârâj, let the mandate once go forth; your slave is ready.

Swamiji: First, on a pretty small scale, start a relief centre, where the poor and the distressed may obtain relief and the diseased may be nursed. Helpless people having none to look after them will be relieved and served there, irrespective of creed or colour, do you see?

Sadananda: Just as you command, sir.

Swamiji: There is no greater Dharma than this service of living beings. If this Dharma can be practiced in the real spirit, then "मुक्तिः करफलायते — Liberation comes as a fruit on the very palm of one's hand".

Addressing Girish Babu now, Swamiji said, "Do you know, Girish Babu, it occurs to me that even if a thousand births have to be taken in order to relieve the sorrows of the world, surely I will take them. If by my doing that, even a single soul may have a little bit of his grief relieved, why, I will do it. Well, what avails it all to have only one's own liberation? All men should be taken along with oneself on that way. Can you say why a feeling like this comes up foremost in my mind?

Girish Babu: Ah, otherwise why should Shri Ramakrishna declare you to be greater than all others in spiritual competence?

Saying this, Girish Babu took leave of us all to go elsewhere on some business.

X

Translated from Bengali
From the Diary of a Disciple

The disciple is Sharatchandra Chakravarty, who published his records in a Bengali book, Swami-Shishya-Samvâda, in two parts. The present series of "Conversations and Dialogues" is a revised translation from this book. Five dialogues of this series have already appeared in the Complete Works, Volume V.

Place: The Alambazar Math.

Year: 1897.

After Swamiji's first return to Calcutta from the West, he always used to place before the zealous young men who visited him the lofty ideals of renunciation, and anyone expressing his desire of accepting Sannyasa would receive from him great encouragement and kindness. So, inspired by his enthusiasm some young men of great good fortune gave up their worldly life in those days and became initiated by him into Sannyasa. The disciple was present at the Alambazar Math the day the first four of this batch were given Sannyasa by Swamiji.

Often has the disciple heard it from the Sannyasins of the Math that Swamiji was repeatedly requested by his brother-monks not to admit one particular candidate into Sannyasa, whereupon Swamiji replied: "Ah, if even we shrink from working out the salvation of the sinful, the heavy-laden, the humiliated, and the afflicted in soul, who else are to take care of them in this world? No, don't you please stand against me in this matter." So Swamiji's strong opinion triumphed, and always the refuge of the helpless, he resolved out of his great love to give him Sannyasa.

The disciple had been staying at the Math for the last two days, when Swamiji called him and said: "Well, you belong to the priestly class; tomorrow you get them to perform their Shrâddha, and the next day I shall give them Sannyasa. So get yourself ready by consulting the books of ceremonials today." The disciple bowed this mandate of Swamiji, and the ceremony was duly gone through.

But the disciple became very much depressed at the thought of the great sternness of Sannyasa. Swamiji detecting his mental agitation asked him, "Well, I see, you feel some dread in your mind at all this experience, is it not so?" And when the disciple confessed it to be so Swamiji said: "From this day these four are dead to the world, and new bodies, new thoughts, new garments will be theirs from tomorrow — and shining in the glory of Brahman they will live like flaming fire! '— Not by work, nor by progeny, nor by wealth, but by renunciation alone some (rare ones) attained Immortality' (Kaivalya Upanishad)."

After the ceremony, the four Brahmacharins bowed at the feet of Swamiji. He blessed them and said, "You have the enthusiasm to embrace the loftiest vow of human life; blessed indeed is your birth, blessed your family, blessed the mothers who held you in their womb! '— The whole family-line becomes hallowed, the mother achieves her highest!'"

That day after supper, Swamiji talked of the ideal of Sannyasa alone. To the zealous candidates for Sannyasa, he said: The real aim of Sannyasa is "— For one's highest freedom and for the good of the world". Without having Sannyasa none can really be a knower of Brahman — this is what the Vedas and the Vedanta proclaim. Don't listen to the words of those who say, "We shall both live the worldly life and be knowers of Brahman." That is the flattering self-consolation of cryptopleasure-seekers. He who has the slightest desire for worldly pleasures, even a shred of some such craving, will feel frightened at the thought of the path you are going to tread; so, to give himself some consolation he goes about preaching that impossible creed of harmonising Bhoga and Tyâga. That is all the raving of lunatics, the frothing of the demented — idle theories contrary to the scriptures, contrary to the Vedas. No freedom without renunciation. Highest love for God can never be achieved without renunciation. Renunciation is the word — "नान्यः पन्था विद्यते अयनाय — There's no other way than this." Even the Gita says, "— The sages know Sannyasa to be the giving up of all work that has desire for its end."

Nobody attains freedom without shaking off the coils of worldly worries. The very fact that somebody lives the worldly life proves that he is tied down to it as the bond-slave of some craving or other. Why otherwise will he cling to that life at all? He is the slave either of lust or of gold, of position or of fame, of learning or of scholarship. It is only after freeing oneself from all this thraldom that one can get on along the way of freedom. Let people argue as loud as they please, I have got this conviction that unless all these bonds are given up, unless the monastic life is embraced, none is going to be saved, no attainment of Brahmajnâna is possible.

Disciple: Do you mean, sir, that merely taking up Sannyasa will lead one to the goal?

Swamiji: Whether the goal is attained or not is not the point before us now. But until you get out of this wheel of Samsâra, until the slavery of desire is shaken off, you can't attain either Bhakti or Mukti. To the knower of Brahman, supernatural powers or prosperity are mere trivialities.

Disciple: Sir, is there any special time for Sannyasa, and are there different kinds of it?

Swamiji: There is no special time prescribed for a life of Sannyasa. The Shruti says: "— Directly the spirit of renunciation comes, you should take to Sannyasa." The Yogavâsishtha also says:

— "Owing to life itself being frail and uncertain, one should be devoted to religion even in one's youth. For who knows when one's body may fall off?"

The Shâstras are found to speak of four kinds of Sannyasa: (1) Vidvat, (2) Vividishâ, (3) Markata, (4) Âtura. The awakening of real renunciation all at once and the consequent giving up of the world through Sannyasa is something that never happens unless there are strong Samskâras or tendencies, developed from previous birth. And this is called the Vidvat Sannyasa. Vividisha Sannyasa is the case of one who, out of a strong yearning for the knowledge of the Self through the pursuit of scriptural study and practice, goes to the man of realisation and from him embraces Sannyasa to give himself up to those pursuits. Markata Sannyasa is the case of a man who is driven out of the world by some of its chastisements such as the death of a relative or the like and then takes to Sannyasa, though in such a case the renouncing spirit does not endure long. Shri Ramakrishna used to say of it, "With this kind of renunciation one hastens away to the up-country and then happens to get hold of a nice job; and then eventually perhaps arranges to get his wife brought over to him or perhaps takes to a new one!" And last, there is another kind of Sannyasa which the Shastras prescribe for a man who is lying on his death-bed, the hope of whose life has been given up. For then, if he dies, he dies with the holiest of vows upon him, and in his next birth the merit of it will accrue to him. And in case he recovers, he shall not go back to his old life again but live the rest of his days in the noble endeavour after Brahmajnana.

Swami Shivananda gave this kind of Sannyasa to your uncle. The poor man died; but through that initiation he will come to a new birth of higher excellence. After all there is no other way to the knowledge of the Self but through Sannyasa.

Disciple: What then, sir, will be the fate of the householders?

Swamiji: Why, through the merit of good Karma, they shall have this renunciation in some future birth of theirs. And directly this renunciation comes, there is an end of all troubles — with no further delay he gets across this mystery of life and death. But then all rules have their exceptions. A few men, one or two, may be seen to attain the highest freedom by the true fulfilment of the householder's Dharma, as we have amongst us Nâg Mahâshaya, for instance.

Disciple: Sir, even the Upanishads etc. do not clearly teach about renunciation and Sannyasa.

Swamiji: You are talking like a madman! Renunciation is the very soul of the Upanishads. Illumination born of discriminative reflection is the ultimate aim of Upanishadic knowledge. My belief, however, is that it was since the time of Buddha that the monastic vow was preached more thoroughly all over India, and renunciation, the giving up of sense-enjoyment, was recognised as the highest aim of religious life. And Hinduism has absorbed into itself this Buddhistic spirit of renunciation. Never was a great man of such renunciation born in this world as Buddha.

Disciple: Do you then mean, sir, that before Buddha's advent there was very little of the spirit of renunciation in the country, and there were hardly any Sannyasins at all?

Swamiji: Who says that? The monastic institution was there, but the generality of people did not recognise it as the goal of life; there was no such staunch spirit for it, there was no such firmness in spiritual discrimination. So even when Buddha betook himself to so many Yogis and Sâdhus, nowhere did he acquire the peace he wanted. And then to realise the Highest he fell back on his own exertions, and seated on a spot with the famous words, "— Let my body wither away on this seat" etc., rose from it only after becoming the Buddha, the Illumined One. The many monasteries that you now see in India occupied by monks were once in the possession of Buddhism. The Hindus have only made them their own now by modifying them in their own fashion. Really speaking, the institution of Sannyasa originated with Buddha; it was he who breathed life into the dead bones of this institution.

Swami Ramakrishnananda, a brother-disciple of Swamiji, interposed, "But the ancient law-books and Puranas are good authority that all the four Ashramas had existed in India before Buddha was born." Swamiji replied, "Most of the Puranas, the codes of Manu and others, as well as much of the Mahâbhârata form but recent literature. Bhagavân Buddha was much earlier than all that." "On that supposition," rejoined Swami Ramakrishnananda, "discussions about Buddhism would be found in the Vedas, Upanishads, the law-books, Puranas, and the like. But since such discussions are not found in these ancient books, how can you say that Buddha antedated them all? In a few old Puranas, of course, accounts of the Buddhistic doctrine are partially given; but from these, it can't be concluded that the scriptures of the Hindus such as the law-books and Puranas are of recent date."

Swamiji: Please read history, (Evidently, during the argumentation, Swamiji was taking his stand on the conclusions of modern historical studies, thereby giving his encouragement and support to such new efforts and methods. But we know from one of his letters to Swami Swarupananda (C.W. modern scholars and worked out the pre-Buddhiscic origin of much of modern Hinduism.) and you will find that Hinduism has become so great only by absorbing all the ideas of Buddha.

Swami Ramakrishnananda: It seems to me that Buddha has only left revivified the great Hindu ideas, by thoroughly practicing in his life such principles as renunciation, non-attachment, and so on.

Swamiji: But this position can't be proved. For we don't get any history before Buddha was born. If we accept history only as authority, we have to admit that in the midst of the profound darkness of the ancient times, Buddha only shines forth as a figure radiant with the light of knowledge.

Now the topic of Sannyasa was resumed and Swamiji said: Wheresoever might lie the origin of Sannyasa, the goal of human life is to become a knower of Brahman by embracing this vow of renunciation. The supreme end is to enter the life of Sannyasa. They alone are blessed indeed who have broken off from worldly life through a spirit of renunciation.

Disciple: But many people are of opinion nowadays, sir, that with the increase of wandering monks in the country, much harm has been done to its material progress. They assert it on the ground that these monks idly roam about depending on householders for their living, that these are of no help to the cause of social and national advancement.

Swamiji: But will you explain to me first what is meant by the term material or secular advancement?

Disciple: Yes, it is to do as people in the West are doing by securing the necessaries of life through education, and promoting through science such objects in life as commerce, industry, communications, and so on.

Swamiji: But can all these be ever brought about, if real Rajas is not awakened in man? Wandering all over India, nowhere I found this Rajas manifesting itself. It is all Tamas and Tamas! The masses lie engulfed in Tamas, and only among the monks could I find this Rajas and Sattva. These people are like the backbone of the country. The real Sannyasin is a teacher of householders. It is with the light and teaching obtained from them that householders of old triumphed many a time in the battles of life. The householders give food and clothing to the Sadhus, only in return for their invaluable teachings. Had there been no such mutual exchange in India, her people would have become extinct like the American Indians by this time. It is because the householders still give a few morsels of food to the Sadhus that they are yet able to keep their foothold on the path of progress. The Sannyasins are not idle. They are really the fountain-head of all activity. The householders see lofty ideals carried into practice in the lives of the Sadhus and accept from them such noble ideas; and this it is that has up till now enabled them to fight their battle of life from the sphere of Karma. The example of holy Sadhus makes them work out holy ideas in life and imbibe real energy for work. The Sannyasins inspire the householders in all noble causes by embodying in their lives the highest principle of giving up everything for the sake of God and the good of the world, and as a return the householders give them a few doles of food. And the very disposition and capacity to grow that food develops in the people because of the blessings and good wishes of the all-renouncing monks. It is because of their failure to understand the deeper issues that people blame the monastic institution. Whatever may be the case in other countries, in this land the bark of householders' life does not sink only because the Sannyasins are at its helm.

Disciple: But, sir, how many monks are to be found who are truly devoted to the good of men?

Swamiji: Ah, quite enough if one great Sannyasin like Shri Ramakrishna comes in a thousand years! For a thousand years after his advent, people may well guide themselves by those ideas and ideals he leaves behind. It is only because this monastic institution exists in the country that men of his greatness are born here. There are defects, more or less, in all the institutions of life. But what is the reason that in spite of its faults, this noble institution stands yet supreme over all the other institutions of life? It is because the true Sannyasins forgo even their own liberation and live simply for doing good to the world. If you don't feel grateful to such a noble institution, lie on you again and again!

While speaking these words, Swamiji's countenance became aglow. And before the eyes of the disciple he shone as the very embodiment of Sannyasa.

Then, as if realising deep within his soul the greatness of this institution, self-absorbed, he broke forth in sweetest symphony:

— "Brooding blissful in mind over the texts of the Vedanta, quite contented with food obtained as alms and wandering forth with a heart untouched by any feeling of grief, thrice blessed are the Sannyasins, with only their loin-cloth for dress."

Resuming the talk, he went on: For the good of the many, for the happiness of the many is the Sannyasin born. His life is all vain, indeed, who, embracing Sannyasa, forgets this ideal. The Sannyasin, verily, is born into this world to lay down his life for others, to stop the bitter cries of men, to wipe the tears of the widow, to bring peace to the soul of the bereaved mother, to equip the ignorant masses for the struggle for existence, to accomplish the secular and spiritual well-being of all through the diffusion of spiritual teachings and to arouse the sleeping lion of Brahman in all by throwing in the light of knowledge. Addressing then his brothers of the Order, he said: Our life is "— for the sake of our self-liberation as well as for the good of the world". So what are you sitting idle for? Arise, awake; wake up yourselves, and awaken others. Achieve the consummation of human life before you pass off — "Arise, awake, and stop not till the goal is reached."

XI

Translated from Bengali
From the Diary of a Disciple

The disciple is Sharatchandra Chakravarty, who published his records in a Bengali book, Swami-Shishya-Samvâda, in two parts. The present series of "Conversations and Dialogues" is a revised translation from this book. Five dialogues of this series have already appeared in the Complete Works, Volume V.

Place: The house of the late Babu Navagopal Ghosh, Ramakrishnapur, Howrah.

Year: 6th February, 1898.

Today the festival of installing the image of Shri Ramakrishna was to come off at the residence of Babu Navagopal Ghosh of Ramakrishnapur, Howrah. The Sannyasins of the Math and the householder devotees of Shri Ramakrishna had all been invited there.

Swamiji with his party reached the bathing ghat at Ramakrishnapur. He was dressed in the simplest garb of ochre with turban on his head and was barefooted On both sides of the road were standing multitudes of people to see him. Swamiji commenced singing the famous Nativity Hymn on Shri Ramakrishna —

"Who art Thou laid on the lap of a poor Brahmin mother", etc., and headed a procession, himself playing on the Khol. (A kind of Indian drum elongated and narrows at both ends.) All the devotees assembled there followed, joining in the; chorus.

Shortly after the procession reached its destination, Swamiji went upstairs to see the chapel. The chapel was floored with marble. In the centre was the throne and upon it was the porcelain image of Shri Ramakrishna. The arrangement of materials was perfect and Swamiji was much pleased to see this.

The wife of Navagopal Babu prostrated herself before Swamiji with the other female members of the house and then took to fanning him. Hearing Swamiji speaking highly of every arrangement, she addressed him and said, "What have we got to entitle us to the privilege of worshipping Thâkur (the Master, Lord)? — A poor home and poor means! Do bless us please by installing him here out of your own kindness!

In reply to this, Swamiji jocosely said, "Your Thakur never had in his fourteen generations such a marble floored house to live in! He had his birth in that rural thatched cottage and lived his days on indifferent means. And if he does not live here so excellently served, where else should he live?" Swamiji's words made everybody laugh out.

Now, with his body rubbed with ashes and gracing the seat of the priest, Swamiji himself conducted the worship, with Swami Prakashananda to assist him. After the worship was over, Swamiji while still in the worship-room composed extempore this Mantra for prostration before Bhagavan Shri Ramakrishna:

— "I bow down to Ramakrishna, who established the religion, embodying in himself the reality of all religions and being thus the foremost of divine Incarnations."

All prostrated before Shri Ramakrishna with this Mantra. In the evening Swamiji returned to Baghbazar.

XII

Translated from Bengali
From the Diary of a Disciple

The disciple is Sharatchandra Chakravarty, who published his records in a Bengali book, Swami-Shishya-Samvâda, in two parts. The present series of "Conversations and Dialogues" is a revised translation from this book. Five dialogues of this series have already appeared in the Complete Works, Volume V.

Place: Balaram Babu's residence, Calcutta.

Year: 1898.

Swamiji had been staying during the last two days at Balaram Babu's residence at Baghbazar. He was taking a short stroll on the roof of the house, and the disciple with four or five others was in attendance. While walking to and fro, Swamiji took up the story of Guru Govind Singh and with his great eloquence touched upon the various points in his life — how the revival of the Sikh sect was brought about by his great renunciation, austerities, fortitude, and life-consecrating labours — how by his initiation he re-Hinduised Mohammedan converts and took them back into the Sikh community — and how on the banks of the Narmada he brought his wonderful life to a close. Speaking of the great power that used to be infused in those days into the initiates of Guru Govind, Swamiji recited a popular Dohâ (couplet) of the Sikhs:

The meaning is: "When Guru Govind gives the Name, i.e. the initiation, a single man becomes strong enough to triumph over a lakh and a quarter of his foes." Each disciple, deriving from his inspiration a real spiritual devotion, had his soul filled with such wonderful heroism! While holding forth thus on the glories of religion, Swamiji's eyes dilating with enthusiasm seemed to be emitting fire, and his hearers, dumb-stricken and looking at his face, kept watching the wonderful sight.

After a while the disciple said: "Sir, it was very remarkable that Guru Govind could unite both Hindus and Mussulmans within the fold of his religion and lead them both towards the same end. In Indian history, no other example of this can be found."

Swamiji: Men can never be united unless there is a bond of common interest. You can never unite people merely by getting up meetings, societies, and lectures if their interests be not one and the same. Guru Govind made it understood everywhere that the men of his age, be they Hindus or Mussulmans, were living under a regime of profound injustice and oppression. He did not create any common interest, he only pointed it out to the masses. And so both Hindus and Mussulmans followed him. He was a great worshipper of Shakti. Yet, in Indian history, such an example is indeed very rare.

Finding then that it was getting late into the night, Swamiji came down with others into the parlour on the first floor, where the following conversation on the subject of miracles took place.

Swamiji said, "It is possible to acquire miraculous powers by some little degree of mental concentration", and turning to the disciple he asked, "Well, should you like to learn thought-reading? I can teach that to you in four or five days."

Disciple: Of what avail will it be to me, sir?

Swamiji: Why, you will be able to know others' minds.

Disciple: Will that help my attainment of the knowledge of Brahman?

Swamiji: Not a bit.

Disciple: Then I have no need to learn that science. But, sir, I would very much like to hear about what you have yourself seen of the manifestation of such psychic powers.

Swamiji: Once when travelling in the Himalayas I had to take up my abode for a night in a village of the hill-people. Hearing the beating of drums in the village some time after nightfall, I came to know upon inquiring of my host that one of the villagers had been possessed by a Devatâ or good spirit. To meet his importunate wishes and to satisfy my own curiosity, we went out to see what the matter really was. Reaching the spot, I found a great concourse of people. A tall man with long, bushy hair was pointed out to me, and I was told that person had got the Devata on him. I noticed an axe being heated in fire close by the man; and after a while, I found the red-hot thing being seized and applied to parts of his body and also to his hair! But wonder of wonders, no part of his body or hair thus branded with the red-hot axe was found to be burnt, and there was no expression of any pain in his face! I stood mute with surprise. The headman of the village, meanwhile, came up to me and said, "Mahârâj, please exorcise this man out of your mercy." I felt myself in a nice fix, but moved to do something, I had to go near the possessed man. Once there, I felt a strong impulse to examine the axe rather closely, but the instant I touched it, I burnt my fingers, although the thing had been cooled down to blackness. The smarting made me restless and all my theories about the axe phenomenon were spirited away from my mind! However, smarting with the burn, I placed my hand on the head of the man and repeated for a short while the Japa. It was a matter of surprise to find that the man came round in ten or twelve minutes. Then oh, the gushing reverence the villagers showed to me! I was taken to be some wonderful man! But, all the same, I couldn't make any head or tail of the whole business. So without a word one way or the other, I returned with my host to his hut. It was about midnight, and I went to bed. But what with the smarting burn in the hand and the impenetrable puzzle of the whole affair, I couldn't have any sleep that night. Thinking of the burning axe failing to harm living human flesh, it occurred again and again to my mind, "There are more things in heaven and earth, Horatio, than are dreamt of in your philosophy."

Disciple: But, could you later on ever explain the mystery, sir?

Swamiji: No. The event came back to me in passing just now, and so I related it to you.

He then resumed: But Shri Ramakrishna used to disparage these supernatural powers; his teaching was that one cannot attain to the supreme truth if the mind is diverted to the manifestation of these powers. The layman mind, however, is so weak that, not to speak of householders, even ninety per cent of the Sâdhus happen to be votaries of these powers. In the

West, men are lost in wonderment if they come across such miracles. It is only because Shri Ramakrishna has mercifully made us understand the evil of these powers as being hindrances to real spirituality that we are able to take them at their proper value. Haven't you noticed how for that reason the children of Shri Ramakrishna pay no heed to them?

Swami Yogananda said to Swamiji at this moment, "Well, why don't you narrate to our Bângâl (Lit. A man from East Bengal, i.e. the disciple.) that incident of yours in Madras when you met the famous ghost-tamer?"

At the earnest entreaty of the disciple Swamiji was persuaded to give the following account of his experience:

Once while I was putting up at Manmatha Babu's (Babu Manmatha Nath Bhattacharya, M.A., late Accountant General, Madras.) place, I dreamt one night that my mother had died. My mind became much distracted. Not to speak of corresponding with anybody at home, I used to send no letters in those days even to our Math. The dream being disclosed to Manmatha, he sent a wire to Calcutta to ascertain facts about the matter. For the dream had made my mind uneasy on the one hand, and on the other, our Madras friends, with all arrangements ready, were insisting on my departing for America immediately, and I felt rather unwilling to leave before getting any news of my mother. So Manmatha who discerned this state of my mind suggested our repairing to a man living some way off from town, who having acquired mystic powers over spirits could tell fortunes and read the past and the future of a man's life. So at Manmatha's request and to get rid of my mental suspense, I agreed to go to this man. Covering the distance partly by railway and partly on foot, we four of us — Manmatha, Alasinga, myself, and another — managed to reach the place, and what met our eyes there was a man with a ghoulish, haggard, soot-black appearance, sitting close to a cremation ground. His attendants used some jargon of South Indian dialect to explain to us that this was the man with perfect power over the ghosts. At first the man took absolutely no notice of us; and then, when we were about to retire from the place, he made a request for us to wait. Our Alasinga was acting as the interpreter, and he explained the requests to us. Next, the man commenced drawing some figures with a pencil, and presently I found him getting perfectly still in mental concentration. Then he began to give out my name, my genealogy, the history of my long line of forefathers and said that Shri Ramakrishna was keeping close to me all through my wanderings, intimating also to me good news about my mother. He also foretold that I would have to go very soon to far-off lands for preaching religion. Getting good news thus about my mother, we all travelled back to town, and after arrival received by wire from Calcutta the assurance of mother's doing well.

Turning to Swami Yogananda, Swamiji remarked, "Everything that the man had foretold came to be fulfilled to the letter, call it some fortuitous concurrence or anything you will."

Swami Yogananda said in reply, "It was because you would not believe all this before that this experience was necessary for you."

Swamiji: Well, I am not a fool to believe anything and everything without direct proof. And coming into this realm of Mahâmâya, oh, the many magic mysteries I have come across alongside this bigger magic conjuration of a universe! Maya, it is all Maya! Goodness! What rubbish we have been talking so long this day! By thinking constantly of ghosts, men become ghosts themselves, while whoever repeats day and night, knowingly or unknowingly, "I am the eternal, pure, free, self-illumined Atman", verily becomes the knower of Brahman.

Saying this, Swamiji affectionately turned to the disciple and said, "Don't allow all that worthless nonsense to occupy your mind. Always discriminate between the real and the unreal, and devote yourself heart and soul to the attempt to realise the Atman. There is nothing higher than this knowledge of the Atman; all else is Maya, mere jugglery. The Atman is the one unchangeable Truth. This I have come to understand, and that is why I try to bring it home to you all. "One Brahman there is without a second", "There is nothing manifold in existence" (Brihadâranyaka, IV. iv. 19)

All this conversation continued up to eleven o'clock

at highs. After that, his meal being finished, Swamiji retired for rest. The disciple bowed down at his feet to bid him good-bye. Swamiji asked, "Are you not coming tomorrow?"

Disciple: Yes, sir, I am coming, to be sure. The mind longs so much to meet you at least once before the day is out.

Swamiji: So good night now, it is getting very late.

Discovery Publisher is a multimedia publisher whose mission is to inspire and support personal transformation, spiritual growth and awakening. We strive with every title to preserve the essential wisdom of the author, spiritual teacher, thinker, healer, and visionary artist.

www.ingramcontent.com/pod-product-compliance
Lightning Source LLC
Chambersburg PA
CBHW080242170426
43192CB00014BA/2535